FOOTBALL GROUNDS *from the air*

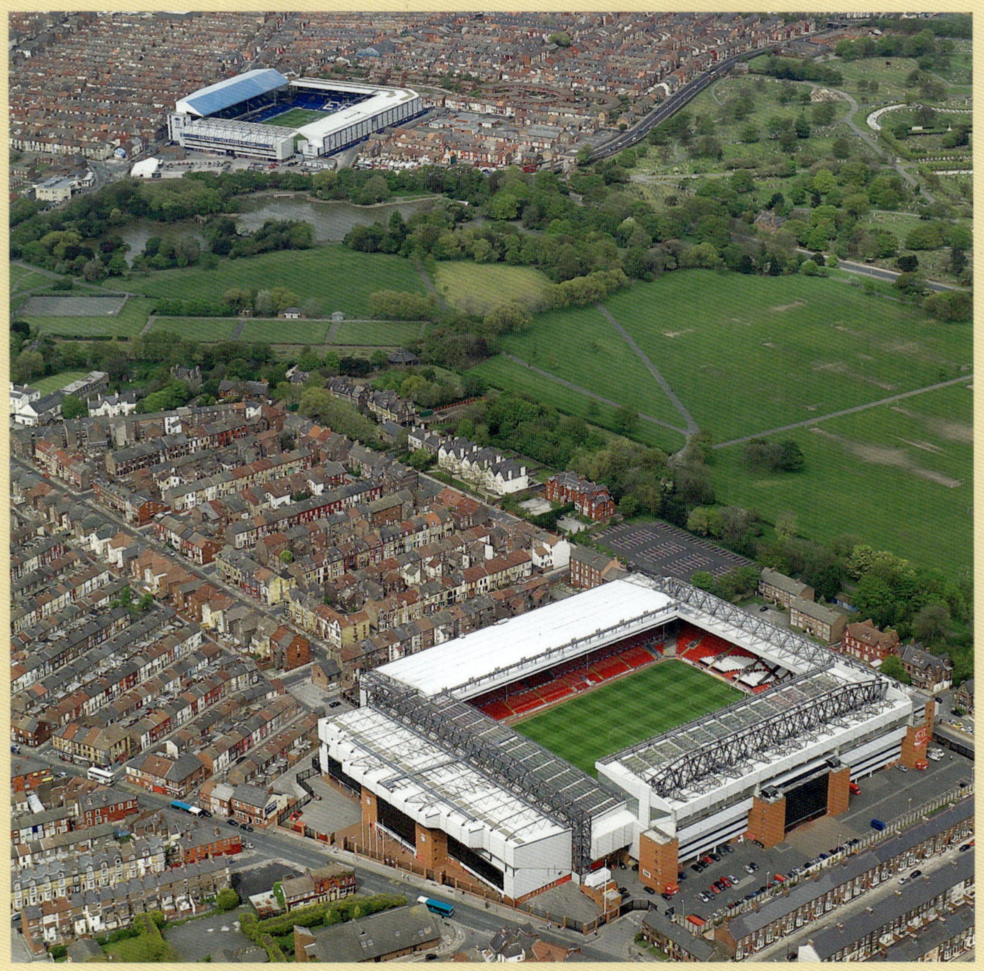

Photographs by **Ian Hay** FLIGHTIMAGES

Text by **Cassandra Wells**

MYRIAD
LONDON

CONTENTS

First published in 2006 by Myriad Books Limited 35 Bishopsthorpe Road, London SE26 4PA

ISBN 1 904 736 56 4
EAN 978 1 904 736 56 1

Designed by Jerry Goldie Graphic Design
Printed in China

www.myriadbooks.com

ABERDEEN

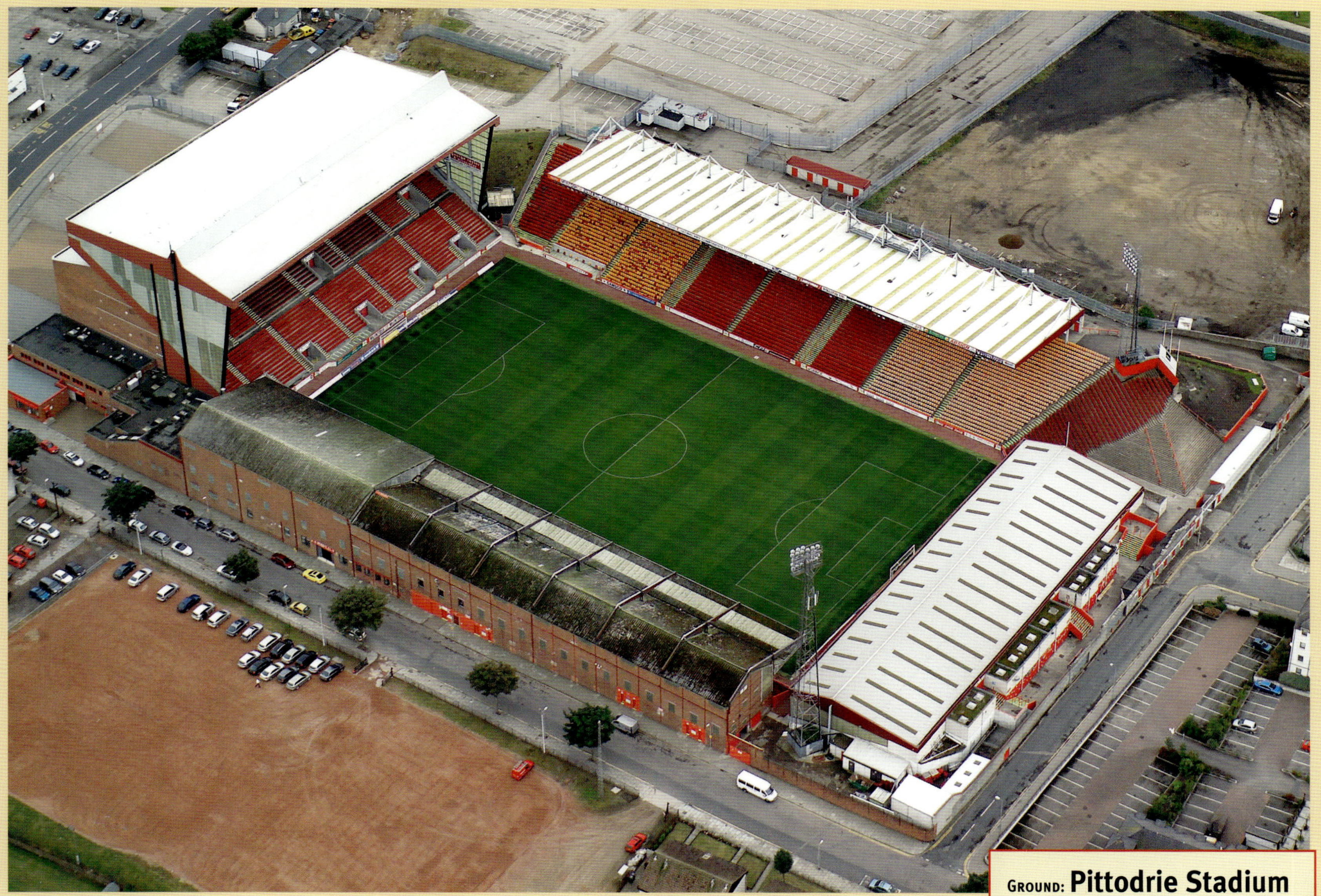

Aberdeen was formed in 1891 and the team played at several grounds before ending up at Pittodrie, a former dung heap used by the police. Despite its grimy beginnings, Pittodrie was made suitable for football in 1899. In 1903 Aberdeen amalgamated with two other sides, Victoria United and Orion, and the newly merged club played their first game there in 1903. The club joined the Second Division in 1904 and paid £5,668 to buy Pittodrie outright. A pavilion was the first building to be erected at the ground but it was not until the 1920s that major building work took place. In 1925 the Main Stand was built and the country's first ever dug-out was hollowed out by the touchline. Aberdeen started a trend and gradually all other football grounds introduced dug-outs for players, coaches and managers. The end terrace was covered in 1934 and three years later a corner stand was built next to the Main Stand.

It was the 1950s before any further changes were made to the ground. In 1954 the club recorded its highest ever crowd of 45,061 for a Cup tie against Hearts and four years later the club built a cover over the Beach End, leaving only the south side without shelter. Fire burned down much of the Main Stand in 1971, three years after the club had first started putting benches on the terraces. In 1978 Pittodrie claimed the title of the first all-seater stadium in Britain. Despite reducing the ground's capacity to 24,000, the alterations met with support from the fans. The 1980s saw further modifications to the ground, including executive boxes, a new roof on the Merkland Road End and undersoil heating, all of which aimed to make watching home games a more pleasant experience. A new £4.5m two-tiered stand was opened at the Beach End in 1993, bringing total capacity up to 22,199.

GROUND: Pittodrie Stadium

ADDRESS: Pittodrie Stadium, Pittodrie Street, Aberdeen AB24 5QH

MAIN TEL: 01224 650 400

BOX OFFICE: 0871 983 1903

WEBSITE: www.afc.co.uk

CAPACITY: 22,199

HOME COLOURS: red shirts, white shorts

CLUB NICKNAME: the Dons

PITCH DIMENSIONS: 101m x 66m (110 x 72 yards)

FOUNDED: 1903

RECORD ATTENDANCE: 45,061 vs Heart of Midlothian, March 13 1954

MOST PROLIFIC SCORER: Joe Harper (199)

RECORD WIN: 13-0 vs Peterhead, January 9 1932

RECORD DEFEAT: 0-8 vs Celtic, January 30 1965

Arsenal

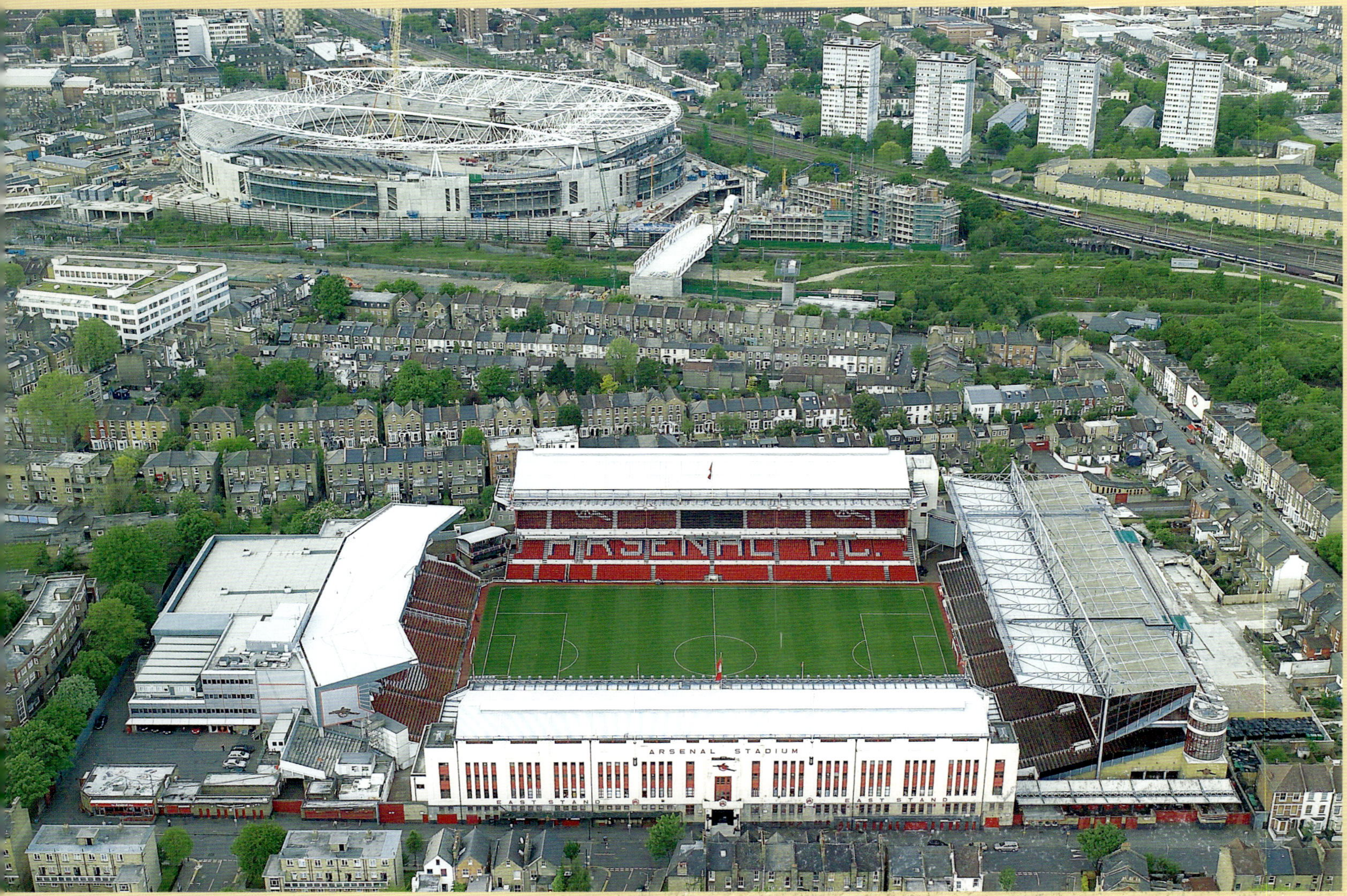

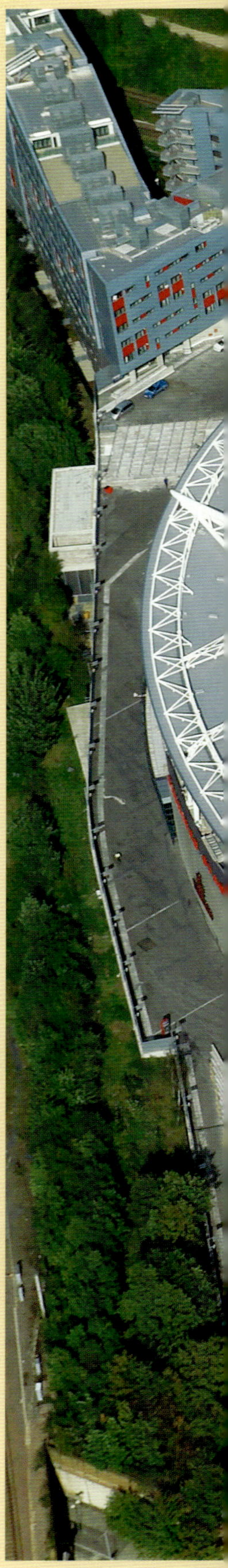

Above: work in progress on the new Emirates Stadium at Ashburton Grove, with Highbury in the foreground

Arsenal started life as a team called Dial Square in 1886, based in Woolwich, south-east London. They changed their name to Royal Arsenal in 1887 and to Woolwich Arsenal in 1891. Their early games were played on Woolwich Common but they moved to Manor Field in 1888, where they remained for the next 26 years. Despite being successful in the League, which they joined in 1893, their gates were low and they went into voluntary liquidation in 1910. Henry Norris, owner of Fulham FC, bought the struggling club and moved them to Highbury, north London, in 1913 much to the annoyance of their neighbours Spurs and Clapton Orient. After the First World War, Arsenal rejoined the First Division where they have remained since 1919. Architect Claude Waterlow Ferrier was commissioned to design a stadium for Arsenal, and he set about using an Art Deco style for the ground. In 1931 he extended the terraces at each end and began building the West Stand. The 1930s also saw success on the pitch: Arsenal won the League five times and the FA Cup twice. In 1935 an AFC monogrammed roof was added to the Laundry End Terrace; in the same season the club recorded its highest attendance when 73,295 turned out to see Arsenal take on Sunderland. In 1936 the East Stand was replaced and looked almost identical to Ferrier's West Stand. The 1970s saw more seats installed at Highbury, and further development came in the 1980s when the club added executive boxes to the Clock End. In 1991 the club drew up plans to rebuild the North Stand in order to increase capacity. The club had to play in front of just three stands in the 1992/93 season as the bulldozers moved in and a mural took the place of the fans on the North Bank. The new two-tiered North Stand opened in 1993. The Clock End and the East and West Terraces were next to be developed bringing a total capacity of 38,500 all-seated.

In February 2004 Arsenal began building a 60,000 all-seater stadium just five minutes from Highbury at Ashburton Grove on the site of a disused railway goods yard.

At the beginning of the 2006-7 season Arsenal moved into the new Emirates Stadium. The new ground consists of a four-tier bowl with an all-seated capacity of 60,432.

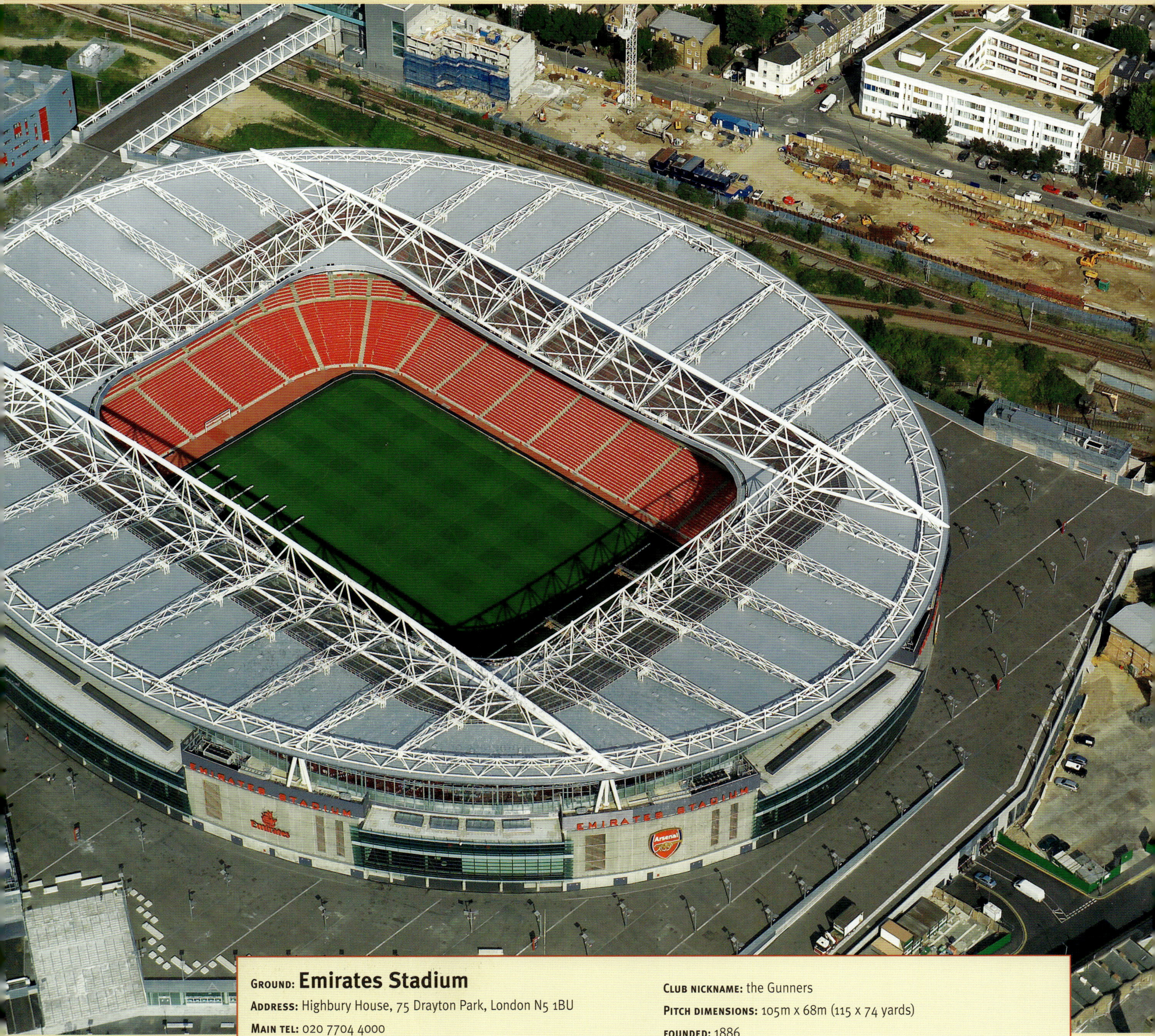

Ground: **Emirates Stadium**

Address: Highbury House, 75 Drayton Park, London N5 1BU

Main tel: 020 7704 4000

Box office: 020 7704 4040

Website: www.arsenal.com

Capacity: 60,432

Home colours: red shirts with white sleeves, white shorts with red trim, white and red hooped socks

Club nickname: the Gunners

Pitch dimensions: 105m x 68m (115 x 74 yards)

Founded: 1886

Record attendance: (at Highbury) 73,295 vs Sunderland, March 9 1935

Record attendance: (at Emirates) 60,132 vs Reading, March 3 2007

Most prolific scorer: Thierry Henry (226)

Record win: 12-0 vs Loughborough Town, March 12 1900

Record defeat: 0-8 vs Loughborough Town, December 8 1896

Aston Villa

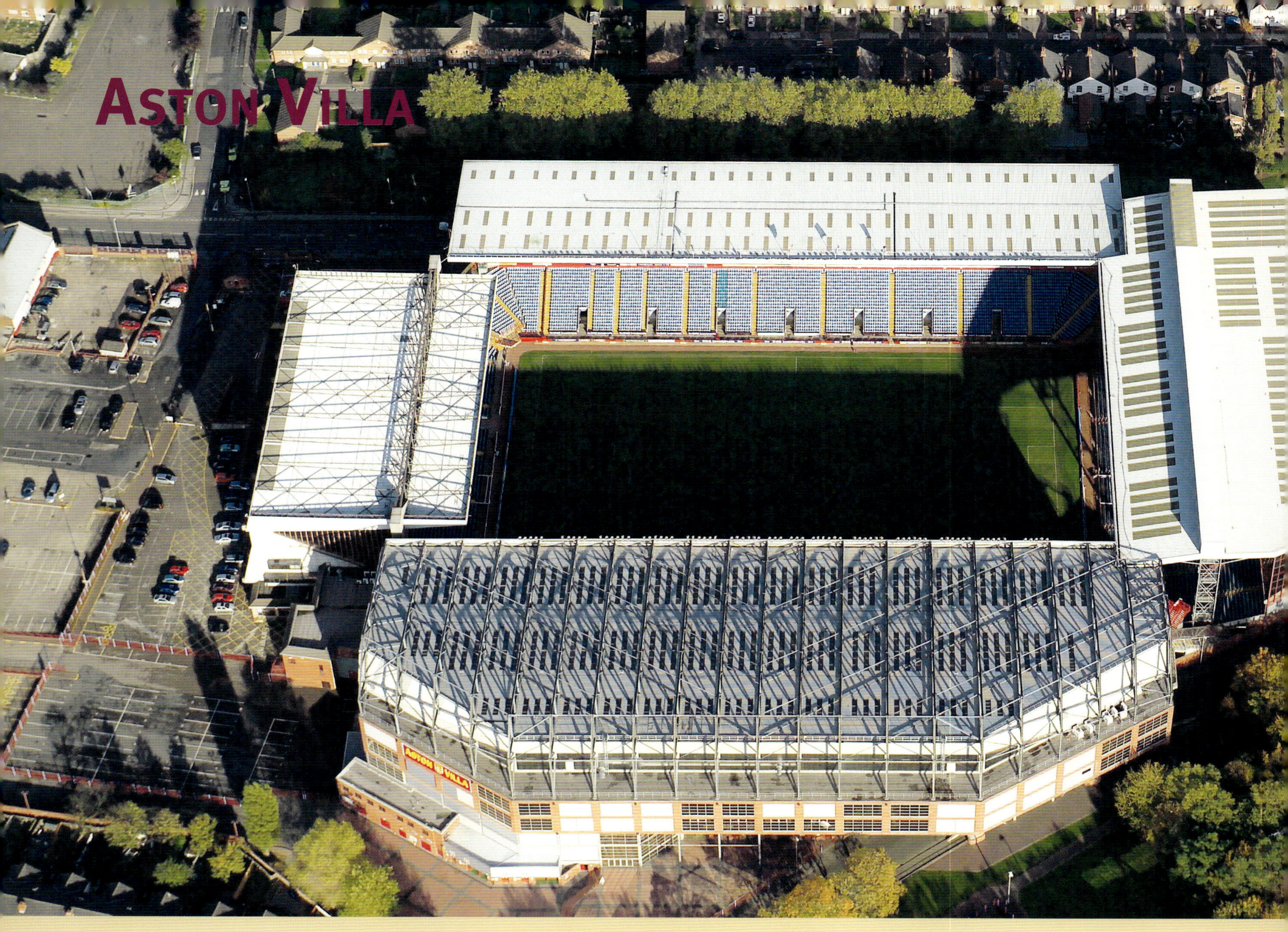

Aston Villa was formed by members of the Villa Cross Wesleyan Chapel in 1874. The club moved to the Aston Lower grounds in 1896 after spending 20 years at a basic ground on Wellington Road. The site was a leisure park dating back to the 1870s but had fallen into a state of disrepair. Villa began developing the ground, building a main stand on what had been a sub-tropical garden. Banking was raised on the other three sides of the ground and a basic barrel roof was added to the Trinity Road side. The ground opened in 1897, the same year Villa won the League and Cup double. Attendances continued to rise and prior to the First World War Villa were drawing in regular crowds of 26,000. In 1914 Villa realised their plans for future development of the ground. The work began with the removal of the concrete cycle path, which had run around the pitch; both end terraces were banked and another terrace added to the front of the Witton Lane Stand. After the war the Trinity Road Stand was built, a stand which was so extravagant in design it cost the club £89,810. The Holte End was extended during the Second World War and in 1946 Villa Park saw its highest ever crowd of 76,588. Villa Park's selection as a location for World Cup games brought about further development with seats being added to the ground's terracing. The two-tiered North Stand was built in 1977, with further development coming in the light of the Taylor report. In 1990 the

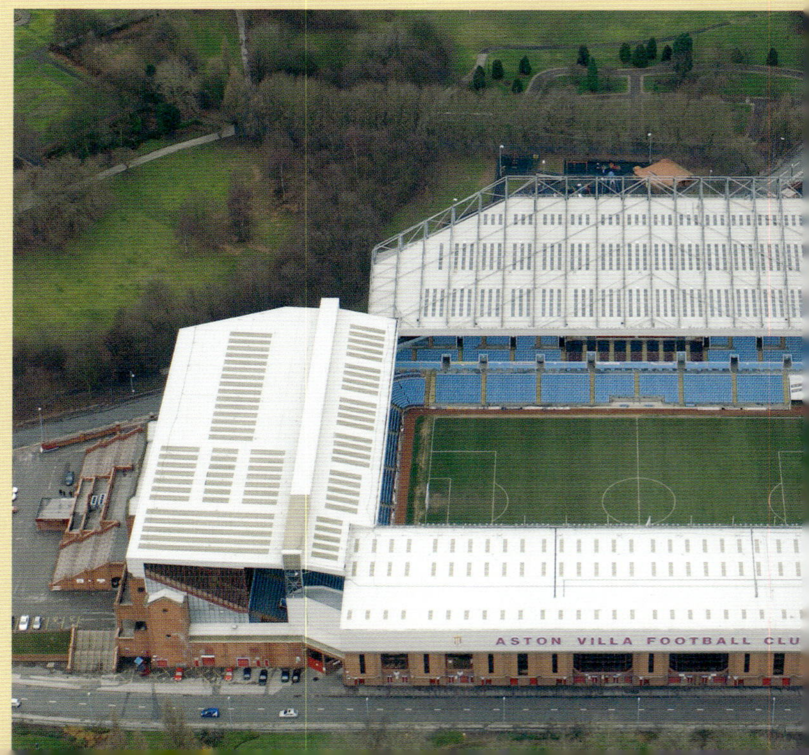

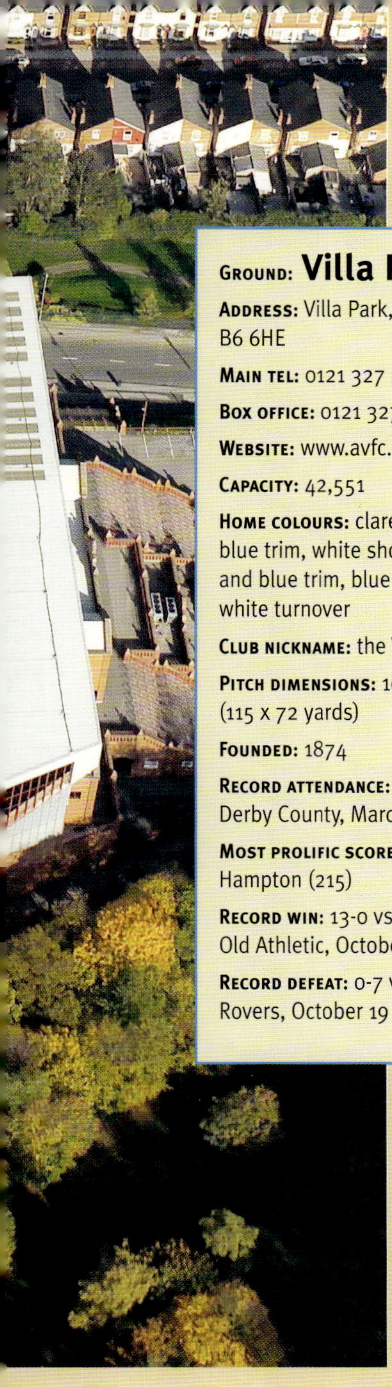

GROUND: **Villa Park**

ADDRESS: Villa Park, Birmingham B6 6HE

MAIN TEL: 0121 327 2299

BOX OFFICE: 0121 327 5353

WEBSITE: www.avfc.co.uk

CAPACITY: 42,551

HOME COLOURS: claret shirts with blue trim, white shorts with claret and blue trim, blue socks with white turnover

CLUB NICKNAME: the Villans, Villa

PITCH DIMENSIONS: 105m x 69m (115 x 72 yards)

FOUNDED: 1874

RECORD ATTENDANCE: 76,588 vs Derby County, March 2 1946

MOST PROLIFIC SCORER: Harry Hampton (215)

RECORD WIN: 13-0 vs Wednesbury Old Athletic, October 30 1886

RECORD DEFEAT: 0-7 vs Blackburn Rovers, October 19 1899

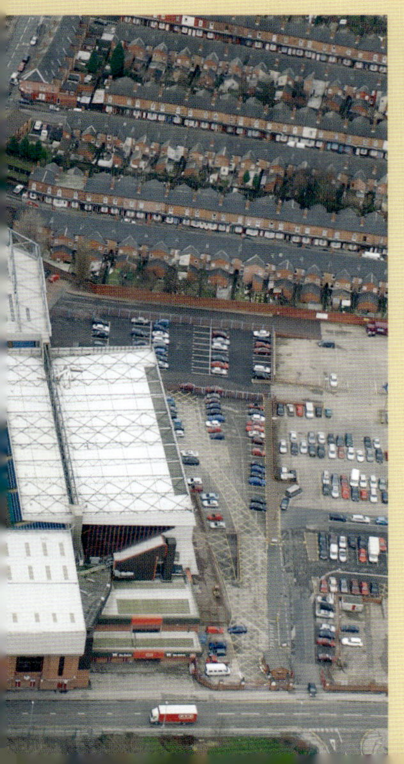

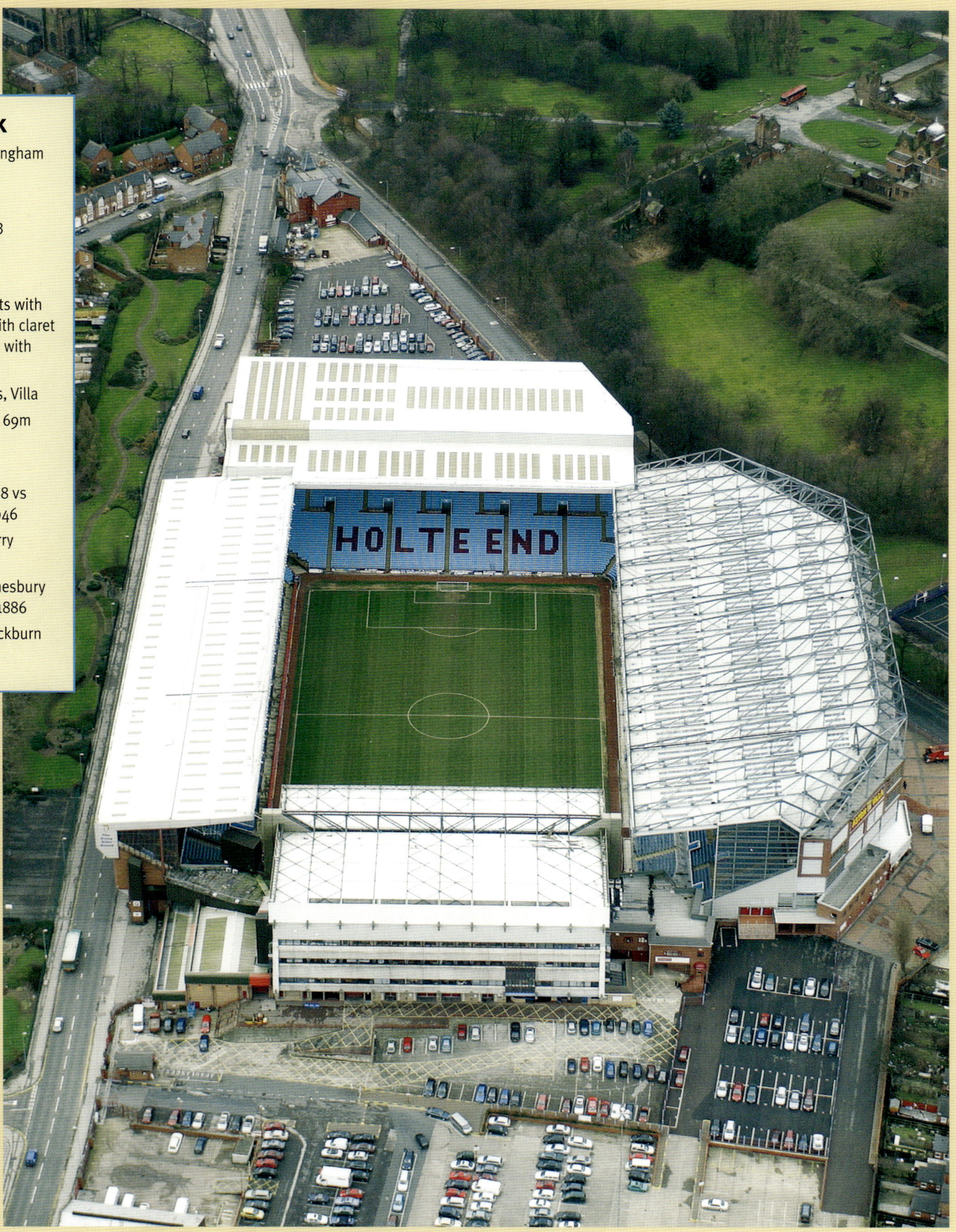

Holte End terracing was updated and the roof extended but as a result of poor planning the whole structure had to be demolished in 1994 and replaced with a two-tier stand. Trinity Road Stand was refurbished in time for the 1996 European Championships. In order to maintain a capacity in excess of 40,000 the club set about planning to redevelop the Witton Lane Stand (now the Doug Ellis Stand), and by the end of 2002 the capacity was up to 42,551. There are plans for further development, extending and filling in the corners of the North Stand to bring capacity up to 51,000.

BARNSLEY

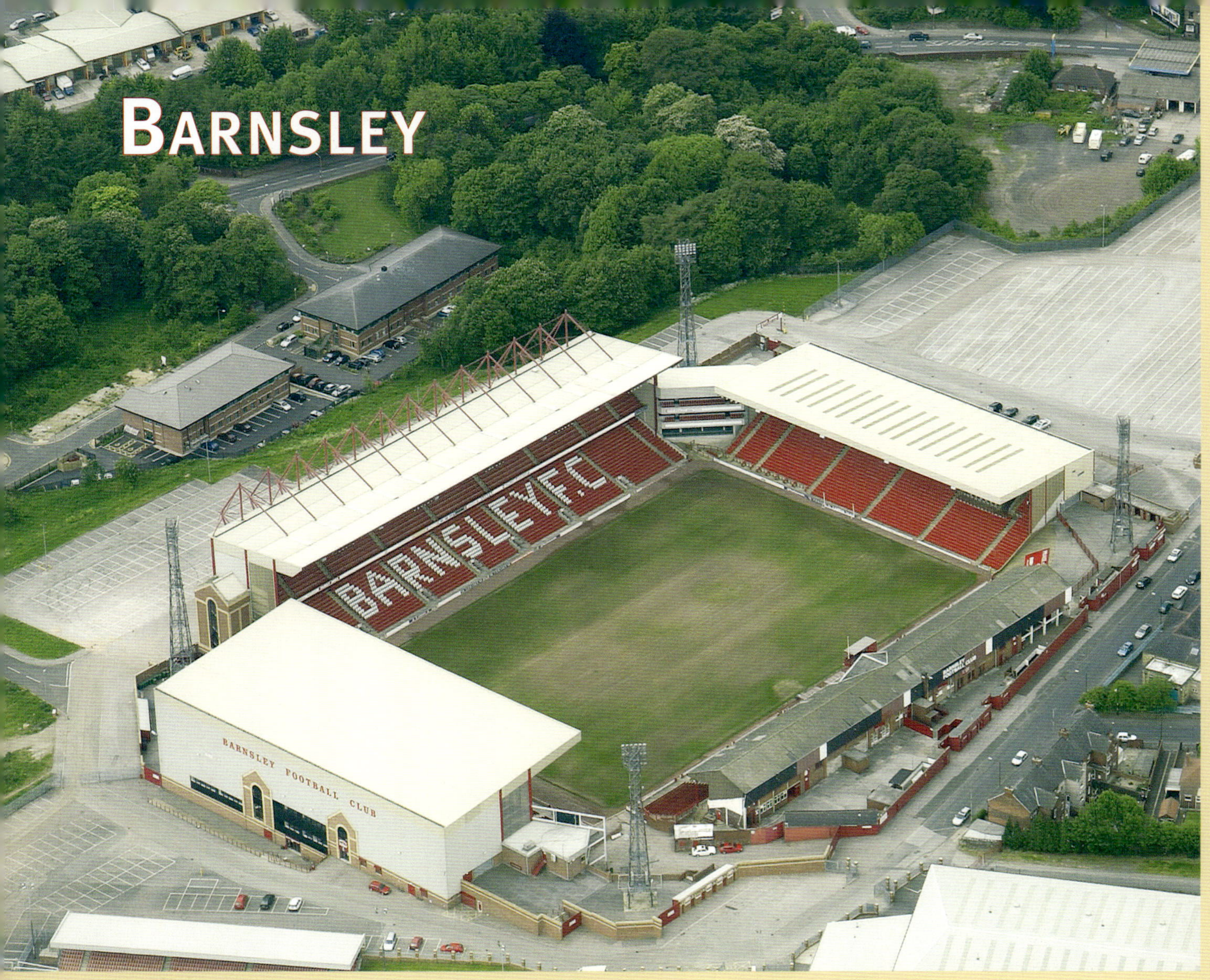

Barnsley's roots date back to 1887, when the Reverend Tiverton Preedy established a football team called Barnsley St Peter's. In 1888 the club began playing on a field situated where Oakwell stands today. The first stand was built in 1895 but was soon blown down during a gale. After significant levelling of the pitch, the Tykes dropped "St Peter's" from their name in 1897. It was a further seven years before they built another stand, the Main Stand (now the West Stand). The next significant building work took place in the late 1940s when the Pontefract Road End was covered, and what is now the Brewery Stand was extended. In 1982, a three-tiered corner structure was added to the Kop specifically for disabled supporters and the club spent money improving the terraces to bring the capacity up to 36,987. Barnsley's success in the League, which coincided with the Taylor report, meant they were required to instal seating in a ground which, until then, had only 2,164 seats. The first stand to get seats was the East Stand, a two-tiered structure capable of holding 7,200 fans. This opened in 1993. The club was not as financially sound as other clubs in the division and struggled to meet the 1994 deadline for becoming all-seater. Their solution was to put temporary seating in the Kop and to close off the two remaining terraces. A year later, seats were added to the West Stand, and the Pontefract Road End was knocked down and replaced by the Enterprise Plc Stand, bringing capacity up to 19,073. In 1999 the Kop was redeveloped and is now a single-tiered stand for away fans. There are plans to develop the West Stand at some point in the future.

Ground: **Oakwell**

Address: Oakwell Stadium, Barnsley, South Yorkshire S71 1ET

Main tel: 01226 211 211

Box office: 01226 211 211

Website: www.barnsleyfc.co.uk

Capacity: 23,009

Home colours: red shirts, white shorts, red socks

Club nickname: the Tykes

Pitch dimensions: 101m x 69m (110 x 75 yards)

Founded: 1887

Record attendance: 40,255 vs Stoke City, February 15 1936

Most prolific scorer: Ernest Hine (123)

Record win: 9-0 vs Loughborough Town, January 28 1899

Record defeat: 0-9 vs Notts County, November 19 1927

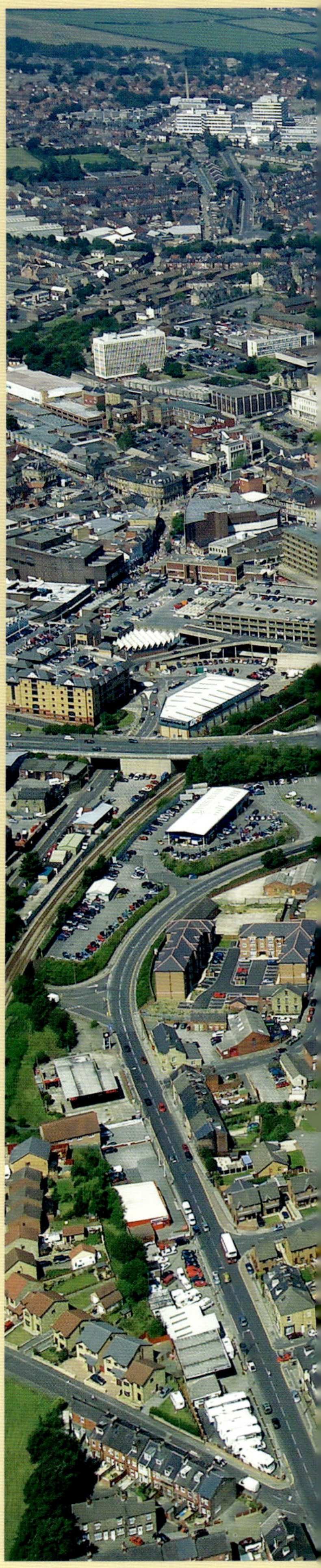

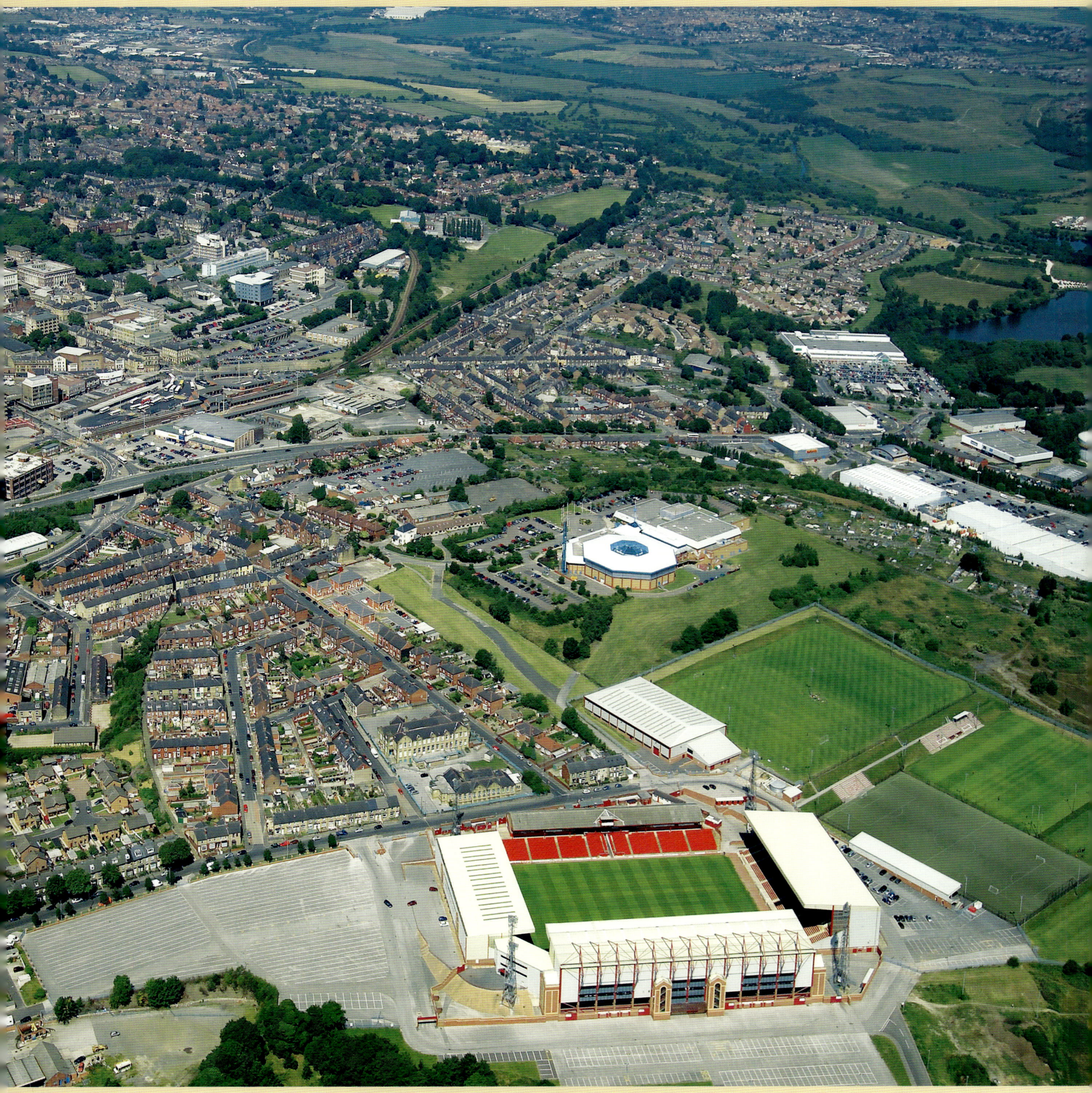

Birmingham City

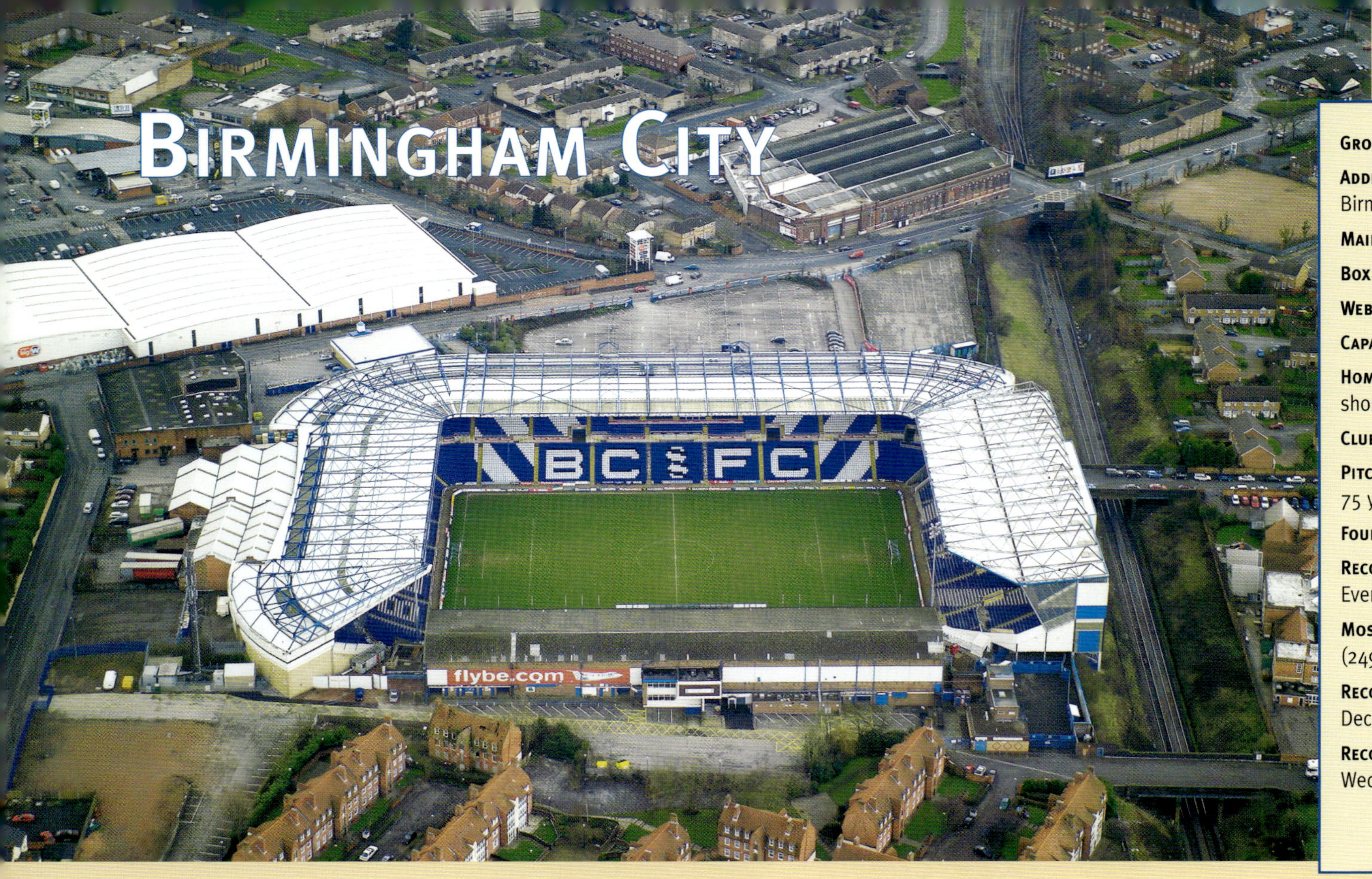

Ground: **St Andrews**
Address: St Andrews Ground, Birmingham B9 4NH
Main tel: 0844 557 1875
Box office: 0844 557 1875
Website: www.bcfc.com
Capacity: 30,016
Home colours: blue shirts, blue shorts, blue and white socks
Club nickname: the Blues
Pitch dimensions: 105m x 69m (115 x 75 yards)
Founded: 1875
Record attendance: 66,844 vs Everton, February 11 1939
Most prolific scorer: Joe Bradford (249)
Record win: 12-0 vs Walsall T Swifts, December 17 1892
Record defeat: 1-9 vs Sheffield Wednesday, December 13 1930

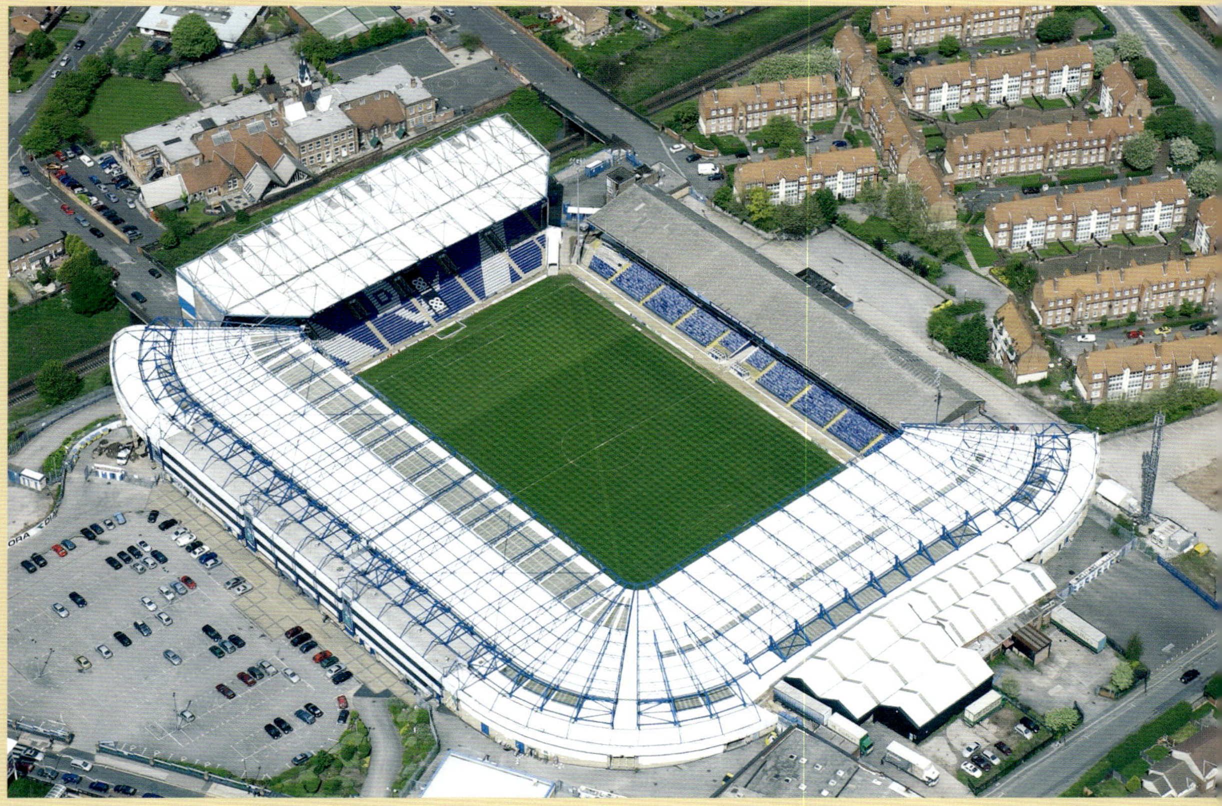

Birmingham City FC started life as the Small Heath Alliance in 1875. Their first pitch was on waste ground on Arthur Street but as their crowd of followers grew, they moved to Muntz Street, where they remained for the next 29 years. The club turned professional in 1885 and changed their name to Birmingham FC in 1905. The Blues moved to St Andrews in 1906, onto a ground that had been previously occupied by gypsies, who are said to have laid a curse on it. The massive main stand was built and in order to raise the height of the ground beneath terracing on the Coventry Road End, locals were encouraged to dump rubbish on the site. A Kop terrace was built on top of the accumulated spoil, with a capacity of 48,000. Terrace covers had been put on top of the Railway End and the Kop by the time the ground recorded its highest gate ever of 66,844 in 1939. During the Second World War the curse returned: the ground was damaged by bombs over 20 times and the Main Stand burned down when a fireman inadvertently used petrol instead of water to put out a brazier. Birmingham had to move, first to Leamington and then to Villa Park until 1943, while their ground was repaired. They emerged from the war with a new name, Birmingham City FC. The Kop reopened in 1947 and the new two-tiered Main Stand opened in 1954. Success in Europe funded the building of the Railway End Stand in 1963-4. The 1980s saw a run of bad luck, and by 1989 the Blues found themselves in the Third Division. March 1993 saw the Blues' fortunes improve as David Sullivan took over ownership of the club. Sullivan drew up plans for a £4.5m development of the Kop and Tilton Road End, which opened in 1994; in 1999 the Railway End was redeveloped and there are now plans to develop the Main Stand.

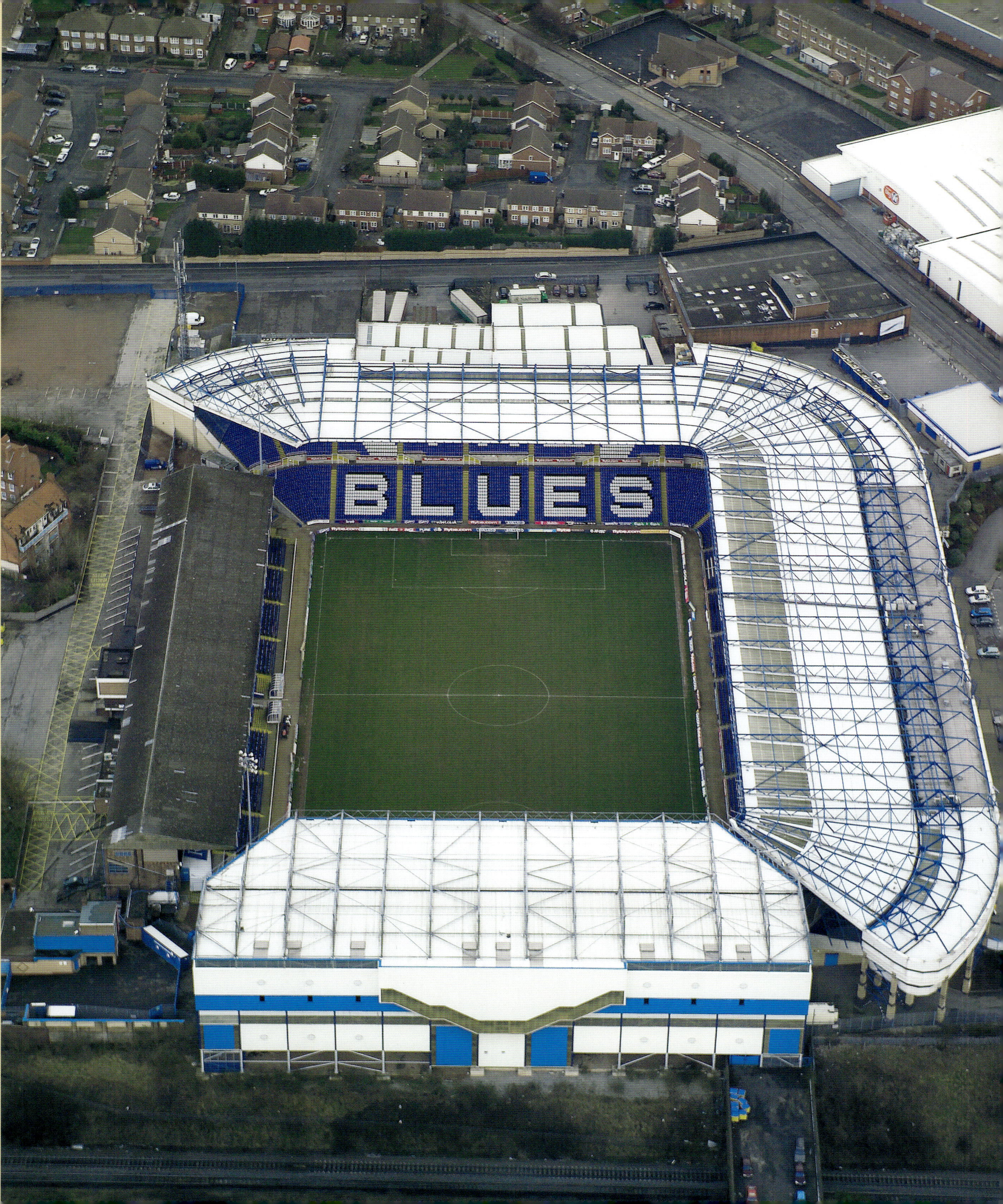
BLUES

Blackburn Rovers

Blackburn Rovers was formed in 1875 by a group of former public schoolboys. It took the club a year before they settled at their first ground, Oozehead, to play regular matches. The club moved a further four times before settling at Ewood Park in 1890. During this time they had become the first real giants of English football, winning the FA Cup three years in a row from 1884 and again in 1890. In 1905 Laurence Cotton, a textile baron, set about transforming the ground. Between 1905-1914 he spent an estimated £12,000 on players and £33,000 on ground improvements. First came a pitched roof on the Darwen End, followed by the building of the Main Stand and the Nuttall Street Stand. Further improvements in 1914 came after Rovers had won the League title, when the Riverside Stand was built. By 1913 the capacity was 70,866. Little changed at the ground until 1960, when an FA Cup final appearance helped to fund a cantilevered roof over the Blackburn End. In 1980 safety regulations brought the capacity at Ewood Park down to 23,400 and tough times followed. In 1983 just 3,797 turned up to see the last game of the season. Fire checks in 1985 saw the upper tier of the Riverside End and the terrace below closed. In 1987 Rovers' fortunes improved and Chairman Bill Fox persuaded his friend, Jack Walker, to help re-build the Riverside Stand. This would be the start of a remarkable relationship. In 1991 Walker decided to buy a 62% share in the Rovers and set about transforming the club in the same spirit as previous chairman Laurence Cotton some 90 years earlier. He spent £13m on the team in his first 18 months and then drew up plans for the building of three two-tiered stands. This proposed development incensed some local people as houses and a mill were to be to be demolished. Regardless of this, the council approved the plans and in 1993 the developments began. When the Jack Walker Stand opened in November 1994 the capacity was 31,367.

Ground: Ewood Park

Address: Ewood Park, Blackburn, Lancashire BB2 4JF

Main tel: 0871 702 1875

Box office: 0871 222 1444

Website: www.rovers.co.uk

Capacity: 31,367

Home colours: blue and white halved shirts, white shorts with a blue trim, white socks with blue trim

Club nickname: Rovers

Pitch dimensions: 105m x 69m (115 x 76 yards)

Founded: 1875

Record attendance: 62,522 vs Bolton Wanderers, March 2 1929

Most prolific scorer: Simon Gurner (168)

Record win: 11-0 vs Rossendale, October 13 1884

Record defeat: 0-8 vs Arsenal, February 25 1933

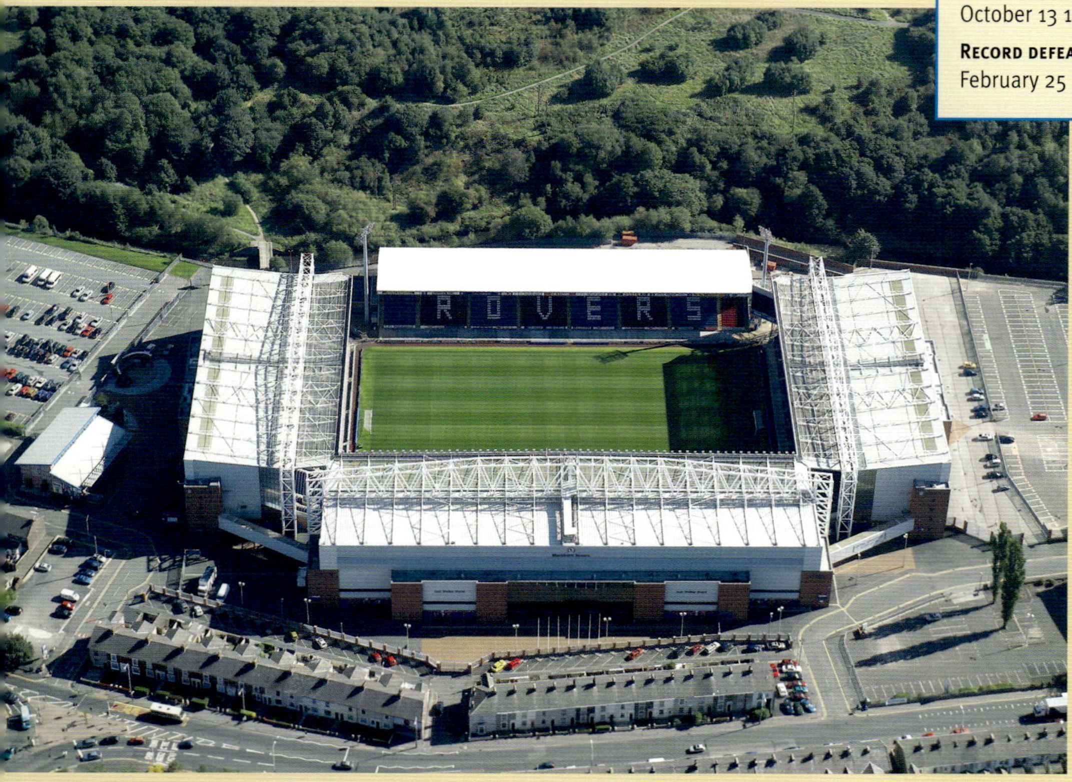

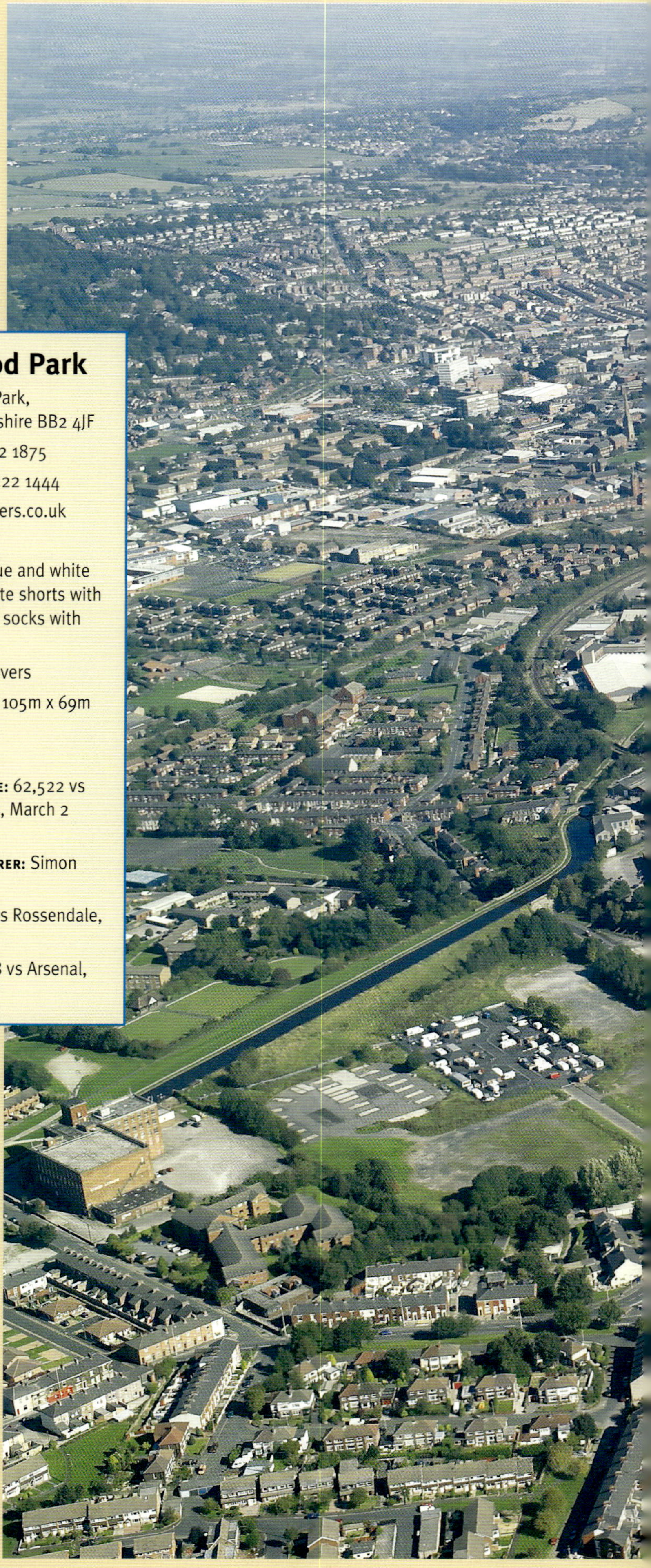

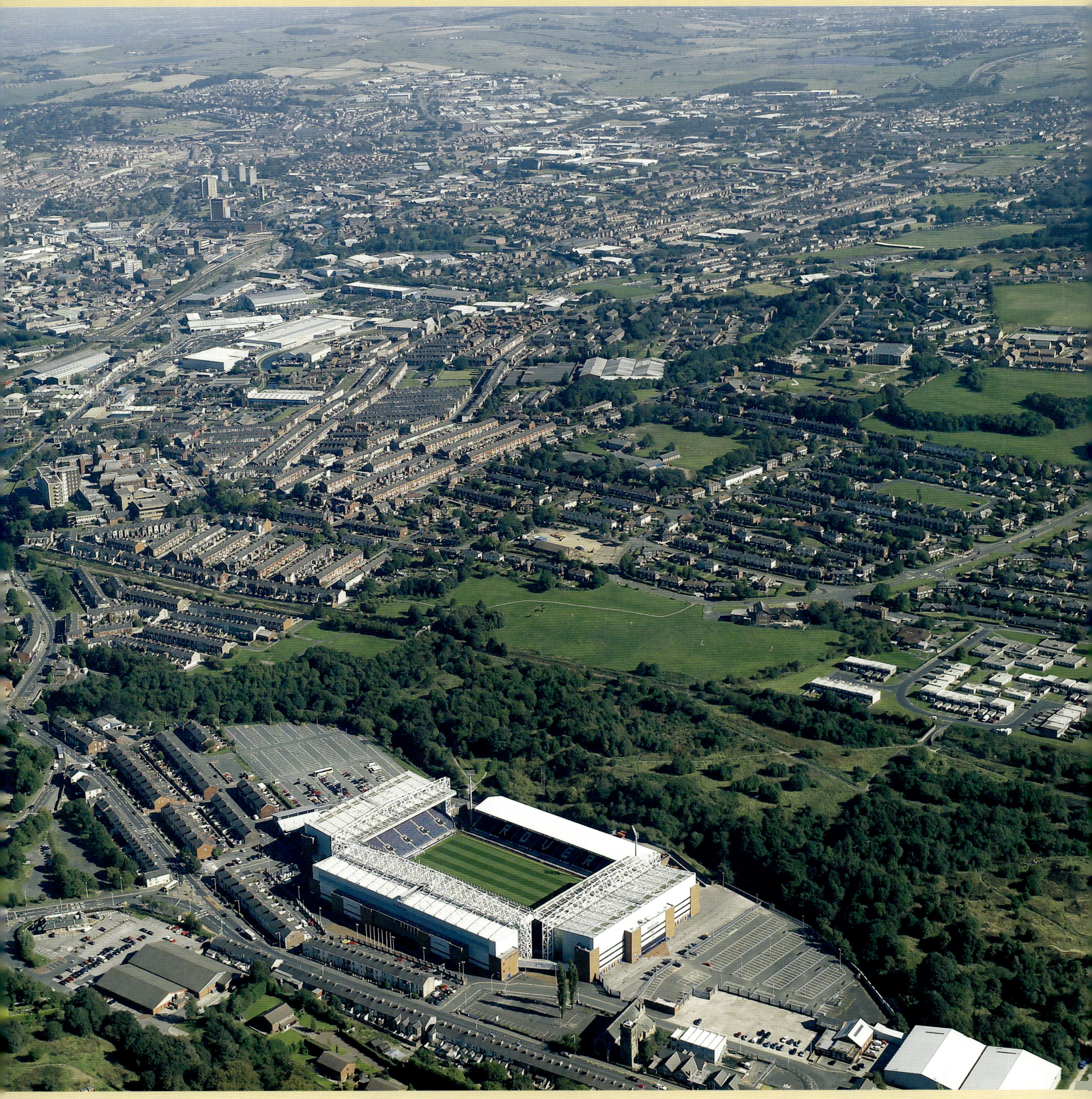

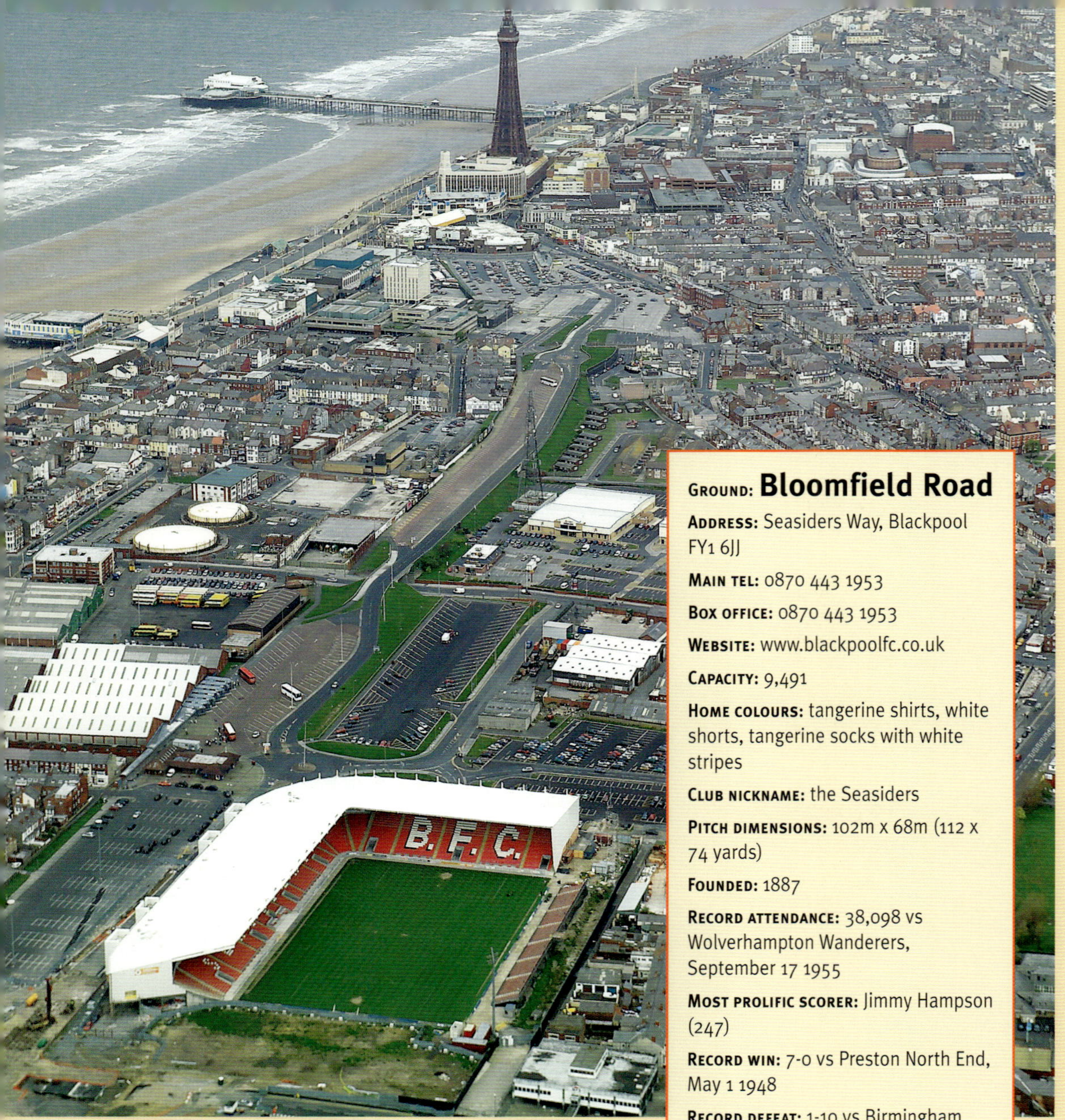

Ground: Bloomfield Road
Address: Seasiders Way, Blackpool FY1 6JJ
Main tel: 0870 443 1953
Box office: 0870 443 1953
Website: www.blackpoolfc.co.uk
Capacity: 9,491
Home colours: tangerine shirts, white shorts, tangerine socks with white stripes
Club nickname: the Seasiders
Pitch dimensions: 102m x 68m (112 x 74 yards)
Founded: 1887
Record attendance: 38,098 vs Wolverhampton Wanderers, September 17 1955
Most prolific scorer: Jimmy Hampson (247)
Record win: 7-0 vs Preston North End, May 1 1948
Record defeat: 1-10 vs Birmingham City, February 2 1901

Blackpool

Blackpool formed in 1887 and played their first games at Raikes Hall, a Victorian leisure park. The club moved twice and after merging with local rivals South Shore in 1899, Blackpool moved to Bloomfield Road. The ground had just one 300-seater stand until 1917 and, when fire burned it down, it was replaced by the West Stand. This was followed shortly afterwards by the building of the Motor Stand and in 1925 the two-tiered South Stand. On winning promotion to the First Division, the Motor Stand was moved to the north-west corner, a Kop was constructed in its place capable of holding 12,000 fans and a roof was added to the East Stand. During the Second World War, the RAF used Bloomfield Road as a training ground. After they moved out, a new roof was added to the Kop, which offered shelter to the record 38,098 fans who packed in to see the Seasiders take on Wolves in the League in 1955. The previous nine seasons were the most successful in the club's history: they reached the FA Cup final three times, winning it in 1953. During the 1970s seats were added to the East Terrace, and the roof over the Kop was removed. A novel response to similar concerns about the West Stand saw alternate rows of seats being removed. By 1990 capacity was down to 10,000 and the ground was in a sorry state of repair. The Seasider's fortunes have since improved and plans are in place for a 16,000 all-seater stadium. By 2002 the West and North Stands had been replaced by a 7,700-seater cantilevered stand. The South Stand was demolished in 2003 and there is a temporary stand on the east side where away fans sit.

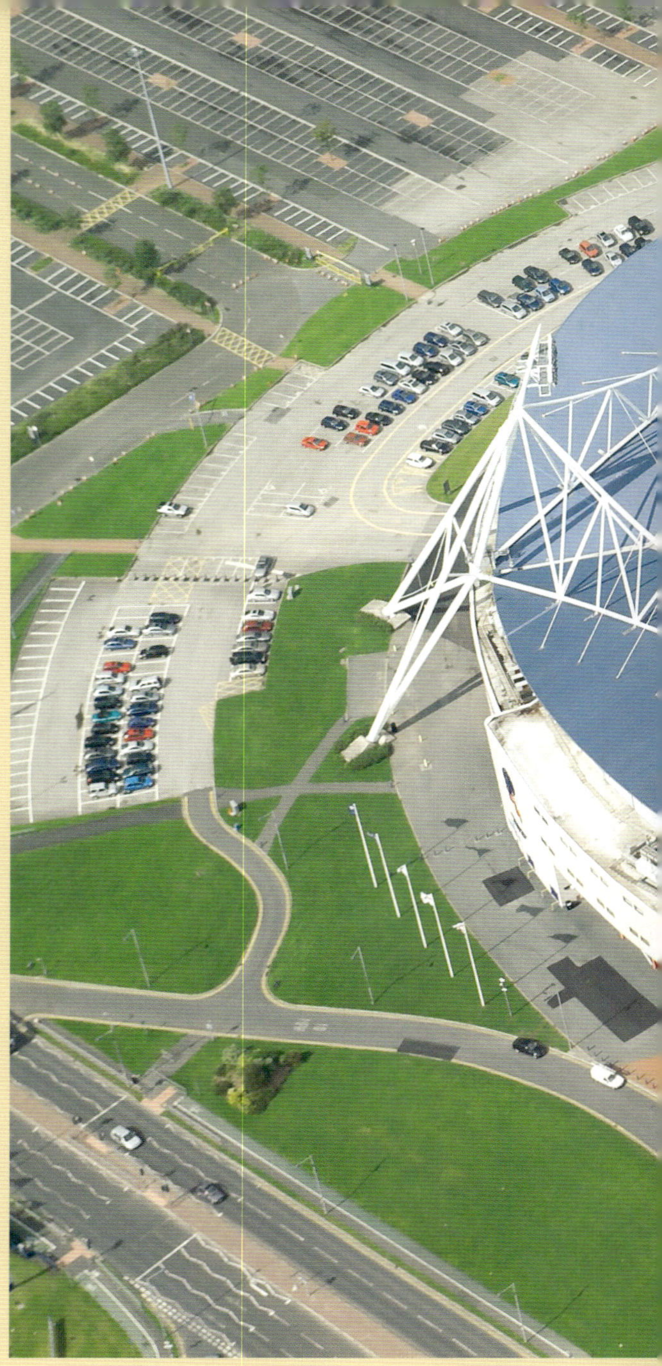

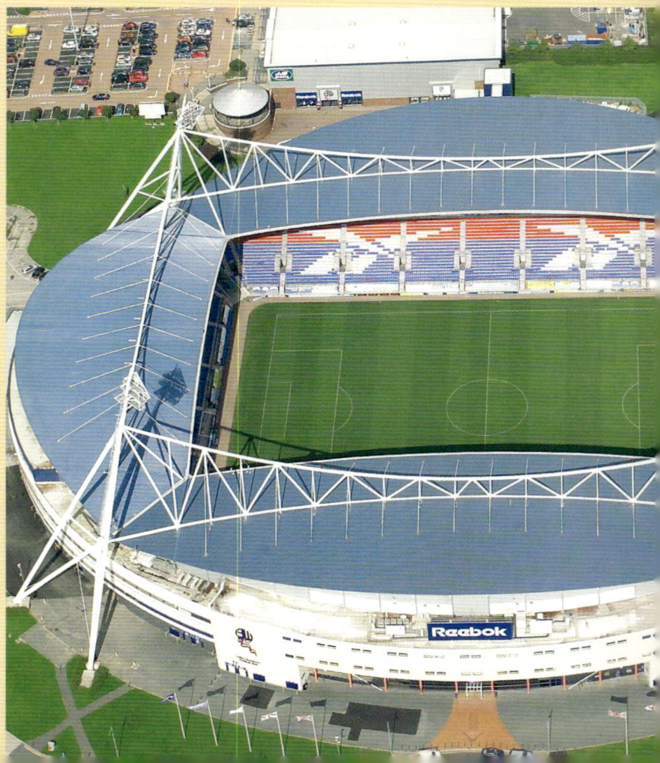

BOLTON WANDERERS

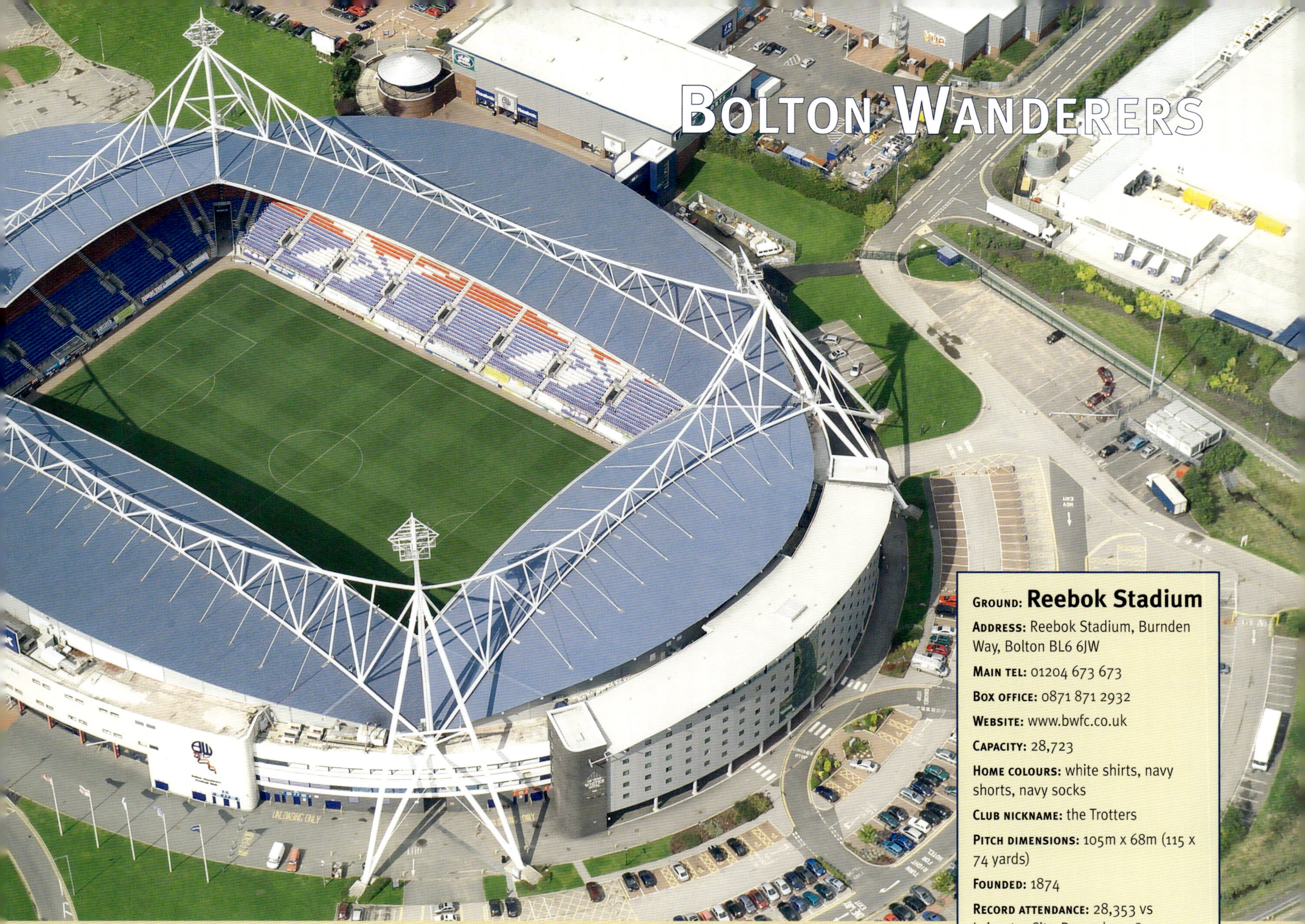

GROUND: Reebok Stadium

ADDRESS: Reebok Stadium, Burnden Way, Bolton BL6 6JW

MAIN TEL: 01204 673 673

BOX OFFICE: 0871 871 2932

WEBSITE: www.bwfc.co.uk

CAPACITY: 28,723

HOME COLOURS: white shirts, navy shorts, navy socks

CLUB NICKNAME: the Trotters

PITCH DIMENSIONS: 105m x 68m (115 x 74 yards)

FOUNDED: 1874

RECORD ATTENDANCE: 28,353 vs Leicester City, December 28 2003

MOST PROLIFIC SCORER: Nat Lofthouse (255)

RECORD WIN: 13-0 vs Sheffield United, February 1 1890

RECORD DEFEAT: 1-9 vs Preston North End, December 12 1887

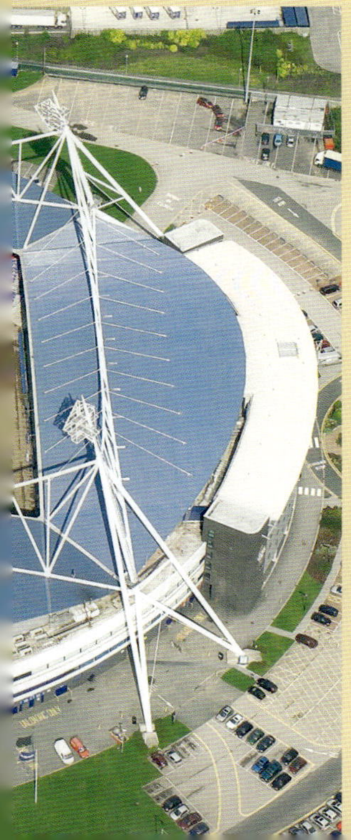

Bolton Wanderers started as a Sunday school team called Christ Church FC, playing on Park Recreation Ground. They moved to Dick Cockle's Field on Pikes Lane in 1877, where the club had a row with the vicar and left to become Bolton Wanderers. In 1881 they moved to a proper sports ground on Pikes Lane, which had two small stands. In 1893 rising rents led Wanderers to bid farewell to Pikes Lane and build a new ground on wasteland. That ground, Burnden Park, would remain home to the Trotters for 102 years. Wanderers were one of the 12 founding members of the Football League, although the League title is one they have never won. Their success has always been with the FA Cup, a prize they have won four times, the last time being in 1958 when Trotters' legend Nat Lofthouse scored both of Bolton's goals against Manchester United. Their first attempt at winning the FA Cup came in 1904 however, and despite losing the final, the money raised meant they could build a main stand and terrace and cover the Great Lever End. The 1920s saw three FA Cup wins for Bolton, and again more ground improvements followed with the new Burnden Stand being built. Little changed at the ground for the following 70 years. The 1980s were the next major period of change for the club, as their fortunes had faded, and the club had sunk from the First Division to the Fourth. Crowds dropped to an all-time low of 2,902 and, to raise revenue, the Trotters sold some of their land at the Railway End to a local superstore. By the 1990s, Bolton's fortunes had reversed; they reached the Premiership in 1995 and made plans for a 28,700 all-seater stadium. The impressive Reebok Stadium opened in 1997, the same season Colin Todd took Wanderers back to the Premiership.

Bournemouth

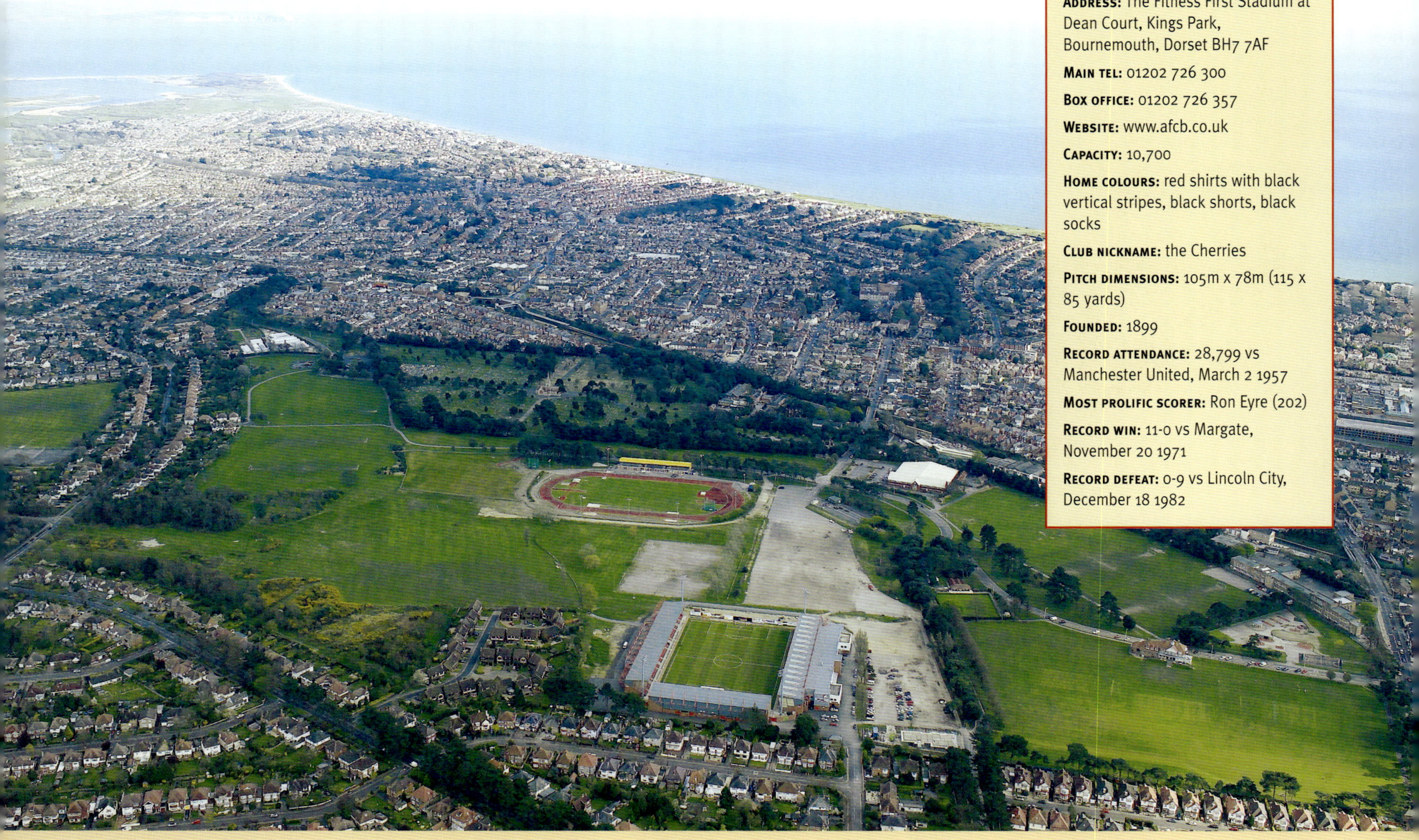

Ground: **The Fitness First Stadium**

Address: The Fitness First Stadium at Dean Court, Kings Park, Bournemouth, Dorset BH7 7AF

Main tel: 01202 726 300

Box office: 01202 726 357

Website: www.afcb.co.uk

Capacity: 10,700

Home colours: red shirts with black vertical stripes, black shorts, black socks

Club nickname: the Cherries

Pitch dimensions: 105m x 78m (115 x 85 yards)

Founded: 1899

Record attendance: 28,799 vs Manchester United, March 2 1957

Most prolific scorer: Ron Eyre (202)

Record win: 11-0 vs Margate, November 20 1971

Record defeat: 0-9 vs Lincoln City, December 18 1982

Bournemouth formed in 1899 as Boscombe FC. The club played their first games at Pokesdown, followed by a spell at King's Park. In 1910 the club moved to Dean Court, a former gravel pit. The facilities were not completed by the time the ground opened and players had to change in a nearby hotel. The club changed its name to Bournemouth and Boscombe Athletic in 1923 when it joined the League. The ground had fairly basic facilities with just one 400-seater stand. However, success on the pitch under the management of Leslie Knighton saw them begin to develop Dean Court. First came the 3,700-seater Main Stand, dressing rooms and a boardroom, which opened in 1927. Many of the materials used came from the Empire Exhibition at Wembley. Next a covered terrace at the south end was opened in 1936. The Cherries' successful cup run in 1957 saw the club's highest ever gate of 28,799 against Manchester United and enough funds to pay for the New Stand. The club officially changed its name to AFC Bournemouth in 1970, although many fans may not have noticed the change. An ill-fated purchase of land behind the North Stand and subsequent plans to build a new stand saw the club's finances take a battering. The first building blocks of the new structure were eventually demolished in 1984 and land sold off for housing. It was 1992 before any further development took place at Dean Court: the Main Stand had new seats added and executive boxes fitted. Finally, in 2001, the club redeveloped the ground. The pitch was rotated 90° and three new single-tiered cantilevered stands were built. The south end remains open, although the club plan to build a fourth stand to bring capacity up to 12,000.

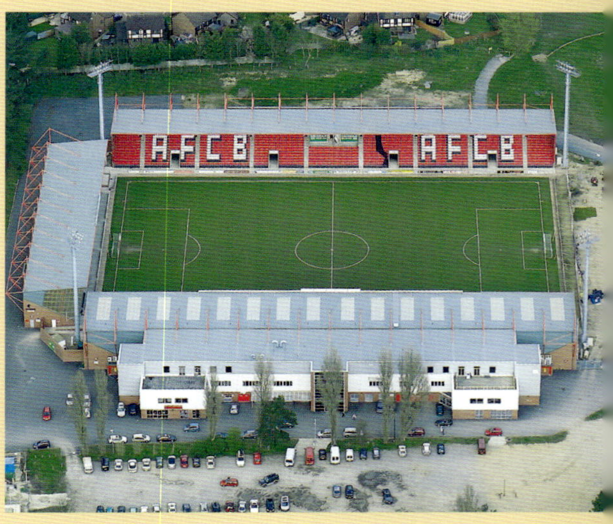

Bradford City

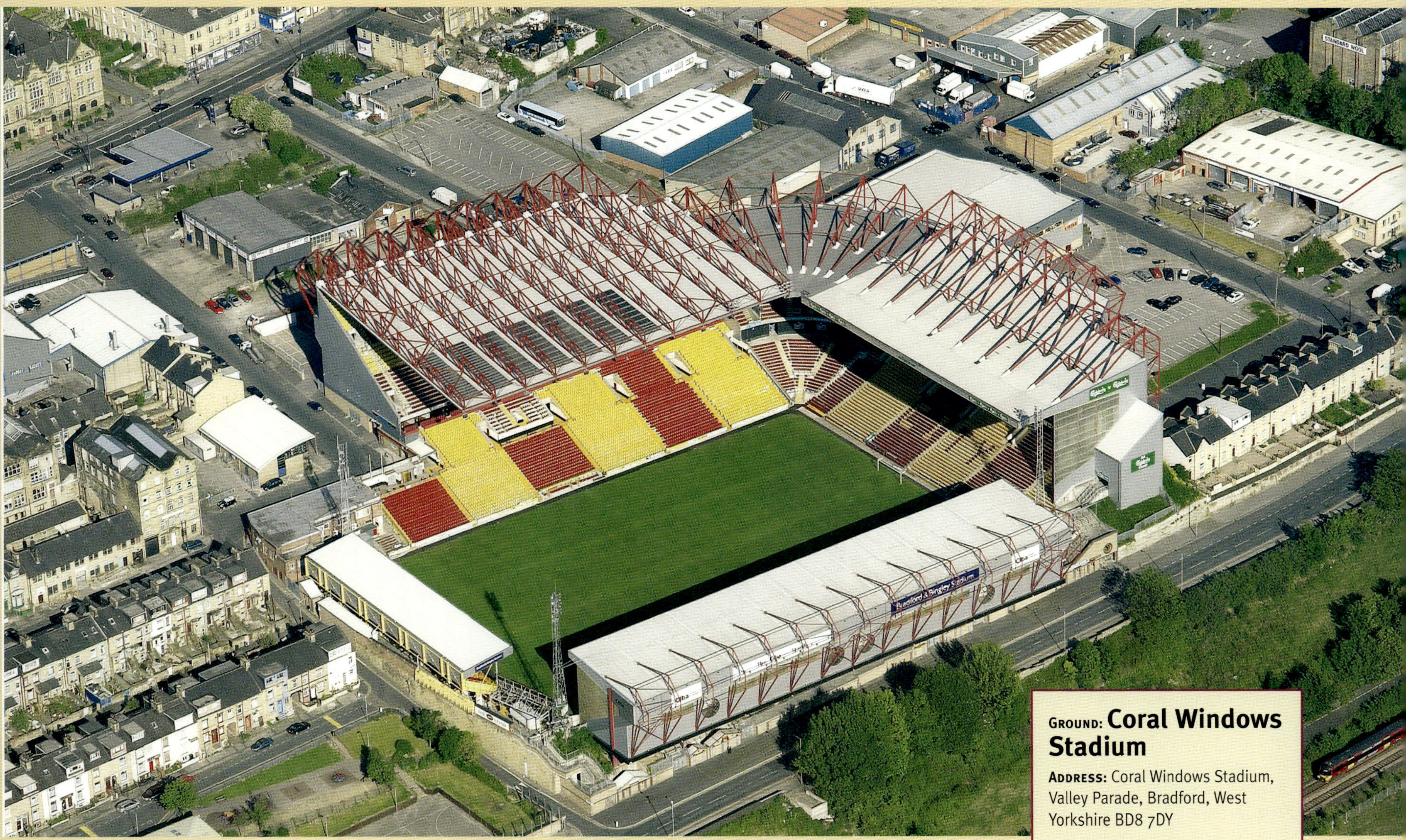

Ground: Coral Windows Stadium

Address: Coral Windows Stadium, Valley Parade, Bradford, West Yorkshire BD8 7DY

Main tel: 01274 773 355

Box office: 01274 770 012

Website: www.bradfordcityfc.co.uk

Capacity: 25,136

Home colours: claret and amber striped shirts, black shorts, claret and amber socks

Club nickname: the Bantams

Pitch dimensions: 103m x 64m (113 X 70 yards)

Founded: 1903

Record attendance: 39,146 vs Burnley, March 11 1911

Most prolific scorer: Bobby Campbell (121)

Record win: 11-1 vs Rotherham United, August 25 1928

Record defeat: 1-9 vs Colchester United, December 30 1961

Bradford City was formed in 1903. All the players came from Manningham Rugby Club, a team that had decided to switch codes and try their luck at football rather than rugby. The facilities at Valley Parade were fairly basic and players had to change in a nearby shed. The ground was redeveloped after the club won promotion to the First Division in 1908. The 3,500-seater Main Stand was the first to be built. Unusually the land on which the stand was erected had to be carved out of a hillside. Next came the development of the Manningham End Terrace: it was doubled in size and renamed the Nunn's Kop. Then on the Midland Road side of the ground a covered terrace was built capable of holding 8,000 fans. By 1911 the club was doing well on the pitch and saw its highest ever gate of 39,146 in an FA Cup game against Burnley in 1911. Bradford went on to win the FA Cup that season. No further development took place until 1951, when the Midland Road Stand was demolished after being certified unsafe. A replacement stand was opened in 1954 but this only lasted until 1960 when the structure was declared dangerous. Valley Parade remained three-sided until 1966, when the pitch was moved closer to the Main Stand and a narrow terrace for supporters was installed on the Midland Road side. In 1970 the Midland Road Terrace was roofed and seats added to the Main Stand. On May 11 1985 a fire, started by a cigarette, burned down the entire Main Stand, killing 56 fans and seriously injuring 200 more. The Bradford fire had serious repercussions for safety at football grounds across the country. The club moved to nearby Odsal for 14 months while Valley Parade was rebuilt. A 4,390-seater stand was opened in 1986 where the Main Stand had stood; the other sides were fitted with seats in subsequent years, with capacity now reaching 25,136.

Brentford

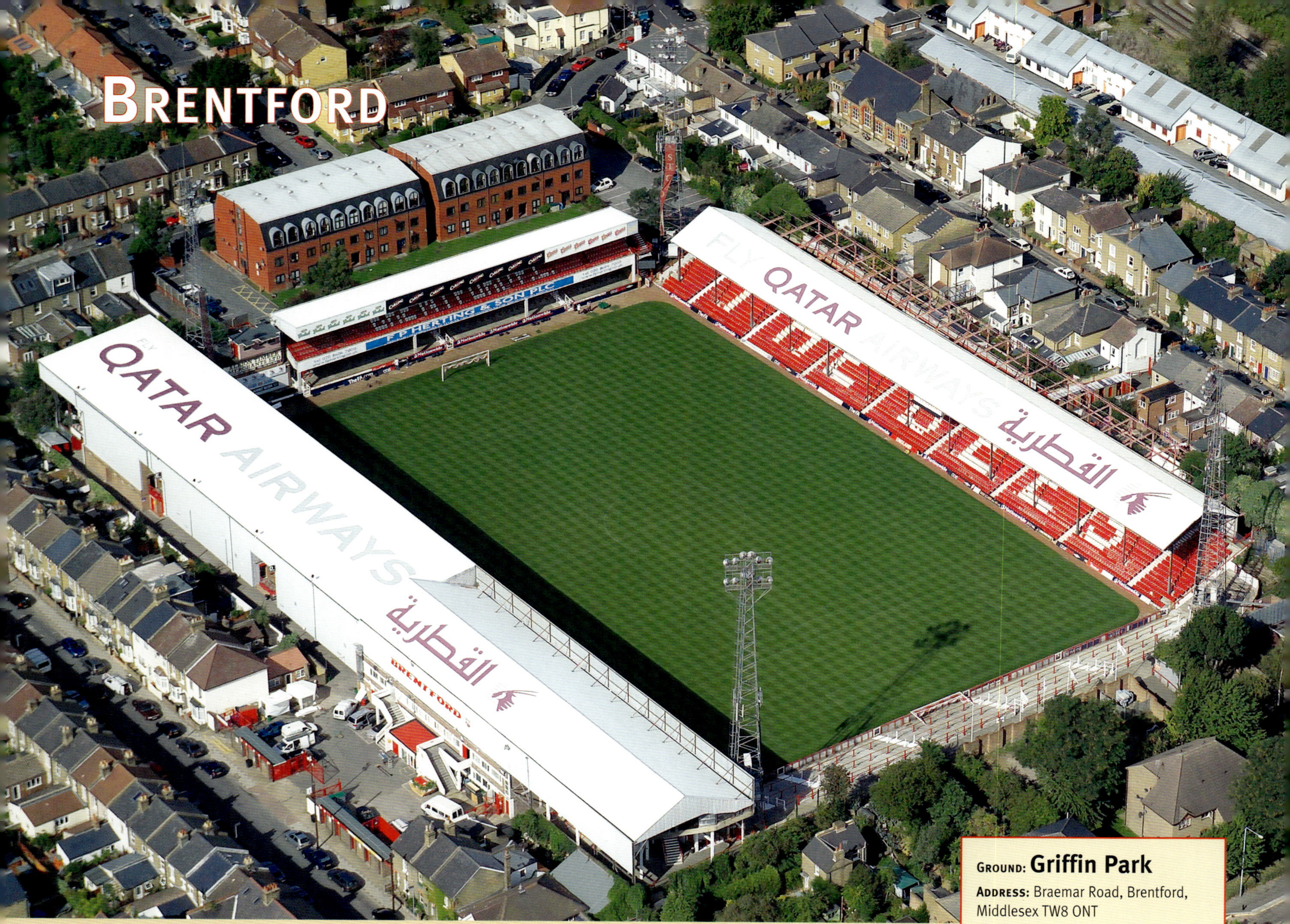

Brentford was formed by members of the local rowing club in 1889. The team played on a variety of local pitches until 1894, when they moved to Shotter's Field. Just four years later they moved to the Cross Roads before moving to Boston Park cricket ground; it was not until 1904 that they found a permanent home on a former orchard next to the Griffin pub. The Bees moved two of the stands from Boston Park, which formed the Main Stand and the Flower Pot Stand. The Main Stand was judged to be unsafe before it even opened and it was 1927 before Brentford had enough money to fund the new Main Stand. The Bees' performances on the pitch saw them rise steadily through the divisions and by 1935 there were covers over the New Road Terrace and the Brook Road End Terrace, and seats were added to the Main Stand. Just before the war, 39,626 fans crammed in to Griffin Park to see the Bees take on Preston North End in the FA Cup. Subsequently, Brentford's fortunes on the pitch declined and there was little development to the ground in the following three decades. An idea was floated to sell the ground to QPR in the 1960s; however, the Bees remained at Griffin Park. In 1983 fire burned down half of the Main Stand and the introduction of new safety measures following the fire at Bradford threw the Bees' finances into turmoil. They sold off some land for development to help fund the building in 1986 of the two-tiered Brook Road Stand, since nicknamed "the Wendy House". The Ealing Road Terrace, which remained an open terrace until 2007, has since been covered and the other two sides have all-seater stands. The club has announced plans to sell Griffin Park and move to a purpose-built 25,000 all-seater stadium to be sited on the edge of Gunnersbury Park.

Ground: **Griffin Park**

Address: Braemar Road, Brentford, Middlesex TW8 ONT

Main tel: 0845 345 6442

Box office: 0845 345 6442

Website: www.brentfordfc.co.uk

Capacity: 12,763

Home colours: red and white vertical striped shirts, black shorts, black socks

Club nickname: the Bees

Pitch dimensions: 100m x 67m (110 x 73 yards)

Founded: 1889

Record attendance: 39,626 vs Preston North End, March 5 1938

Most prolific scorer: Jim Towers (153)

Record win: 9-0 vs Wrexham, October 15 1963

Record defeat: 0-7 vs Swansea City, November 11 1924

BRIGHTON & HOVE ALBION

Brighton & Hove Albion's roots go back to a team called Brighton United which formed in 1898. After the team disbanded, Brighton & Hove Rangers formed, and then in 1901 they became Brighton and Hove Albion and played at a field on Dyke Road. A year later they played a game at the Goldstone Ground, which was at the time home to Hove FC. The teams agreed to a long-term ground-share, although in 1908 Hove sold their lease in its entirety to the Seagulls and Hove FC moved to Hove Park. The Goldstone Ground had a pavilion on one side and a small stand at the south end. The club began to redevelop the ground in 1920, erecting a terrace at the north end. In 1958 the West Stand was built and by December that year, 36,747 fans packed in to see the Seagulls take on Fulham in the FA Cup. The late 1970s and early 1980s saw Brighton's fortunes on the pitch take off. They spent four seasons in the First Division and almost beat Manchester United in the FA Cup final. Despite these successes, the Goldstone Ground was in a sorry state of repair, and the club's finances were not much better. In 1995 the ground was sold to developers, with no replacement secured. The Seagulls left the Goldstone Ground in May 1997 to ground-share with Gillingham. They remained there for two seasons before returning to Brighton to play at the Withdean Athletics Stadium in 1999. An athletics track surrounds the pitch, and at one end is a completely open stand. The South Stand holds 4,500 seats and the North Stand can hold 1,500 fans. The other end is open with uncovered seating. Plans for Brighton to move to a new purpose-built 22,000 capacity stadium have been approved.

GROUND: Withdean Stadium

ADDRESS: Withdean Stadium, Tongdean Lane, Brighton BN1 5JD

MAIN TEL: 01273 695 400

BOX OFFICE: 01273 776 992

WEBSITE: www.seagulls.co.uk

CAPACITY: 8,850

HOME COLOURS: blue and white striped shirts, white shorts, blue socks

CLUB NICKNAME: the Seagulls

PITCH DIMENSIONS: 100m x 68m (110 x 75 yards)

FOUNDED: 1901

RECORD ATTENDANCE: (at the Goldstone Ground) 36,747 vs Fulham, December 27 1958

MOST PROLIFIC SCORER: Tommy Cook (114)

RECORD WIN: 9-1 vs Newport County, April 18 1951

RECORD DEFEAT: 0-9 vs Middlesbrough, August 23 1958

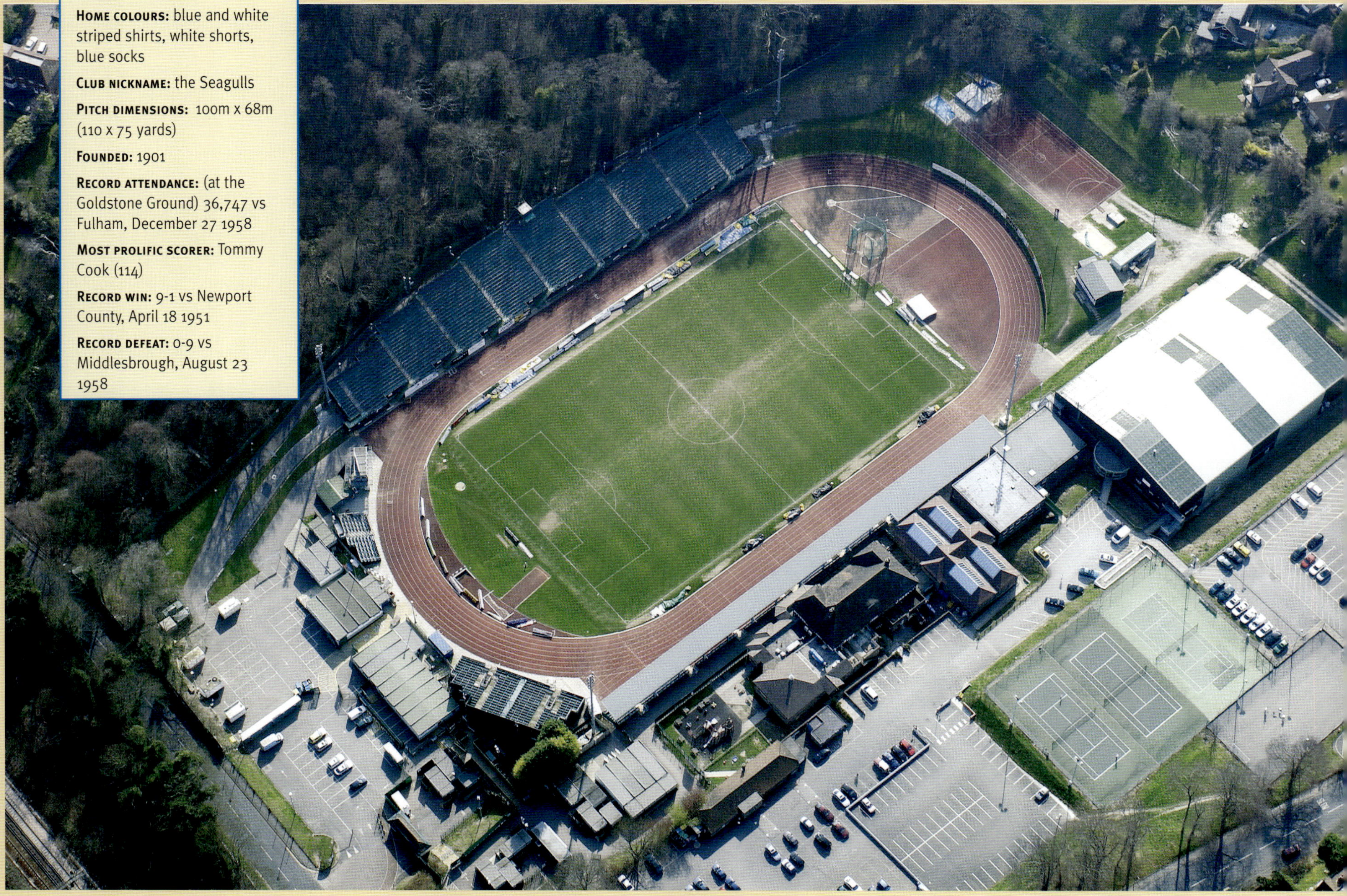

Bristol City

Bristol City was formed in 1894 as Bristol South End but changed its name to Bristol City in 1897. The Robins played their first games at St John's Lane. Ashton Gate was initially used by Bedminster FC, who merged with Bristol City in 1900. It was 1904 before the Robins officially made Ashton Gate their home ground. They immediately began building on the ground, starting off with the Main Stand on the west side, and moving one of the original stands to the east side. A roof was added to the South Terrace, although this blew down in 1916. The team's successes on the pitch saw them reach second place in the First Division in 1907, just six years after joining the League. However, their good fortune on the pitch did not last. In 1928 they had to sell players to fund the building of the Covered End Terrace. A year later a fire burned down one of the two original stands and the club almost had to sell Ashton Gate. The Main Stand was destroyed during the war, and it was replaced by a grandstand in 1953. A new stand was erected on the east side of the ground in 1970, just in time for City's promotion to the First Division. The Robins then dropped in record time to the bottom of the Fourth Division. Despite their finances being in a sorry state, Ashton Gate was in a fairly good state of repair. The club carried out further development in 1991 when seats were added to the Covered End Terrace and the paddock in front of the Grandstand. The Blackthorn Atyeo Stand was opened in 1994 on the site of the former Open End, behind one of the goals. The Micra Wedlock Stand is opposite and is used by away fans. The Main Stand was renamed the Williams Stand, and is a single-tiered structure. Opposite is the Dolman Stand, the ground's only two-tiered stand. While capacity is now 21,479, the Robins have ambitious plans to redevelop the ground into a 30,000 all-seater stadium starting with the new Micra Wedlock Stand.

Ground: **Ashton Gate**

Address: Ashton Gate Stadium, Ashton Road, Bristol BS3 2EJ

Main tel: 0871 222 6666

Box office: 0871 222 6666

Website: www.bcfc.co.uk

Capacity: 21,479

Home colours: red shirts, red shorts, white socks

Club nickname: the Robins

Pitch dimensions: 105m x 69m (115 x 75 yards)

Founded: 1894

Record attendance: 43,335 vs Preston North End, February 16 1935

Most prolific scorer: John Atyeo (314)

Record win: 9-0 vs Aldershot, December 28 1946

Record defeat: 0-9 vs Coventry City, April 28 1934

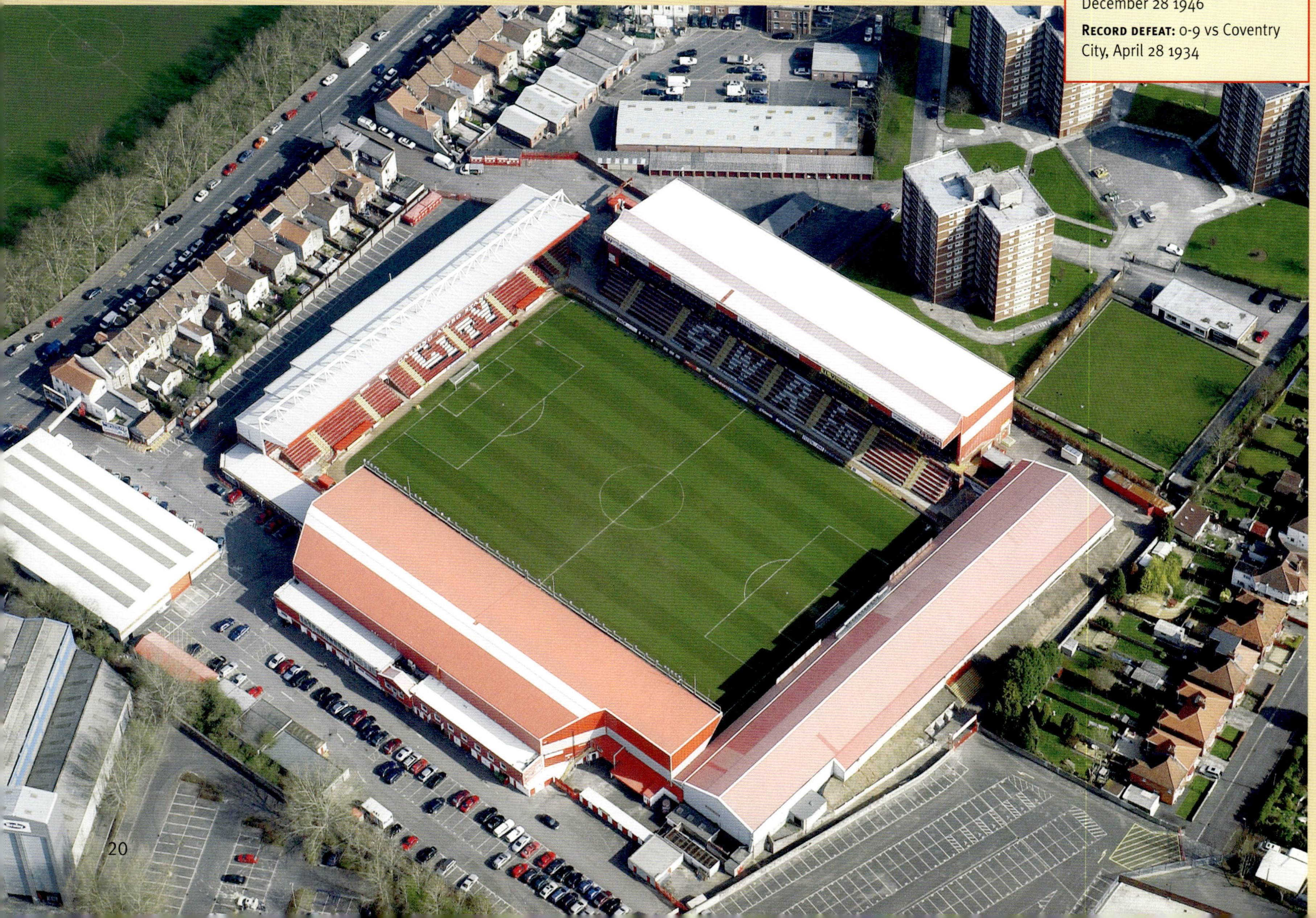

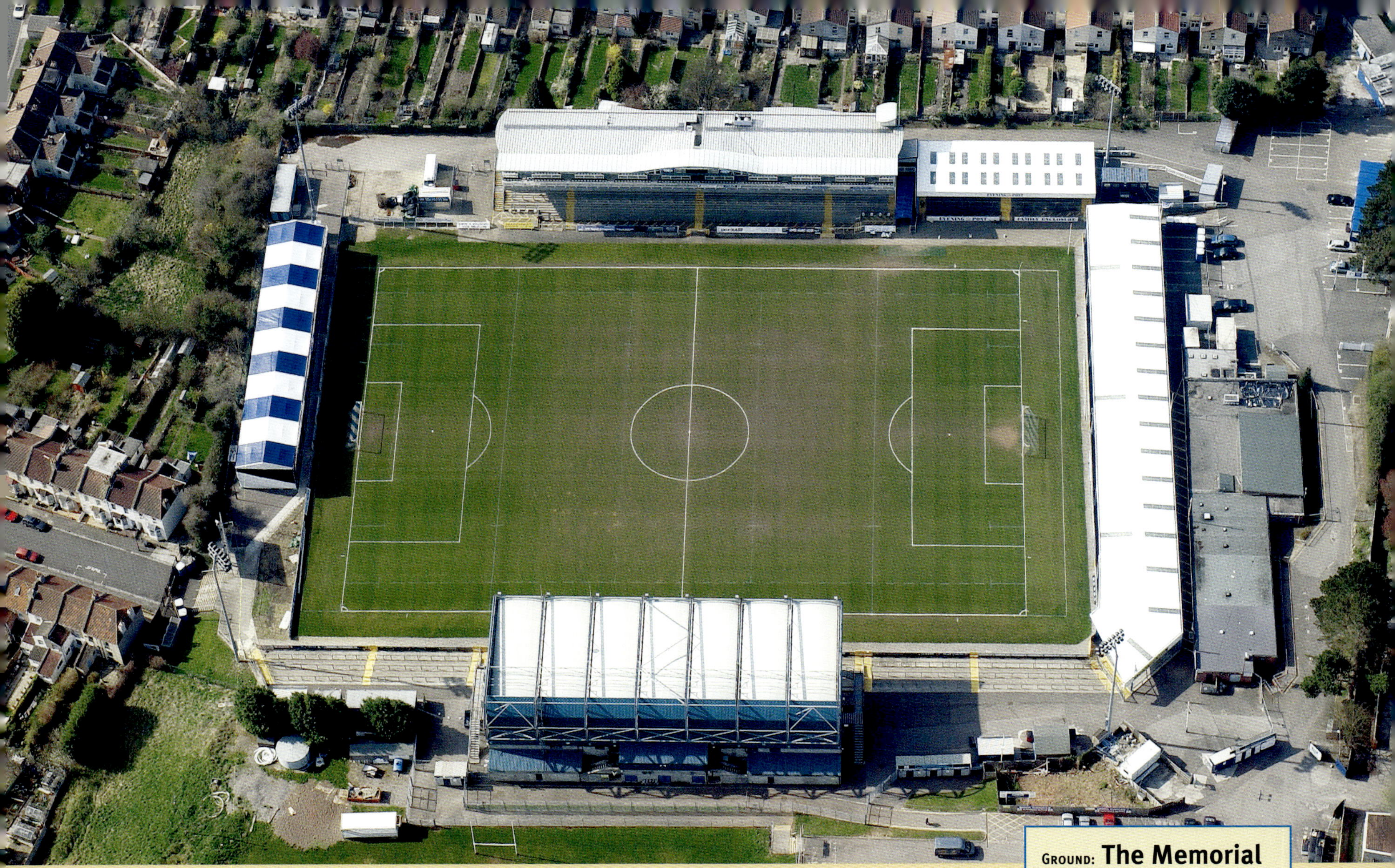

Bristol Rovers

Bristol Rovers began in 1883 as the Black Arabs. After playing at a number of grounds they eventually took over the Eastville Football and Athletic Ground, previously owned by Bristol Harlequins Rugby Club, in 1897. The club changed their name to Bristol Eastville Rovers, although they dropped the "Eastville" in 1898. The club began ground improvements by adding a roof to the north side, to go with the 500-seater stand on the south side. They joined the Third Division in 1920 and were able to pay for the new South Stand in 1924. A dog track was added in 1932 in an effort to raise much-needed funds; despite this the Pirates had to sell Eastville to the greyhound company in 1940. They remained as tenants at Eastville, built the new North Stand in 1958 and covered the Tote End Terrace in 1961. The previous year, the Pirates took on Preston North End in the FA Cup and 38,472 fans crammed into Eastville. The lease came up for renewal in 1979, but a fierce legal battle between the club and their landlords ensued. After the South Stand burned down in 1980, Rovers were forced to move in with their most hated rivals, Bristol City. An out-of court settlement saw Rovers continue to play at Eastville with a hefty annual rent. They finally left the ground in 1986 and moved to Bath City's ground, Twerton Park. Local rivalries made their presence felt when, in 1990, a group of Bristol City fans set fire to the Main Stand at Twerton Park. In 1996 Rovers moved back to Bristol to share a ground with Bristol Rugby Union Football Club at The Memorial Ground in Filton Avenue. At the time there was just the Main Stand to the east and an uncovered terrace to the north. They became joint owners of the ground with the rugby club in May 1998, and took full control in July of the same year when Bristol Rugby Club went into receivership. Rovers have since embarked on a total redevelopment programme to bring capacity at The Memorial Ground up to 18,500.

Ground: The Memorial Stadium

Address: the Memorial Ground, Filton Avenue, Horfield, Bristol BS7 0AQ

Main tel: 0117 909 6648

Box office: 0117 909 6648

Website: www.bristolrovers.co.uk

Capacity: 11,916

Home colours: blue and white quartered shirts, white shorts, blue socks

Club nickname: the Pirates, Rovers

Pitch dimensions: 101m x 65m (110 x 71 yards)

Founded: 1883

Record attendance: 11,883 vs Leeds United, September 14 2007

Most prolific scorer: Geoff Bradford (245)

Record win: 7-0 vs Brighton and Hove Albion, November 29 1952

Record defeat: 0-12 vs Luton Town, April 13 1936

BURNLEY

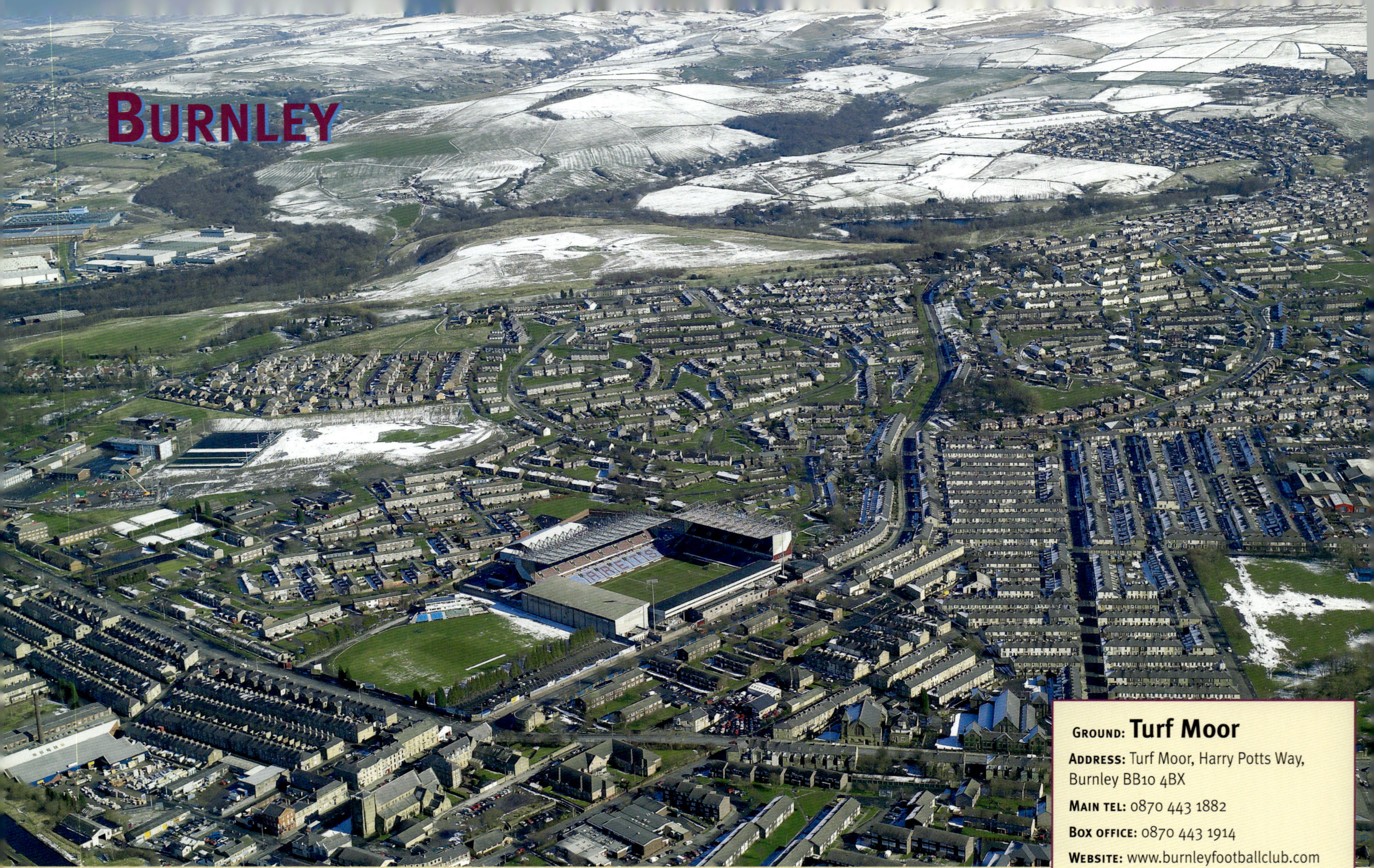

GROUND: Turf Moor

ADDRESS: Turf Moor, Harry Potts Way, Burnley BB10 4BX

MAIN TEL: 0870 443 1882

BOX OFFICE: 0870 443 1914

WEBSITE: www.burnleyfootballclub.com

CAPACITY: 22,546

HOME COLOURS: claret shirt, white shorts, white socks

CLUB NICKNAME: the Clarets

PITCH DIMENSIONS: 105m x 67m (115 x 73 yards)

FOUNDED: 1882

RECORD ATTENDANCE: 54,775 vs Huddersfield, February 23 1924

MOST PROLIFIC SCORER: George Beel (178)

RECORD WIN: 9-0 vs Darwen, January 9 1892

RECORD DEFEAT: 0-10 vs Aston Villa, August 29 1925

Above: Turf Moor, with Burnley Cricket Club alongside

Burnley was formed from a rugby team in 1882 and was known as Burnley Rovers for its first year of existence. In 1883, after dropping "Rovers" from their name, they moved to Turf Moor, where the club remains. The first stand to be built was an 800-seater stand on the south side and covers were added to each end. In 1908 the club built the Main Stand along one side and the so-called Star Stand on the other side. The team was well-supported and in 1924 recorded its highest ever attendance with 54,775 fans packing in to see the Clarets take on Huddersfield in the FA Cup. Between the wars concrete terracing was added to the Long Side Terrace and a roof was added in 1954. The club continued to develop the stands and seats, together with underfloor heating, were added to the Cricket Field End in 1969. The system of heating was extremely expensive and was done away with just two years later. A new single-tiered main stand was opened in 1974, named the Bob Lord Stand after the club's chairman. The Taylor report saw more changes at Turf Moor: the much-loved Long Side Terrace was cleared and the North Stand built in its place, a two-tiered cantilevered structure with 8,000 seats. A second two-tiered stand was also built at the east end of the ground, bringing capacity up to 22,546. There are plans for the club to develop the Cricket Field Stand by buying land currently owned by the cricket club. These have been put on hold while the club tries to find an alternative venue for the cricket club.

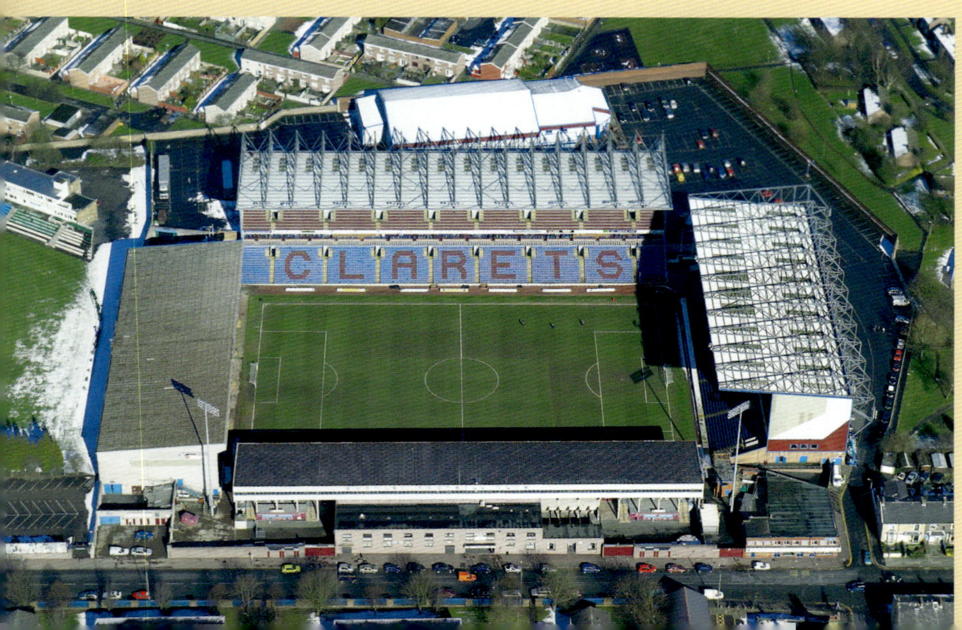

Cardiff City

Cardiff City emerged from Riverside FC, a team formed in 1899 from players at the Riverside Cricket Club. Ninian Park was then a rubbish tip between Sloper Road and the Taff Vale railway line. When the club turned professional in 1909, they bought a seven-year lease on the ground but before their first game against Aston Villa the players still had to clear debris from the pitch. The ground was fairly basic, with a small wooden grandstand on the Sloper Road side. The team won promotion in their first season in the League, finished runners-up in the First Division in 1924 and in 1927 they won the FA Cup. During this successful period the club built the Canton Stand at the north end and, following their FA Cup success, they built a roof over the Grangetown End Terrace. A bad run of form followed, and when in 1937 the Main Stand burned down, Cardiff were languishing in Division Three. By 1952 they were back in the First Division and gates were averaging 38,000. Despite being relegated again, the club continued to develop the ground and by 1960 they were back in the top flight. The ground was frequently used for Welsh internationals – 51 in total between 1946-76. The Safety of Sports Grounds Act in 1977 saw the capacity at Ninian Park slashed to 10,000 while it was improved. The Grangetown End roof was demolished and the banking was cut down. Bad performances on the pitch coupled with boardroom bickering saw Cardiff hit an all-time low in 1991 when just 1,629 fans turned up to see them defeated by Aldershot, and they almost went into liquidation. They were saved by millionaire holiday resort owner Rick Wright, who ploughed £2m into the club. In 1991 more seats were installed in the Main Stand, the Bob Bank and the Canton Stand, and the Grangemouth End was restored. Sam Hamman bought the club in 2000 and has been investing heavily in the ground and the squad; by the end of the 2004 season the capacity was up to 20,376.

Right: Ninian Park with the Millennium Stadium in the background

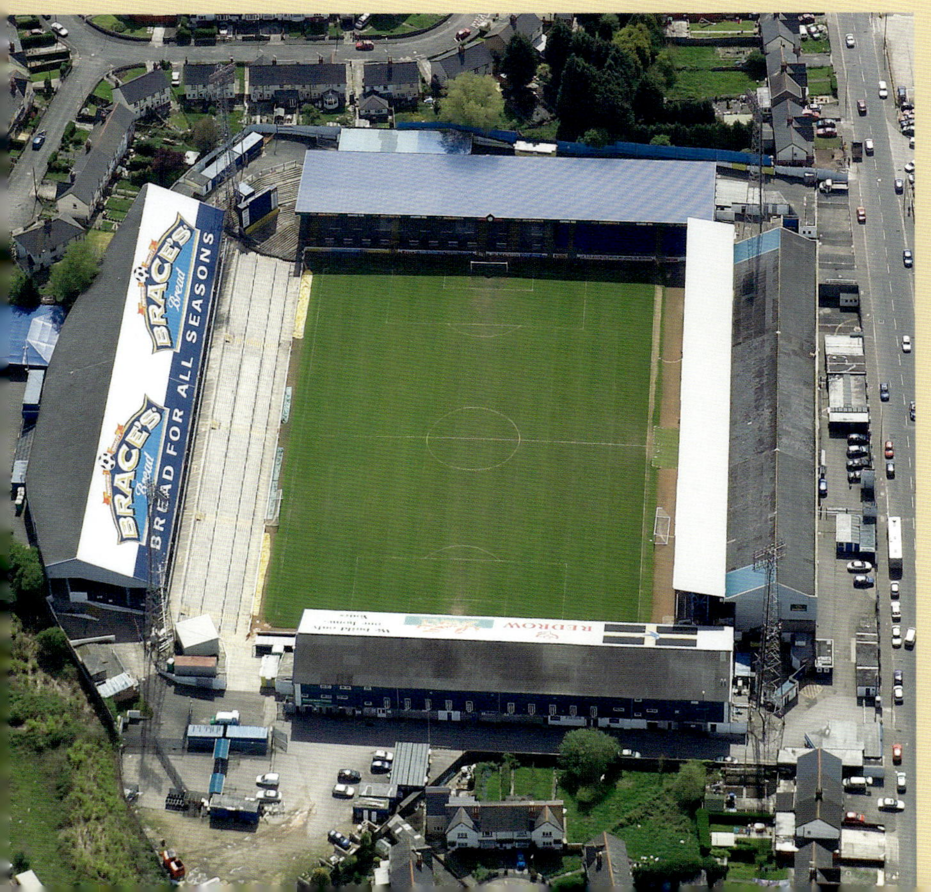

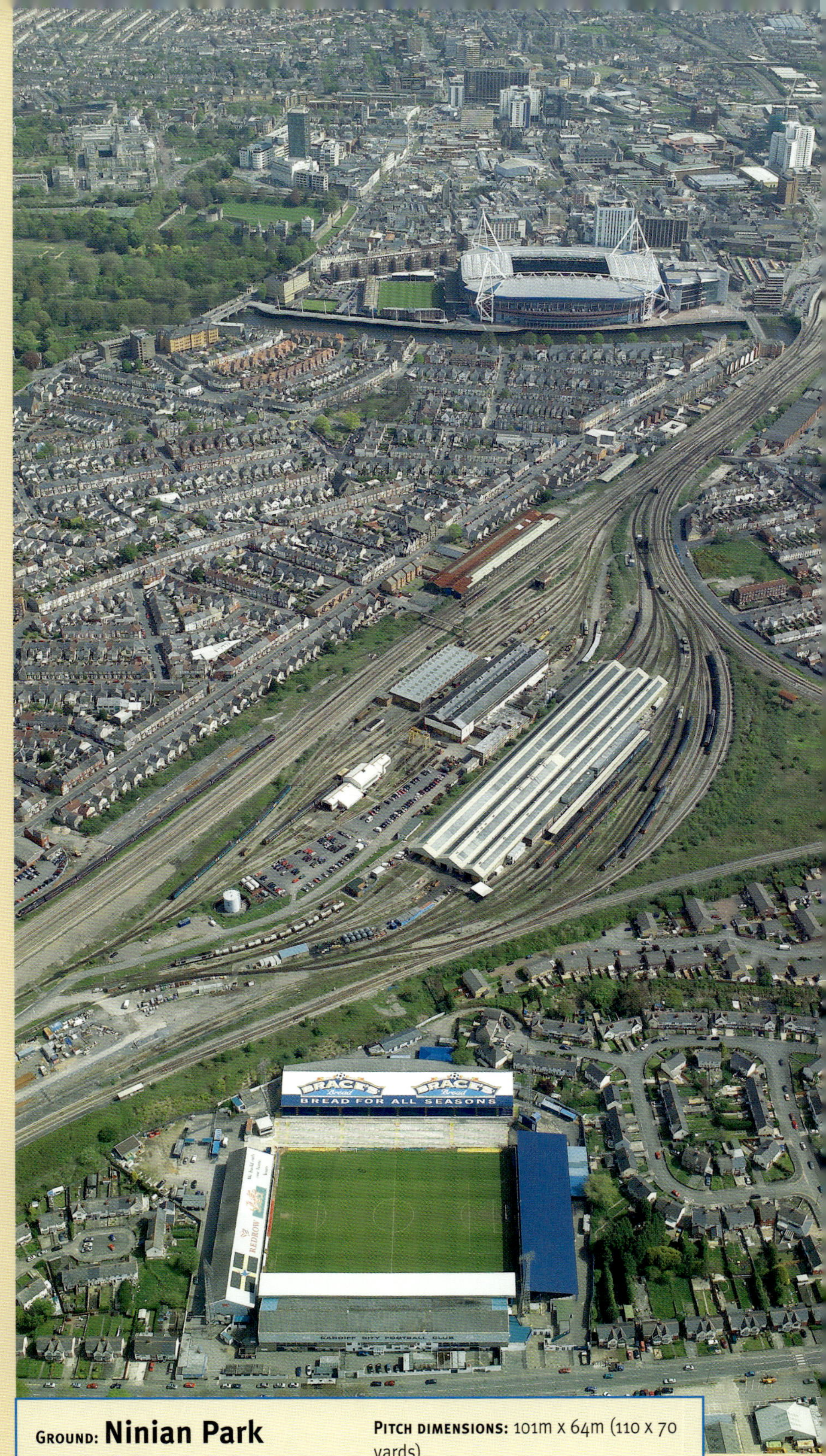

Ground: Ninian Park

Address: Ninian Park, Sloper Road, Cardiff CF11 8SX

Main tel: 029 2022 1001

Box office: 0845 345 1400

Website: www.cardiffcity.co.uk

Capacity: 20,376

Home colours: blue shirts, white shorts, white socks

Club nickname: the Bluebirds

Pitch dimensions: 101m x 64m (110 x 70 yards)

Founded: 1899

Record attendance: 57,893 vs Arsenal, April 22 1953

Most prolific scorer: Len Davies (128)

Record win: 8-0 vs Enfield, November 28 1931

Record defeat: 2-11 vs Sheffield United, January 1 1926

Celtic

Celtic was formed in 1888 as a charitable trust for the Catholic communities in Glasgow's East End. The club played games at a ground called Celtic Park from 1888 until 1892. When they could no longer afford the rent, they moved to a former brickyard in Parkhead and took the name Celtic Park to their new home. The club quickly built a grandstand and a pavilion with terracing on both ends. In 1898 the club's director James Grant paid for the Grant Stand to be built; this was unusual in that it was on stilts and had padded seats and windows along the front and side. The windows proved to be a less than successful innovation as they often steamed up. The ground was used for various sporting activities as well as football, including the World Cycling Championships, athletics meetings and a speedway race. The Grant Stand was demolished in 1929 and the South Stand built in its place. By 1938 Celtic Park recorded its largest ever crowd of 92,000 in an Old Firm clash with Rangers. The next major changes to the ground took place between 1957-71, reflecting the success the Bhoys were having on the pitch. The Rangers End was covered following Celtic's European Cup triumph in 1967. In 1986 the club added a new front to the South Stand in readiness for the club's centenary; however Celtic's reluctance to add more seats cost them dear in the aftermath of the Hillsborough disaster. Celtic's debts were high and a plan was announced to move the club to a new 52,000 all-seater stadium. The fans were not keen on the planned move and began boycotting games. As debts soared, the club faced receivership until Fergus McCann, a Canadian businessman, took over the club. He ditched the planned move and began developing Celtic Park into an all-seater stadium. Now the ground is fully enclosed, with three new two-tier stands and the older Main Stand bringing the all-seater capacity up to 60,832.

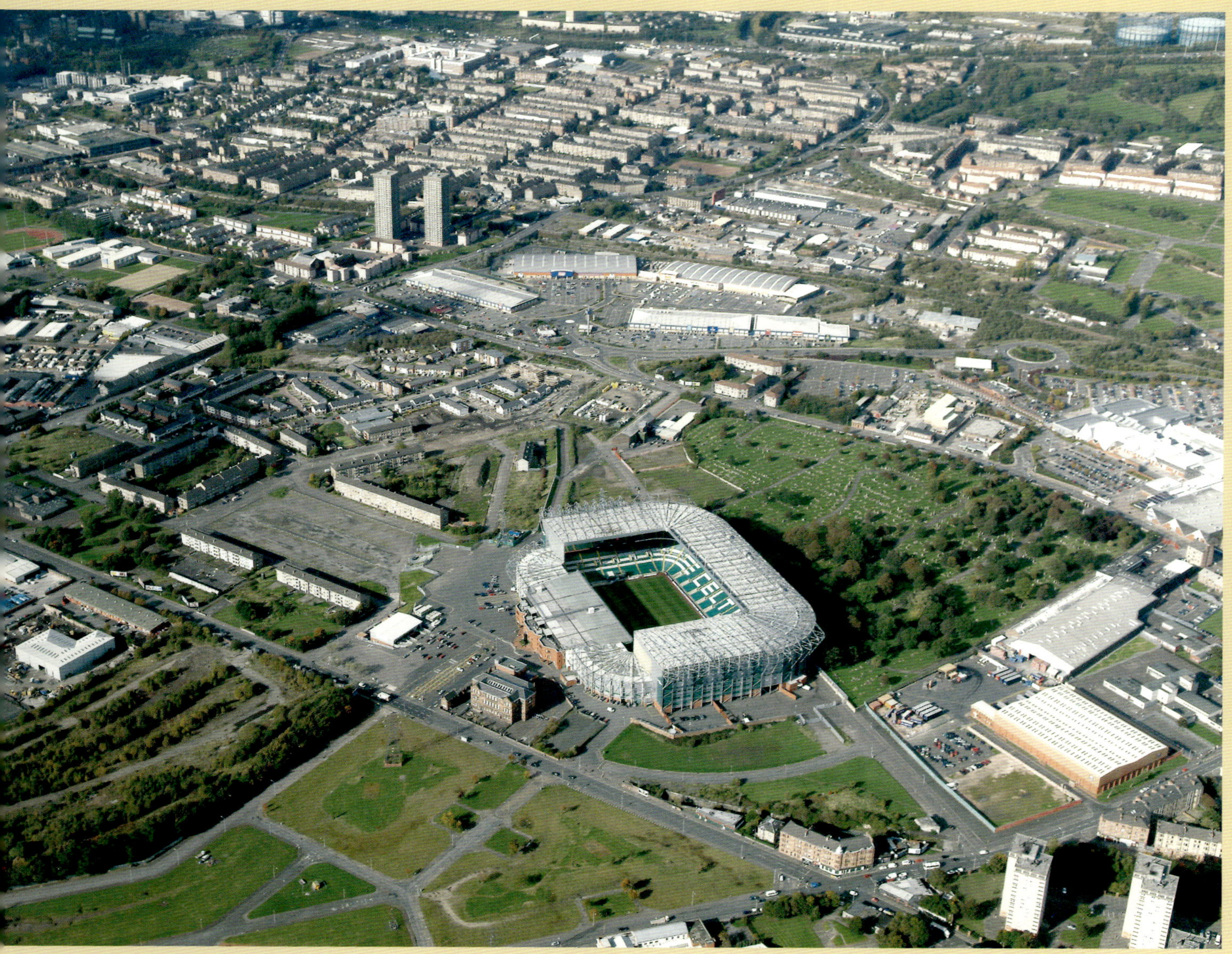

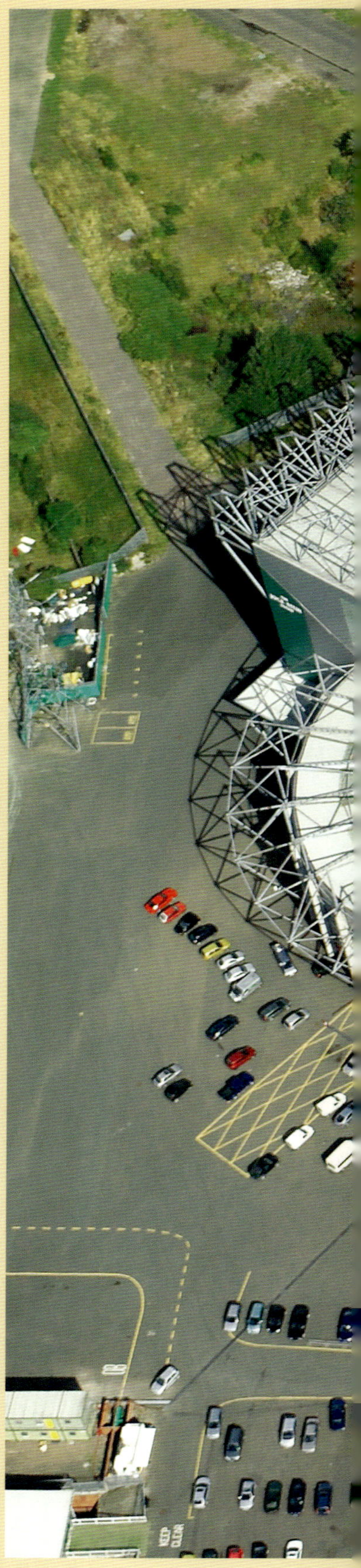

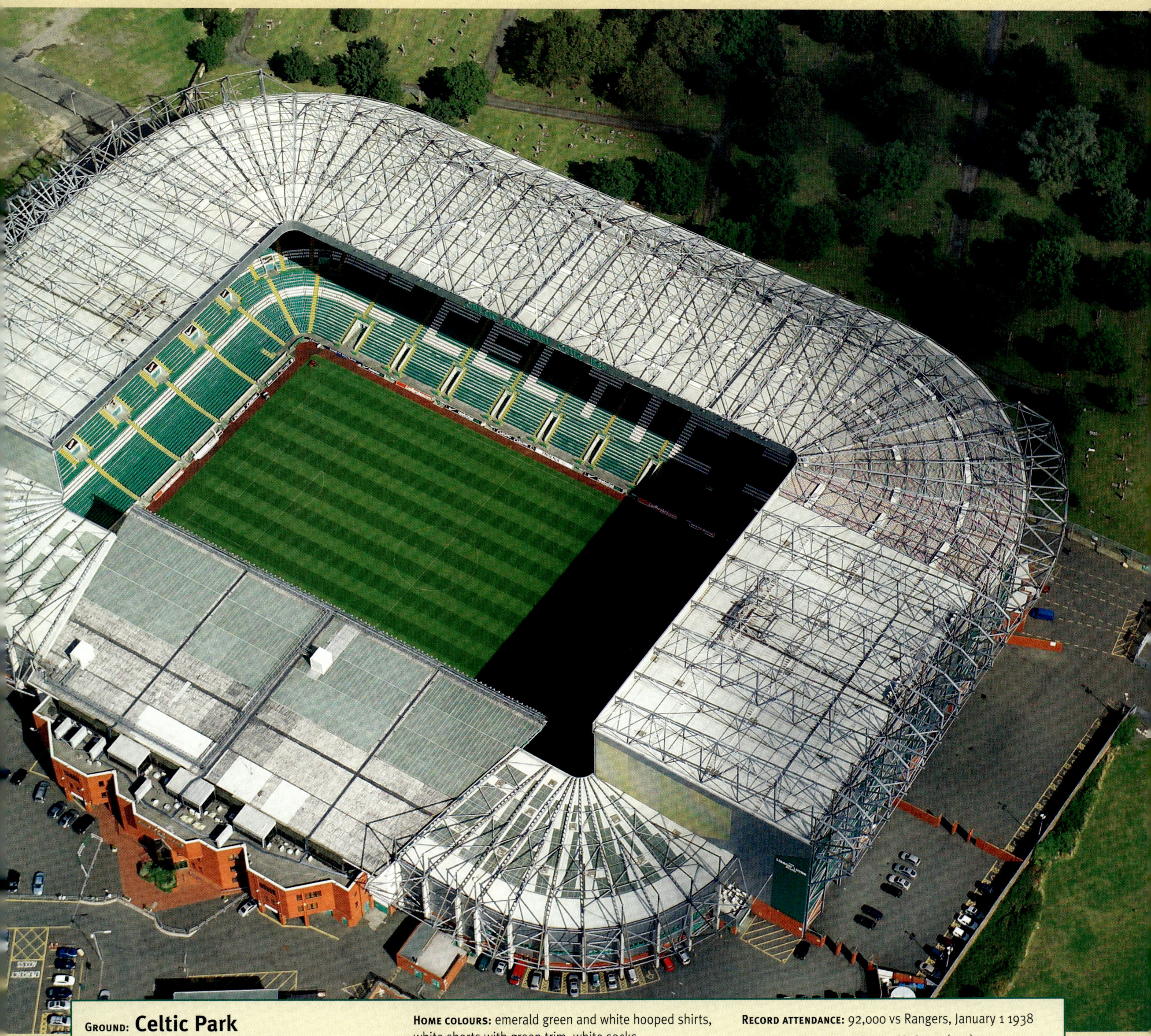

Ground: **Celtic Park**
Address: Celtic Park, Glasgow G40 3RE
Main tel: 0871 226 1888
Box office: 0871 226 1888
Website: www.celticfc.net
Capacity: 60,832

Home colours: emerald green and white hooped shirts, white shorts with green trim, white socks
Club nickname: the Bhoys
Pitch dimensions: 105m x 68m (115 x 74 yards)
Founded: 1888

Record attendance: 92,000 vs Rangers, January 1 1938
Most prolific scorer: James McGrory (397)
Record win: 11-0 vs Dundee, October 10 1895
Record defeat: 0-8 vs Motherwell, April 30 1937

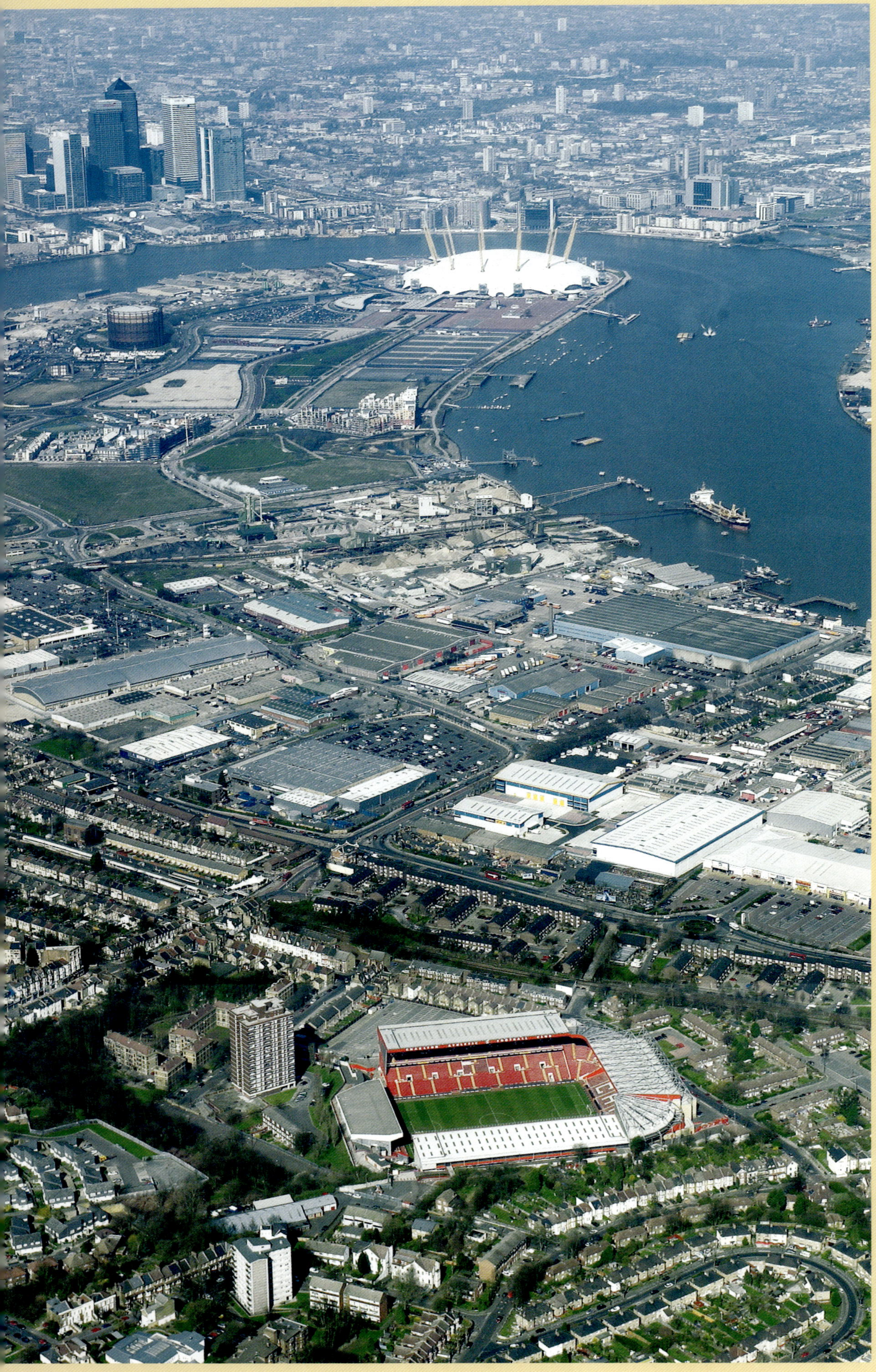

Charlton Athletic

Charlton Athletic was formed in 1905 by a group of teenagers. The team played at four grounds before arriving at The Valley in 1919. At the time The Valley was a chalk and sand pit known as "the swamp". Volunteers helped to dig out a pitch and banking was formed at either end. By 1921 the club had turned professional and built the Main Stand on the west side of the pitch; the ground was famed for its vast East Terrace. In 1923 the club decided to leave The Valley and move to a ground called The Mount. Charlton moved back to The Valley after just one season. The club had run up huge debts and were facing a bleak future until the Gliksten brothers stepped in with a £100,000 rescue package in 1931. Success on the pitch under the management of Jimmy Seed saw the fan base swell and in 1938 The Valley recorded its highest ever gate of 75,031. Despite winning the FA Cup in 1947, the club did not carry out any further development until 1950 when a few hundred seats were added to the Main Stand paddock. In the 1980s the club announced plans to make the ground all-seater. However, poor financial decisions meant Charlton had to leave The Valley in 1985 and moved in with local rivals Crystal Palace. New directors and a massive campaign by the club's dedicated fans led to an announcement in 1989 that Charlton would be moving back to The Valley. Fans and directors alike helped clear the overgrown pitch but in 1990 Greenwich Council turned down the plans. After forming a political party, the fans finally achieved their goal and despite having to spend a further season at Upton Park, the club moved back to The Valley in 1992. Since then the ground has been totally redeveloped with the large single-tiered East Stand and two-tiered North and West Stands; the Jimmy Seed Stand remains a small single-tiered structure. The north-east and north-west corners have been filled in and there are plans for the redevelopment of the East Stand, the south-east corner and the Jimmy Seed Stand to eventually bring capacity up to 40,000.

Left: The Valley with the Millennium Dome, Canary Wharf and the river Thames in the background

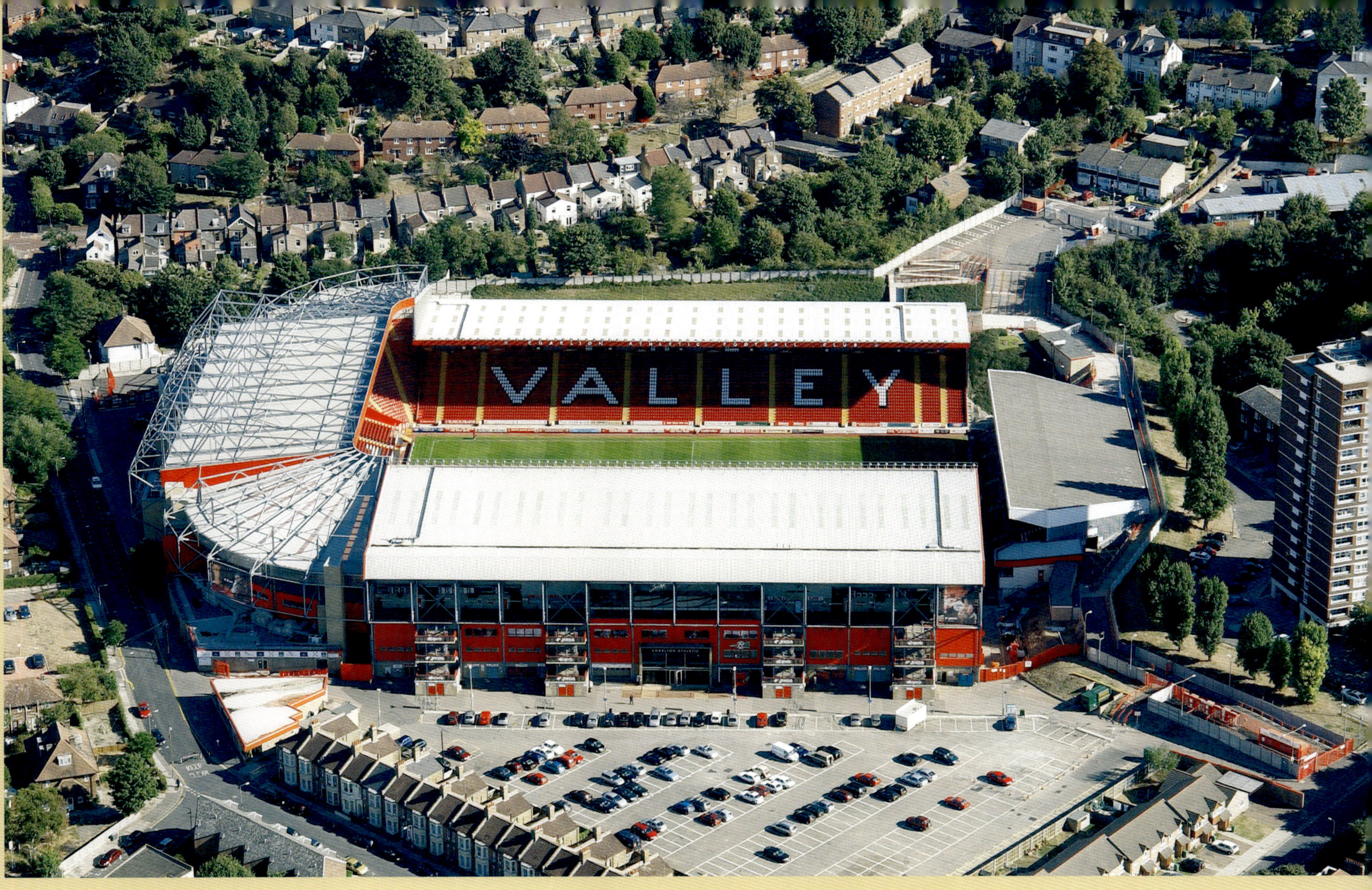

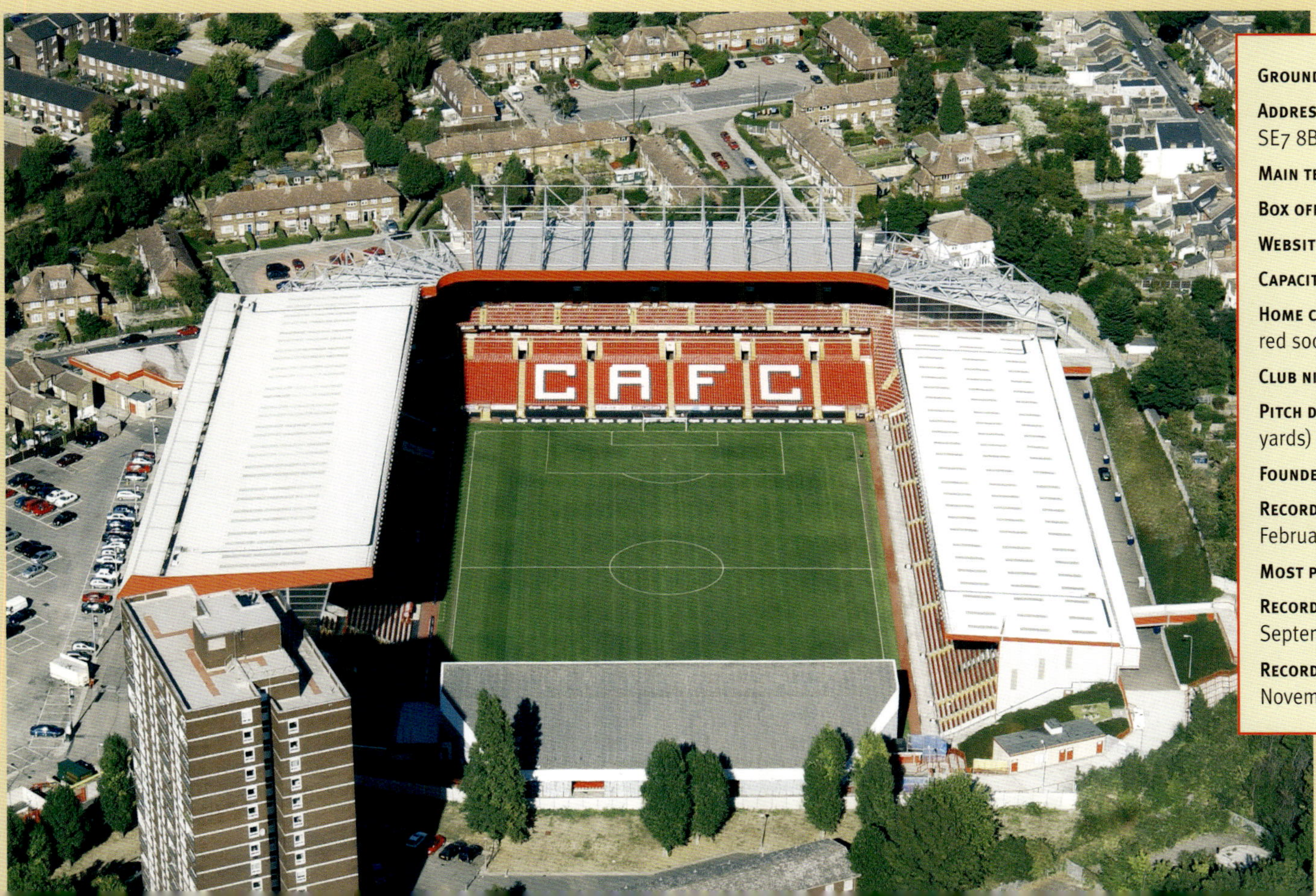

GROUND: **The Valley**

ADDRESS: The Valley, Floyd Road, Charlton SE7 8BL

MAIN TEL: 020 8333 4000

BOX OFFICE: 0871 226 1905

WEBSITE: www.cafc.co.uk

CAPACITY: 27,111

HOME COLOURS: red shirts, white shorts, red socks

CLUB NICKNAME: the Addicks, the Valiants

PITCH DIMENSIONS: 102m x 67m (112 x 73 yards)

FOUNDED: 1905

RECORD ATTENDANCE: 75,031 vs Aston Villa, February 12 1938

MOST PROLIFIC SCORER: Stuart Leary (153)

RECORD WIN: 8-1 vs Middlesbrough, September 12 1953

RECORD DEFEAT: 1-11 vs Aston Villa, November 14 1959

Chelsea

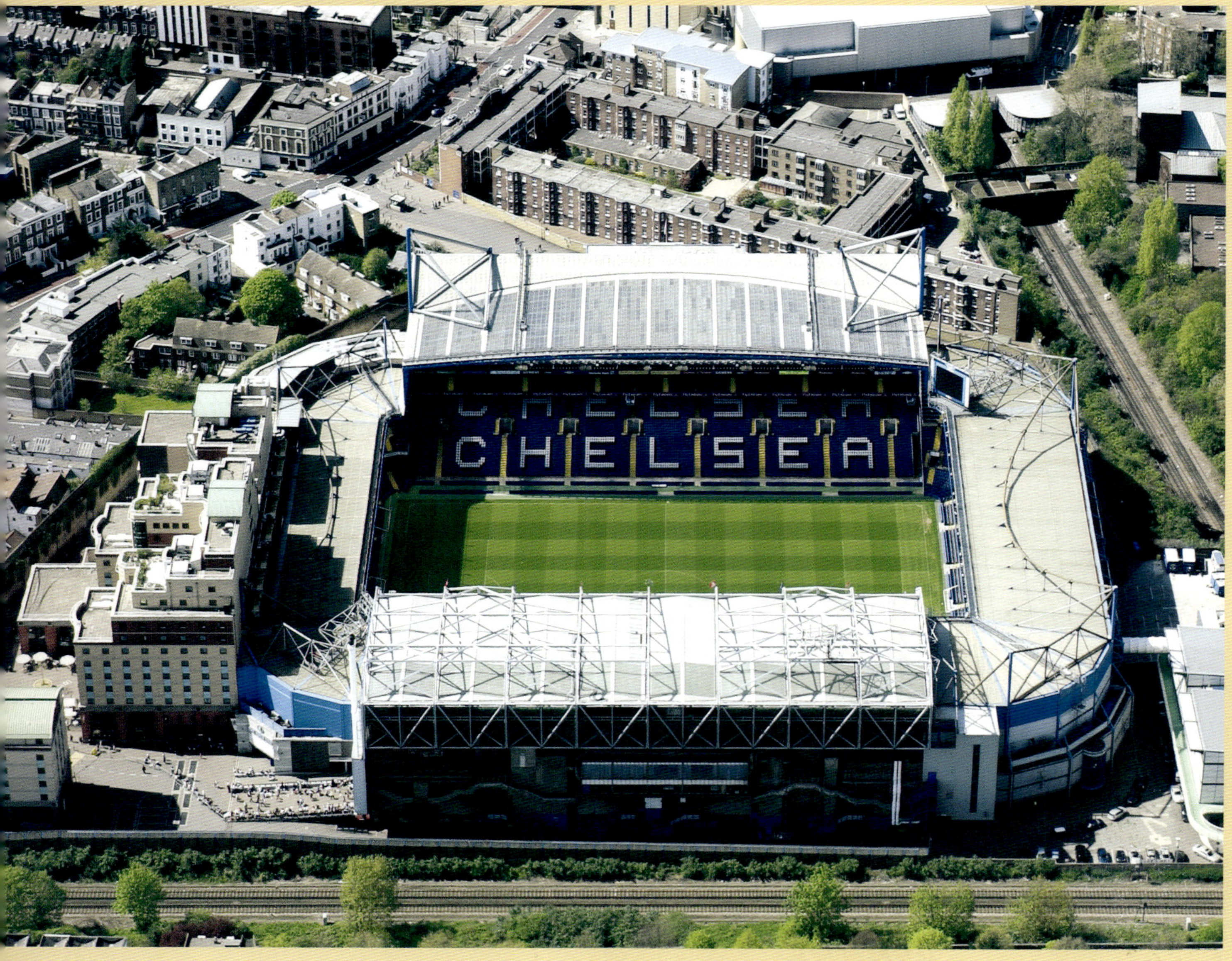

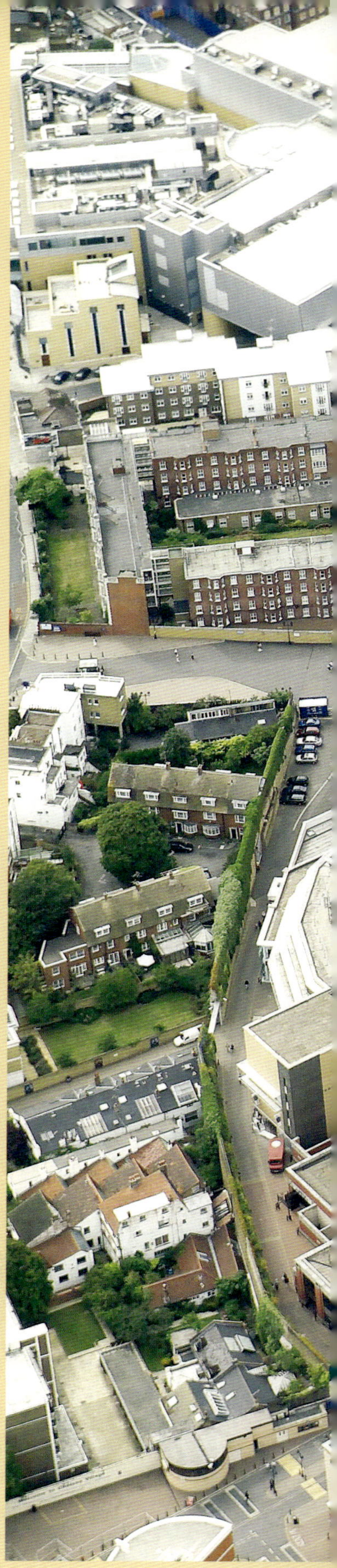

Chelsea was formed in 1905 but their ground, Stamford Bridge, came into being almost 30 years earlier in 1877, when the London Athletic Club developed it as a running track from an orchard and market garden. In 1904 Gus Mears took over the ownership of the ground and developed it into a venue for cycling, athletics and football. Mears commissioned the Scottish architect, Archibald Leitch, to design the 5,000-seater Main Stand. Mears and his friend Fred Parker established Chelsea FC in 1905. Chelsea had a remarkably successful first season and by 1907 their promotion to the First Division saw them attracting the highest gates in the League. Despite staging FA Cup finals and other sporting events, the cub did not invest much money in the ground. It was not until 1935 that a cover was added to the Fulham Road Terrace. This was the same year the club recorded its highest ever gate of 82,905 in a game against Arsenal. In 1939 a 2,500-seater stand was erected on the north-east corner, on stilts above the terracing. A new north stand was opened in 1945, but it was during the 1960s and 1970s when major development took place at the Bridge. At the time the West Stand was built, the team were going through one of their most successful periods ever, winning the League Cup in 1965 and the FA Cup in 1970. They also won the European Cup Winners' Cup in 1971. In 1971 plans were drawn up for the three-tier East Stand, the first stand in the £5.5m development. The stand opened in 1974 but Chelsea's luck took a turn for the worse. They were heavily in debt, they were relegated to the Second Division and gates were dropping. In the 1982/83 season gates twice dropped to below 7,000. It was in this season that Ken Bates took over as chairman. Over the following 20 years, Chelsea Village was developed. Two new all-seater stands were built at each end and corner stands added. In 2001 the West Stand was rebuilt, a two-tiered stand bringing capacity up to 42,449.

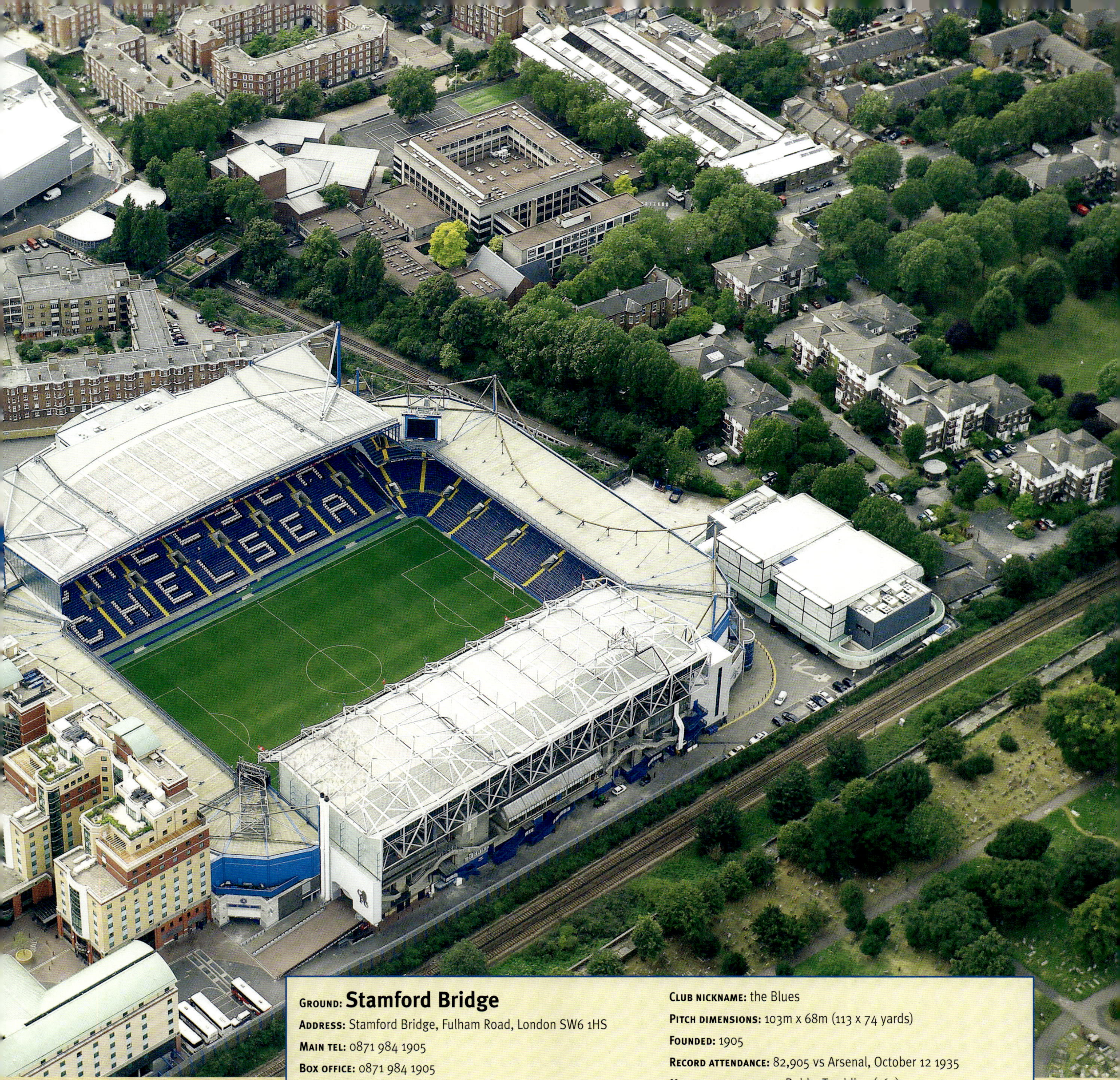

Above: Stamford Bridge with the Chelsea Village Hotel in the foreground

Ground: **Stamford Bridge**

Address: Stamford Bridge, Fulham Road, London SW6 1HS

Main tel: 0871 984 1905

Box office: 0871 984 1905

Website: www.chelseafc.com

Capacity: 42,449

Home colours: royal blue shirts with white and amber trim, royal blue shorts with white and blue trim, white socks with blue and amber trim

Club nickname: the Blues

Pitch dimensions: 103m x 68m (113 x 74 yards)

Founded: 1905

Record attendance: 82,905 vs Arsenal, October 12 1935

Most prolific scorer: Bobby Tambling (164)

Record win: 13-0 vs Jeunesse Hautcharage, September 29 1971

Record defeat: 1-8 vs Wolverhampton Wanderers, December 26 1953

CHESTERFIELD

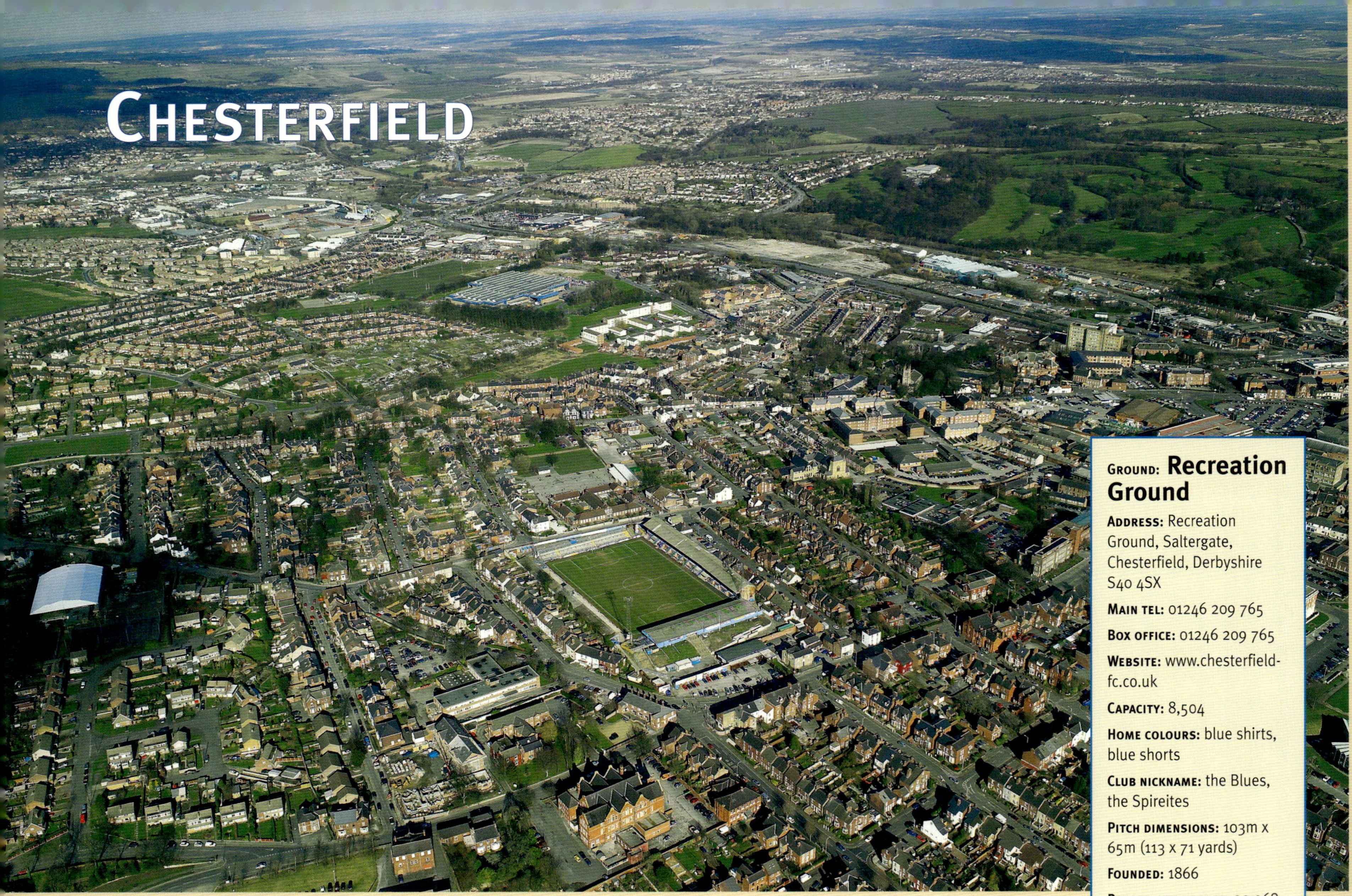

GROUND: Recreation Ground

ADDRESS: Recreation Ground, Saltergate, Chesterfield, Derbyshire S40 4SX

MAIN TEL: 01246 209 765

BOX OFFICE: 01246 209 765

WEBSITE: www.chesterfield-fc.co.uk

CAPACITY: 8,504

HOME COLOURS: blue shirts, blue shorts

CLUB NICKNAME: the Blues, the Spireites

PITCH DIMENSIONS: 103m x 65m (113 x 71 yards)

FOUNDED: 1866

RECORD ATTENDANCE: 30,968 vs Newcastle United, April 7 1939

MOST PROLIFIC SCORER: Ernie Moss (161)

RECORD WIN: 10-0 vs Glossop, January 17 1903

RECORD DEFEAT: 0-10 vs Gillingham, September 5 1987

Chesterfield can trace its roots back to 1866 and a team originally called Chesterfield Town. The club settled at the Recreation Ground in 1887 after playing at various local grounds. At the turn of the century a small stand stood along the east side of the pitch, and a pavilion was built in 1914. After a 10-year spell in the League between 1899 and 1909, Chesterfield FC rejoined the League in 1921, but it was not until the 1930s that they began developing the ground. The Main Stand was opened in 1936, and just three years later a record attendance of 30,968 watched the Spireites take on Newcastle United in a Second Division match. A successful Cup run in the 1950s funded a cover over the Compton Street Terrace, and in 1961 a cover was added to the Kop. The Spireites were the last League club to instal floodlights. After several failed attempts, the Recreation Ground finally erected floodlights in 1967. The various acts aiming to improve safety at football grounds, which came into force in the 1980s and 1990s, saw capacity at the Recreation Ground drop from 19,750 to 8,504. Chesterfield, like many other clubs, found the financial commitments needed to meet the new regulations extremely demanding. Its location, with surrounding housing, means further development of some of the stands and terraces would be difficult if not impossible. The Compton Street Terrace was replaced by an all-seater stand in 2002; however it appears the death knell has now sounded for the Recreation Ground. The club has now announced plans to move to a 10,000-capacity stadium on the site of a former glass factory.

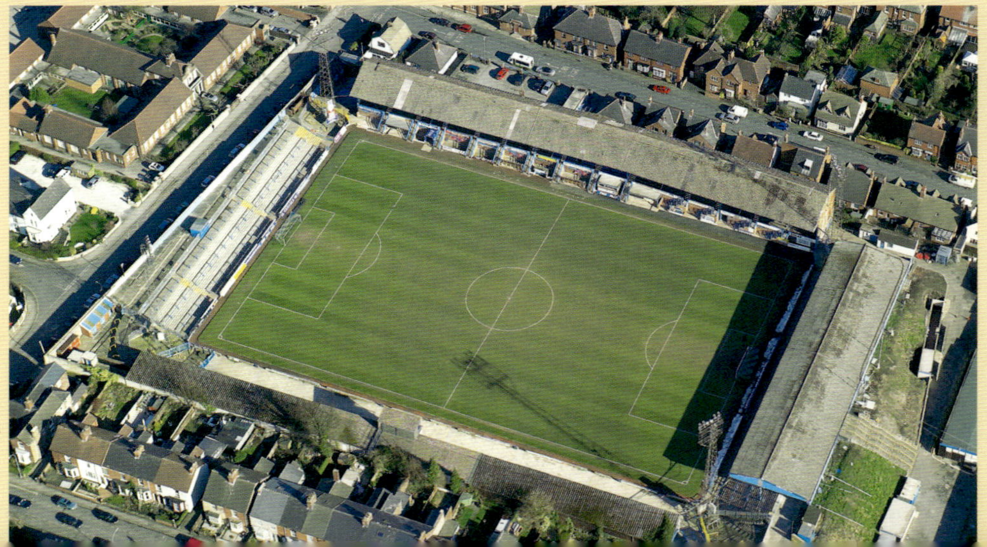

Colchester United

Colchester United formed in 1937, although the club can trace its roots back to Colchester Town, an amateur team formed in 1873. Town played at various sites before moving to Layer Road in 1909. Layer Road had been used by the army previously, and during the First World War the army moved back in to use the ground for drilling practice. In 1919 Colchester Town bought the ground and began developing it. The club built the Main Stand in 1932 and added a cover to the terracing opposite. In 1937 the team turned professional and changed their name to Colchester United. They added a roof to the Layer Road End, and during the Second World War POWs built wooden terracing beneath it. An excellent Cup run in 1948 saw attendances at Layer Road grow, and the following season a record 19,072 fans packed in to see the Us take on Reading in the Cup. Colchester joined the League in 1950, and continued to develop the ground. The terraces had roofs fitted in 1956 and floodlights were put up in 1959. Little else changed until 1985 when, in the aftermath of the Bradford fire, new safety regulations were introduced which slashed Layer Road's capacity from 14,000 to 4,000. In a bid to save money, the Us took the unusual step of banning away fans, which was intended to cut policing bills. Unfortunately the idea backfired and attendances dropped to their lowest levels ever. By 1990 the club found themselves playing in the GM Vauxhall Conference and, with ever increasing debts, had to sell Layer Road to the council. United returned to the League in 1992 and carried out further improvements to the Barside Popular Terrace and the Clock End. Visiting spectators are now mostly housed in the small Layer Road End.

Ground: **Layer Road**

Address: Layer Road, Colchester, Essex CO2 7JJ

Main tel: 0871 226 2161

Box office: 0871 226 2161

Website: www.cu-fc.com

Capacity: 6,375

Home colours: blue and white striped shirts, white shorts, white socks

Club nickname: the Us

Pitch dimensions: 101m x 64m (110 x 70 yards)

Founded: 1937

Record attendance: 19,072 vs Reading, November 27 1948

Most prolific scorer: Martyn King (131)

Record win: 9-1 vs Bradford City, December 30 1961

Record defeat: 0-8 vs Leyton Orient, October 15 1989

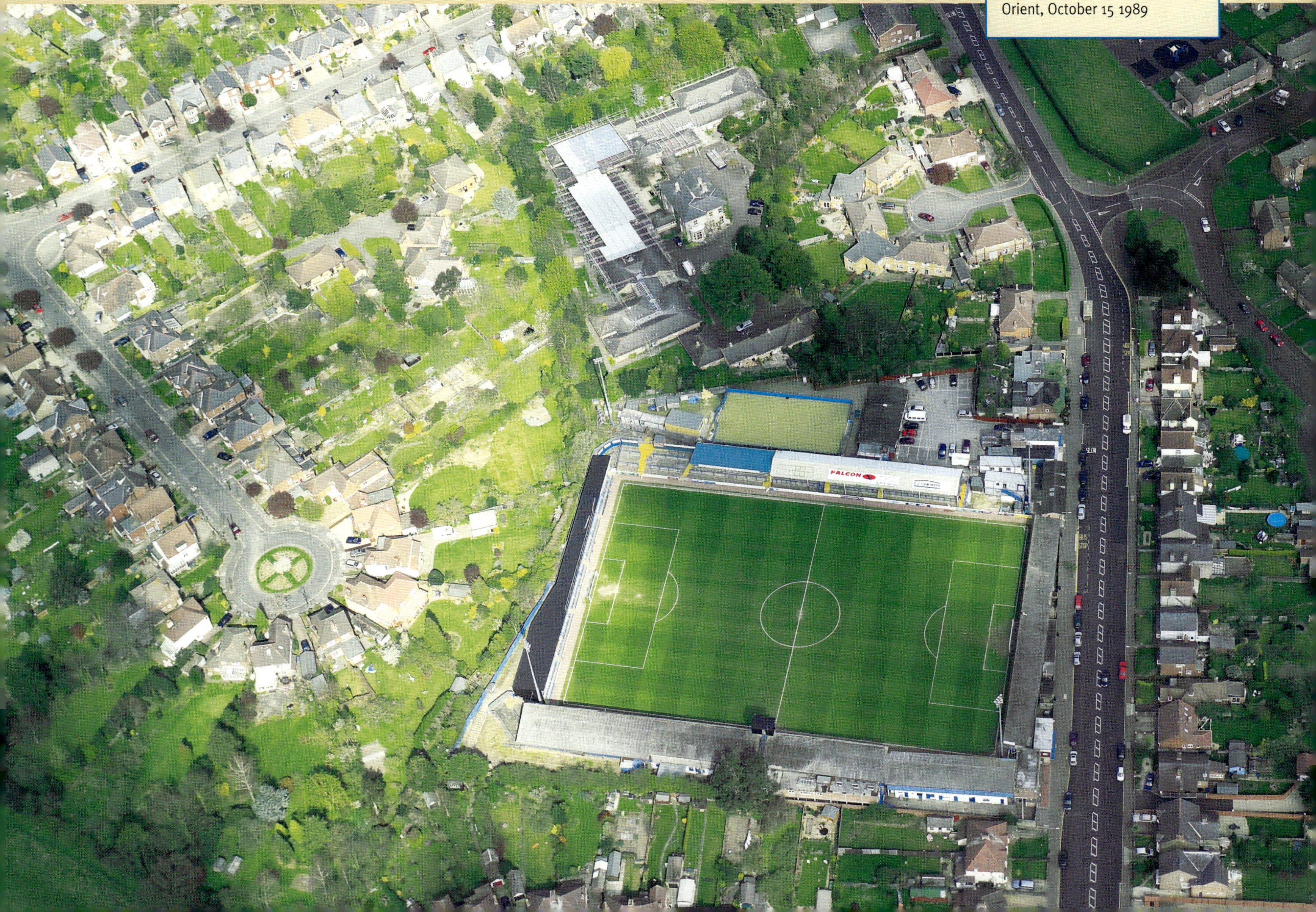

Coventry City

Coventry City FC was founded in 1883 by workers at the local Singer factory, a manufacturer of bicycles. The club played at various grounds before moving to Highfield Road in 1899. City joined the Southern League in 1908 and a good run in the Cup two years later helped to finance a new stand with a roof on the Thackhall Street side. They joined the League in 1919 and further developments were made to the ground, including the erection of the Kop in 1922 and a cover over the West Terrace. The Main Stand was built to replace the original stand on the south side of the pitch, and the club bought Highfield Road outright in 1936. Two years later terracing was extended at the Kop's north corner, known as the Crow's Nest. The ground was not badly hit during the Blitz; the pitch was destroyed but little else was damaged. Jimmy Hill's appointment as manager in 1961 brought in sweeping changes, and not just to the kit (which was previously blue and white). The club rose from the Third to the First Division in just six years and the ground was developed to reflect this success. The Thackhall Street Stand had seats added and the new Sky Blue Stand was built. The Sky Blues' support base increased rapidly and in 1967, 51,455 fans saw Jimmy Hill's side take on local rivals Wolves and beat them on their way to win the Second Division title race. When Hill returned as chairman, more significant changes were introduced. In 1981 Highfield Road became England's first all-seater stadium, but disapproval from fans saw terraces reintroduced a few seasons later. During the 1990s the new all-seater East Stand (formerly the Kop) was built and the Main Stand re-roofed. The 2004/5 season was the club's last at Highfield Road and they have now moved to the 32,500 Ricoh Arena. This stylish stadium has an unusual Sky Blues' Wall of Fame on the back of the East Stand.

Ground: **Ricoh Arena**

Address: Ricoh Arena, Phoenix Way, Foleshill, Coventry CV6 6GE

Main tel: 0870 421 1987

Box office: 0870 421 1987

Website: www.ccfc.co.uk

Capacity: 32,500

Home colours: sky blue shirts, sky blue shorts, sky blue socks

Club nickname: the Sky Blues

Pitch dimensions: 105m x 68m (115 x 74 yards)

Founded: 1883

Record attendance: (at Ricoh Arena) 28,120 vs Middlesbrough, January 28 2006

Most prolific scorer: Clarrie Bourton (171)

Record win: 9-0 vs Bristol City, April 28 1934

Record defeat: 2-10 vs Norwich City, March 15 1930

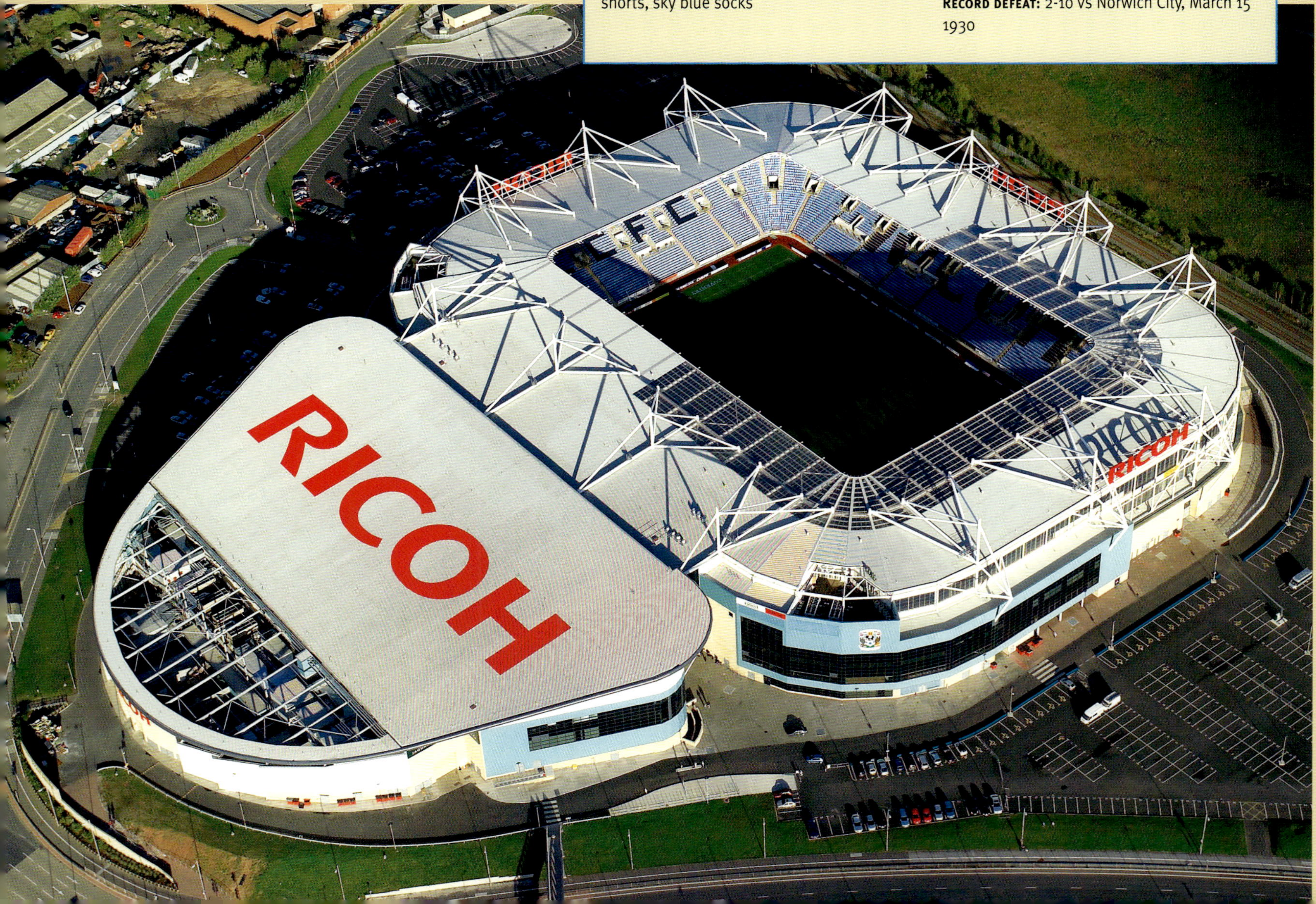

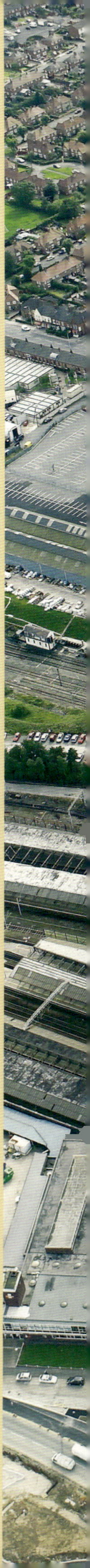

Crewe Alexandra

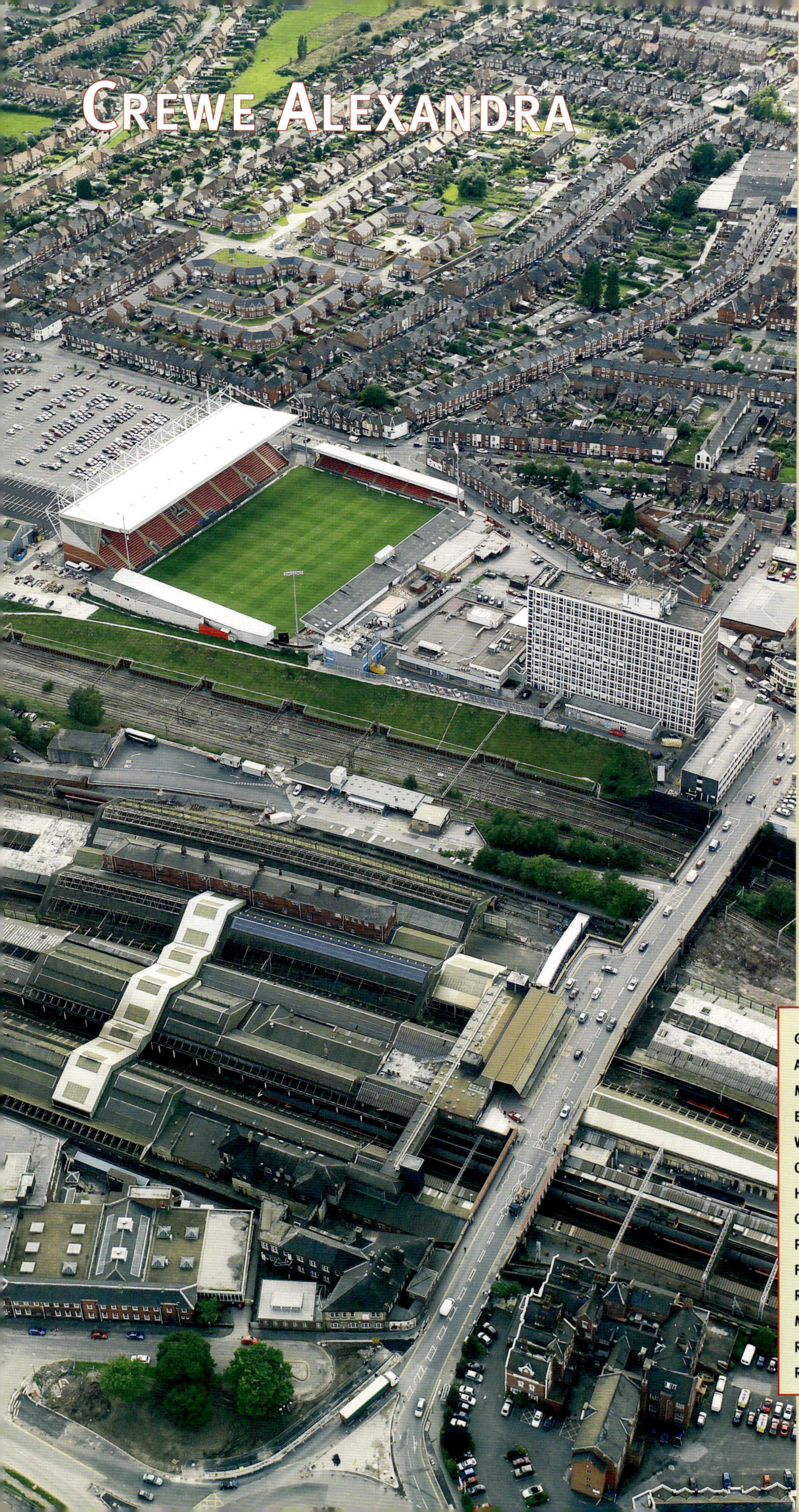

Crewe Alexandra formed in 1877, although their roots go back to an athletics club founded in 1866. The club's name "Alexandra" is thought to have been in honour of Princess Alexandra, who married Prince Edward in 1863. Early games were played at Nantwich Road, where a recreation ground had the capacity to stage cricket, football and cycling. Crewe reached the semi-finals of the FA Cup in 1888, an achievement they have never since matched or beaten. They moved grounds twice in 1896, before returning to the recreation ground. In 1906 the building of new railway lines forced the club to move again, this time to Gresty Road. The ground had a stand on each side of the pitch and some embankments. It was 1921 when Crewe joined the League for a second time after a short spell from 1892-1896. The original Main Stand burned down in 1932 and a new one was built in its place, on the south side of the pitch. A record 20,000 supporters saw Crewe take on Spurs in the FA Cup in 1960, but little development took place over the course of the next 30 years, except for the rebuilding of the Popular Side in the 1970s. Gresty Road was transformed during the 1990s however. Seats were added to all of the existing stands, and the Gresty Road End had a cantilevered roof added in 1995 along with 994 seats. The Popular Side had seats added and the roof is now supported with just two poles instead of 12 columns. A large, single-tiered cantilevered stand, the Air Products Stand, was built in 1999 to replace the Railtrack Stand. It now dominates one whole side of the ground, and has a capacity of 7,000. There are plans to develop the Blue Bell BMW Stand (formerly the Popular Side) and turn it into a two-tiered stand.

Ground: **Alexandra Stadium**

Address: Alexandra Stadium, Gresty Road, Crewe CW2 6EB

Main tel: 01270 213 014

Box office: 01270 252 610

Website: www.crewealex.net

Capacity: 10,066

Home colours: red shirts, white shorts, red socks

Club nickname: the Railwaymen

Pitch dimensions: 100m x 66m (109 x 72 yards)

Founded: 1877

Record attendance: 20,000 vs Tottenham Hotspur, January 30 1960

Most prolific scorer: Bert Swindells (126)

Record win: 8-0 vs Rotherham United, October 1 1932

Record defeat: 2-13 vs Tottenham Hotspur, February 3 1960

CRYSTAL PALACE

Crystal Palace was formed in 1905 when the club took up residence at the Crystal Palace Park ground, which was then England's national stadium. In 1915 the team moved to the Herne Hill cycle and athletics ground as the Admiralty had taken over its ground. In 1918 Palace moved to the Nest, a ground situated opposite Selhurst station. In 1919 Crystal Palace paid £2,570 for a former brickfield, Selhurst Park. It took a further five years for the site to be prepared. The club's plans for development were fairly modest, with one stand and minimal terracing. The Main Stand was built to a similar design to those at Chelsea and Fulham. A healthy rise in gates followed its opening, despite the club being relegated. In the 1950s the ground fell into a state of disrepair as the Eagles languished in the Third and Fourth Divisions. The 1960s were more successful. Following the installation of floodlights in 1962, chairman Arthur Wait persuaded Real Madrid to play a friendly at Selhurst Park. The uncovered Park Side was developed in 1969 into a stand with a 42m deep roof covering the original banking. In 1979 a record 51,482 saw Palace win the Second Division championship. Palace spent the next 12 seasons yo-yoing between the First and Third Divisions. The 1980s also signalled the first ever long-term ground-sharing plans at Selhurst

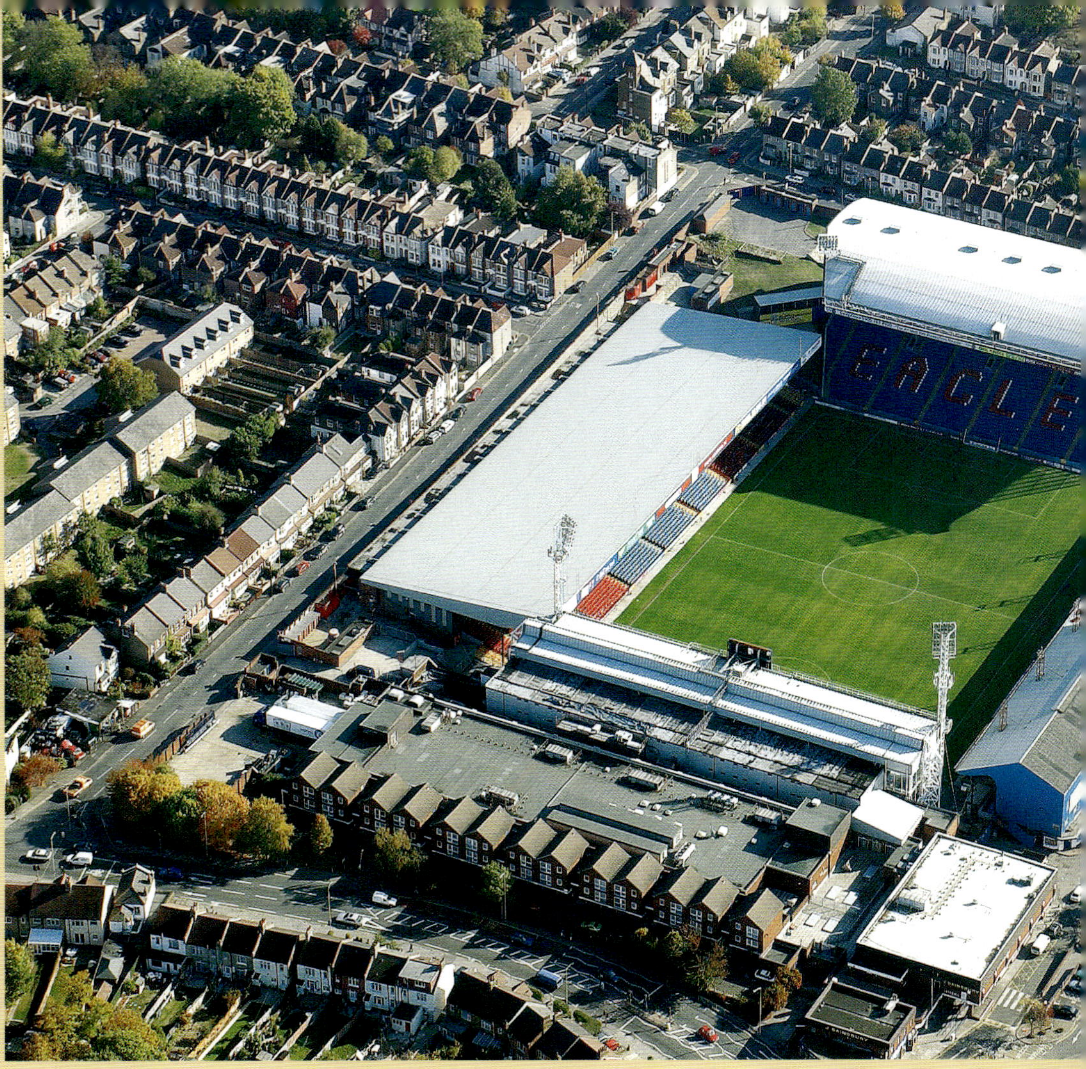

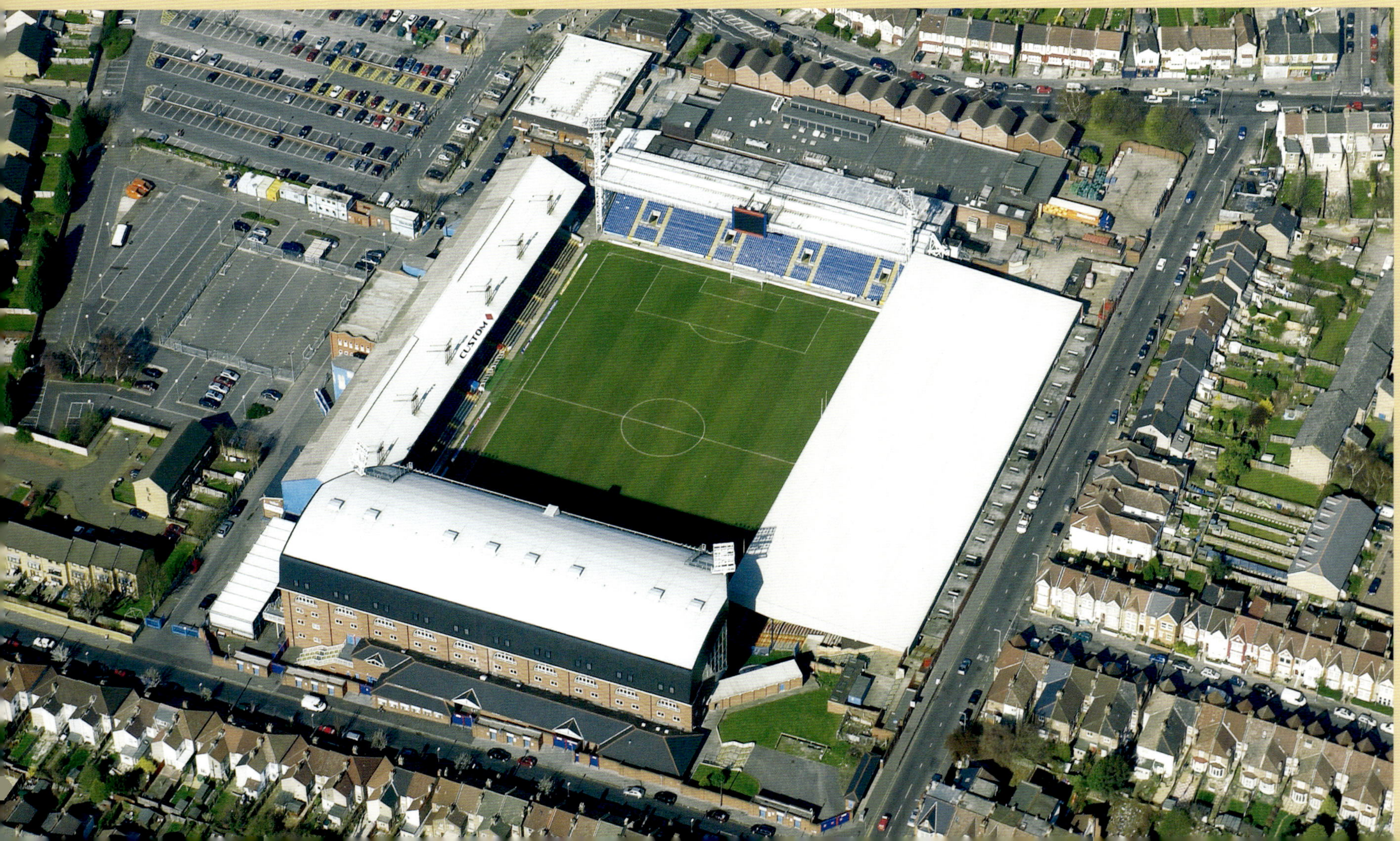

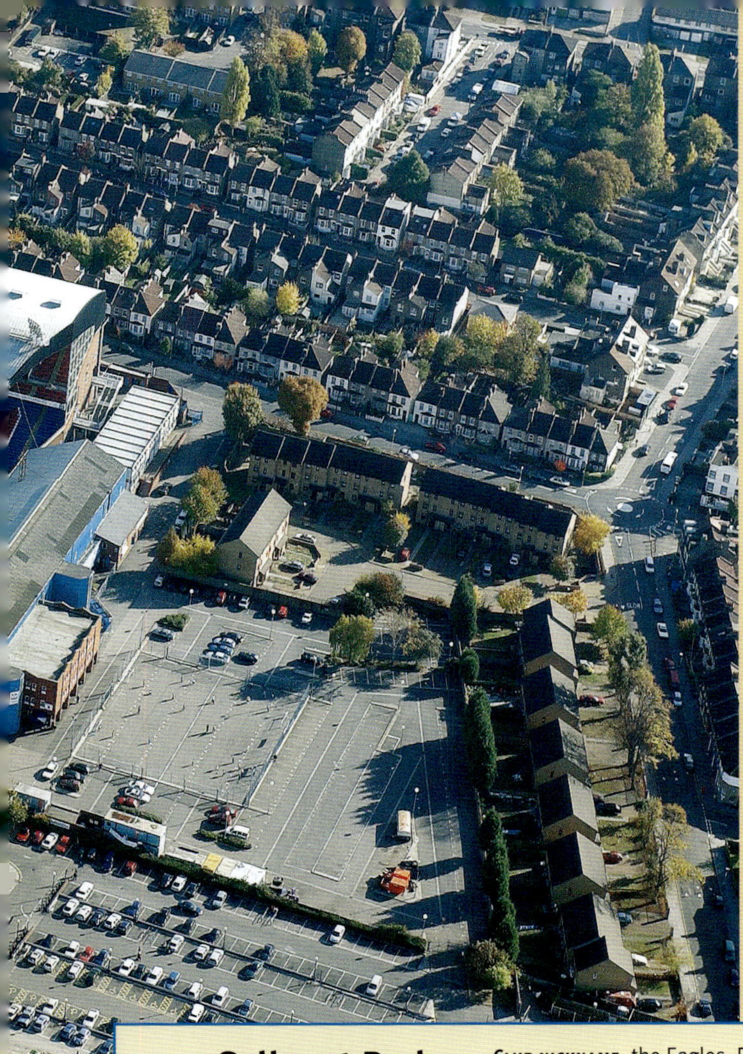

Ground: **Selhurst Park**

Address: Selhurst Park, Whitehorse Lane, London SE25 6PU

Main tel: 020 8768 6000

Box office: 0871 200 0071

Website: www.cpfc.co.uk

Capacity: 26,309

Home colours: red and blue striped shirts, red shorts, red socks with blue tops

Club nickname: the Eagles, Palace

Pitch dimensions: 101m x 68m (110 x 74 yards)

Founded: 1905

Record attendance: 51,482 vs Burnley, May 11 1979

Most prolific scorer: Peter Simpson (153)

Record win: 9-0 vs Barrow, October 11 1959

Record defeat: 0-9 vs Burnley, February 10 1909

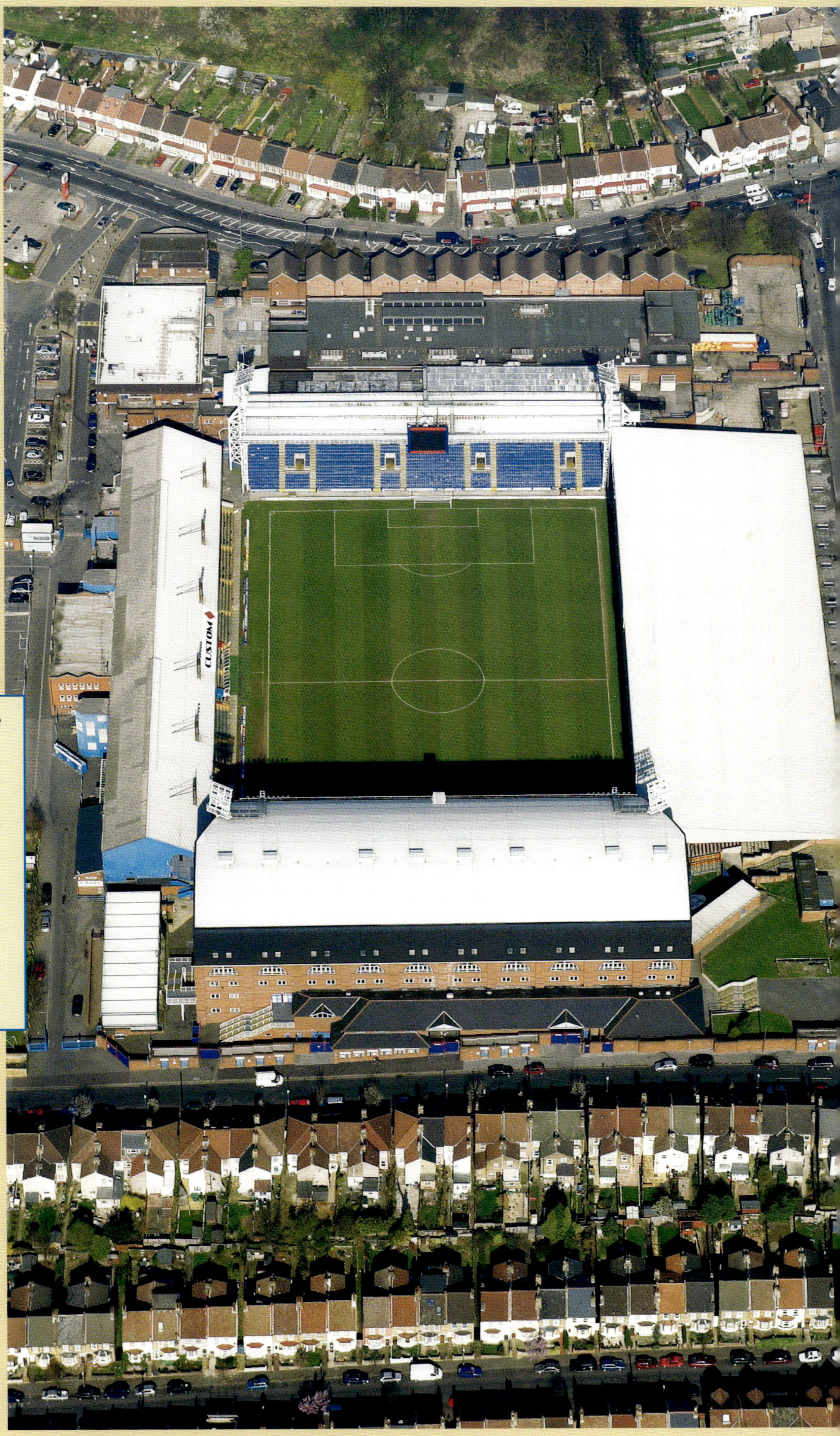

Park, firstly with local rivals Charlton Athletic and then with Wimbledon. The 1990s saw more major development; the Arthur Wait Stand was converted to an all-seater, a hospitality block was built behind the Main Stand and the Whitehorse Lane Stand was developed. The most significant development, however, was to the Holmesdale Road Stand. Built into a natural embankment and surrounded by houses, building work was always going to be difficult; however, structural engineers worked their magic and a massive structure, which took more than a year to build, was finally opened in August 1995, raising the capacity to 26,309. Plans to expand the Main Stand were opposed by local residents and now the club may look for a new site.

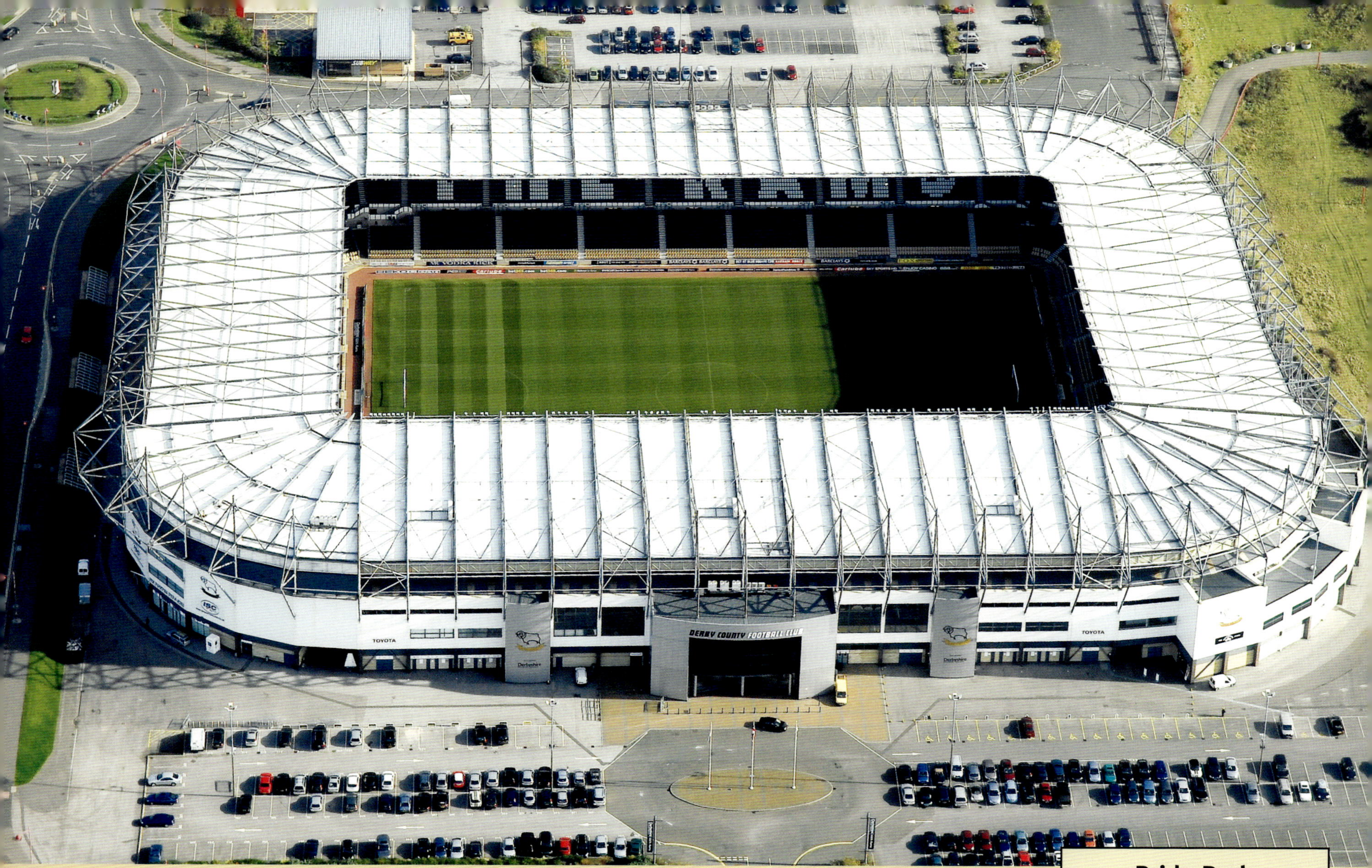

Derby County

Players from Derby County Cricket Club formed Derby County FC in 1884. Their first pitch was part of the cricket ground, which was in the middle of a race-course. Derby soon tired of rescheduling games that clashed with race meetings, and in 1895 they moved to a baseball ground that owner Francis Ley had built after a visit to the US. The Baseball Ground was very enclosed however, and in 1923 Derby received an offer to move to Osmanton Park stadium. They turned this offer down and in 1924 they bought the Baseball Ground from Francis Ley. In 1925 the Popular Side was concreted, and a year later the Rams went back up to the First Division, which funded further ground developments. A two-tiered stand, opened in 1933, was built where the Osmanton Terrace and Catcher's Corner had stood. By the start of WWII all four sides of the Baseball Ground had been rebuilt and covered. The Rams returned to the First Division in 1969 under the management of Brian Clough; this was the same year the Ley Stand opened, and a record 41,826 fans crammed in to see Derby take on Spurs. Crowd trouble in the late 1970s and 1980s saw fences and barriers erected throughout the ground, and calls by local residents for the club to move. In the 1980s the club was struggling under massive debts and they were relegated to the Third Division. These problems were eased when Robert Maxwell took over as chairman in 1984. The fences came down in 1989 and after the Taylor report the club developed plans to rebuild the stadium. They were offered another chance to leave the ground, this time to go to Pride Park. Yet again the club turned the offer down and began working on plans for a 28,000 all-seater Baseball Ground. However, in 1995, after seeing the success of Middlesbrough's relocation they moved to Pride Park. The £16m project took 46 weeks and at the start of the 1997/98 season the Rams began playing at Pride Park, a 33,597 all-seater stadium.

Ground: Pride Park

Address: Pride Park Stadium, Derby DE24 8XL

Main tel: 0871 472 1884

Box office: 0871 472 1884

Website: www.dcfc.co.uk

Capacity: 33,597

Home colours: white shirts with black trim, black shorts with white trim, white socks

Club nickname: the Rams

Pitch dimensions: 105m x 68m (115 x 74 yards)

Founded: 1884

Record attendance: 33,475 vs Rangers, May 1 2006

Most prolific scorer: Steve Bloomer (292)

Record win: 9-0 vs Wolverhampton Wanderers, January 10 1891

Record defeat: 2-11 vs Everton, January 18 1889

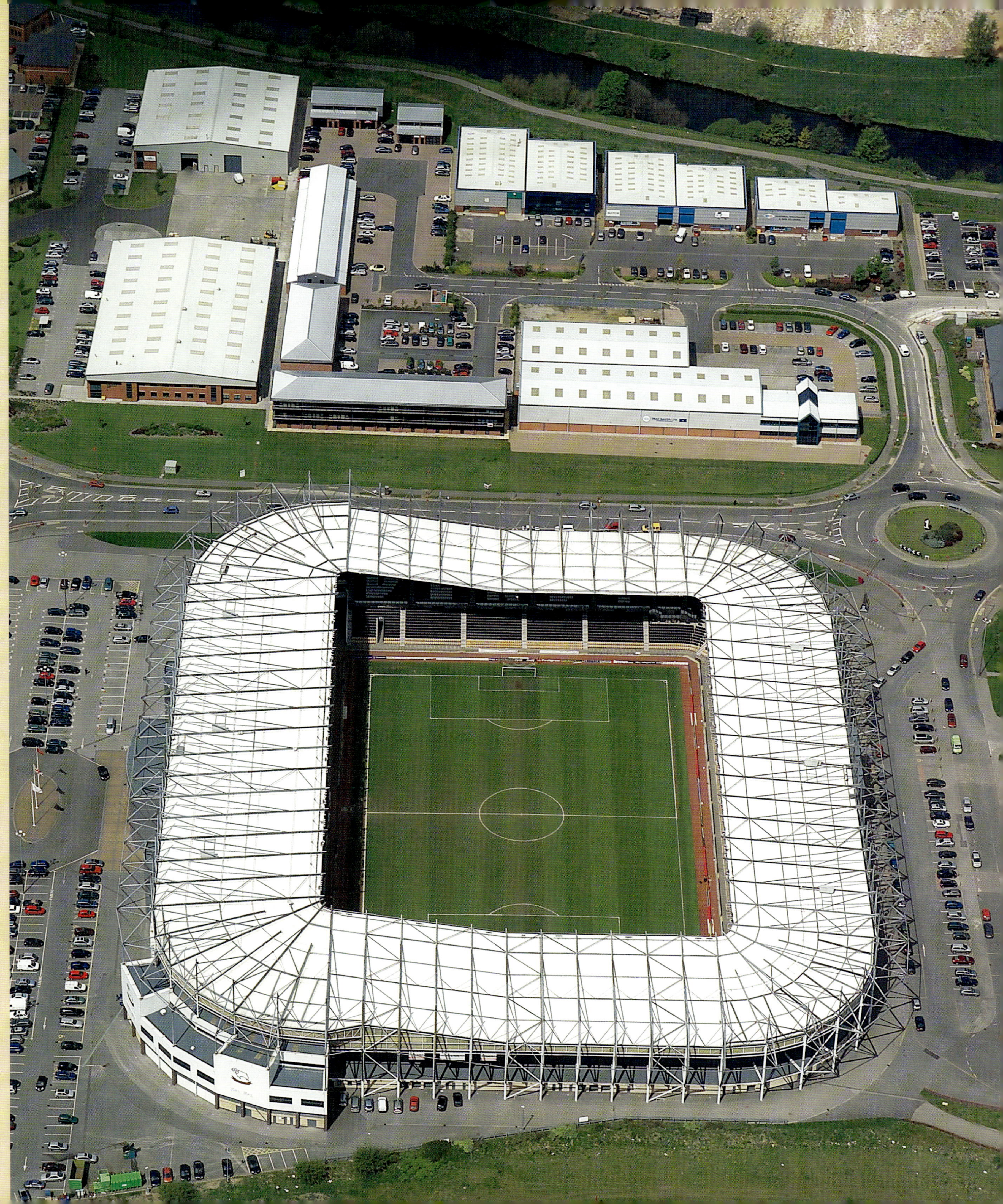

Doncaster Rovers

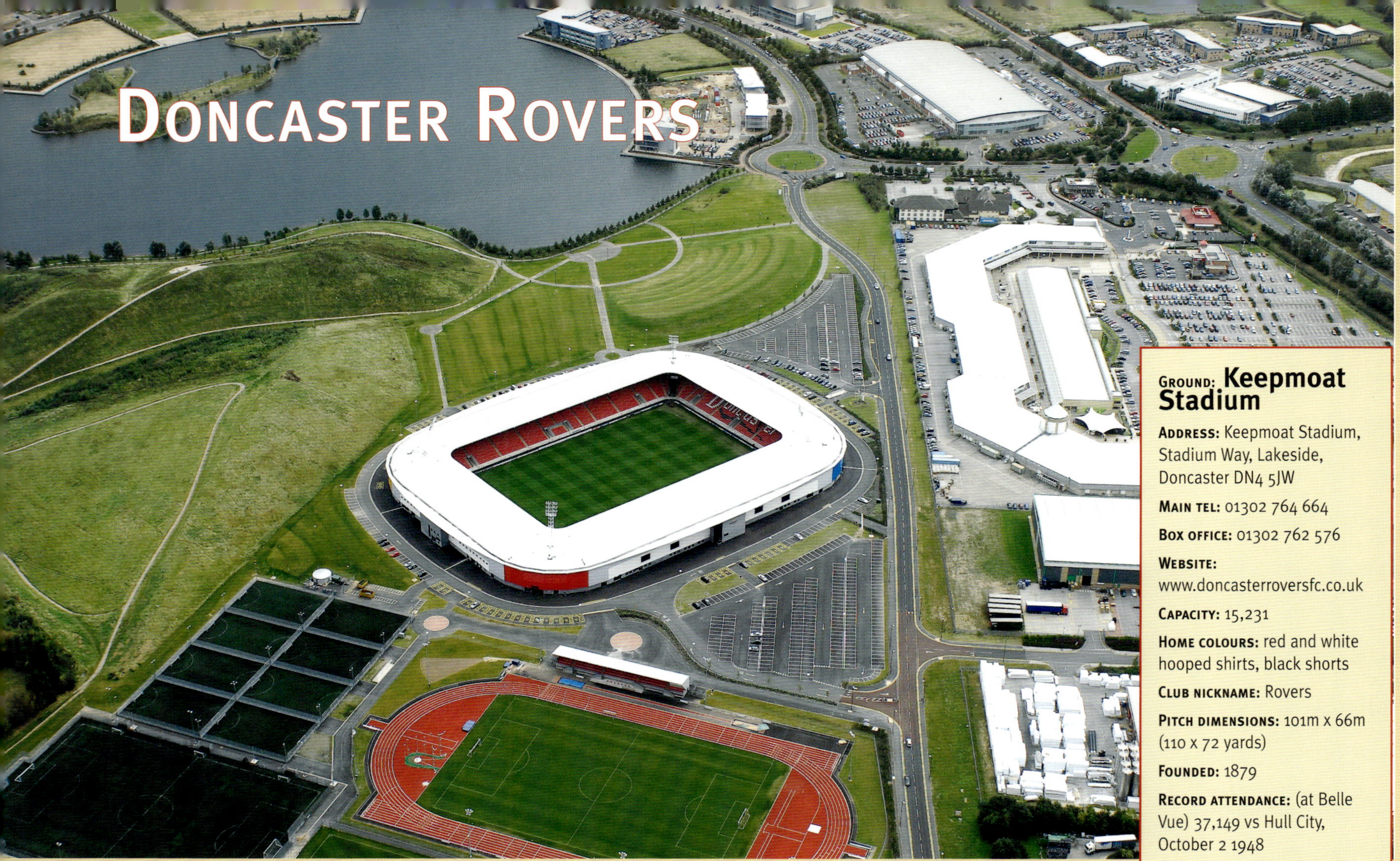

Ground: Keepmoat Stadium

Address: Keepmoat Stadium, Stadium Way, Lakeside, Doncaster DN4 5JW

Main tel: 01302 764 664

Box office: 01302 762 576

Website: www.doncasterroversfc.co.uk

Capacity: 15,231

Home colours: red and white hooped shirts, black shorts

Club nickname: Rovers

Pitch dimensions: 101m x 66m (110 x 72 yards)

Founded: 1879

Record attendance: (at Belle Vue) 37,149 vs Hull City, October 2 1948

Most prolific scorer: Tom Keetley (180)

Record win: 10-0 vs Darlington, January 25 1964

Record defeat: 1-6 vs Fulham, March 15 1958

Above: with its superb leisure and sports facilities, the Keepmoat Stadium is part of the Lakeside Sports Complex

Doncaster Rovers formed in 1879 and played on various grounds before settling at Belle Vue in 1922. The club initially played on the fields between Belle Vue and the racecourse, then settled at the Intake Ground. This was taken over by the army during the First World War. Rovers re-formed in 1920 and acquired the lease for Belle Vue, then called Low Pastures, but had to spend two seasons at Bennetthorpe while the ground was developed. Ash was transported from local coal tips to form the base of the pitch and to create banking on three sides. Rovers transported the Main Stand from Bennetthorpe and positioned this on the Town End slope; they also built a main stand on the Bawtry Road side. This stand was extended and a cover added to the Popular Side, which then had to be moved so the terracing could be expanded. By the time Rovers played Hull City in a Third Division game, 37,149 people packed in and capacity was at 40,000. Little positive development has taken place at Belle Vue since the early days. Capacity was severely reduced as a result of increasing safety regulations, sheer misfortune and criminal damage. The Bennetthorpe Stand was taken down in the aftermath of the Bradford fire, the cover over the Popular Side was removed after the banking that supported it began subsiding and a lower cover was added to the front half in 1989. The Main Stand was gutted by fire in 1995. Doncaster Rovers' promotion back to the League in 2003 has however seen some much-needed planning for the future. In 2007 the club, along with the Doncaster Dragons Rugby Club and the Doncaster Belles Ladies Football Club moved to the new 15,231-capacity Keepmoat Stadium, about a mile and a half from Belle Vue.

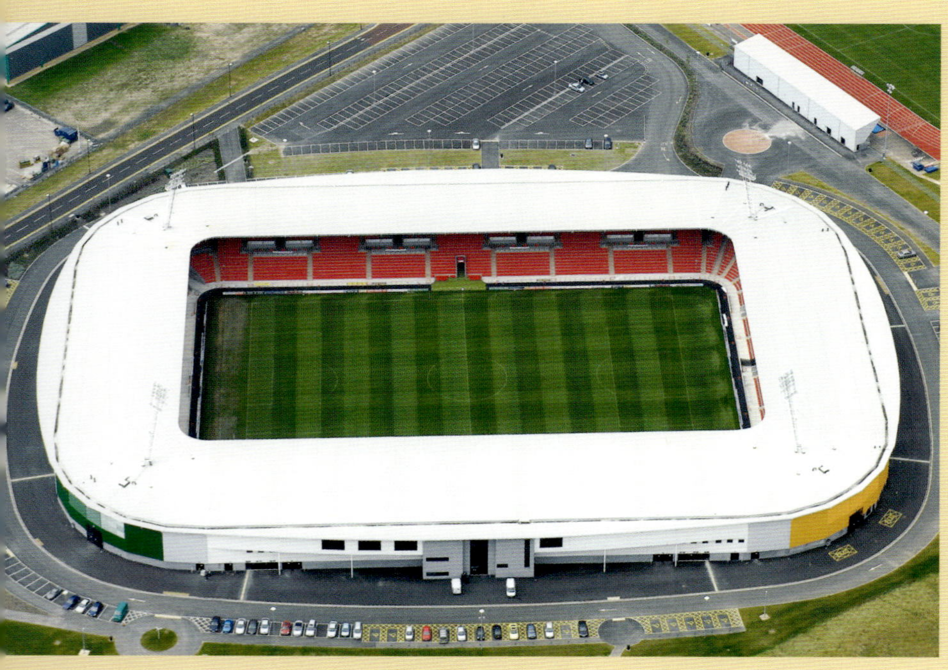

Dundee

Dundee formed in 1893 and played their early games at Carolina Port. The club moved to Dens Park in 1898 and its first game took place there in 1899. The club brought the grandstand with them and erected it on the south side of the pitch and installed an uncovered stand on the north side and embankments at each end. The Dark Blues took on full ownership of the ground in 1919, buying it for £5,000, and began to develop it shortly afterwards. They built terracing on three sides and the Main Stand was erected along the north side in 1921, the same year the original grandstand burned down. In 1953 a record 43,024 fans saw Dundee take on Rangers in the Cup. Few further improvements were made until 1959, when a roof was added to the South Side Terrace and in the 1960s a roof was added to the West Terrace. Following the Safety of Sports Grounds Act in 1975, seats were installed along the South and West Terraces. There have been several attempts to get Dundee and Dundee United to embark on a ground-sharing initiative, although both clubs have resisted. In the early 1990s, mounting debts saw plans put forward for a new stadium for both clubs to share, although once again these were not taken seriously by either club. In 1991 Canadian Ron Dixon bought the club and he began developing the ground in 1994. As well as paying off the club's debts, he financed a complete renovation of the Main Stand and added a greyhound racing track around the pitch in a bid to raise more revenue from the ground. Malcolm Reid bought the club in 1995 and in 1999 new stands were built at each end of the ground. New seats were also added to the South Stand bringing capacity up to 12,085.

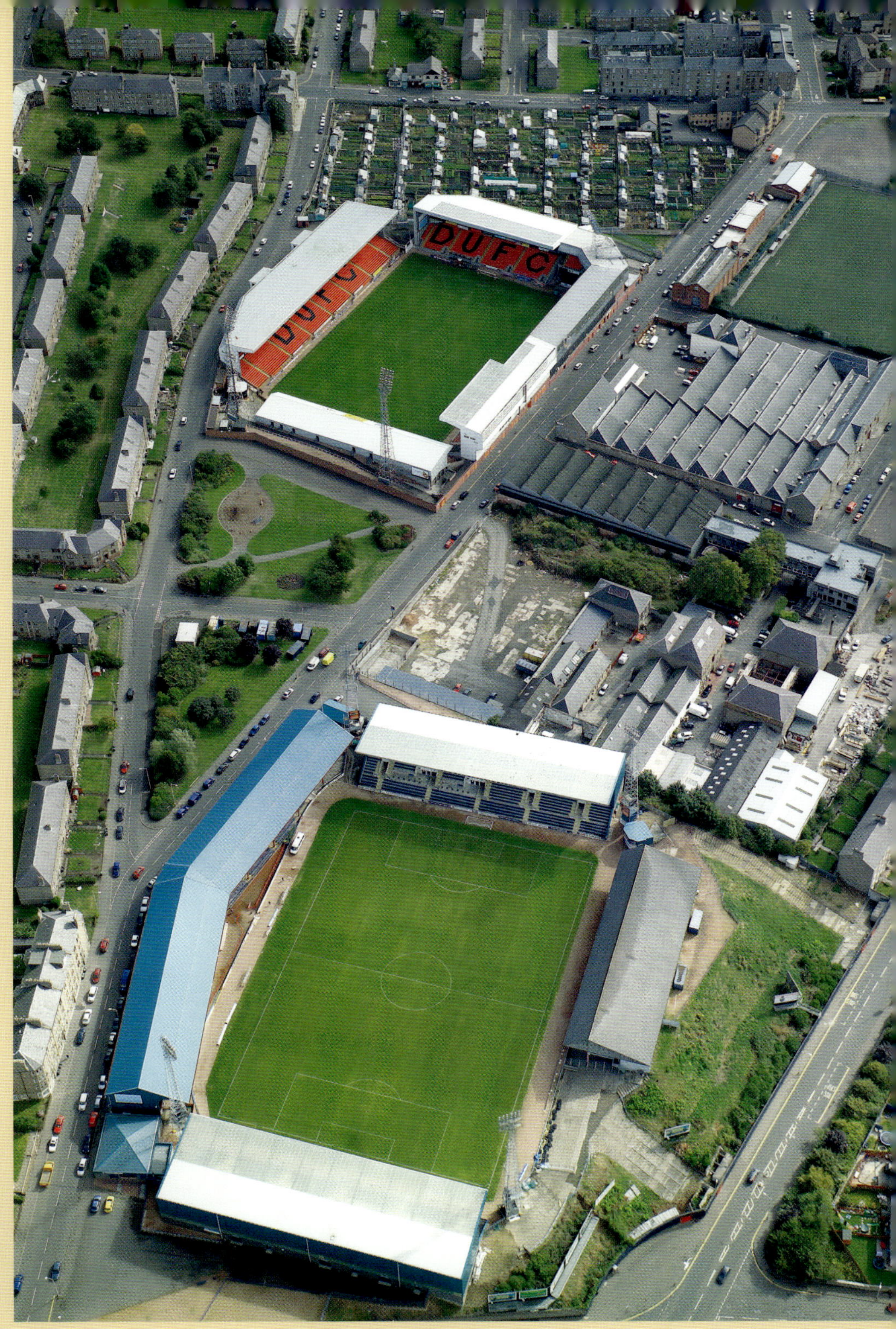

Right: Dens Park lies a few hundred yards fromTannadice Park, the home of close rivals Dundee United

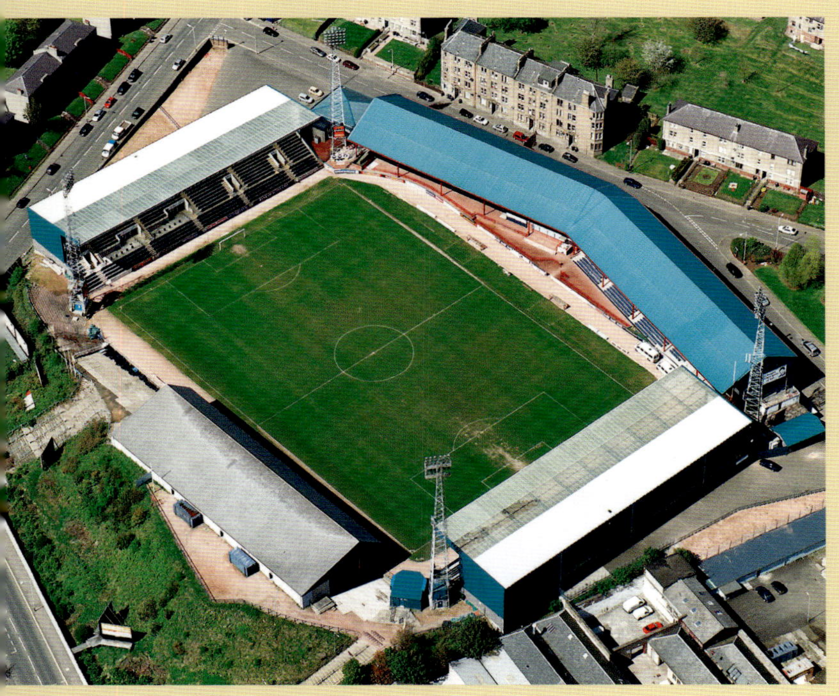

Ground: Dens Park

Address: Dens Park Stadium, Sandeman Street, Dundee DD3 7JY

Main tel: 01382 889 966

Box office: 01382 889 966

Website: www.thedees.co.uk

Capacity: 12,085

Home colours: dark blue, red and white shirts, white shorts, dark blue socks

Club nickname: the Dark Blues or the Dees

Pitch dimensions: 101m x 66m (110 x 72 yards)

Founded: 1893

Record attendance: 43,024 vs Rangers, February 7 1953

Most prolific scorer: Alan Gilzean (113)

Record win: 10-2 vs Queen of the South, December 1 1962

Record defeat: 0-11 vs Celtic, October 26 1895

Dundee United

Dundee United was formed in 1909 under the name of Dundee Hibernian. The club played games at Clepington Park, which was renamed Tannadice Park the year Dundee Hibernian moved in. The club joined the Scottish Second Division in 1910 but they did not fare well and dropped out of the League completely in 1922. A group of businessmen saved the club, renamed it Dundee United, and the team rejoined the League just a year later. The club bought Tannadice Park but it was not in very good shape and there were insufficient funds to develop the ground. Sleepers were added to the banking and efforts were made to reduce the slope in the pitch but that was as far as the money stretched. It was not until the late 1950s and early 1960s that major development took place. A roof was added to the West End Terrace in 1957 and concrete laid at the Arklay Street End. In 1962 the new L-shaped Main Stand was built and floodlights were installed. In 1966 a record attendance of 28,000 went to Tannadice Park to see Dundee United take on Barcelona in the Inter Cities Fairs Cup. A cover was added to the North Side Terrace in 1979, although the safety regulations of the 1970s and 1980s left Tannadice in serious need of redevelopment. After deciding not to ground-share with nearby rivals Dundee FC, the Terrors installed seats in the West End in 1992. In the same year they also built the two-tiered George Fox Stand on the north side of the pitch. The installation of seats in the East Stand in 1994 turned Tannadice Park into an all-seater stadium. The Main Stand (now called the Jerry Kerr Stand) was extended in 1997 so that it stretched the length of the pitch. Capacity at Tannadice Park is now 14,209.

Ground:
Tannadice Park

Address: Tannadice Park, Tannadice Street, Dundee DD3 7JW

Main tel: 01382 833 166

Box office: 01382 833 166

Website: www.dundeeunitedfc.co.uk

Capacity: 14,209

Home colours: tangerine shirts, tangerine shorts, tangerine socks

Club nickname: the Terrors or the Arabs

Pitch dimensions: 101m x 66m (110 x 72 yards)

Founded: 1909

Record attendance: 28,000 vs Barcelona, November 16 1966

Most prolific scorer: Peter McKay (158)

Record win: 14-0 vs Nithsdale Wanderers, January 17 1931

Record defeat: 1-12 vs Motherwell, January 23 1954

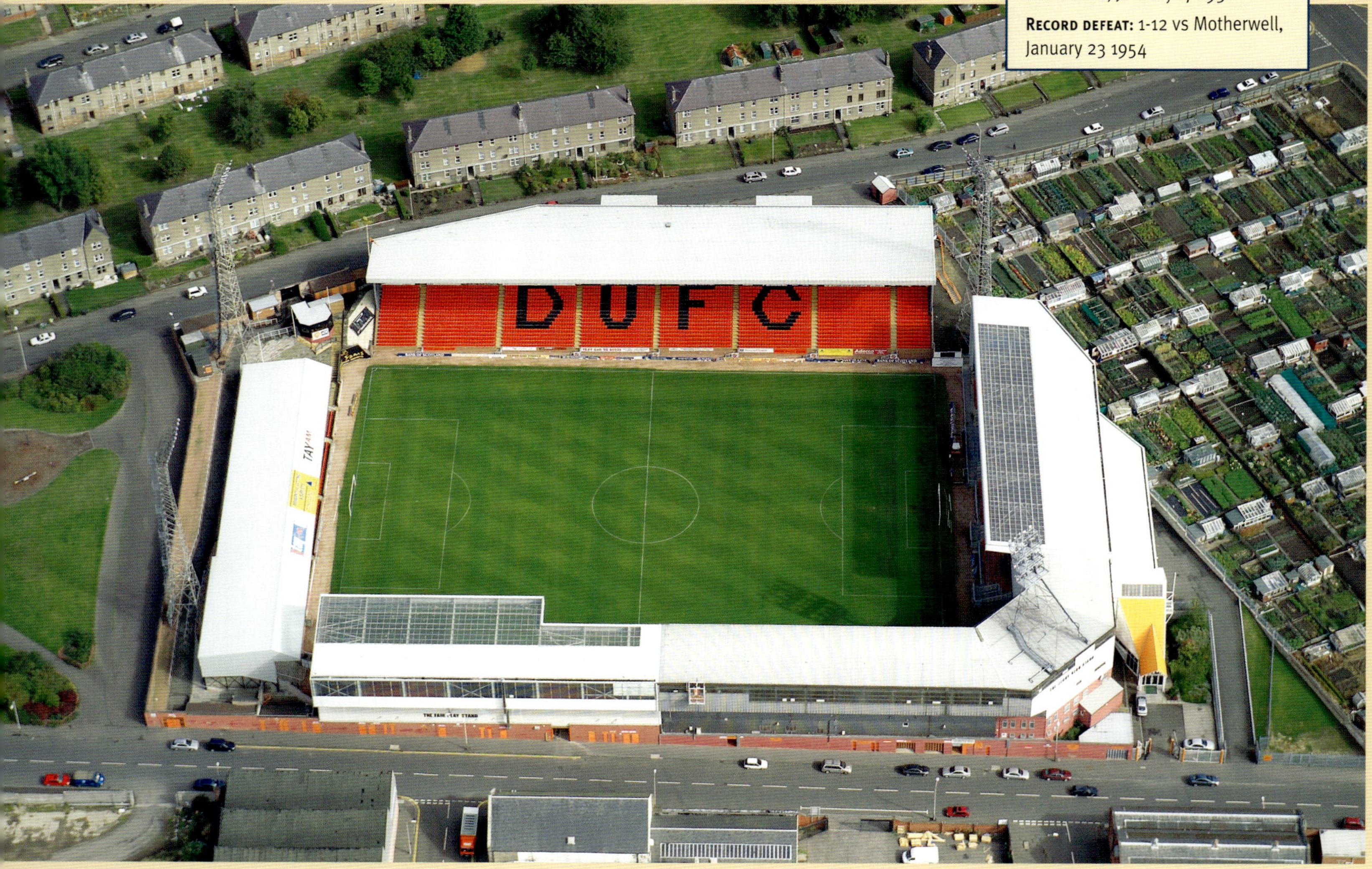

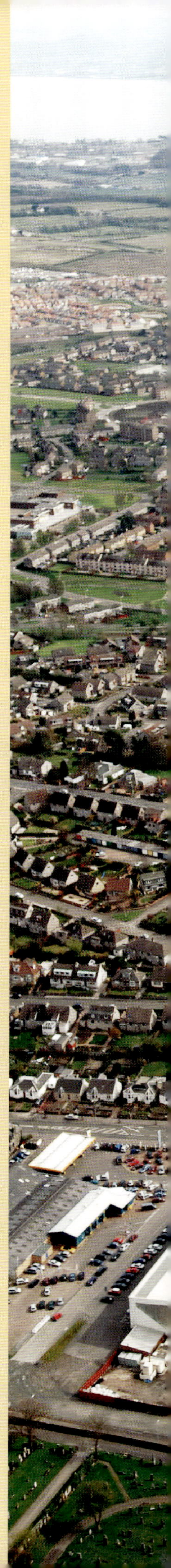

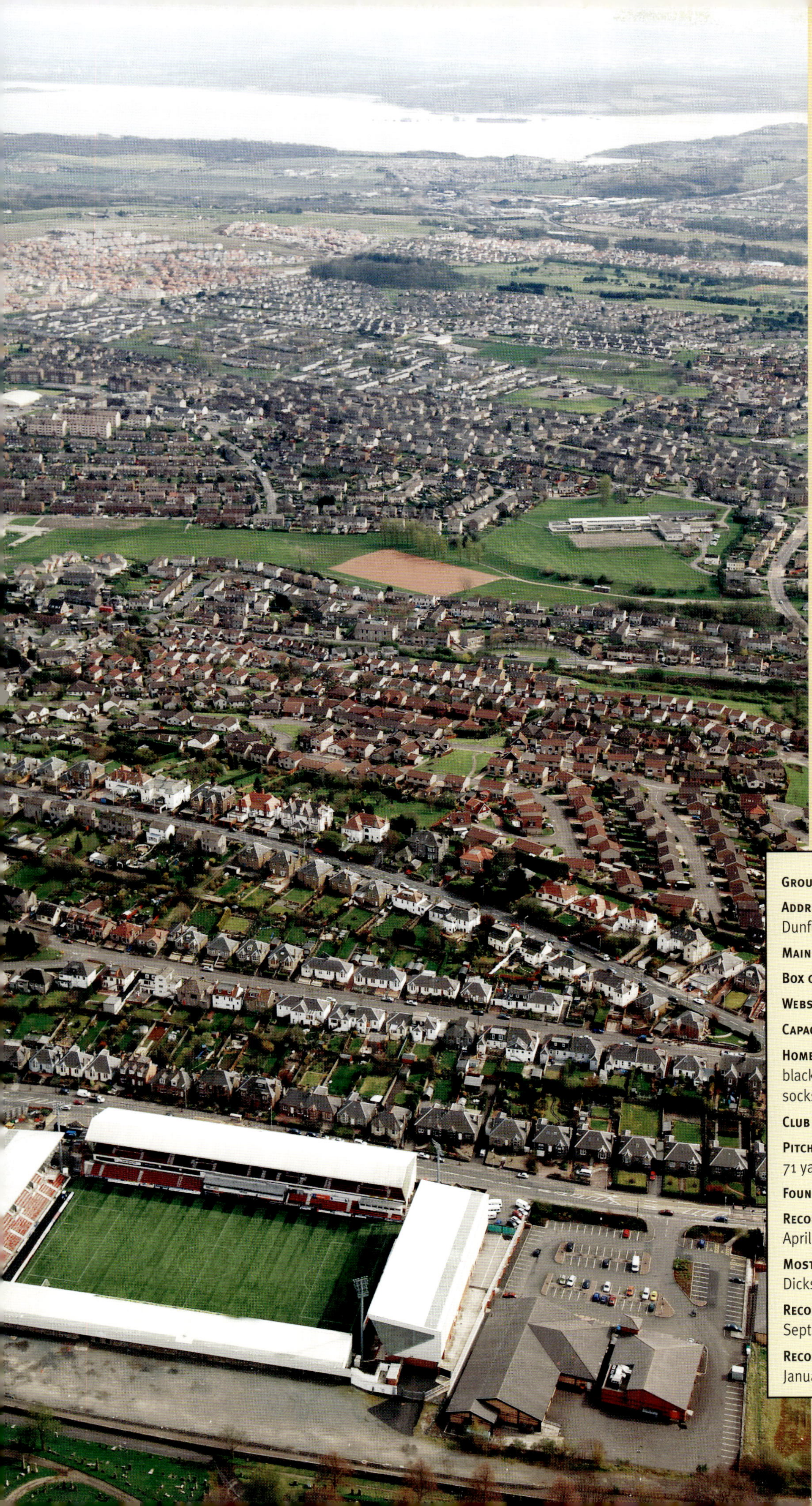

Dunfermline Athletic

Dunfermline Athletic formed in 1885 from members of a local cricket team. East End Park was originally owned by the North British Railway and the club bought it from them after the First World War. A pavilion stood on the south side and cinder banking ran around the rest of the pitch. The Pars added a stand to the south side in 1926 as well as extending the banking in time for their promotion to the First Division. Demotion back to the Second Division followed quickly. By 1930 the club had introduced greyhound racing to the ground to try and ease their financial troubles. With better results on the field, Dunfermline soon found themselves back in the First Division. The club installed a roof on the North Terrace in 1934 and developed the East Terrace a year later. Little was developed around the ground until the 1960s. The two-tiered Main Stand was opened in 1962, partly funded by Dunfermline's victory in the Scottish FA Cup in 1961. A roof was built over the North Terrace in 1965 and extended to join up with the West Terrace in 1968. East End Park saw a record attendance that same season, with 27,816 turning out to watch the Pars take on Celtic. The 1960s were the glory years for the Pars, winning the Scottish FA Cup again in 1968 and reaching the semi-finals of the European Cup in 1968-69. By the 1980s the team's fortunes had changed and at times attendances dropped to below 1,000. Despite this, the club continued to carry out improvements. During the 1990s development continued and the all-seater Norrie McCathie Stand and the East Stand opened in 1998, bringing capacity up to 12,500.

Ground: **East End Park**

Address: Halbeath Road, Dunfermline, Fife KY12 7RB

Main tel: 01383 724 295

Box office: 0870 300 1201

Website: www.dafc.co.uk

Capacity: 12,500

Home colours: white shirts with black stripes, black shorts, black socks

Club nickname: the Pars

Pitch dimensions: 105m x 65m (115 x 71 yards)

Founded: 1885

Record attendance: 27,816 vs Celtic, April 30 1968

Most prolific scorer: Charles Dickson (154)

Record win: 11-2 vs Stenhousemuir, September 27 1930

Record defeat: 1-7 vs Partick Thistle, January 7 1928

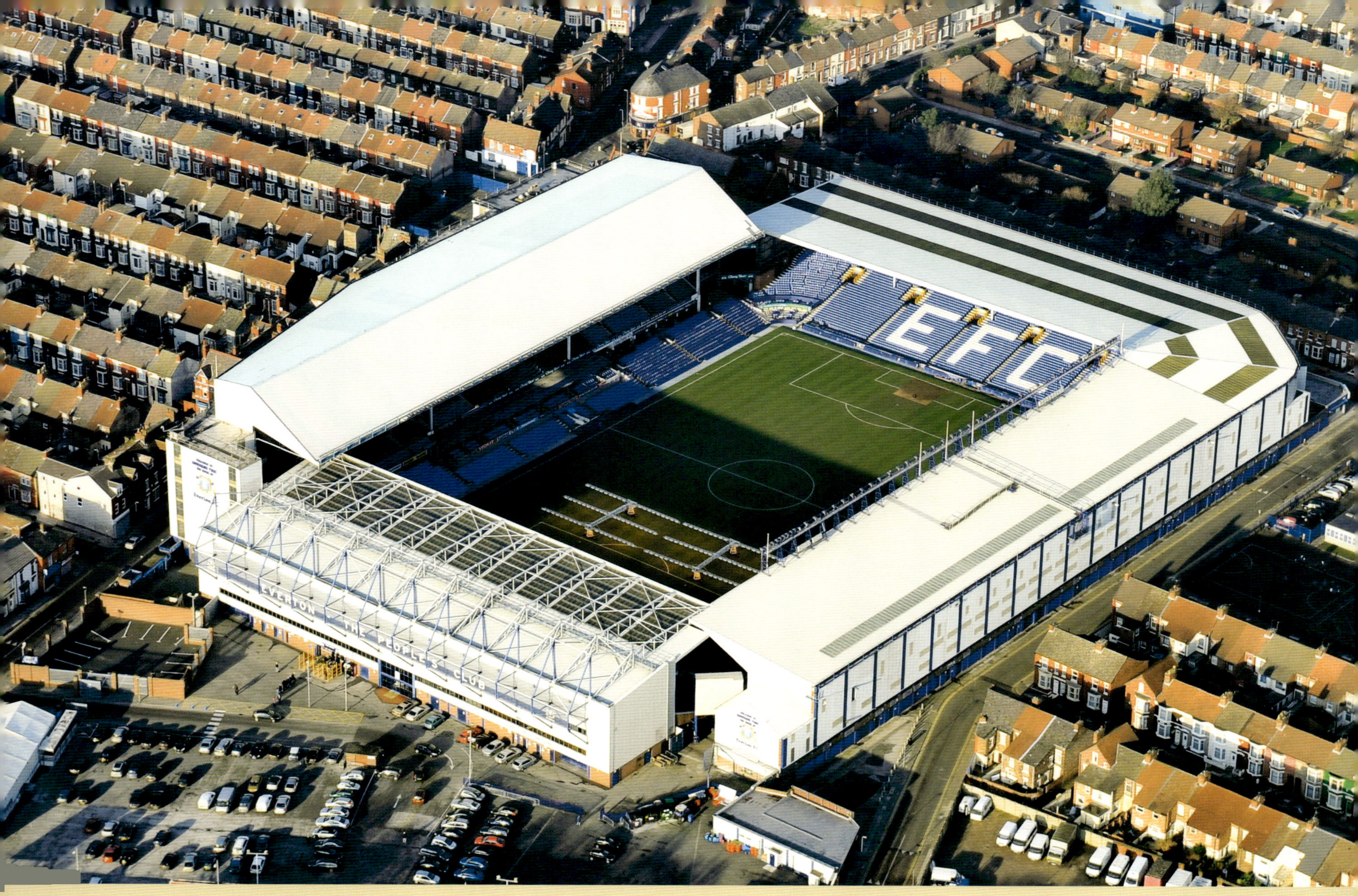

EVERTON

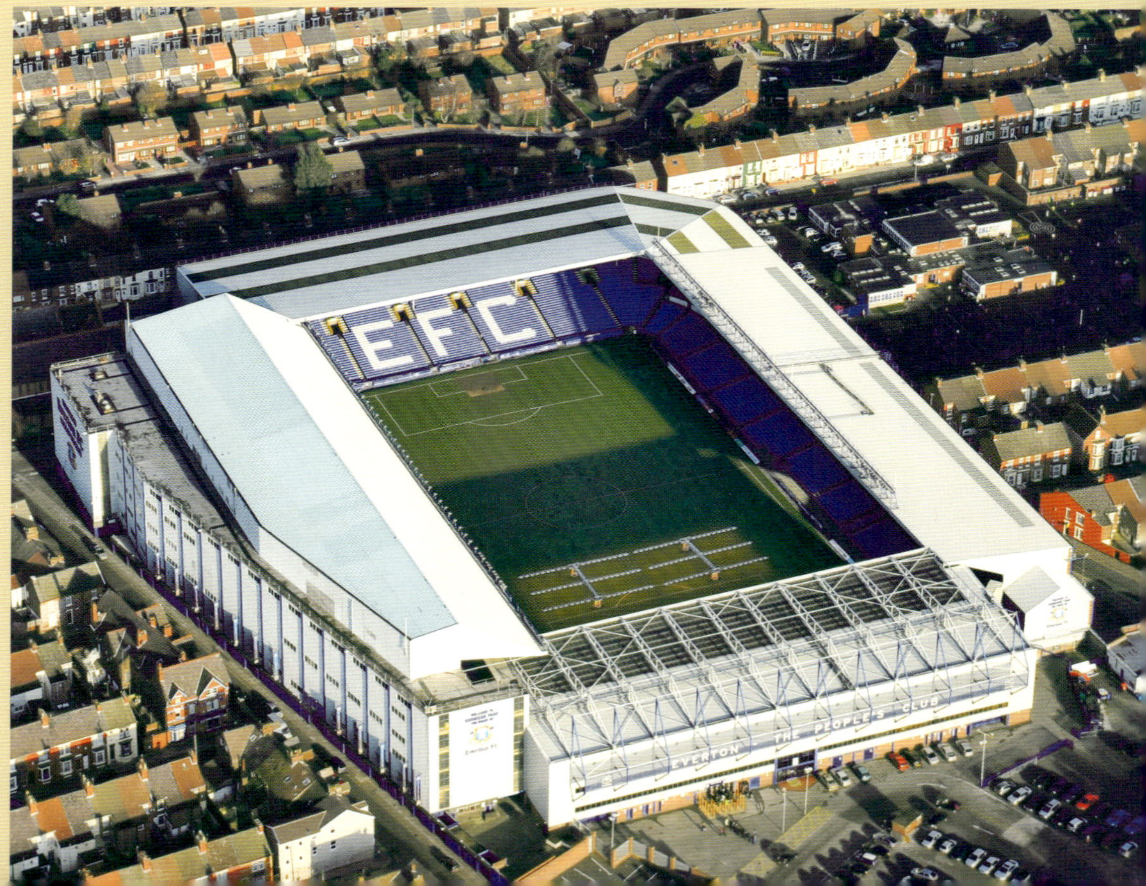

Everton began as St Domingo's FC in 1878, playing games at Stanley Park. In 1884 the club became the first tenants at Anfield, by which time they had changed their name to Everton. A row with their landlord in 1892 prompted them to move to Goodison Park, then called Mere Green. In 1888 the club became founder members of the League, winning the League title in 1891. Everton spent a great deal of money preparing the ground, building two uncovered stands and a third covered stand with seating, as well as improving the pitch. Mere Green was renamed Goodison Park in time for its official opening in 1892. Everton's support was unrivalled at the time, and the FA was so impressed with the ground they allowed the 1894 Cup Final to be played there. In 1895 the Bullens Road Stand was built following the ground's first international. The

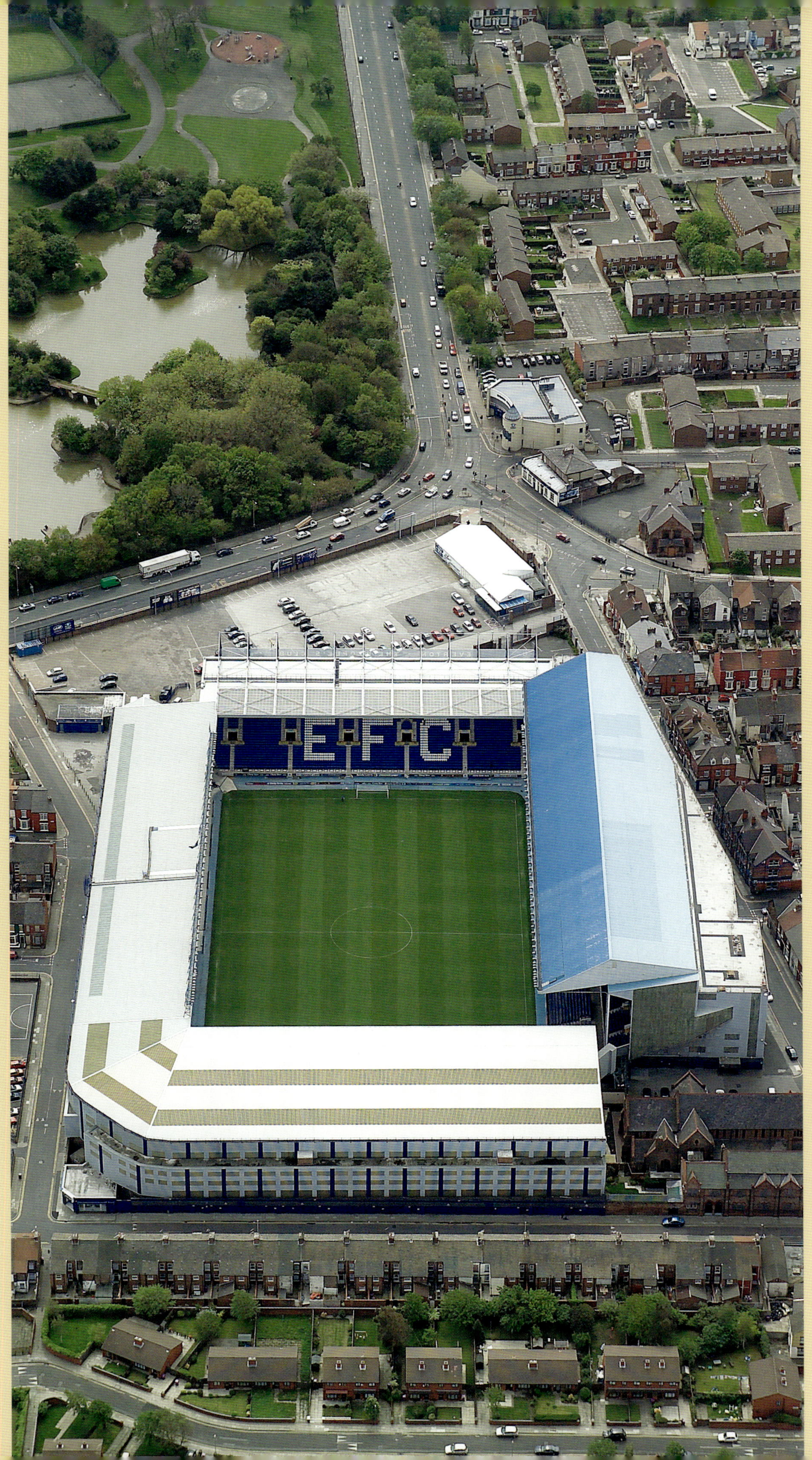

GROUND: **Goodison Park**
ADDRESS: Goodison Park, Liverpool L4 4EL
MAIN TEL: 0870 442 1878
BOX OFFICE: 0870 442 1878
WEBSITE: www.evertonfc.com
CAPACITY: 40,569
HOME COLOURS: royal blue shirts with white trim, white shorts, blue socks
CLUB NICKNAME: the Toffees
PITCH DIMENSIONS: 102m x 71m (112 x 78 yards)
FOUNDED: 1878
RECORD ATTENDANCE: 78,299 vs Liverpool, September 18 1948
MOST PROLIFIC SCORER: Dixie Dean (349)
RECORD WIN: 11-2 vs Derby County, January 18 1890
RECORD DEFEAT: 4-10 vs Tottenham Hotspur, October 11 1958

Goodison Road Terrace was covered and by 1905 the ground was estimated to have a capacity of 55,000. In 1907 Scottish engineer Archibald Leitch built the two-tiered Park End Stand at Goodison before building the magnificent Main Stand in 1909, which had a pitched roof and central gable. It was not until 1926 that the ground saw any more improvements, when the two-tiered stand was built on the Bullens Road side. Twelve years later this was linked to the Gladwys Street end, making Goodison Park the first to have two-tiered stands on all sides. In 1948 the ground saw a record crowd of 78,299 fans cram in for a Merseyside derby against Liverpool. In the 1970s the new three-tier Main Stand replaced Leitch's original and a new roof was erected on the Bullen's Road Stand, which was brought round to cover the Gladwys Street end in 1986. In the aftermath of the Taylor report, seats were added to the remaining terraces, and in 1994 the new single-tier Park End Stand was built. There are now reports that the club will move to a new 55,000 capacity purpose-built stadium at Kirkby, since Goodison Park's capacity remains at 40,569.

FULHAM

Fulham began life in 1879 as Fulham St Andrews, a church team. The club moved grounds eight times before they finally arrived at Craven Cottage in 1896. The ground was on the site of the original Craven Cottage, which was built in 1789 by Baron Craven and burned down in 1888. The team turned professional in 1898 and by 1905 were more successful than their neighbours Chelsea, drawing crowds in the region of 20,000. The club spent £15,000 developing the ground; this included three terraces and a corner pavilion, the Cottage. The only stand to be built was on Stevenage Road, which had an upper tier of seats, a paddock in front covered by a pitched roof and gable in the centre. It was not until the 1960s that further development took place. In 1961 the Hammersmith End was extended and in 1965 it was covered. The Riverside Terrace was replaced by the Riverside Stand in 1971, although the cost of this stand almost bankrupted the club. For the next 20 years Fulham fell into decline, gates dropped and debts stacked up. In the early 1990s the club's future at Craven Cottage looked very doubtful as property developers took over ownership of the ground. In 1991 Fulham started ground-sharing talks with Chelsea, although these never came to fruition. Perhaps Fulham's lowest moment came in January 1996 when they were second from bottom of the Third Division, drawing crowds of around 4,000 and facing an exit from the League. Their fortunes turned completely on May 29 1997 when Harrods' owner Mohammed Al Fayed took over ownership of the club. He brought with him a five-year plan to get the club into the Premiership. Al Fayed spent millions on players and in just four years this dream was realised. He then went about redeveloping the ground. In 2002 Fulham left Craven Cottage to ground-share at QPR's Loftus Road. Rumours circulated that Al Fayed intended to sell the ground. However these reports proved unfounded and at the start of the 2004/05 season the Cottagers moved back to Craven Cottage, to an improved stadium, with a 26,300 capacity.

GROUND: **Craven Cottage**

ADDRESS: Craven Cottage, Stevenage Road, London SW6 6HH

MAIN TEL: 0870 442 1222

BOX OFFICE: 0870 442 1234

WEBSITE: www.fulhamfc.com

CAPACITY: 26,300

HOME COLOURS: white shirts with black and red trim, black shorts, white socks with red and black trim

CLUB NICKNAME: the Cottagers, the Whites

PITCH DIMENSIONS: 102m x 66m (112 x 72 yards)

FOUNDED: 1879

RECORD ATTENDANCE: 49,335 vs Millwall, October 8 1938

MOST PROLIFIC SCORER: Gordon Davies (159)

RECORD WIN: 10-1 vs Ipswich, December 26 1963

RECORD DEFEAT: 0-10 vs Liverpool, September 23 1986

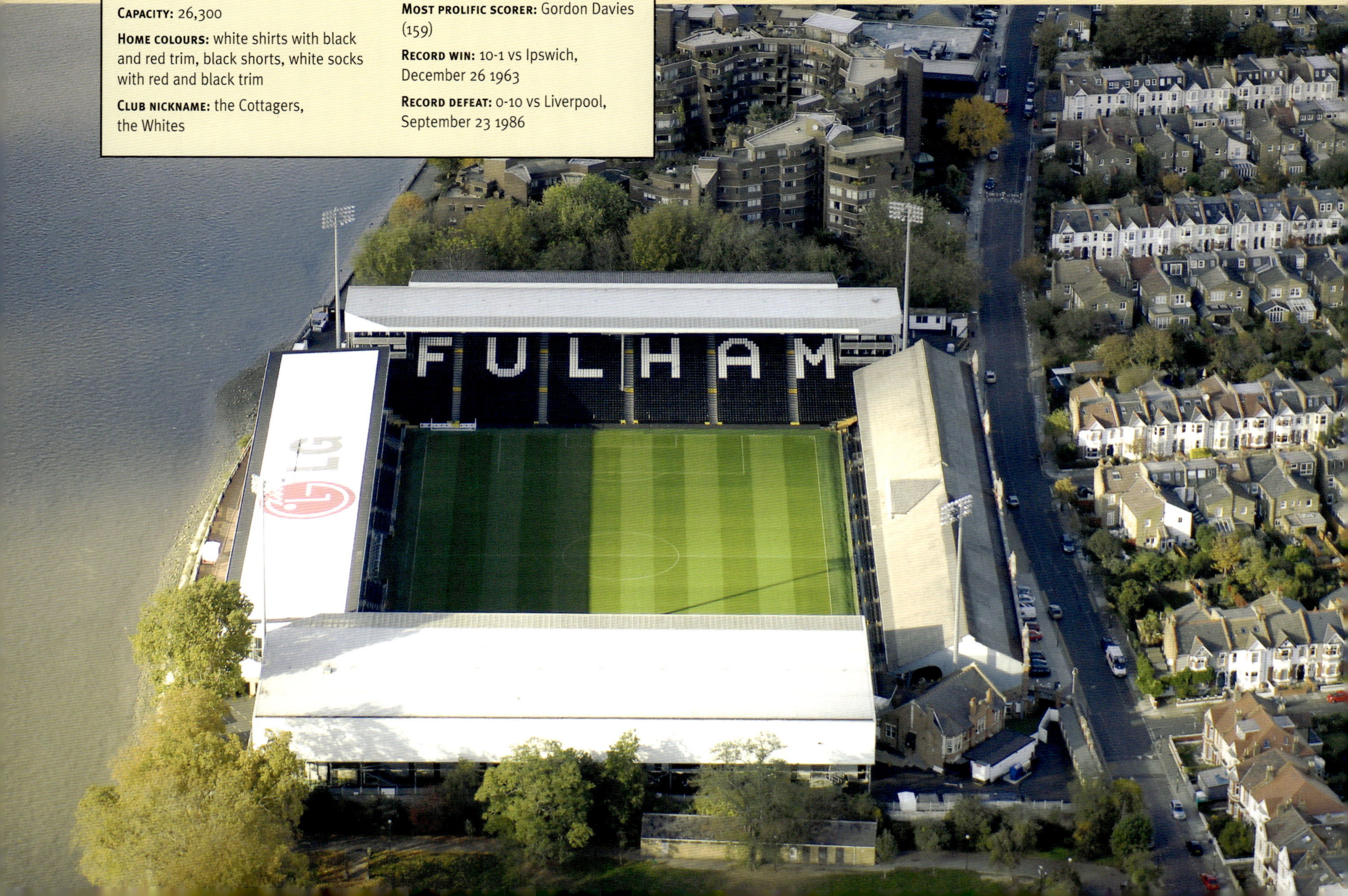

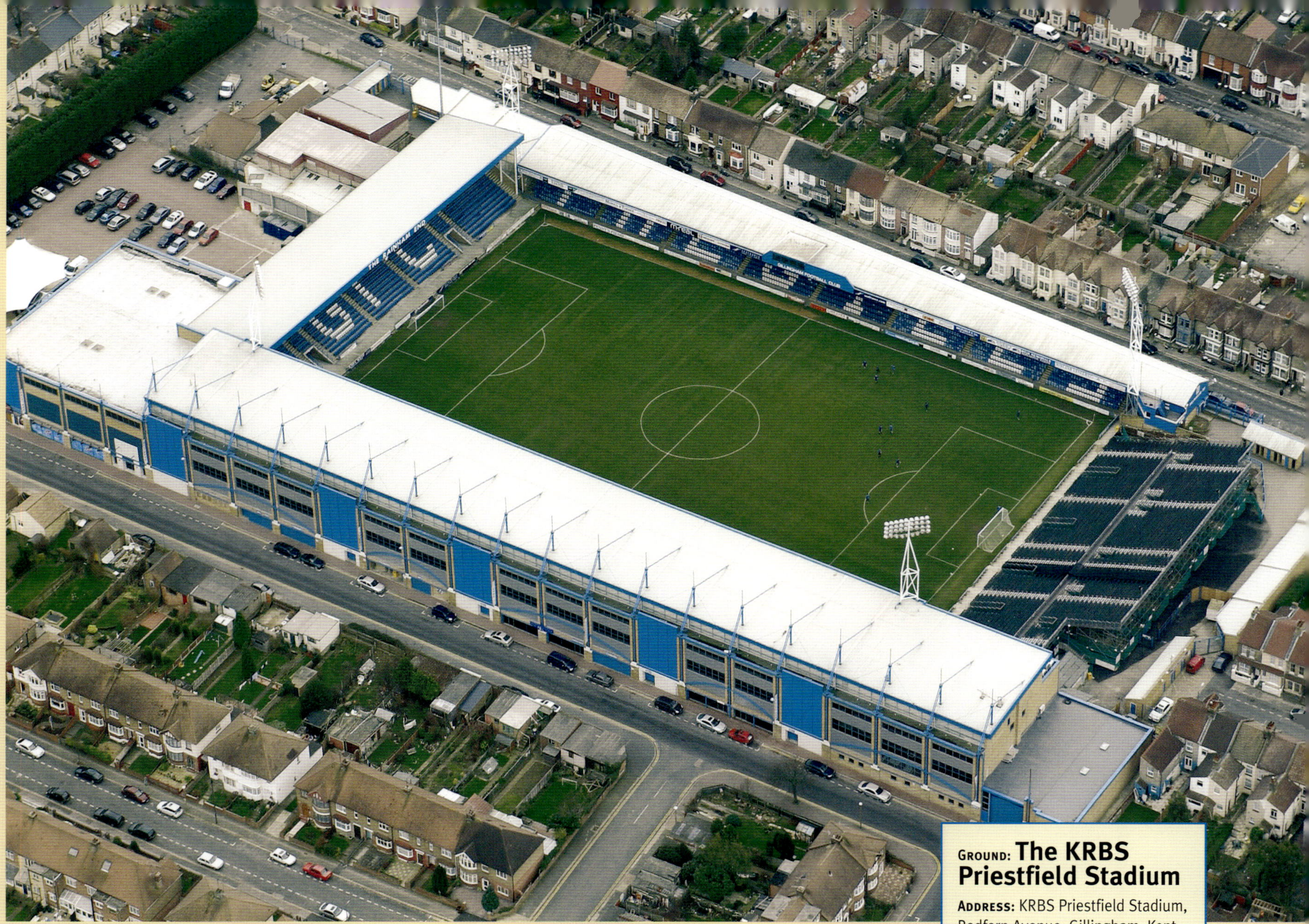

GILLINGHAM

Gillingham's roots can be traced back to a team called Excelsior, which formed in 1893 and played on the Great Lines. In 1893 they changed their name to New Brompton FC and moved to Priestfield Road. A pavilion and a 400-seater wooden stand already stood alongside the pitch; in 1899 a group of dockyard workers built another stand with wooden benches, this time on the Gordon Road side. This simple structure lasted until 1985. The club changed their name to Gillingham FC in 1913 and in 1914 built a main stand, which was blown down by gales a year later. The Gills joined the Third Division in 1920, and spent the next 10 years developing the ground. The club expanded the terracing and added a cover to the Rainham End in 1927. The Gills began expanding their support base in the post-war period, as the local shipyards grew busy. When they took on QPR in the FA Cup in 1948, 23,002 fans packed into the ground and thousands more had to be turned away. The club changed the ground's name in 1947 to the Priestfield Stadium and three years later they rejoined the League. This prompted the club to continue developing the ground, levelling the pitch in 1955 and adding a cover to the Gordon Road Stand. The Gordon Road Stand was forced to close in 1985 following safety legislation. In 1995 Paul Scally took over as chairman and set about completely renovating the site. Along one side of the ground now stands the two-tiered Medway Stand and opposite is the new Gordon Road Stand. The Rainham End has been developed and is now a single-tiered cantilevered stand, and the temporary Brian Moore Stand occupies the space where the Gillingham End Terrace once stood. The club is currently exploring possible suitable sites for a new stadium.

GROUND: The KRBS Priestfield Stadium

ADDRESS: KRBS Priestfield Stadium, Redfern Avenue, Gillingham, Kent ME7 4DD

MAIN TEL: 01634 300 000

BOX OFFICE: 01634 300 000

WEBSITE: www.gillinghamfootballclub.com

CAPACITY: 11,582

HOME COLOURS: blue shirts with white sleeves, blue shorts, blue socks

CLUB NICKNAME: the Gills

PITCH DIMENSIONS: 104m x 69m (114 x 75 yards)

FOUNDED: 1893

RECORD ATTENDANCE: 23,002 vs QPR, January 10 1948

MOST PROLIFIC SCORER: Brian Yeo (135)

RECORD WIN: 10-0 vs Chesterfield, September 5 1987

RECORD DEFEAT: 2-9 vs Nottingham Forest, November 16 1957

Hampden Park

Queen's Park is Scotland's oldest football club dating back to 1867. The club played its early games at Queen's Park Recreation Ground before moving to their own ground, the first Hampden Park on Queen's Drive, in 1873. They moved to Titwood Park in 1883 before moving again to the second Hampden Park in 1884. It was not long before the ground was also being used for Scottish FA Cup finals. The club moved once again in 1903 to a yet larger site, the third Hampden Park, which had a capacity of 65,000. Scottish architect Archibald Leitch designed the ground's two stands on the south side with a pavilion in between and an oval bowl of terracing around the rest of the ground. The club continued to do well, finishing fifth in the Scottish First Division in 1929. Further development took place in the 1930s when the North Stand was built at the back of the Main Stand terracing, bringing the capacity up to 150,000. This led to the ground being used for international games and in 1937, the highest crowd ever to attend a football game – 149,415 fans – packed in to see Scotland play England. Until the 1950s Hampden Park was

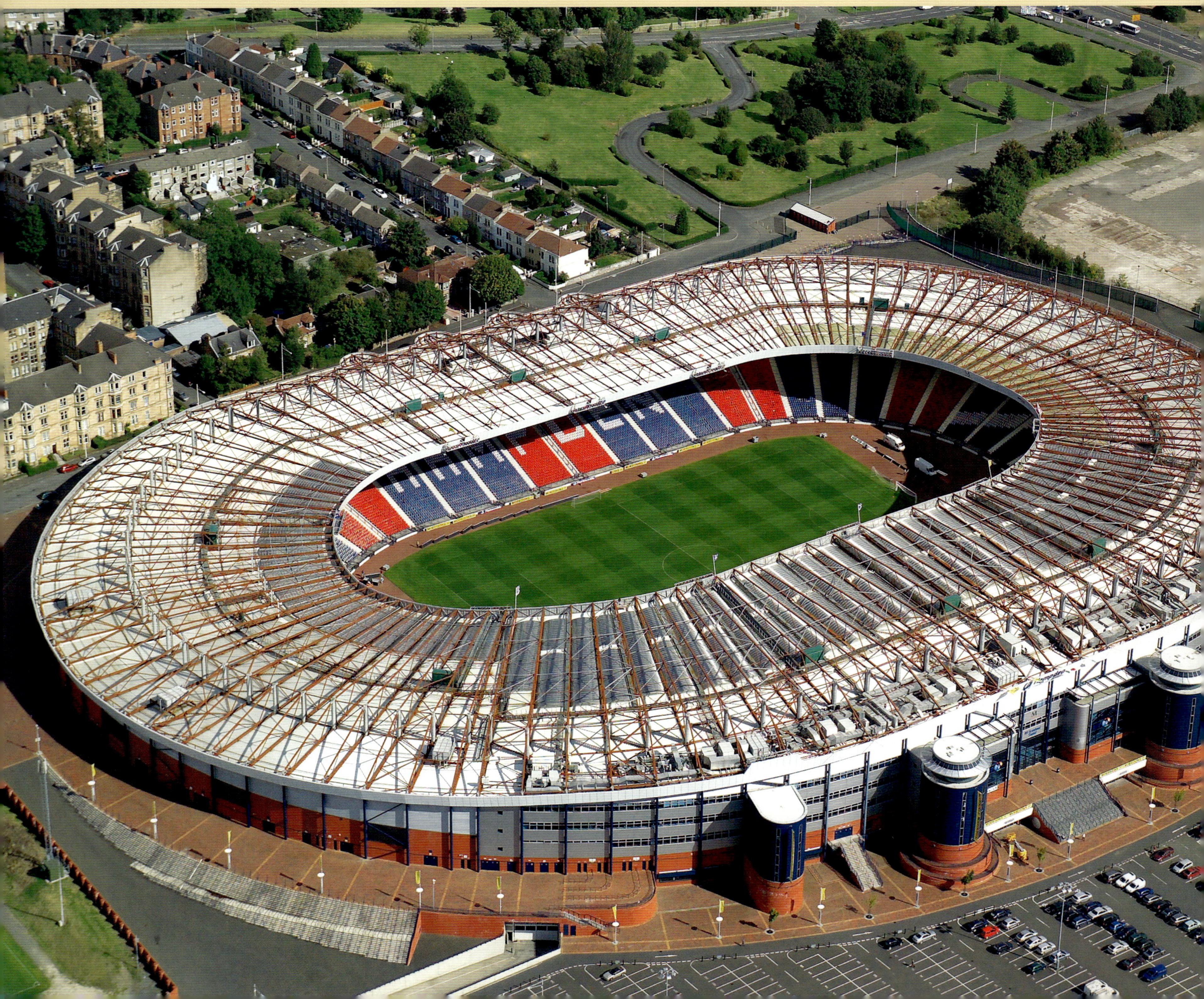

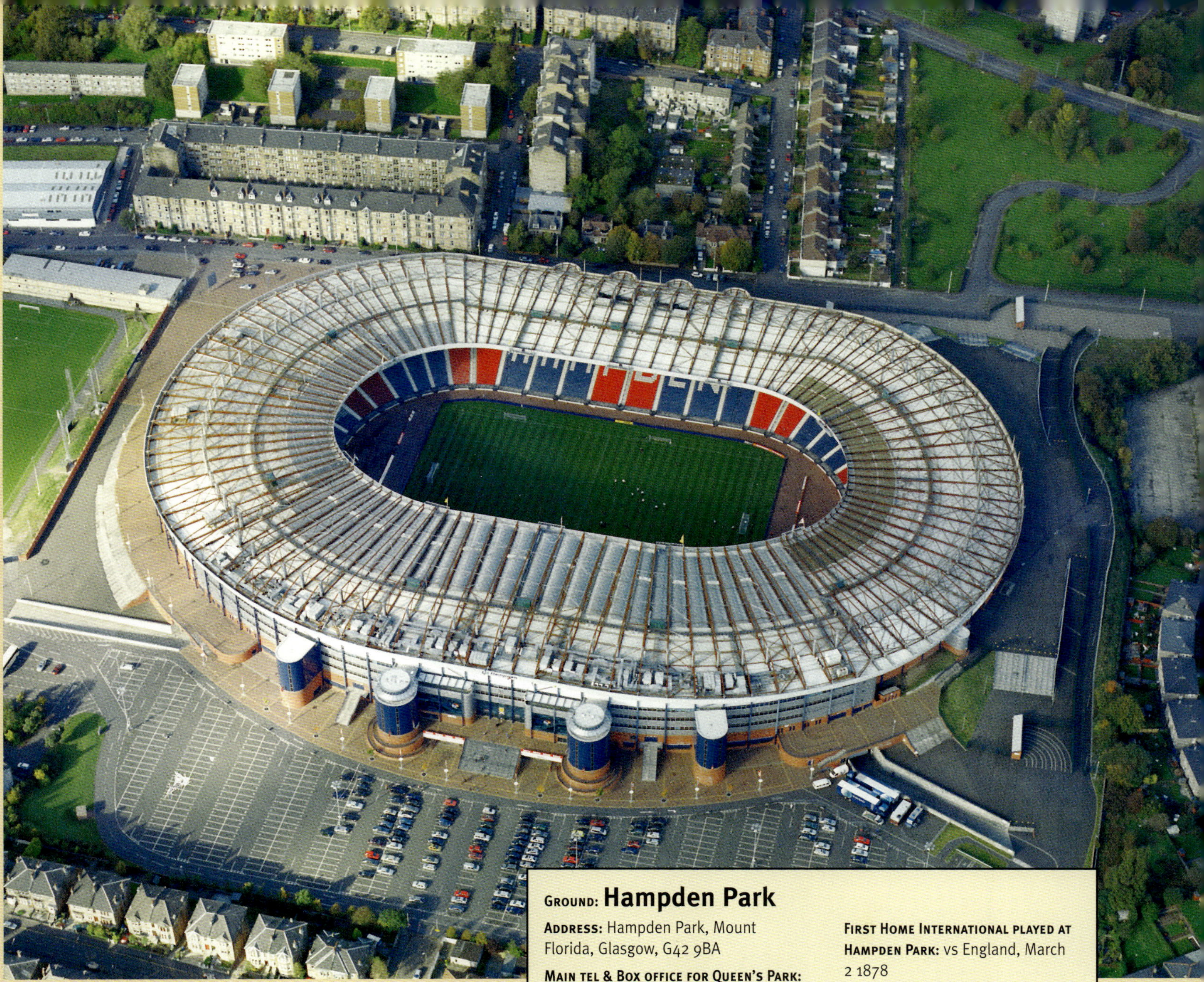

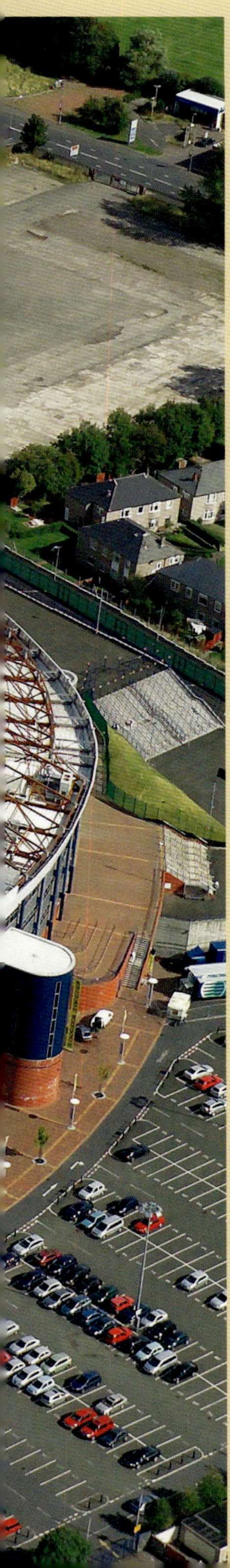

the largest ground in the world. In the 1960s a roof was added to the West Stand but the club lacked funds to carry out more major, and necessary, refurbishments. During the 1970s Hampden Park's future hung in the balance as the Scottish FA tried to decide how the renovations would be funded. By 1981 an appeal had raised the necessary funds to begin redeveloping the ground. The North Stand was demolished and concrete added to the terraces. The next phase was delayed as the Taylor report requirements meant that proposed development was going to be more costly than at first intended. Some commentators even began to question whether it was cost effective to renovate the ground since Ibrox and Murrayfield were so close by. However, eventually a decision was made to develop Hampden Park and in 1992 work began. Seats and roofs were added to the North and East Stands and now the ground has a 52,000 all-seater capacity. Queen's Park remains the only amateur football club still in the Scottish League. Hampden Park will host the atheltics events during the 2014 Commonwealth Games in Glasgow.

GROUND: Hampden Park

ADDRESS: Hampden Park, Mount Florida, Glasgow, G42 9BA

MAIN TEL & BOX OFFICE FOR QUEEN'S PARK: 0141 632 1275

BOX OFFICE FOR INTERNATIONALS: contact Scottish FA

WEBSITE: www.queensparkfc.co.uk www.hampdenpark.co.uk

CAPACITY: 52,000

HOME COLOURS: black and white hooped shirts, white shorts, black socks

CLUB NICKNAME: the Spiders

PITCH DIMENSIONS: 105m x 69m (115 x 75 yards)

FOUNDED: 1867

RECORD CLUB ATTENDANCE: 95,772 vs Rangers, January 12 1929

MOST PROLIFIC SCORER: James McAlpine (163)

RECORD WIN: 16-0 vs St Peter's, August 29 1885

FIRST HOME INTERNATIONAL PLAYED AT HAMPDEN PARK: vs England, March 2 1878

RECORD ATTENDANCE FOR A HOME INTERNATIONAL: 149,415 vs England, April 17 1937, the all-time highest attendance in Europe.

HAMPDEN PARK was the largest stadium in the world until 1950, when the Maracana Stadium in Rio De Janeiro was completed.

THE SCOTTISH CUP is played at Hampden annually in May. The prize is the world's oldest national trophy, the Scottish Football Association Challenge Cup, made in 1873.

HAMPDEN PARK INNOVATIONS & FIRSTS: turnstiles, a press box (1906), a public address system, a car park outside the ground and the world's first all-ticket match in 1884.

Hartlepool United

Hartlepool United was formed in 1908, and was originally known as Hartlepools United. The club took over Victoria Park (then known as the Victoria Ground) from the local rugby club, who had used it from 1886. Originally the Victoria Ground had been a quarry and a rubbish tip. In 1916 a German bombing raid hit the wooden stand that stood on the east side of the pitch and it burned down. The local council planned to improve the road that ran behind the stand, so when United joined the League in 1921 they could only erect a temporary structure with 620 seats in place of the stand. Terraces were later installed and by 1947 a cover had been added at the north end of the ground. The Pool saw a record attendance of 17,426 in 1957 when they took on Manchester United in the FA Cup. The major changes to the Victoria Ground came after Brian Clough took over as manager in 1965; as the team succeeded on the pitch and found themselves in the Third Division, so the £40,000 Mill House Stand was erected. During this time the club dropped the final "s" from their name and became simply Hartlepool United. The club's fortunes took a turn for the worse after Brian Clough's departure and in 1971 their finances left them with no choice other than to sell the ground to the local council. The temporary stand that was erected in 1921 was finally taken down in 1985 and Portakabins installed in its place. The terrace roofs also had to be removed as they were deemed unsafe. The ground underwent significant improvement in the 1990s; two new covers were added to the ends and a new cantilevered stand was built. By the turn of the century the ground had a new name, Victoria Park, and a capacity of 7,629.

Ground: **Victoria Park**

Address: Victoria Park, Clarence Road, Hartlepool TS24 8BZ

Main tel: 01429 272 584

Box office: 01429 272 584

Website: www.hartlepoolunited.co.uk

Capacity: 7,629

Home colours: royal blue and white striped shirts, royal blue shorts, white socks

Club nickname: the Pool

Pitch dimensions: 103m x 70m (113 x 77 yards)

Founded: 1908

Record attendance: 17,426 vs Manchester United, January 5 1957

Most prolific scorer: Ken Johnson (98)

Record win: 10-1 vs Barrow, April 4 1959

Record defeat: 1-8 vs Plymouth Argyle, May 7 1994

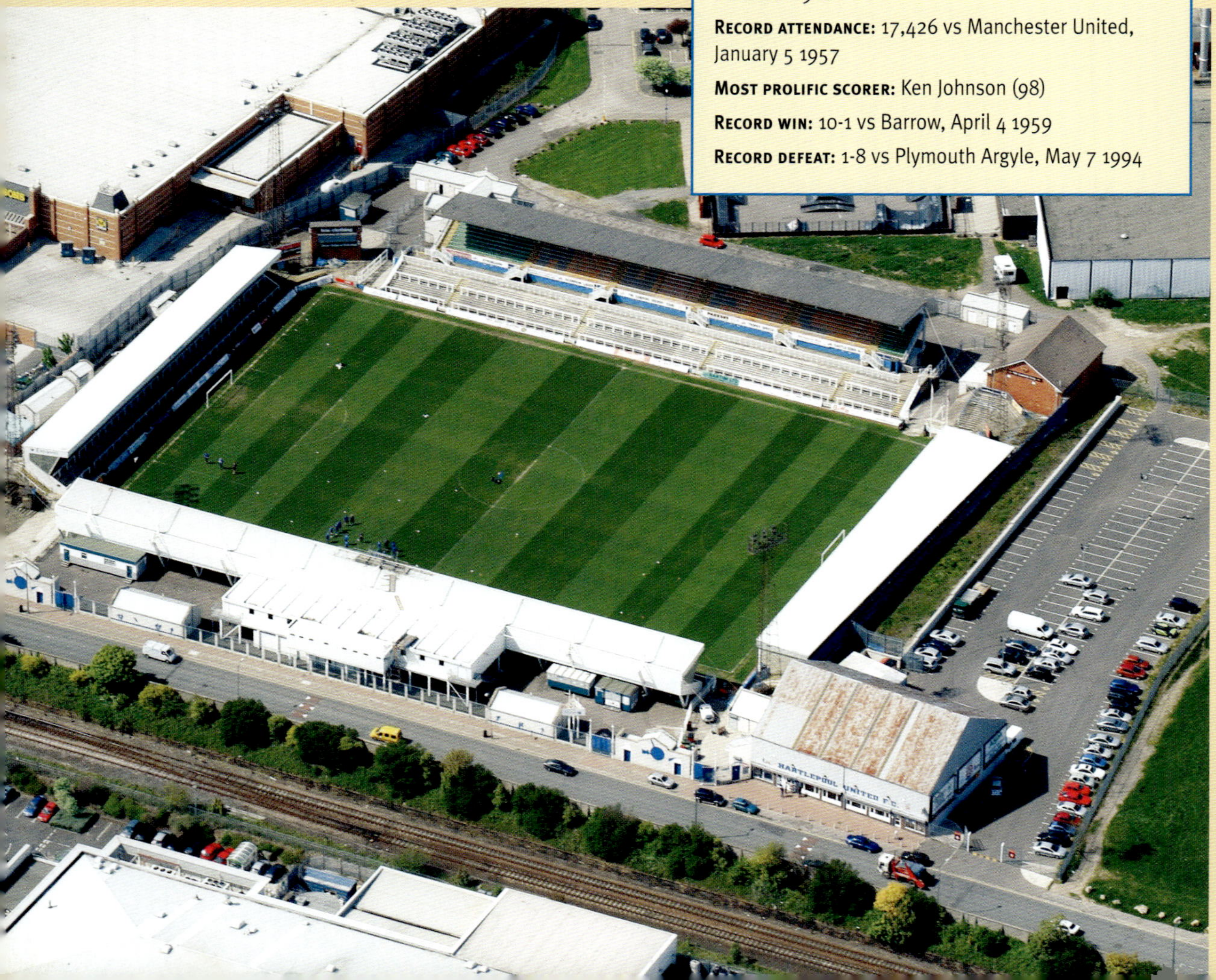

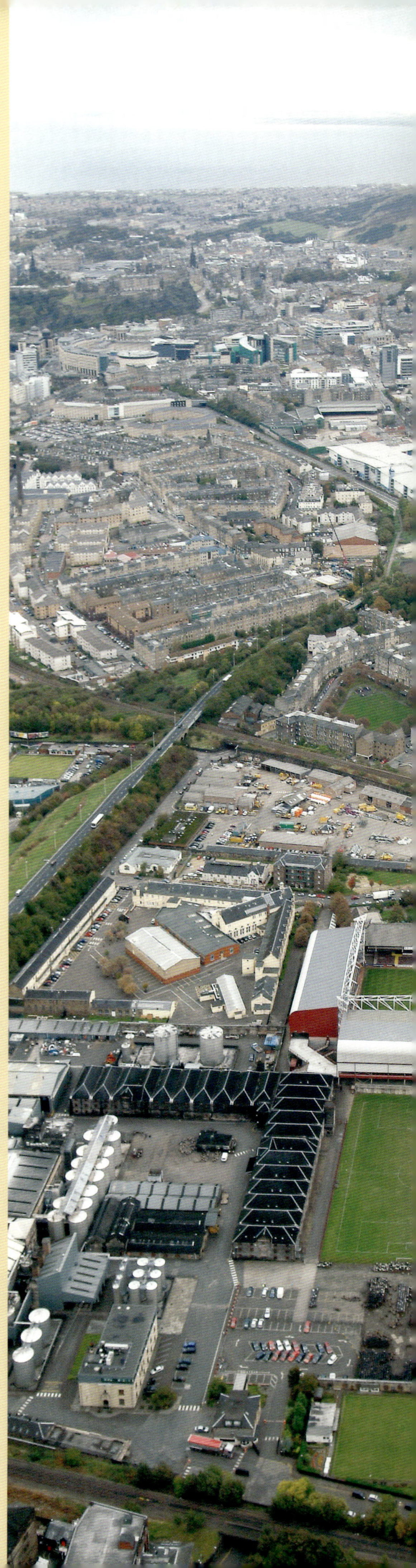

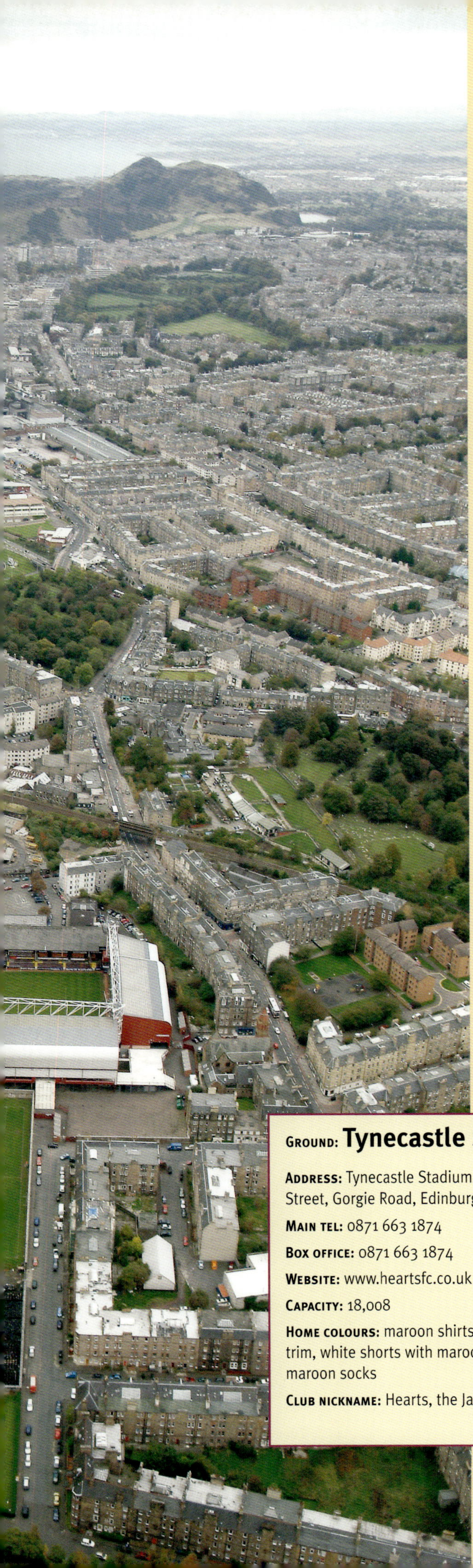

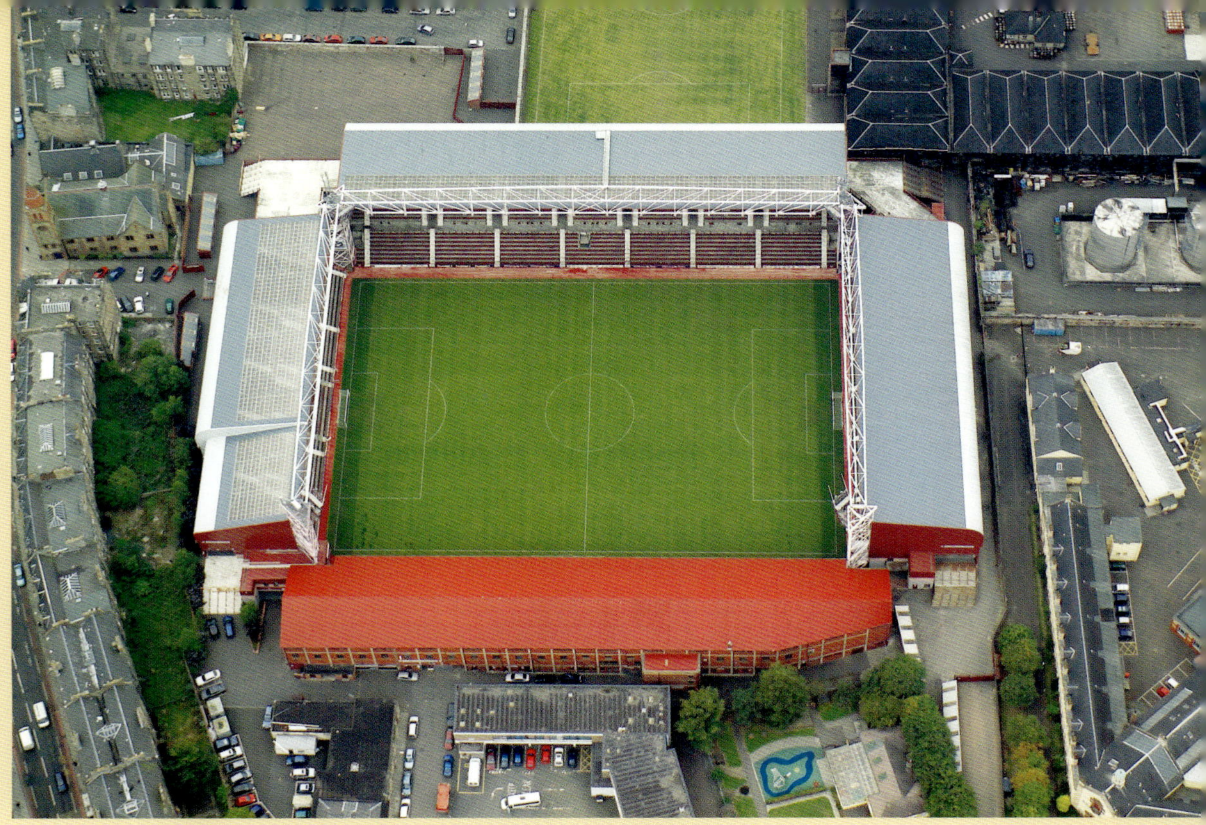

HEART OF MIDLOTHIAN

Heart of Midlothian FC formed in 1874, taking their name from a dance club in Edinburgh. The club began playing games on the East Meadows and at Powderhall before moving to Gorgie Road in 1881. They moved from the first Tynecastle Park across the road to the current Tynecastle Park in 1886. Hearts was a founder member of the Scottish Football League in 1890. In 1903 a pavilion, a stand and a cycle track were installed. By 1914 Hearts had won two League titles and four Cup finals and they began building a main stand. This came complete with an owl on top to frighten off other birds from the ground. In 1926 the club bought the ground and began building up the terraces, although its location between narrow streets, a school and the North British Distillery meant expansion was going to be very difficult. When a record 53,396 fans crammed into the ground for a Cup tie with Rangers the club seriously thought about relocating to Murrayfield; however the outbreak of the Second World War put paid to this plan. The 1950s and 60s saw further successes on the pitch: Hearts won the League twice, the League Cup four times and the Scottish Cup once, all of which helped to fund the concreting of the terraces and a roof on the Wheatfield Street side. Further development came in the wake of the Safety of Sports Ground Act in the 1970s. Hearts' chairman Walter Mercer ploughed £500,000 into developing the ground, adding benches beneath the Wheatfield Street side plus cover and seats to the Main Stand paddock. The Taylor report led Hearts to consider leaving Tynecastle Park as capacity was so limited. In the end, the club decided to redevelop Tynecastle Park. Two all-seater stands were built on the north and west sides in the mid-1990s followed by a new stand on the south side. The club's financial worries continue to haunt them and there are still plans for the club to move to Murrayfield if their finances do not improve.

GROUND: Tynecastle Stadium

ADDRESS: Tynecastle Stadium, McLeod Street, Gorgie Road, Edinburgh EH11 2HL
MAIN TEL: 0871 663 1874
BOX OFFICE: 0871 663 1874
WEBSITE: www.heartsfc.co.uk
CAPACITY: 18,008
HOME COLOURS: maroon shirts with white trim, white shorts with maroon trim, maroon socks
CLUB NICKNAME: Hearts, the Jam Tarts
PITCH DIMENSIONS: 98m x 68m (107 x 74 yards)
FOUNDED: 1874
RECORD ATTENDANCE: 53,396 vs Rangers, February 13 1932
MOST PROLIFIC SCORER: John Robertson (208)
RECORD WIN: 10-3 vs Queens Park, August 24 1912
RECORD DEFEAT: 0-7 vs Hibernian, January 1 1973

Hibernian

Hibernian was formed in 1875 by a group of Irish football enthusiasts. They called the team Hibernian after the Latin name for Ireland. At first they shared a ground with Hearts, then moved three times before arriving at the first Easter Road in 1880, not far from their present ground. In 1891 Hibs disbanded after many of their players left to play for Celtic and developers took over the ground. Two years later they re-formed and found themselves a ground not far from the original Easter Road, which opened in February 1893. Success followed and Hibs won their first League title in 1903. Another ground move was considered but in 1922 they signed a 25-year lease on Easter Road. Development began in 1924, when the pitch was moved sideways, raised banking was built on three sides and a stand on the west side. In 1950 Easter Road recorded its highest ever attendance of 65,480 for a game against Hearts and the East Terrace was extended not long afterwards. The North Terrace was covered over in the 1960s but no further development came until the 1980s. Easter Road was the first Scottish club to instal undersoil heating in 1980; two years later benches were added to the North Stand and in 1985 the height of the East Terrace was reduced. Hibs was floated on the Stock Exchange and shortly afterwards a business plan was put forward which proposed merger with Hearts to form Edinburgh United. Protests from the fans and investment from chairman David Duff saw off the idea. The Taylor report meant the club had to consider either moving or further developing Easter Road. Plans to move four miles away to a 20,000 all-seater ground in Straiton were shelved in 1994 following fierce opposition from fans, so Easter Road had to be developed quickly. Two new stands were built at either end and in 2001 a double-decker stand opened on the west side. Seats have been added to the old east terrace and capacity is now 17,500.

Ground: Easter Road Stadium

Address: Easter Road Stadium, 12 Albion Place, Edinburgh EH7 5QG

Main tel: 0131 661 2159

Box office: 0131 661 1875

Website: www.hibs.org.uk

Capacity: 17,500

Home colours: green and white shirts, white shorts, green socks with white trim

Club nickname: the Hibees

Pitch dimensions: 102m x 68m (112 x 74 yards)

Founded: 1875

Record attendance: 65,860 vs Hearts, January 2 1950

Most prolific scorer: Gordon Smith (364)

Record win: 22-1 vs 42nd Highlanders, September 3 1881

Record defeat: 0-6 vs Celtic, October 15 1960

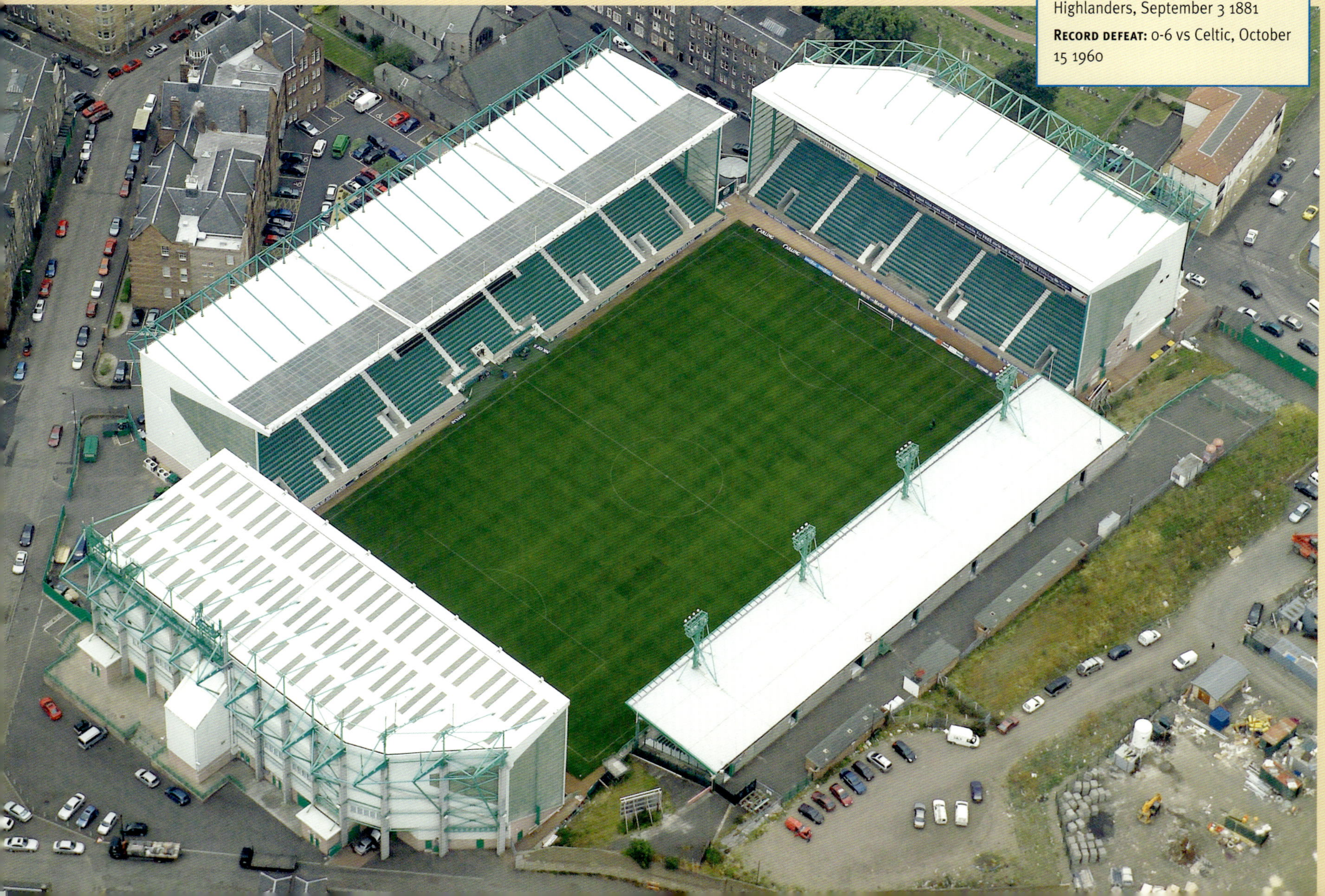

Huddersfield

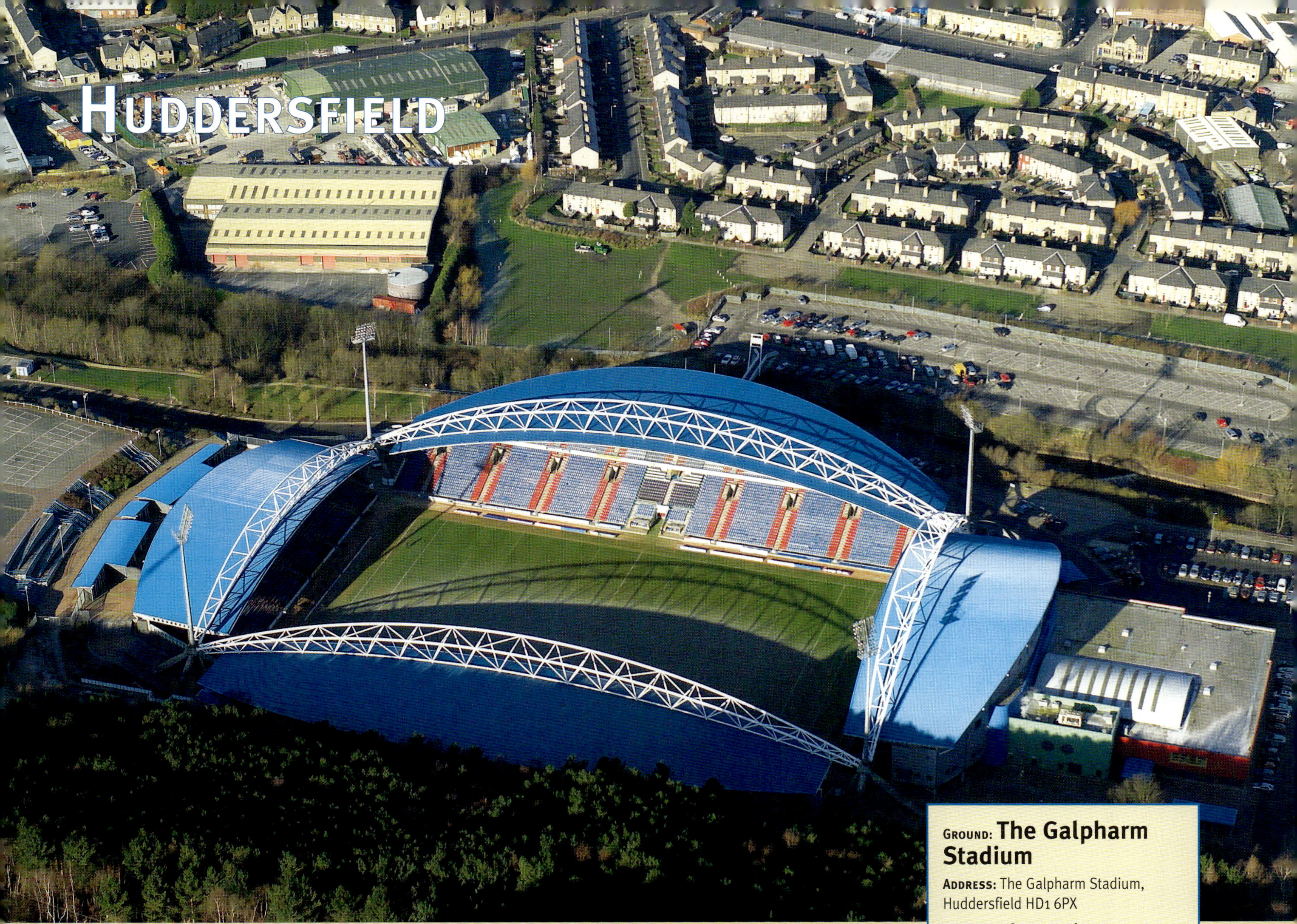

Huddersfield Town FC dates back to 1908; the club first played at Leeds Road, where they remained until 1994. Initially the ground was very underdeveloped, but by 1910, when Town joined the League, the club had turned the pitch 90°, built a 4,000-seater stand along the south side, installed terracing around the pitch and put a cover over the west end. Financial problems beset the club and in 1919 it was announced that Huddersfield planned a move to Elland Road to ground-share with Leeds United. This move never came to fruition. Fortunes revived when the fans helped raise funds and the team began playing better than ever, reaching the FA Cup final twice and winning three League titles during the 1920s. This success saw attendances rise and some development to the ground, including a roof on the Leeds Road End and the erection of a second-hand stand, the Schoolboys Enclosure, built between the Leeds Road End and the West Stand. The Terriers saw a record attendance of 67,037 in 1932 when they took on Arsenal in the FA Cup. Little else changed until fire destroyed the Schoolboys Enclosure and the West Stand in 1950. A new stand opened the following season and a roof was installed over the North Terrace in 1955. By the 1990s, Leeds Road was no longer suited to the pressures of the modern game and in 1994 Town moved across the river Colne to a 24,500 purpose-built stadium, the Alfred McAlpine Stadium. The stadium has won several design awards for its innovative structure, a first for the post-Taylor era of football stadiums. It has four semi-circular stands, three of which opened in 1995, and the last in 1996. Two of the stands, the North Stand and the Lawrence Botley Stand, are two-tier; the other two are single tiers. The ground was renamed The Galpharm Stadium in 2003-4.

Ground: The Galpharm Stadium

Address: The Galpharm Stadium, Huddersfield HD1 6PX

Main tel: 0870 444 4677

Box office: 0870 444 4552

Website: www.htafc.com

Capacity: 24,500

Home colours: blue and white striped shirts, white shorts, white socks

Club nickname: the Terriers

Pitch dimensions: 105m x 69m (115 x 76 yards)

Founded: 1908

Record attendance: (at the Galpharm Stadium) 23,678 vs Liverpool, December 12 1999

Most prolific scorer: Jimmy Glazzard (142)

Record win: 10-1 vs Blackpool, December 13 1930

Record defeat: 1-10 vs Manchester City, November 7 1987

Hull City

Hull City FC formed in 1904 and shared the Boulevard ground with Hull FC, a rugby league club. The ground was closed following crowd trouble at a rugby match and the Tigers moved to the Circle, home of Hull Cricket Club. The club laid out a pitch next to the cricket oval in 1906 and called it Anlaby Road. A main stand was erected in 1914 and covers added to the three sides of terracing in the 1920s. The Tigers remained there until the Second World War, and despite closing down during the war years, the club re-formed in 1944 and moved to Boothferry Park in 1946. The first stand to be built was the 8,000-seater West Stand, followed by a cover over the North Stand. Attendances peaked in the 1940s when a record 55,019 turned up to see City take on Manchester United in the FA Cup. The North Stand was extended in 1950 and seats were added to the upper tier. Boothferry Park was equipped with its own railway station and the first train service began in 1951. The Tigers yet again shared their home with a local rugby league club between 1953-59 when Hull Kingston Rovers moved in. The new South Stand was built in 1964 but City's fortunes slipped and they found themselves in Division Four by the 1980s. The club's finances were in a sorry state and by 1982 the club went into receivership. The ground fell into a bad state of repair and the North Stand was sold off to a supermarket. In 2002 Hull moved back to the Circle, to the Kingston Communications Stadium, a £44m purpose-built ground with a capacity of 25,504 which they share with Hull RLFC. The large two-tiered West Stand and the single-tiered stands on the other three sides completely enclose the stadium. There are plans to add another tier to the East and South Stands.

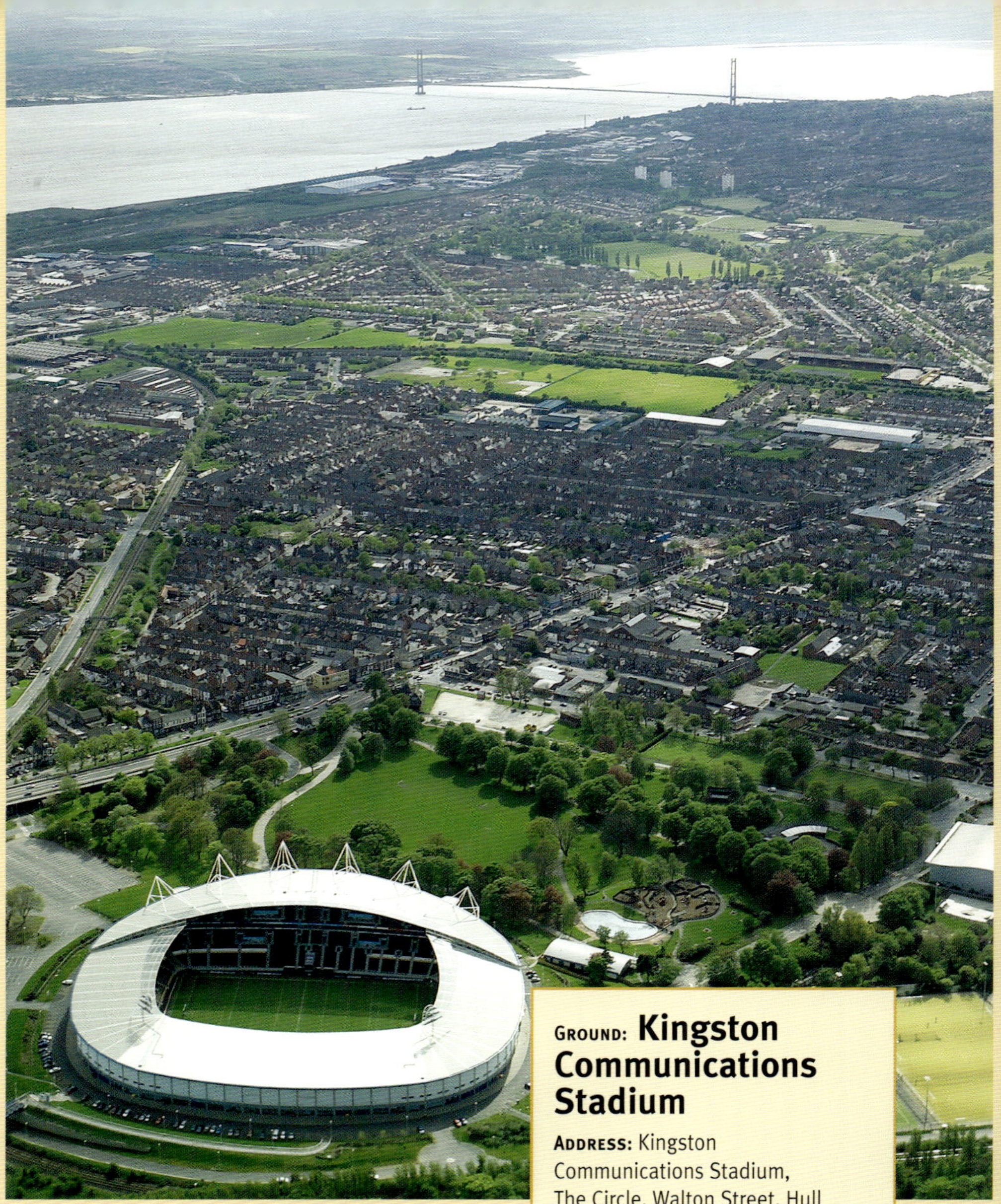

Ground: Kingston Communications Stadium

Address: Kingston Communications Stadium, The Circle, Walton Street, Hull HU3 6HU

Main tel: 08708 370 003

Box office: 0870 837 0004

Website: www.hullcityafc.co.uk

Capacity: 25,504

Home colours: amber shirts with a black and white trim, black shorts with amber stripe, black socks with amber tops

Club nickname: the Tigers

Pitch dimensions: 104m x 71m (114 x 78 yards)

Founded: 1904

Record attendance: (at KC Stadium) 25,280 England U21 vs Holland U21, February 24 2004

Most prolific scorer: Chris Chiltern (195)

Record win: 11-1 vs Carlisle United, January 14 1939

Record defeat: 0-8 vs Wolverhampton Wanderers, November 4 1911

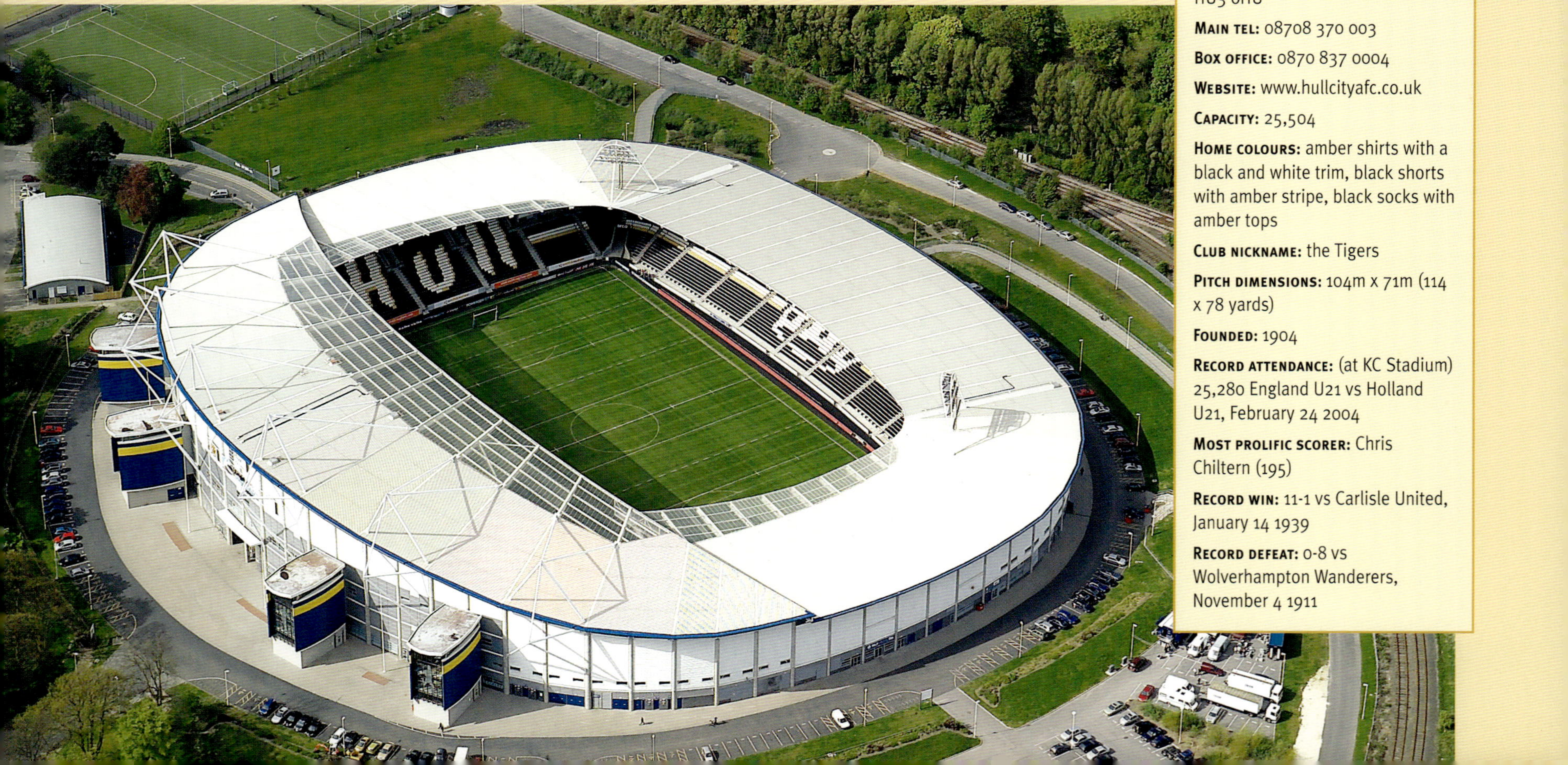

Inverness

Inverness Caledonian Thistle was formed in 1994 following the merger of two clubs – Inverness Thistle and Caledonian both of which date back to 1885. In 1893 there were six clubs in Inverness; the idea of merging some together was first floated in 1937 but was met with fierce resistance. Once the Scottish League announced its plans to expand the number of teams in the League in 1993, further pressure was added to merge two of the Inverness teams. Despite opposition from both sides' fans, Thistle and Caledonian eventually agreed to amalgamate after the Inverness and Nairn Enterprise Board offered to help fund a brand new stadium. While the stadium was being built, the new club, Inverness Caledonian Thistle FC, played home games at Telford Street, former home of Caledonian FC. The ground had a covered seated stand along the south side of the pitch and terracing around the other three sides, two of which were covered. In 1996 the club moved to the Tulloch Caledonian Stadium. The new ground was built on the site of a rifle range on the shores of the inner Moray Firth, giving it perhaps the most dramatic location of any club in Britain. The ground has a large main stand running along one side of the pitch; opposite is a smaller uncovered stand. Following Caley Thistle's promotion to the Scottish Premier League in 2004, the club found itself in trouble as the new ground did not have sufficient capacity (10,000 covered seats). This led to them having to move more than 100 miles away to play home games at Aberdeen's ground, Pittodrie. The SPL amended its capacity requirements, and together with the club's construction of two all-seater stands at either end of the ground, it has finally been able to move back home to a ground which now has a capacity of 7,512.

Ground: Tulloch Caledonian Stadium

Address: Tulloch Caledonian Stadium, East Longman, Inverness IV1 1FF

Main tel: 01463 222 880

Box office: 01463 222 880

Website: www.ictfc.co.uk

Capacity: 7,512

Home colours: royal blue and red shirts, royal blue shorts, white socks

Club nickname: Caley Thistle

Pitch dimensions: 105m x69m (115 x 75 yards)

Founded: 1994

Record attendance: 7,512 vs Rangers, August 6 2005

Most prolific scorer: Iain Stewart (27)

Record win: 8-1 vs Annan Athletic, January 24 1996

Record defeat: 0-4 vs Forfar, May 3 1997

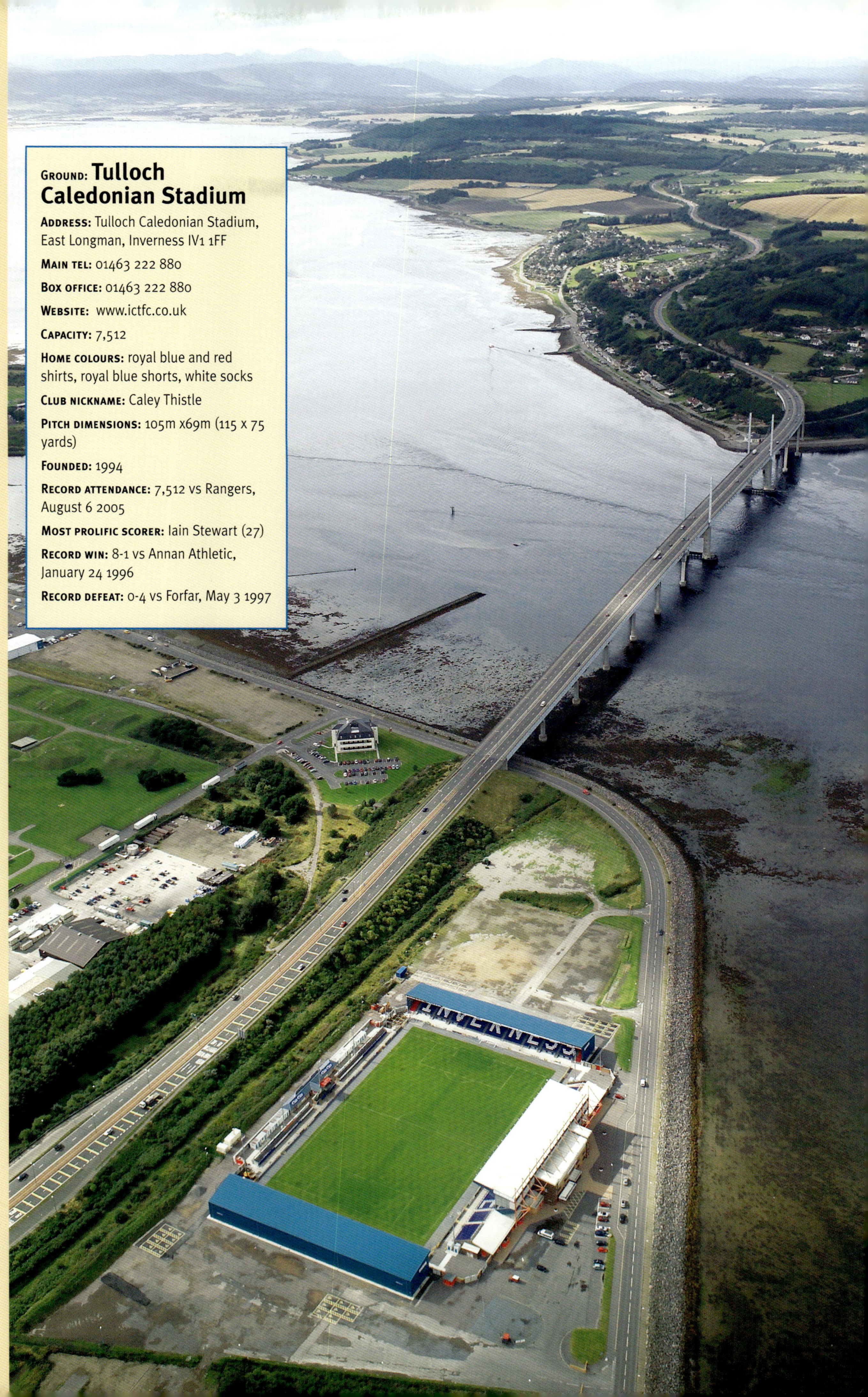

Ipswich Town

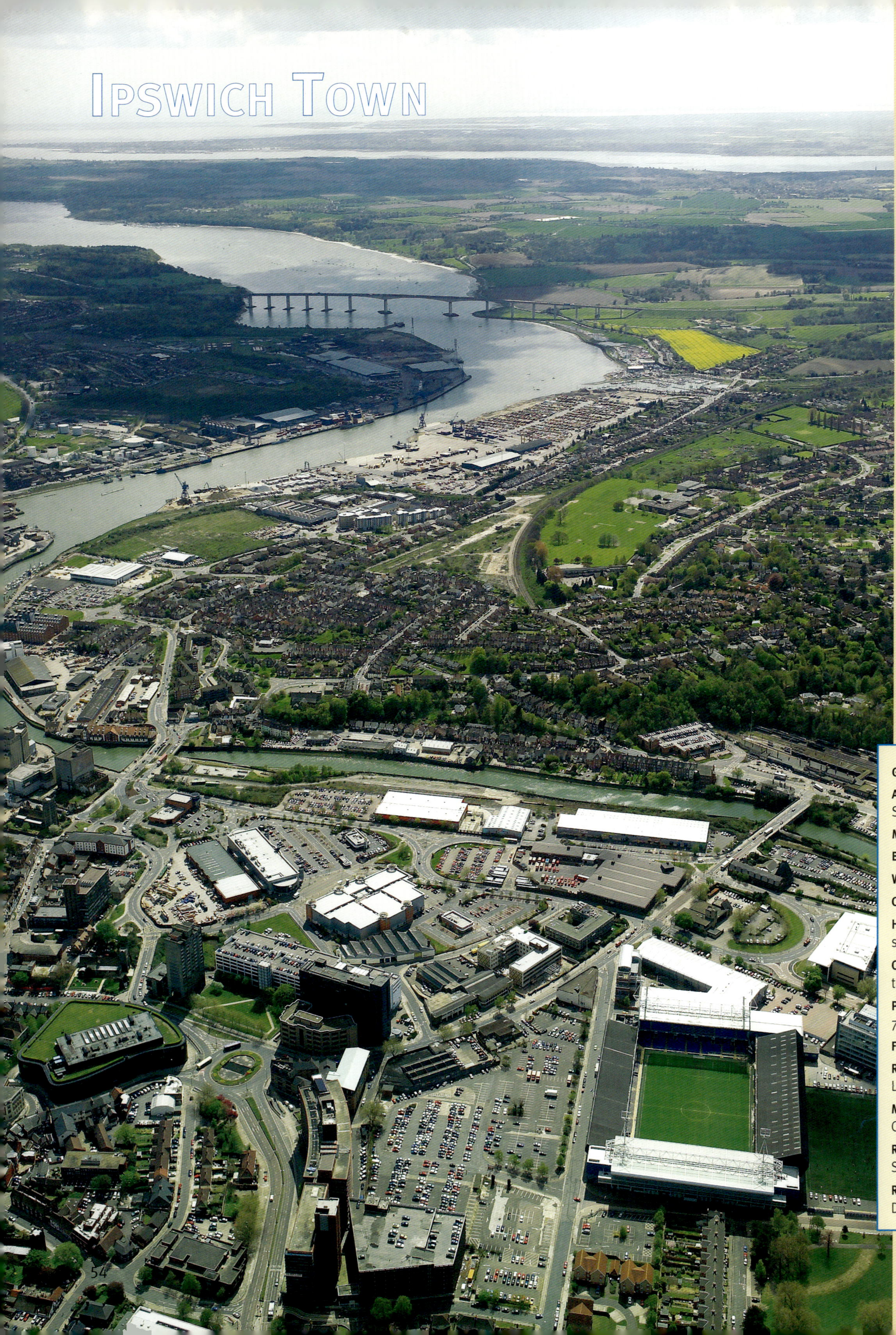

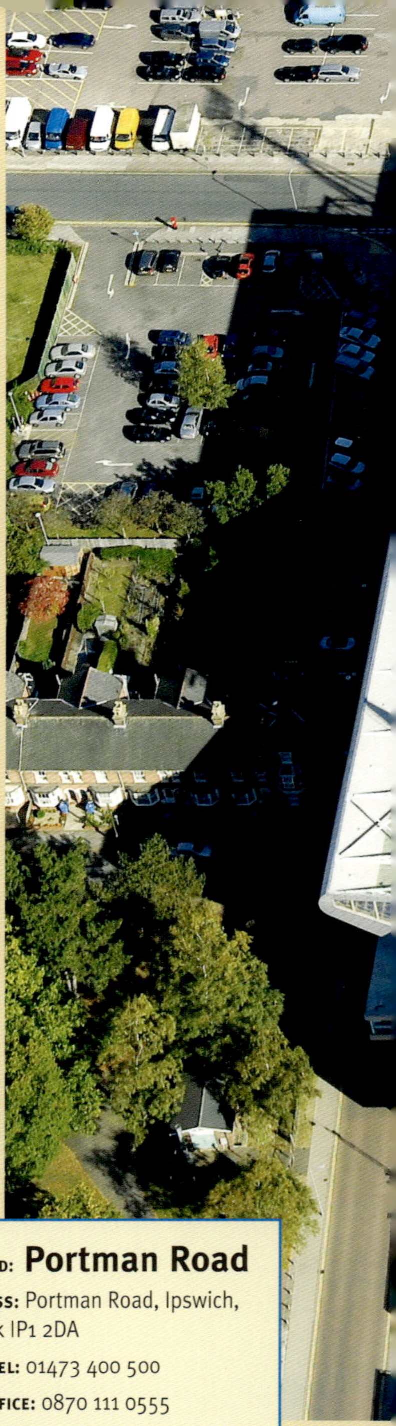

Ground: Portman Road

Address: Portman Road, Ipswich, Suffolk IP1 2DA

Main tel: 01473 400 500

Box office: 0870 111 0555

Website: www.itfc.co.uk

Capacity: 30,300

Home colours: blue shirts, white shorts, blue socks

Club nickname: the Blues, Town, the Tractor Boys

Pitch dimensions: 102m x 64 (112 x 70 yards)

Founded: 1878

Record attendance: 38,010 vs Leeds United, March 8 1975

Most prolific scorer: Ray Crawford (203)

Record win: 10-0 vs Floriana, September 25 1962

Record defeat: 1-10 vs Fulham, December 26 1963

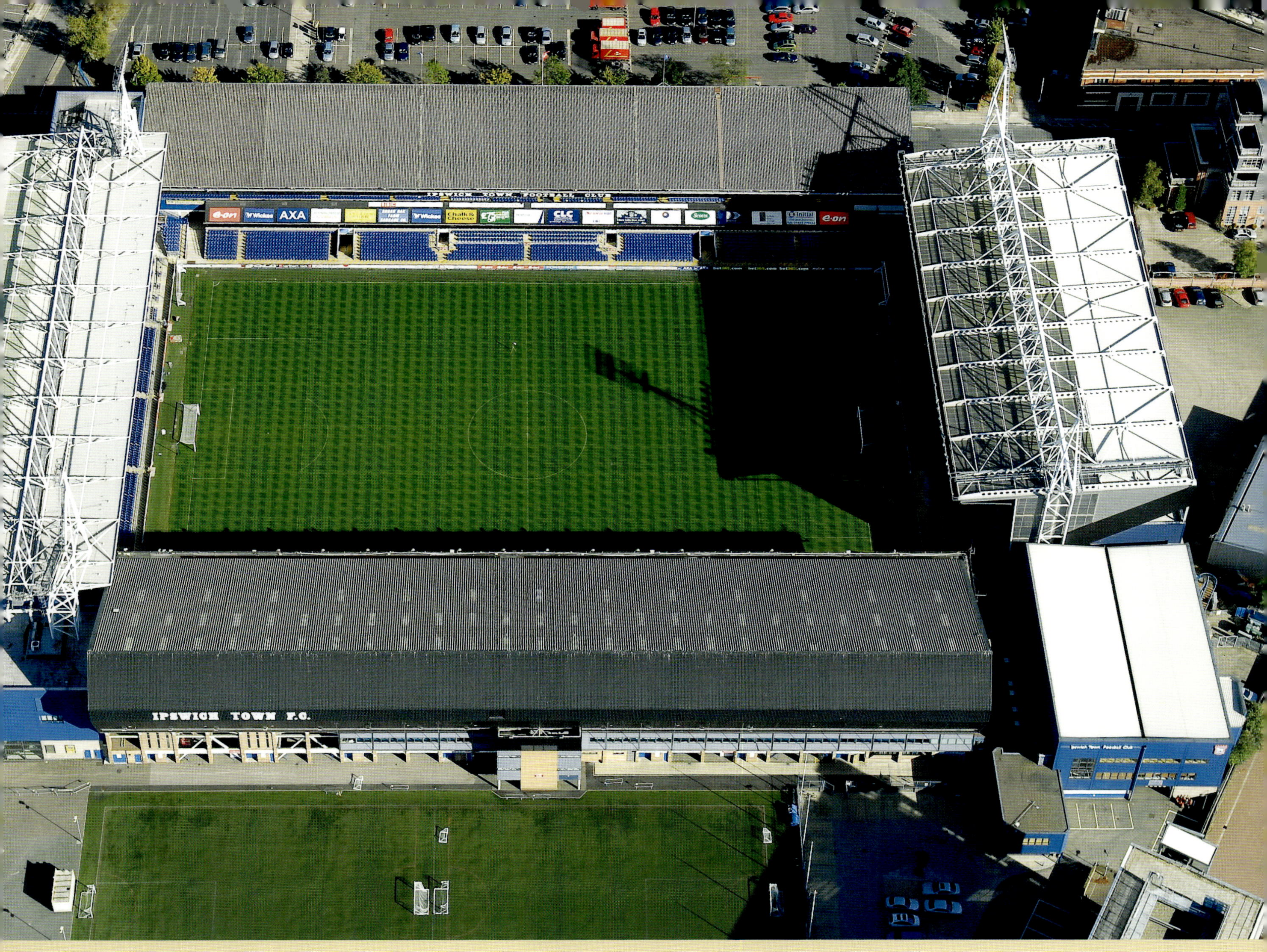

Ipswich began life as Ipswich AFC in 1878. The club's first ground was on Broom Hill, Norwich Road. In 1888 the football team merged with the local rugby team to become Ipswich Town and they moved to Portman Road, the town's best sporting venue. The rugby team broke away in 1893 but Town continued to share Portman Road with East Suffolk Cricket Club. In 1905 the Ipswich Cricket, Football and Athletic Ground Company formed to pay for separate football and cricket pitches. There was a wooden stand along the Portman Road side but nothing else divided the two pitches. Portman Road suffered damage and neglect when the army took over the ground during the First World War. They refused to leave the ground until 1920, by which time the pitch was ruined. Town eventually turned professional in 1936 but the ground still only had one stand. That summer the club put up fencing and terracing, raising the capacity to 15,000. The following year more terracing was added to the Churchman's End and the club added more seats to the East Stand, both of which were further expanded next season when Ipswich joined the League in 1939. After the Second World War the supporter's club raised virtually all the money to fund improvements until 1965. In 1957, under the management of Alf Ramsey, Ipswich was promoted to Division Two. On the basis of this success, the club constructed the West Stand, a two-tier stand with a pitched roof. Between 1972-82 Ipswich continued their footballing success under Bobby Robson and the Blues carried out extensive redevelopment, demolishing the East Stand and replacing it with the Portman Stand. The next major changes took place in the 1980s when the West Stand was extended and renamed the Pioneer Stand. This stand had to be developed just eight years later following the Taylor report when seats were added. Next, seats were installed on both terraces and Portman Road became the first Premier League ground to become all-seater. The development continued and the Greene King, or South Stand, opened in 2001 and a year later the new North Stand was opened, bringing the capacity up 30,300.

KILMARNOCK

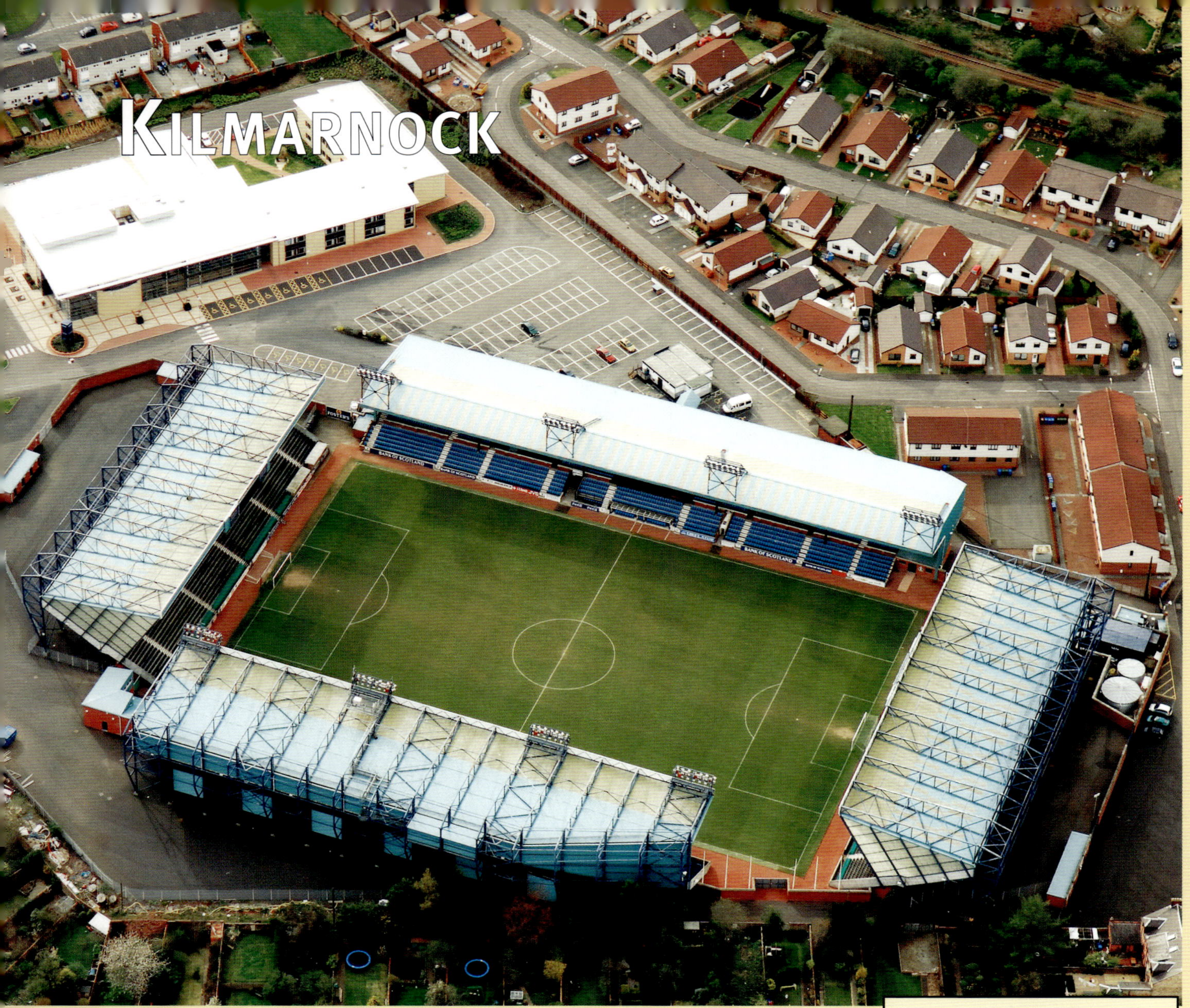

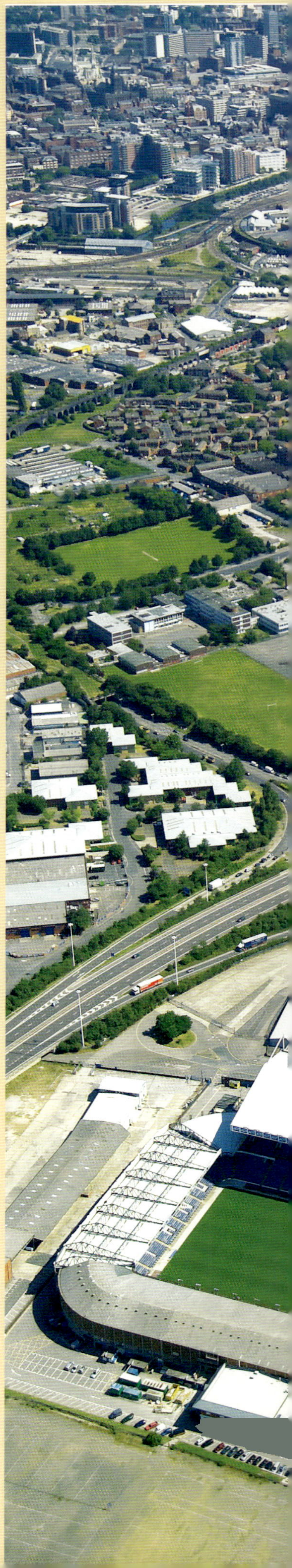

Kilmarnock formed in 1869 and after first concentrating on cricket and then rugby they tried their hand at football. The club moved to Rugby Park in 1877 – a short distance from where the existing stadium lies today – after playing at various local grounds. In 1894 the ground staged an international between Scotland and Wales and Kilmarnock joined the Scottish Football League a year later. The new Rugby Park ground was officially opened in 1899 with a game against Celtic. The ground had a running track around its edge, a pavilion and another stand along the west side. In 1935 a cover was added to part of the south terrace. During the Second World War the army installed massive oil and coal storage tanks at Rugby Park, owing to its closeness to St Marnock's mineral depot. The pitch had to be reconstructed after the war and Italian prisoners of war helped rebuild and extend the North Terrace. After the war, Kilmarnock's fortunes rose and the ground was developed. A roof was added to the East Terrace in 1959 and the new Main Stand was built in 1961. In 1965, a record 35,995 fans packed in to see Killie take on Rangers in the Cup. The 1980s, in contrast, were an era of decline for the club. Kilmarnock sank to the Second Division and attendances dropped to fewer than 2,000. A new board of directors took over in the 1990s with the sole aim of restoring Kilmarnock to the successful team it was in the 1960s. The ground was completely rebuilt in 1994. Three new stands were constructed in shortly under a year: at either end are two-tiered stands each with an electronic scoreboard plus the new East Stand bringing the capacity at Rugby Park up to 18,128.

GROUND: Rugby Park

ADDRESS: Rugby Park, Kilmarnock KA1 2DP

MAIN TEL: 01563 545 300

BOX OFFICE: 01563 545 318

WEBSITE: www.kilmarnockfc.co.uk

CAPACITY: 18,128

HOME COLOURS: blue and white shirts, blue shorts, blue socks

CLUB NICKNAME: Killie

PITCH DIMENSIONS: 105m x68m (115 x 74 yards)

FOUNDED: 1869

RECORD ATTENDANCE: 35,995 vs Rangers, March 10 1962

MOST PROLIFIC SCORER: W Culley (149)

RECORD WIN: 9-2 vs Falkirk, February 8 1964

RECORD DEFEAT: 1-9 vs Celtic, August 13 1908

Leeds United

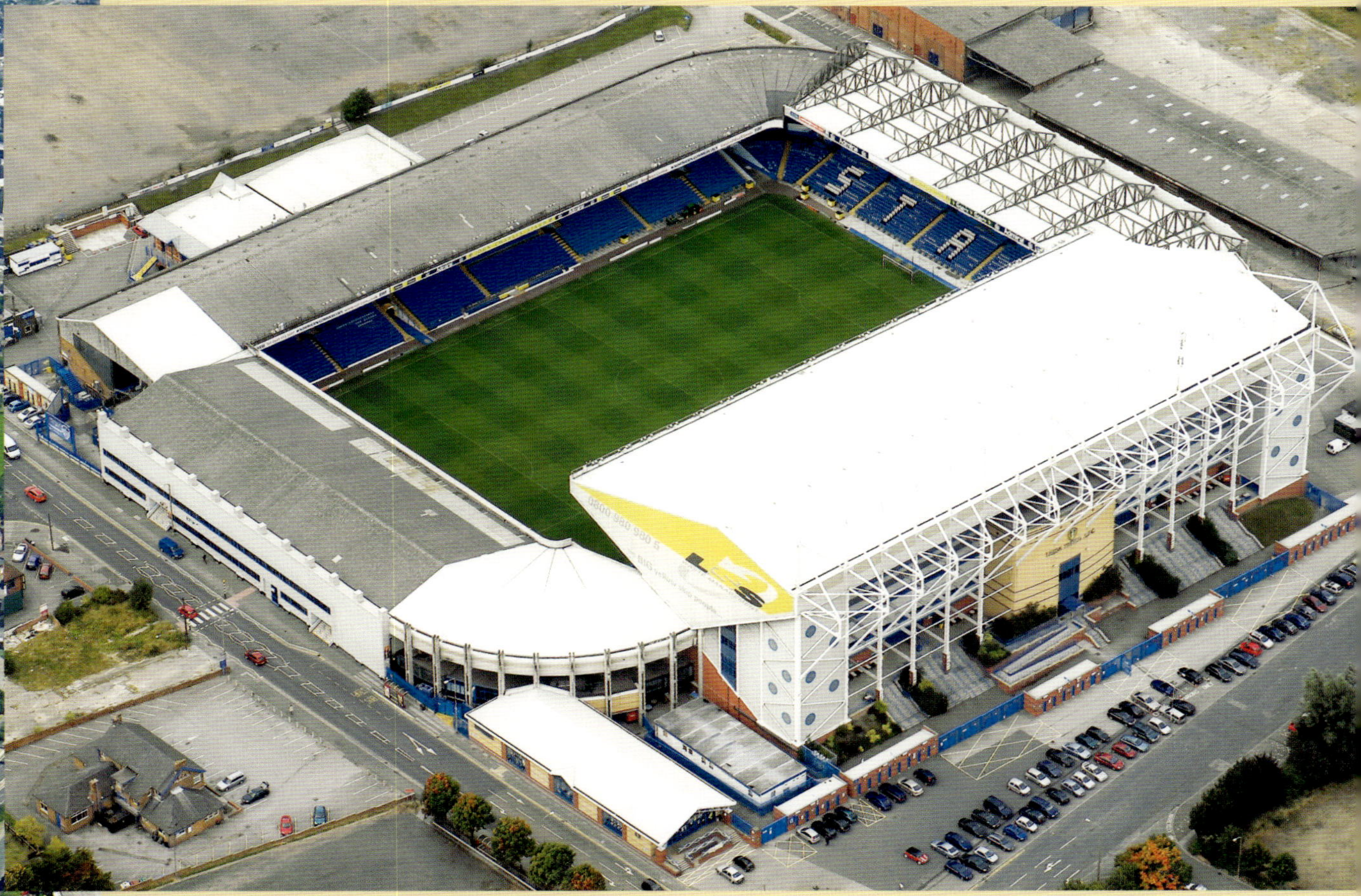

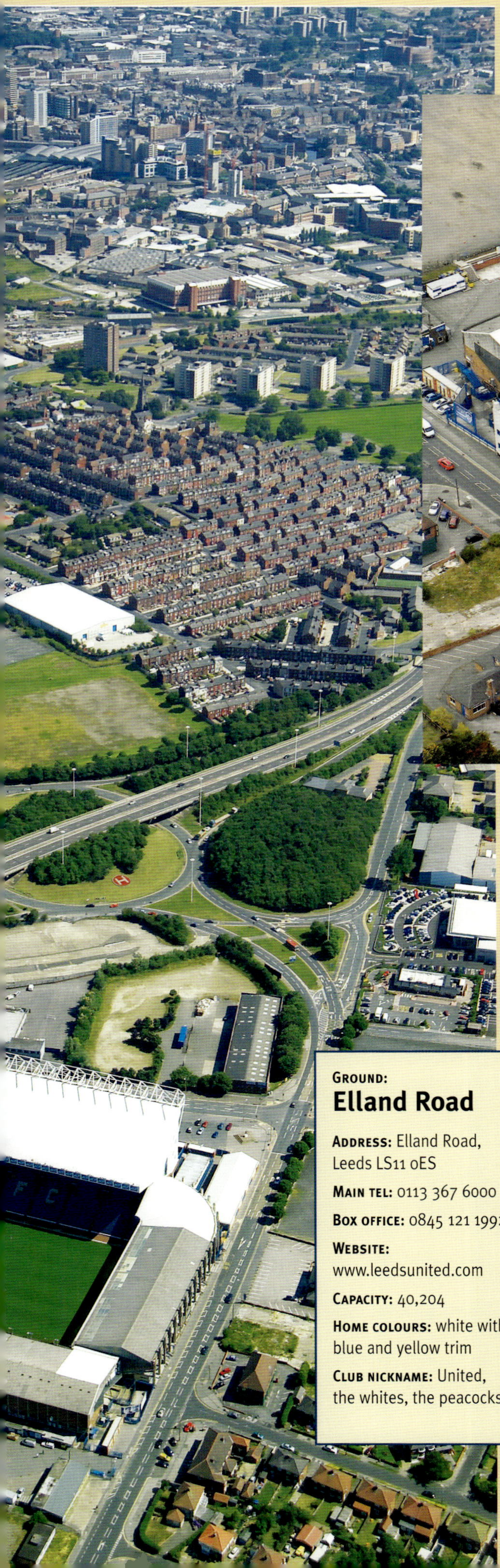

Elland Road began its life as an open grass field, known as the Old Peacock ground, named after the pub which stood opposite. Leeds City Football Club formed in 1904 and took over the ownership of the ground from Holbeck Rugby Club. In 1905 Leeds City built the West Stand and that year more than 22,000 fans saw the club play local rivals Bradford City. During the First World War the army used Elland Road for drilling and shooting practice. Leeds United re-formed in 1920 from the remnants of Leeds City, which was disbanded after the club was accused of making illegal payments to players.

During the 1920s, ground development continued with the erection of the terraces popularly known as the Scratching Shed and the Spion Kop. The most impressive transformations came during the late 1960s, however, in the Don Revie era when support reached record levels. In March 1967 Elland Road saw its highest ever crowd of 57,892 as United battled with Sunderland in the FA Cup. The success of the team brought in money to fund the building of the new Kop in 1968, the season Leeds first became First Division champions. The Scratching Shed was replaced by the South Stand in 1974. At one stage, Leeds' performances began to falter. Revie believed the ground held bad omens and in 1971 he brought in a gypsy to lift the curse. Almost immediately the team's performances improved: Leeds won the FA Cup the following year (1972) and became First Division champions in 1973/4. Hooliganism blighted the club in the 1970s and 80s and Elland Road became the first club in the country to instal a police compound to hold trouble-makers. The East Stand was the last to be completed in 1992-3, the year after Leeds once again won the First Division championship. Now Elland Road boasts the biggest cantilevered stand in the world.

Ground:
Elland Road

Address: Elland Road, Leeds LS11 0ES

Main tel: 0113 367 6000

Box office: 0845 121 1992

Website: www.leedsunited.com

Capacity: 40,204

Home colours: white with blue and yellow trim

Club nickname: United, the whites, the peacocks

Pitch dimensions: 106m x 69m (117 x 76 yards)

Founded: Leeds City 1904; Leeds United 1920

Record attendance: 57,892 vs Sunderland, March 15 1967

Most prolific scorer: John Charles (153 goals)

Record win: 8-0 vs Leics City, April 7 1934

Record defeat: 1-8 vs Stoke City, August 27 1934

Leicester City

Many of Leicester City's founder members lived near Fosse Way in the city's west end so it was not surprising that the team was first known as Leicester Fosse when it was established in 1884. In their first year the team played at the racecourse before moving the following year to Victoria Park. In 1889 Leicester turned professional and moved to Mill Lane, which they left two years later when they found a good site at Filbert Street. While the Filbert Street site was being prepared for football, the team played home games at Aylestone Road Cricket Ground. Filbert Street was then known as Walnut Street and the facilities included a low main stand. It was not until after the First World War that Leicester began major development of the ground and changed their name to Leicester City. In 1921 the new Main Stand was opened, coming complete with mock classical podium and a very grand players' entrance to the pitch with a small window either side of the players' tunnel and brass rails. In 1927 the club built a two-tier stand at the Kop End and moved the Kop to the Filbert Street End. In February 1928, 47,298 fans crammed in to see the Foxes take on Spurs in the FA Cup, the largest-ever crowd at Filbert Street. In the late 1930s, the last remaining open section was covered. The next phase of major development was in the 1970s when the club began converting terraces to seating. The development started in 1971 with the Filbert Street Terrace, which became the North Stand; next the Popular Side was turned into the all-seater East Stand. The 1990s saw further plans for change, and the club considered either building a completely new stand, or turning the pitch 90°. In the end, they opted to do neither and rebuilt the Main Stand. However, this still provided a cramped ground and in 2002 the club moved to the all-seater Walkers Stadium constructed at a short distance from the Filbert Street ground. The new £35m stadium is completely enclosed, with all sides the same height and style.

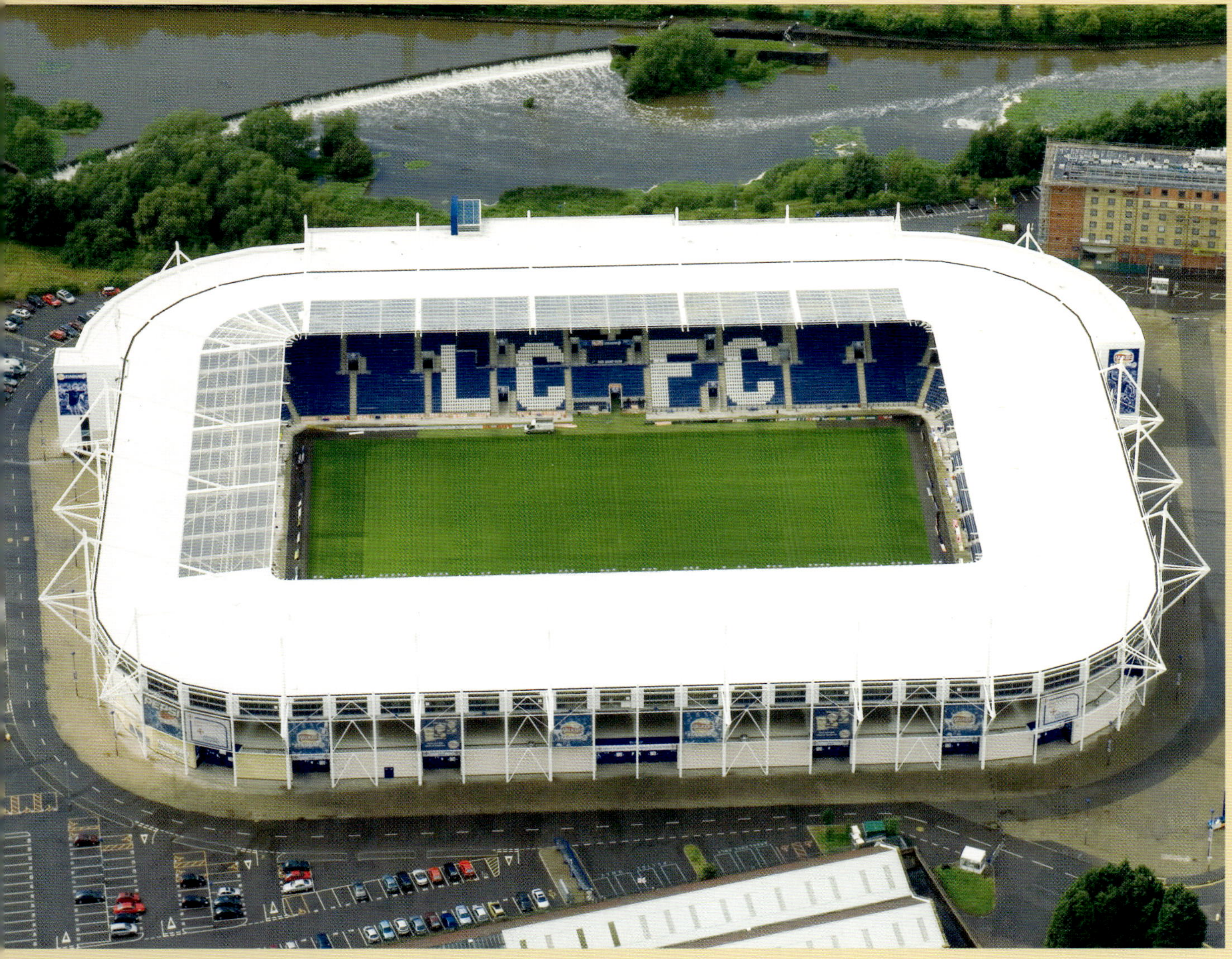

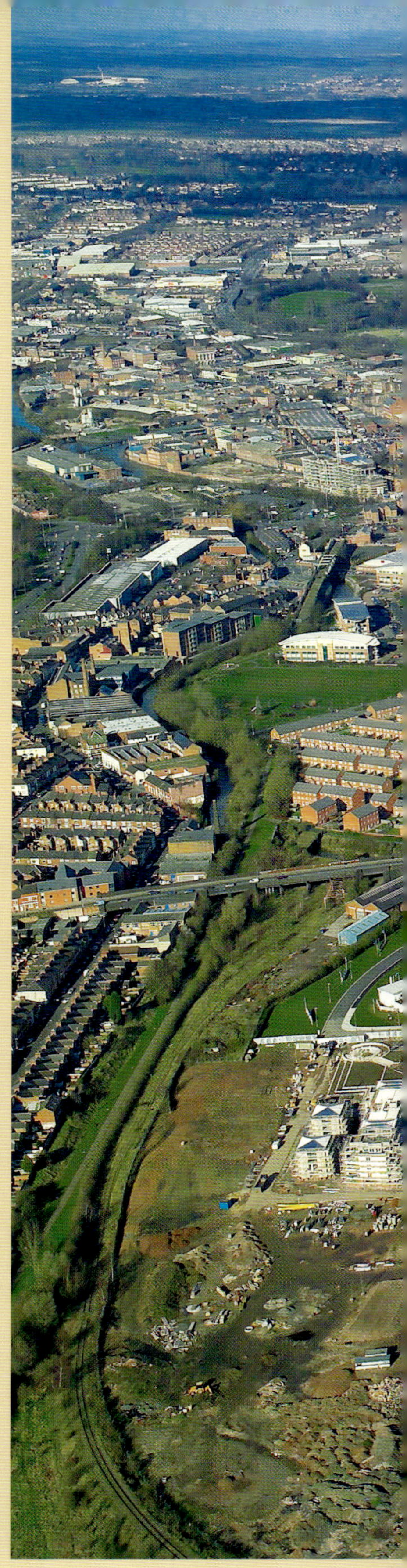

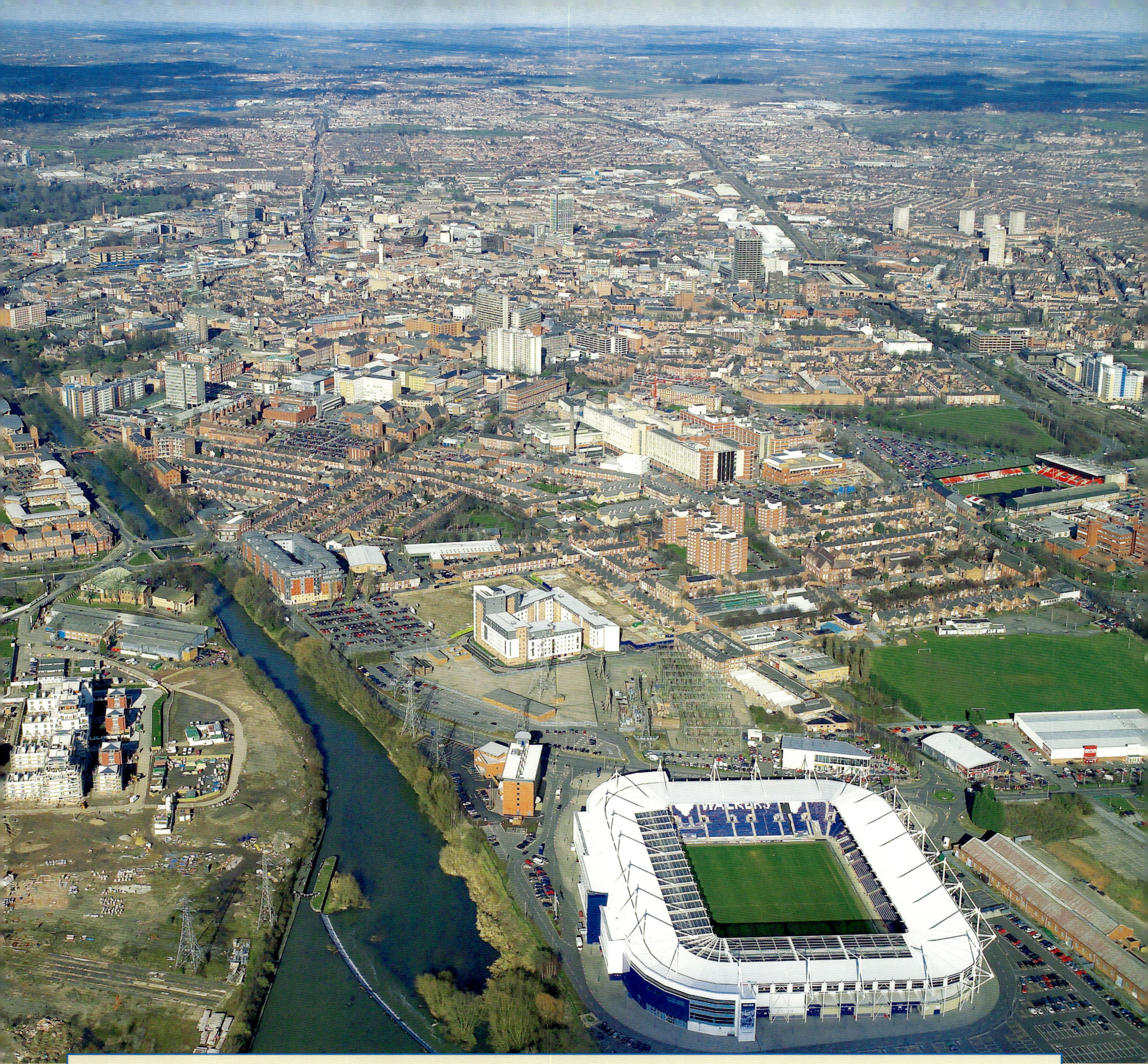

Ground: **Walkers Stadium**
Address: Filbert Way, Leicester LE2 7FL
Main tel: 0844 815 6000
Box office: 0844 815 5000
Website: www.lcfc.co.uk
Capacity: 32,500

Home colours: blue shirts, white shorts, blue socks
Club nickname: the Foxes, the Filberts
Pitch dimensions: 101m x 69m (110 x 76 yards)
Founded: 1884
Record attendance: (at the Walkers Stadium) 32,148 vs Newcastle United, December 26 2003

Most prolific scorer: Arthur Chandler (259)
Record win: 10-0 vs Portsmouth, October 10 1928
Record defeat: 0-12 vs Nottingham Forest, April 21 1909

LIVERPOOL

Anfield was originally home to Everton, who played there from 1884 until 1892, when they had a disagreement with Anfield's owner John Houlding and moved on to Goodison Park. Houlding set up his own team, Liverpool, which was dominated by Scottish players. Major changes took place at Anfield in 1906, the season Liverpool won their second League title. The pitch was raised by five feet and in addition to the two sides which were already covered, a new main stand and south terrace, the Kop, were built. The Kop was one of the tallest terraces in England, complete with a 50ft flagpole and was covered in 1928, when it became Britain's largest covered terrace, with a capacity of 28,000. During the Shankly era of the 1960s, Liverpool carried out further renovations to the ground. The Kemlyn Road Stand was rebuilt and reopened in 1964, the same season that Liverpool won their first FA Cup final. The 1970s saw the Main Stand extended, and the club began buying houses along Kemlyn Road so they could build a second tier on the Kemlyn Road Stand. It was not until 1990 that the final tenants – two elderly sisters – agreed to sell up. April 15 1989 is a day that will forever remain in the memories of Liverpool fans, the date of the Hillsborough disaster, when 96 Liverpool fans were crushed to death. The resulting Taylor report had a massive impact on football grounds across the country. At Anfield plans were drawn up to make the Kop all-seater, so that a tragedy on the scale of Hillsborough could never happen again. It was a sad day for many fans in 1994 when the Kop was finally demolished. Liverpool has now announced plans to move to nearby Stanley Park, to a purpose-built 60,000 all-seater stadium, due to open in 2009. The strong ties many fans feel to Anfield means this move is deeply unpopular with some fans.

Right: Anfield, with Goodison Park, home of its close rival Everton FC in the background. Stanley Park, the proposed site of Liverpool's new ground, separates the two clubs

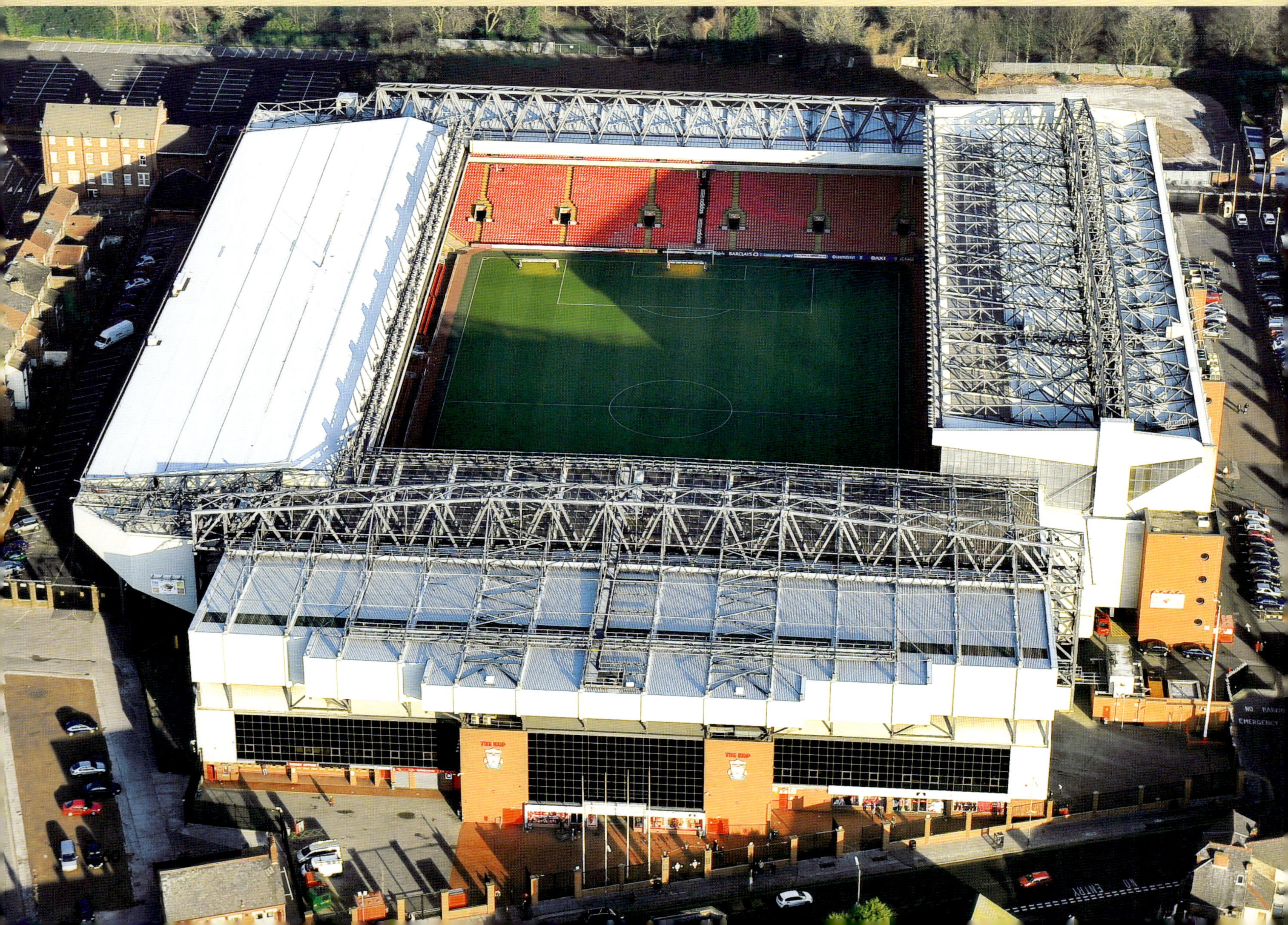

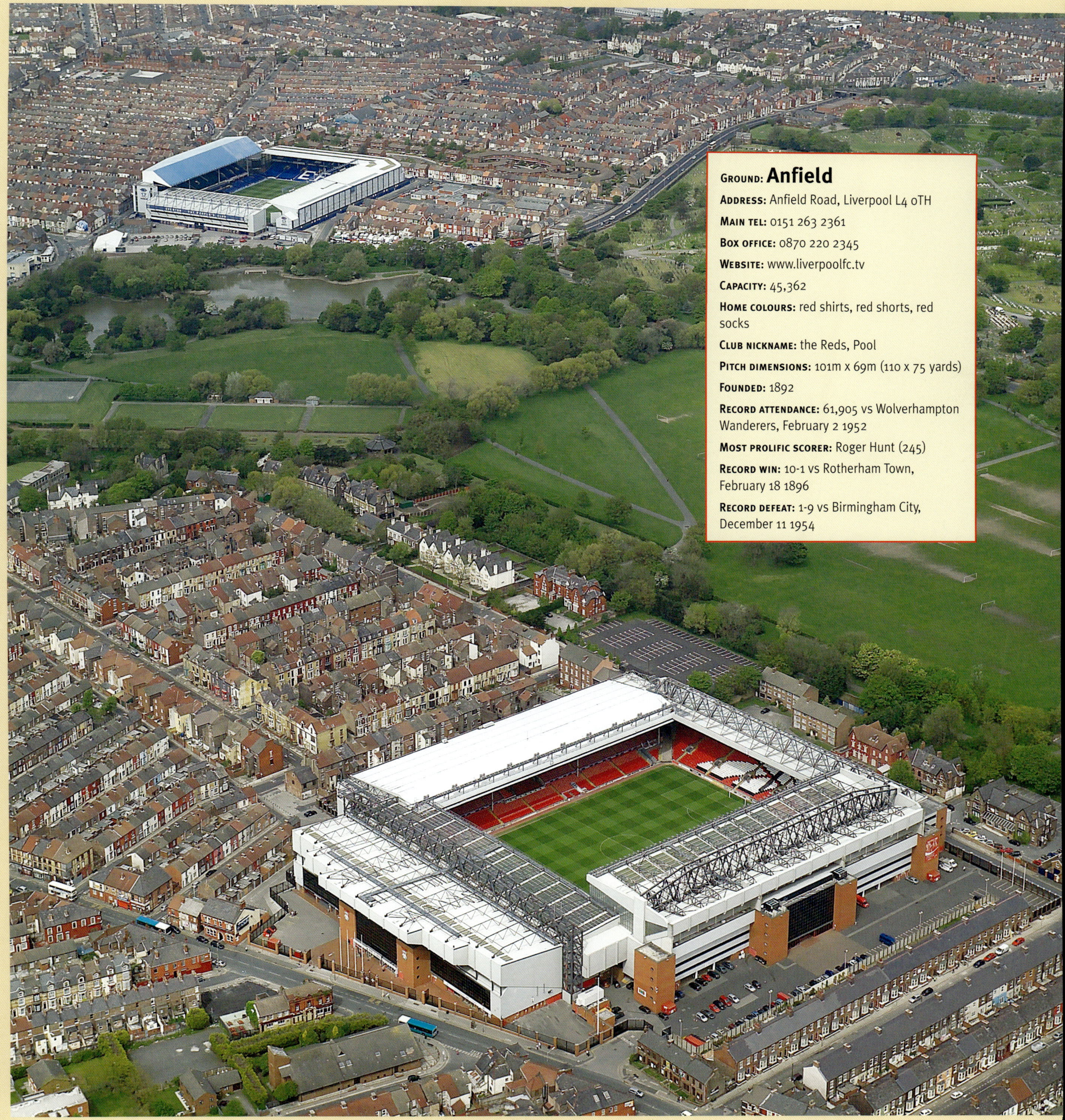

Ground: **Anfield**

Address: Anfield Road, Liverpool L4 0TH

Main tel: 0151 263 2361

Box office: 0870 220 2345

Website: www.liverpoolfc.tv

Capacity: 45,362

Home colours: red shirts, red shorts, red socks

Club nickname: the Reds, Pool

Pitch dimensions: 101m x 69m (110 x 75 yards)

Founded: 1892

Record attendance: 61,905 vs Wolverhampton Wanderers, February 2 1952

Most prolific scorer: Roger Hunt (245)

Record win: 10-1 vs Rotherham Town, February 18 1896

Record defeat: 1-9 vs Birmingham City, December 11 1954

Livingston

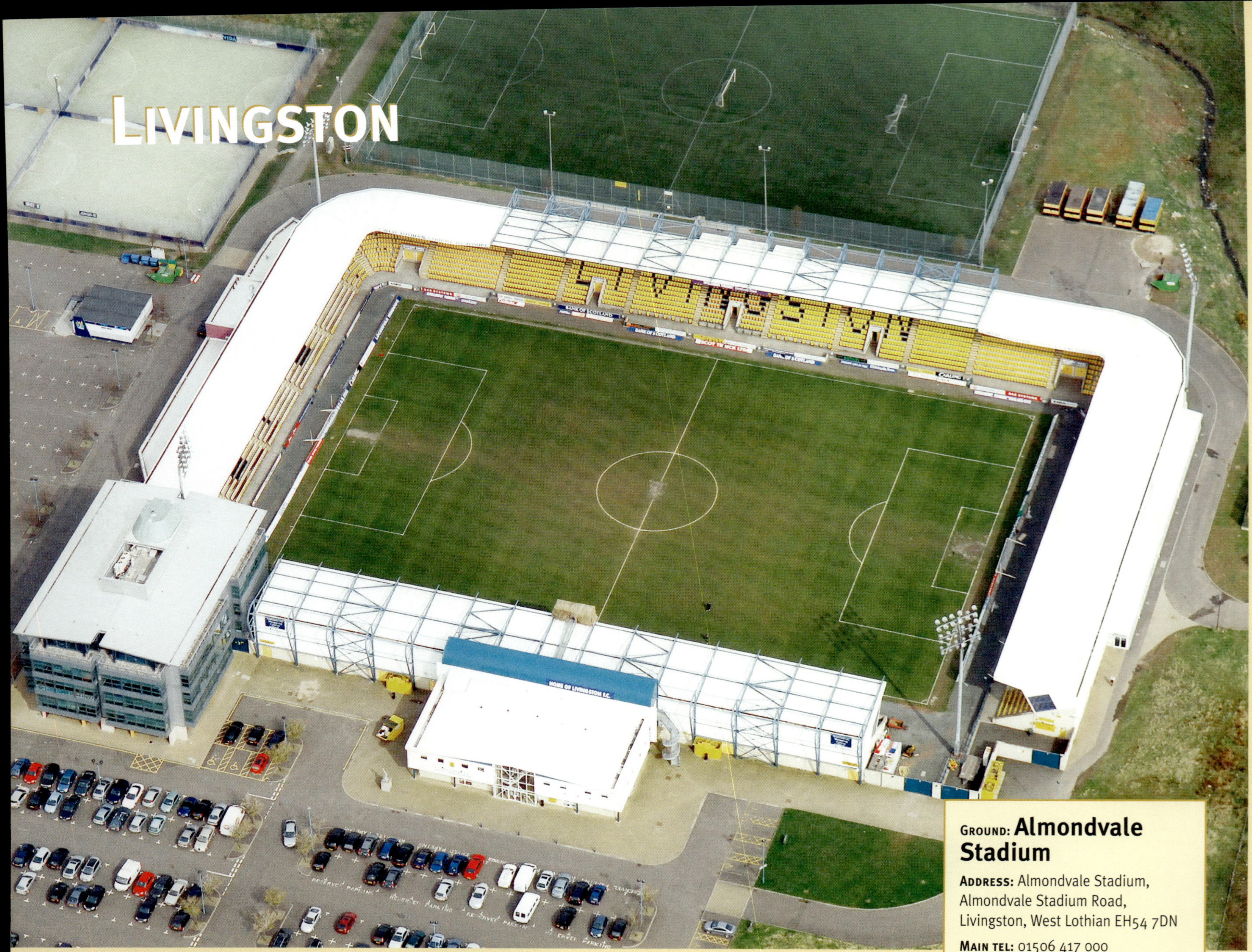

Ground: Almondvale Stadium

Address: Almondvale Stadium, Almondvale Stadium Road, Livingston, West Lothian EH54 7DN

Main tel: 01506 417 000

Box office: 01506 417 000

Website: www.livingstonfc.co.uk

Capacity: 10,112

Home colours: white and gold shirts, black shorts, gold socks

Club nickname: Livi Lions

Pitch dimensions: 101m x 69m (110 x 76 yards)

Founded: 1995

Record attendance: 10,112 vs Rangers, October 27 2001

Most prolific scorer: John McGacghie (21)

Record win: (as Meadowbank Thistle) 6-0 vs Raith Rovers, November 9 1985

Record defeat: (as Meadowbank Thistle) 0-8 vs Hamilton, December 14 1974

Livingston formed in 1995 from Meadowbank Thistle, which itself started out as Ferranti Thistle, a works team dating back to 1943. Meadowbank Thistle found themselves drawing in smaller and smaller crowds and were on the brink of folding when club secretary Bill Hunter had a chance meeting with the Livingston Development Corporation. The first idea they discussed was to move Meadowbank Thistle to East Lothian. However it did not take long for them to agree that a better location would be in the new town of Livingston, West Lothian. Fans of Thistle were not happy – however finances meant there was not much choice. Meadowbank Thistle played its last ever game against Stenhousemuir on the final day of the 1994/95 season and attracted its highest crowd of the season – 463. The following season the new team continued to play at Meadowbank, but this time under their new name, Livingston. The Almondvale Stadium opened in November 1995 at a cost of £5.1m. Around £2m came from the Livingston Development Corporation and half a million came from the Football Trust. It has stands on all sides of the pitch and two corners have been filled in. Since forming as Livingston FC, the club has gone from strength to strength. Starting off in the Scottish Third Division, it rose steadily to the Scottish Premier League, and by the end of the 2001/02 season it finished third and European football beckoned. Despite not lasting long in Europe, Livingston are now drawing in much larger crowds than their previous incarnations ever managed; a record 10,112 packed in to see Livi Lions take on Rangers in the League on October 27 2001.

Luton Town

Luton Town formed in 1885 and played their first games at Dallow Lane, where they remained until 1897 when they moved to Dunstable Road. The club stayed at Dunstable Road for eight years before moving again to Kenilworth Road in 1905. A main stand stood along one edge of the pitch, a covered cinder bank stood on the other side and there was banking at each end. The Main Stand burned down in 1921 and was replaced with a stand from Kempton Racecourse. In 1933 the club bought the ground's freehold and paid for a new terrace to be built opposite the Main Stand; this terrace was known as the Bobbers' Stand (as entrance to this stand cost a bob, one old shilling). In 1935 the Oak Road Terrace was covered and two years later the Kenilworth Road End was extended. In 1955 the Oak Road Terrace was also extended and just four years later a record attendance of 30,069 saw the Hatters take on Blackpool in a Cup match. The club experienced mixed fortunes over the next 20 years, falling to the Fourth Division and climbing back up to the First Division. During this time the club took the decision to relocate, although so far all attempts have proved fruitless. Seats were added to the Bobbers Stand in 1979 but in 1985 these were removed and replaced with executive boxes and an artificial pitch was also installed. The executive boxes reduced capacity so much at Kenilworth Road that the club decided to ban all away fans; to help control this, they introduced a membership card scheme for home fans. This did nothing for the atmosphere at Kenilworth Road and in 1991 away fans were allowed back and the artificial pitch was ripped up and replaced. The club still hopes to relocate and have therefore put any further development of the ground on hold.

Ground:
Kenilworth Road

Address: Kenilworth Road Stadium, 1 Maple Road, Luton LU4 8AW

Main tel: 01582 411 622

Box office: 01582 416 976

Website: www.lutontown.co.uk

Capacity: 10,300

Home colours: white shirts, black shorts, black socks

Club nickname: the Hatters

Pitch dimensions: 101m x 66m (110 x 72 yards)

Founded: 1885

Record attendance: 30,069 vs Blackpool, March 4 1959

Most prolific scorer: Gordon Turner (243)

Record win: 12-0 vs Bristol Rovers, April 13 1936

Record defeat: 0-9 vs Birmingham City, November 12 1898

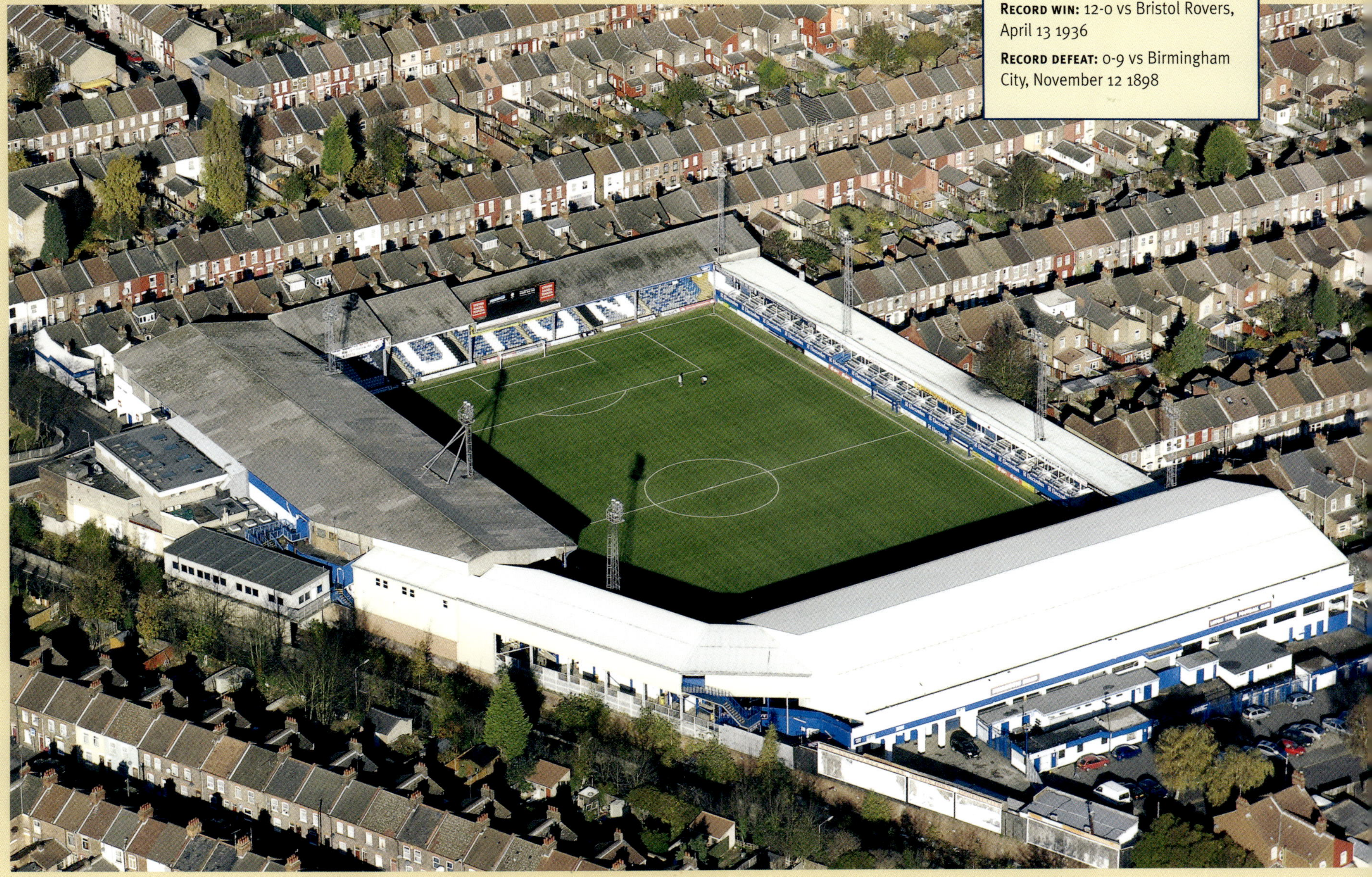

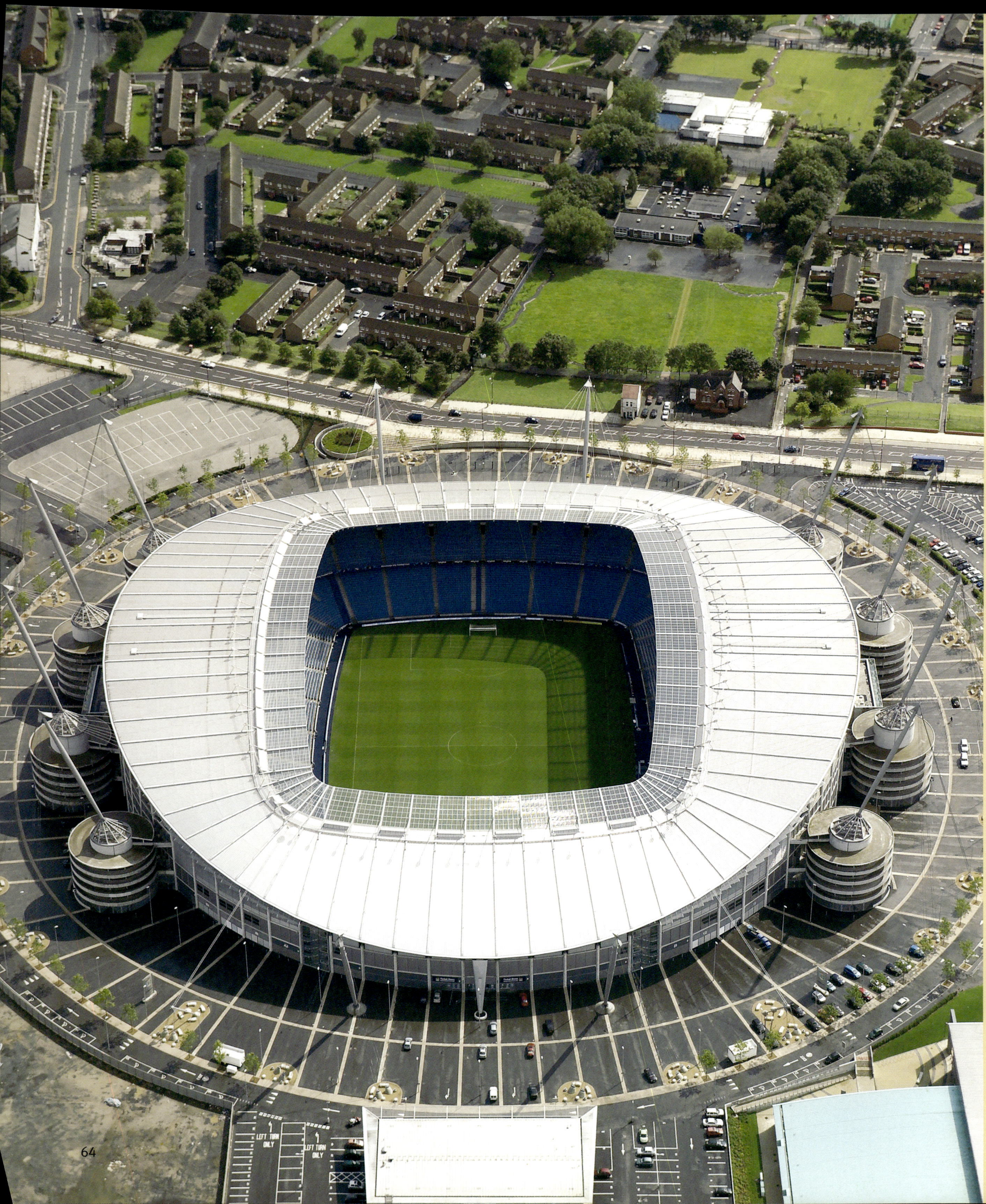
LEFT TURN ONLY
LEFT TURN ONLY

MANCHESTER CITY

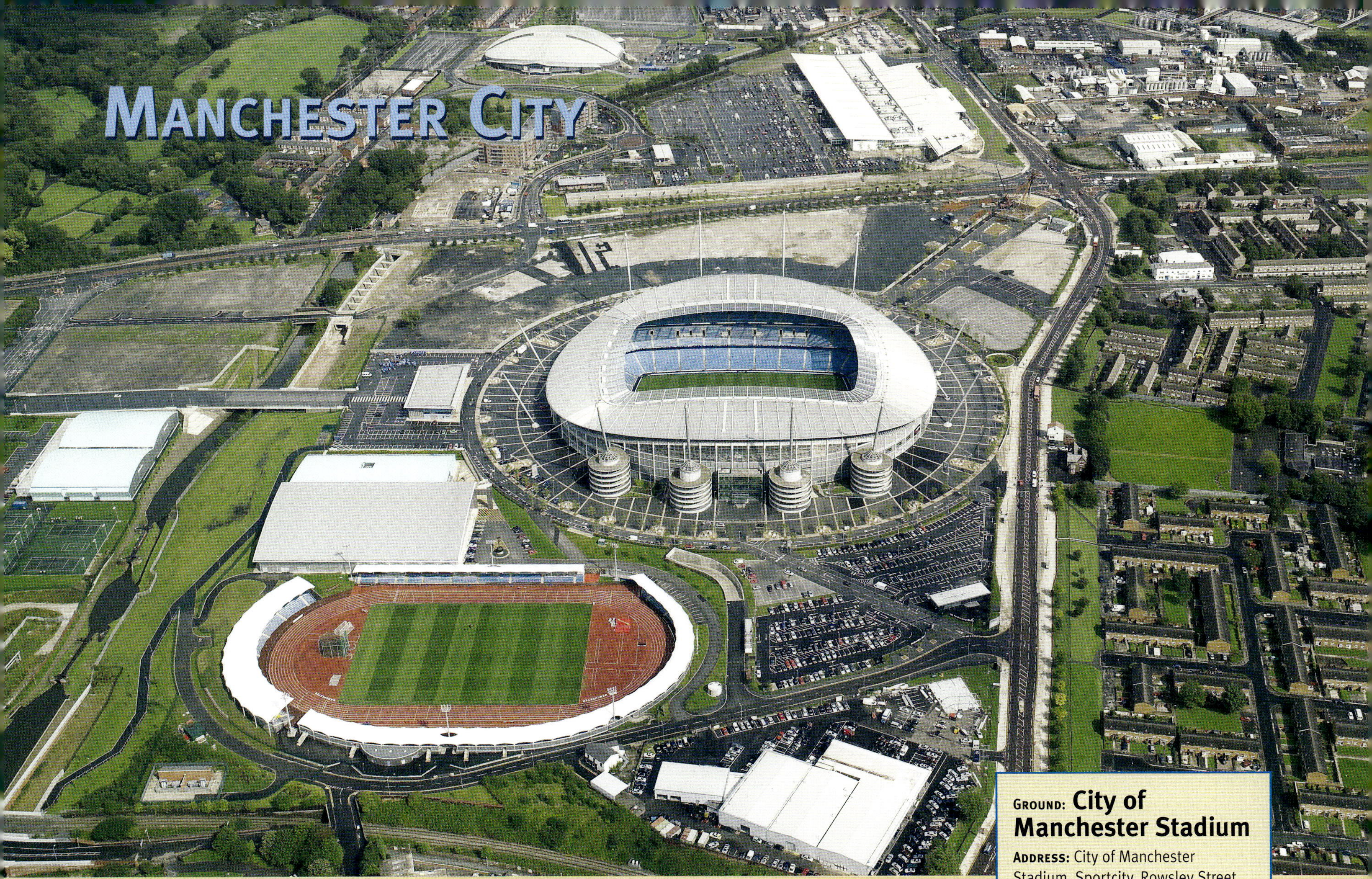

Manchester City's roots go back to an amalgamation between local teams West Gorton and Gorton Athletic in 1887. At first the club played as Ardwick before changing their name to Manchester City in 1894. The team initially played games on Hyde Road, a small ground penned in by a railway line and houses, which had two stands, paid for with the help of a local brewery. In 1920, the Main Stand burned down and the club decided it was time to move. At the start of the 1923 season they opened the doors to their new home at Maine Road. The ground was vast: in the 1920s it had a capacity in excess of 80,000 and regular gates of 37,000, the highest gates in the League. In 1934, 84,569 fans turned out to see City take on Stoke in the Cup. Following the Second World War, local rivals Manchester United became lodgers at Maine Road and profits soared. The Blues spent some of this money on wooden benches, which were installed under the Platt Lane roof in the 1950s. In 1956 City won their third FA Cup and built a roof over the Kippax Terrace, leaving just the Scoreboard End uncovered. This end was replaced by the North Stand in 1971. In 1983 the club replaced the roof on the Main Stand. Following the Taylor report, the Platt Lane Stand was demolished in 1992 and replaced by the Umbro Stand, which cost City £5m and plunged the club into debt. The report's requirements meant the club had to demolish the Kippax Terrace and replace it with an all-seater stand. The new stand cost £11m and brought Maine Road's capacity up to 32,344. Despite spending £19m on development, the club left Maine Road in 2003 and became tenants of the brand new City of Manchester Stadium, built for the 2002 Commonwealth Games. The club spent £20m turning the athletics stadium into a football ground, expanding the stands and bringing them closer to the pitch. The bowl-shaped stadium has a capacity of 48,000 and is totally enclosed by two three-tiered stands and two two-tiered stands.

Above: the City of Manchester Stadium stands at the heart of Sportcity, an area which also contains the National Cycling Centre, the Indoor Athletics Stadium and the National Squash Centre

GROUND: City of Manchester Stadium

ADDRESS: City of Manchester Stadium, Sportcity, Rowsley Street, Manchester M11 3FF

MAIN TEL: 0161 231 3200

BOX OFFICE: 0870 062 1894

WEBSITE: www.mcfc.co.uk

CAPACITY: 48,000

HOME COLOURS: laser blue shirts, white shorts, navy socks

CLUB NICKNAME: the Blues, the Citizens

PITCH DIMENSIONS: 107m x 71m (117 x 78 yards)

FOUNDED: 1887

RECORD ATTENDANCE: (at City of Manchester Stadium) 47,321 vs Liverpool, December 30 2007

MOST PROLIFIC SCORER: Tommy Johnson (158)

RECORD WIN: 10-1 vs Huddersfield, November 7 1987

RECORD DEFEAT: 1-9 vs Everton, September 3 1906

MANCHESTER UNITED

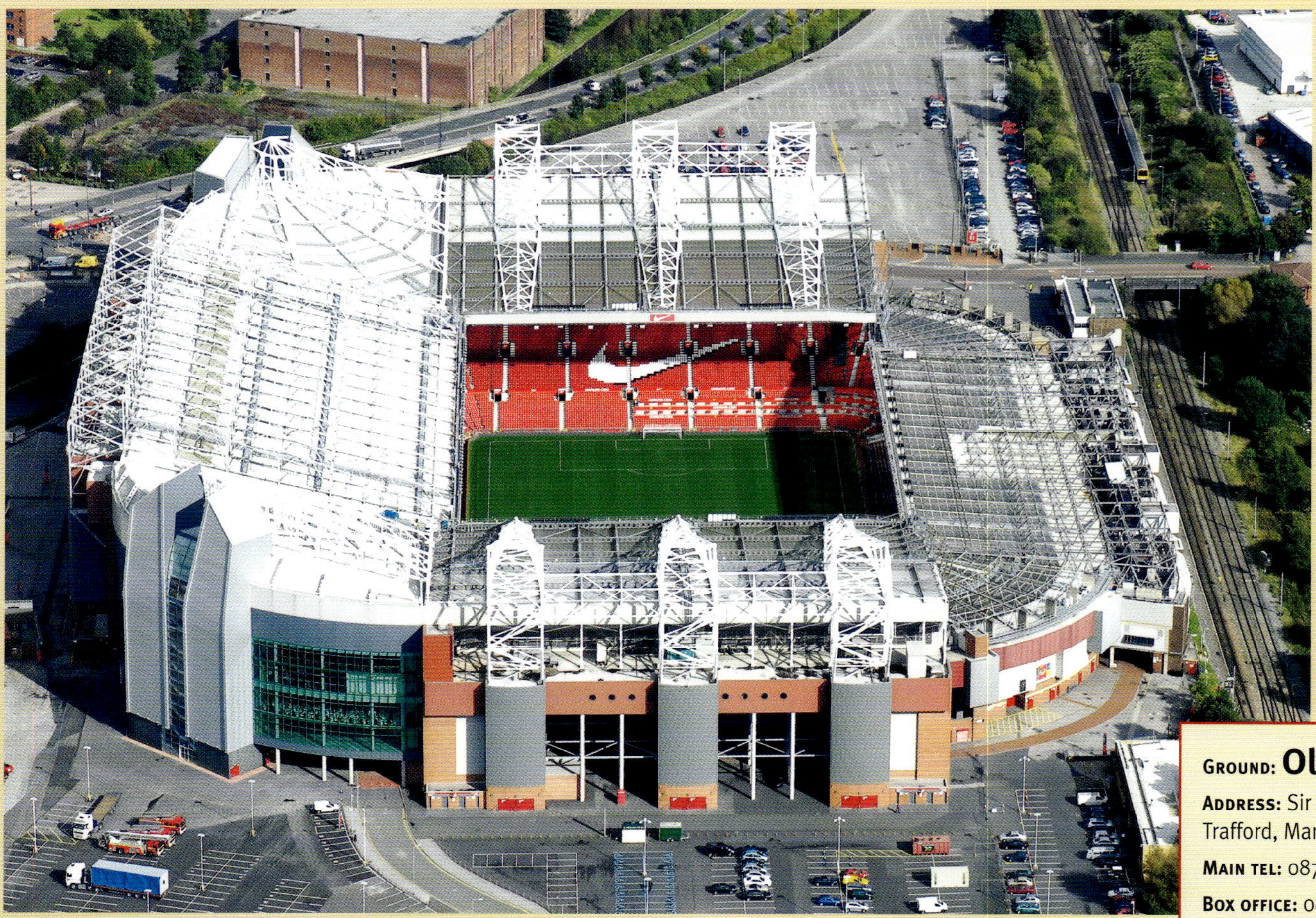

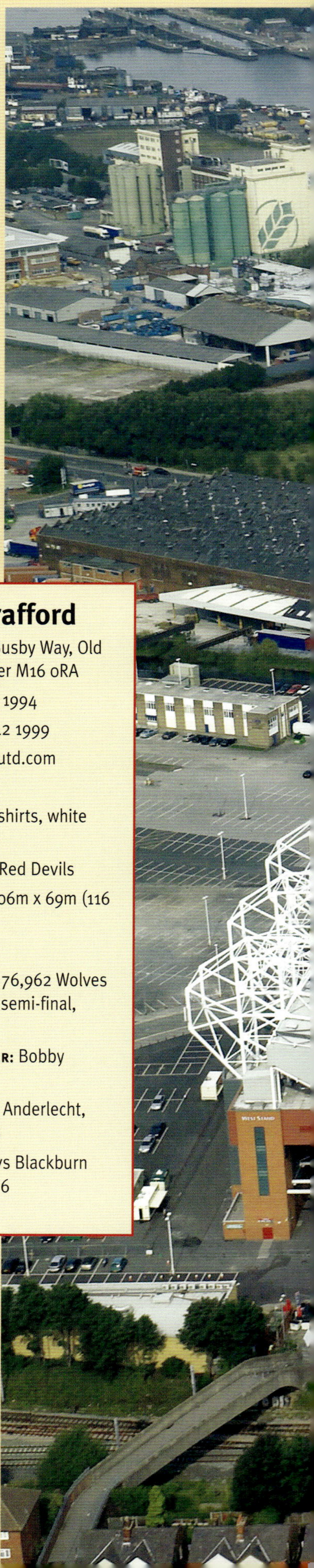

Manchester United began life in 1878 as Newton Heath FC, formed by railway workers from the Lancashire and Yorkshire Railway. The Heathens played early matches on North Road, before moving to Bank Street, Clayton in 1893, a year after joining the League. By 1902 their debts had grown so large they went into liquidation. Local brewer John H Davies rescued the club and changed their name to Manchester United. The club's fortunes on the pitch also changed; by 1906 they were back in the First Division and had cover on all sides of the ground, a main stand with a gallery and a total capacity of 50,000. In 1908 United won their first League title and in 1909 the FA Cup. A year later the club said farewell to Bank Street and moved five miles away to a new ground at Old Trafford. By then Davies had invested £60,000 and had developed the ground into a rectangle with curved corners and a multi-span main stand. In 1931 United were relegated, crowds dropped to 3,500 and the club faced bankruptcy for the second time. Up stepped James Gibson, a wealthy businessman, who cleared the club's debts and funded a cover over the United Road side. The ground was badly damaged during the war, and United began ground-sharing with Manchester City.

Right: Old Trafford with the Manchester Ship Canal. A new footbridge links the Imperial War Museum North and the Lowry Gallery

It was not until 1949 that Old Trafford was repaired and United returned. The pitched roof covering the south-west corner was expanded to cover the Stretford End in 1959, the year after the Munich air crash. The 1960s saw further development at the ground, when Old Trafford was selected as a venue for World Cup games. In 1965 the club built a new two-tiered stand over the United Road Terrace capable of seating 10,000 and holding a further 10,000 standing. This new stand also held the first executive boxes at a European football ground. From then until the 1990s United gradually converted Old Trafford into a fully enclosed all-seater stadium. New plans to expand capacity were drawn up in 1995. The three-tiered North Stand opened in 1996 and second tiers were added to the East and West Stands in 2001. In 2006 north-east and north-west quadrants were opened.

GROUND: Old Trafford

ADDRESS: Sir Matt Busby Way, Old Trafford, Manchester M16 0RA

MAIN TEL: 0870 442 1994

BOX OFFICE: 0870 442 1999

WEBSITE: www.manutd.com

CAPACITY: 76,100

HOME COLOURS: red shirts, white shorts, black socks

CLUB NICKNAME: the Red Devils

PITCH DIMENSIONS: 106m x 69m (116 x 76 yards)

FOUNDED: 1878

RECORD ATTENDANCE: 76,962 Wolves vs Grimsby, FA Cup semi-final, March 25 1939

MOST PROLIFIC SCORER: Bobby Charlton (199)

RECORD WIN: 10-0 vs Anderlecht, September 26 1956

RECORD DEFEAT: 0-7 vs Blackburn Rovers, April 10 1926

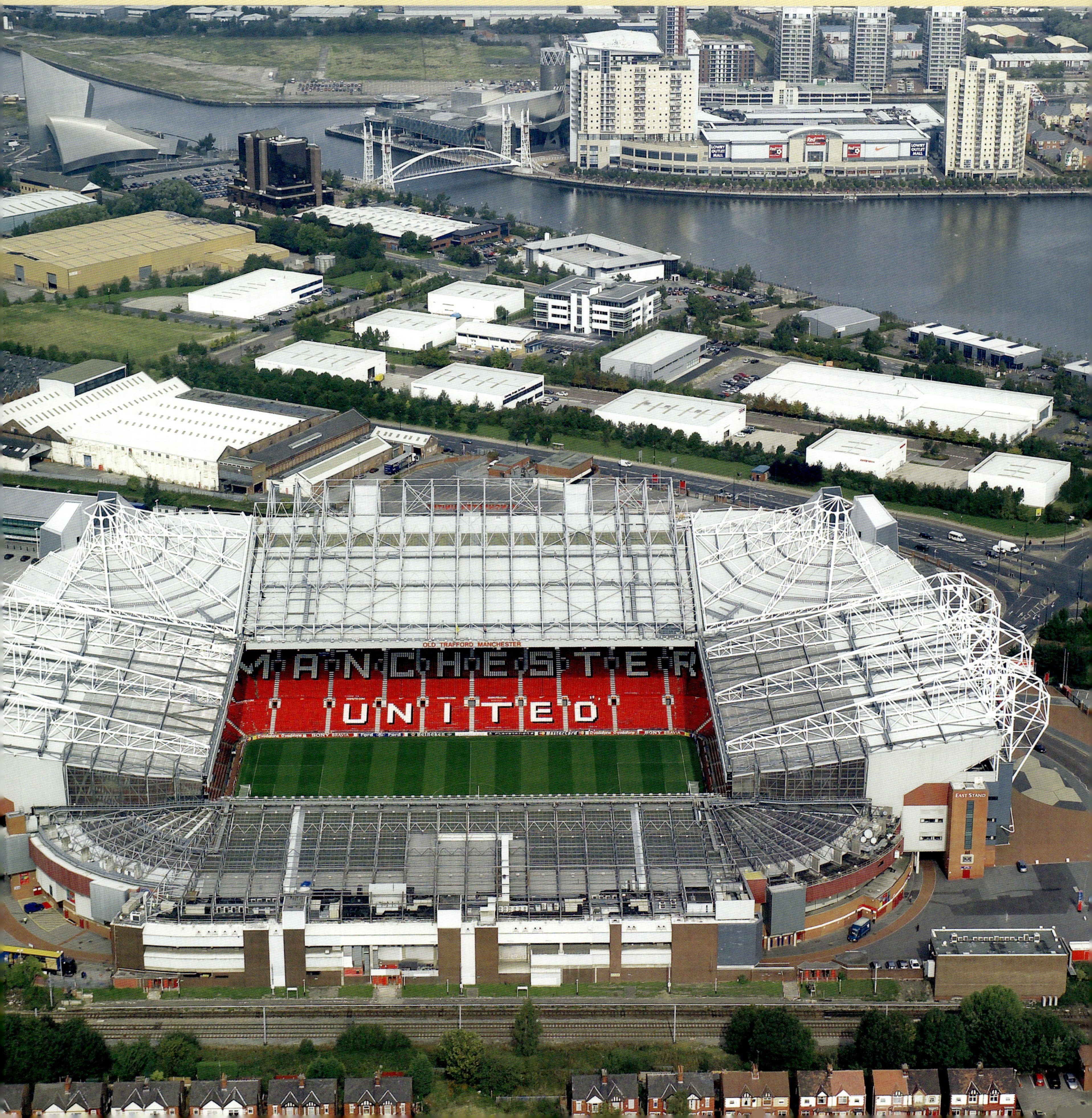
OLD TRAFFORD MANCHESTER
MANCHESTER
UNITED
EAST STAND

Middlesbrough

Although Middlesbrough was founded in 1876, the club did not find themselves a proper home until 1879, when they moved to Breckon Hill Road and again a year later to Middlesbrough Cricket Club, Linthorpe Road. At Linthorpe Road the club built a small stand and in 1899 Boro joined the League. By 1902 it was clear the ground was too small and in 1903 they moved to Ayresome Park. The Scottish architect Archibald Leitch helped the club in its mission to prepare the ground and build a stadium in nine months. He designed a two-tier stand with a semi-circular gable and barrel roof, capable of seating 2,000, and incorporated the old stand from Linthorpe Road into the stadium together with banking at both ends. The next major development came in the 1930s when the South Stand was replaced by a two-tier stand and the West End was given a roof. After the war the club made further improvements to the terracing, and in 1949 the ground held a record 53,596 fans as Boro took on Newcastle. Ayresome Park was selected as a venue for some of the 1966 World Cup matches and the club took on some major ground improvements, including adding a roof to the East End and seats to the North, South and East Terraces. In the following years Middlesbrough's success faltered and support dwindled. In 1986 fire safety checks revealed the ground needed significant attention. Due to Middlesbrough's huge debts, the club was unable to carry out the repairs and had to play home games at Hartlepool. Following the Taylor report, £800,000 was spent on ground improvements: fences were removed, seats were installed in the South and East Stands and plans made for redeveloping the North Stand. In 1994 self-made millionaire Steve Gibson took a 68 per cent share in the club and in April 1995 Boro played their last game at Ayresome Park. At a cost of £12m, the club have now moved to the site of a former petro-chemical storage facility. The two-tiered West Stand and the single tiers on the other three sides totally enclose the new 35,100-seater stadium.

Right: on the banks of the Tees, east of the city centre, the Riverside Stadium has become one of the landmarks of the Middlesbrough skyline

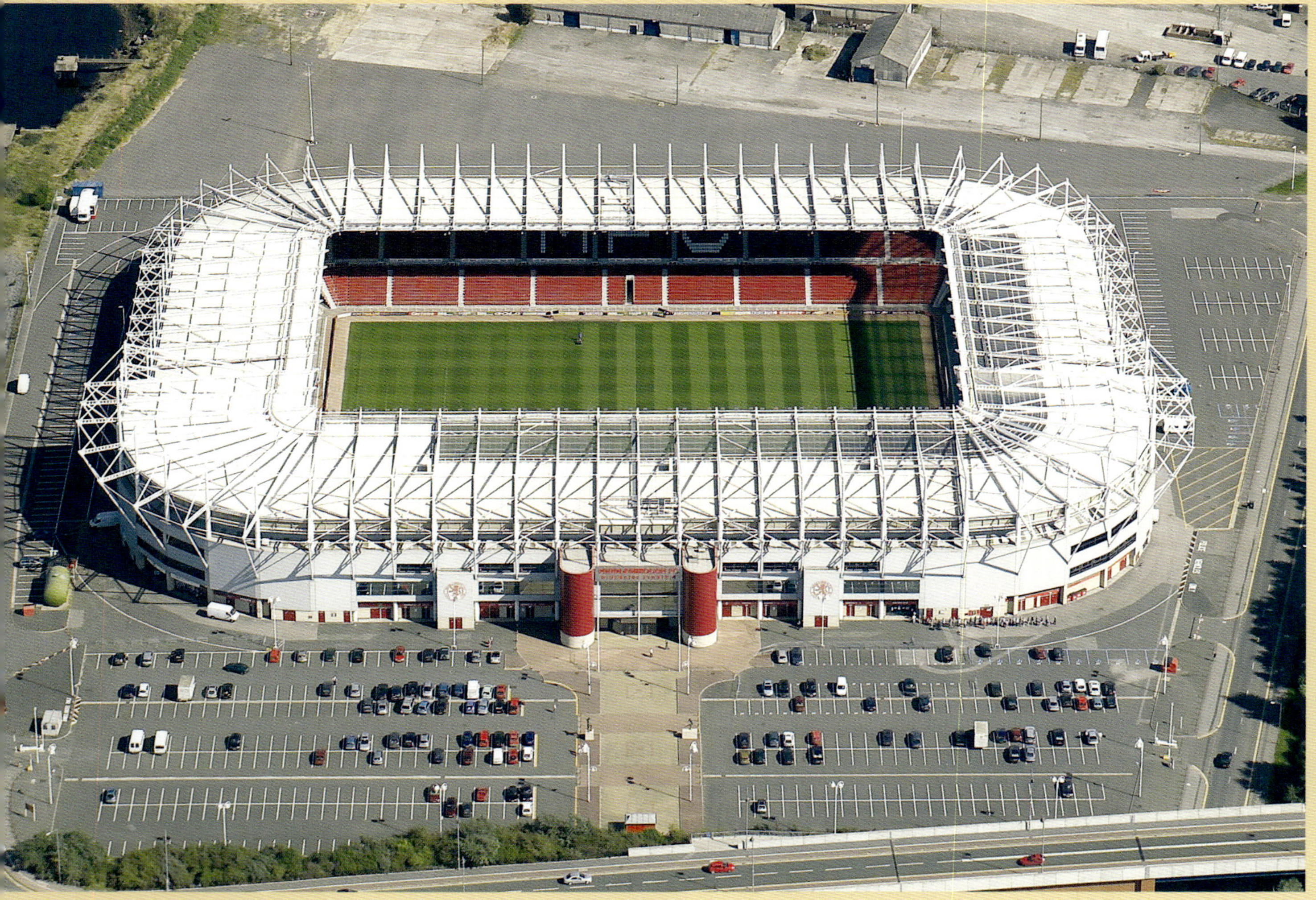

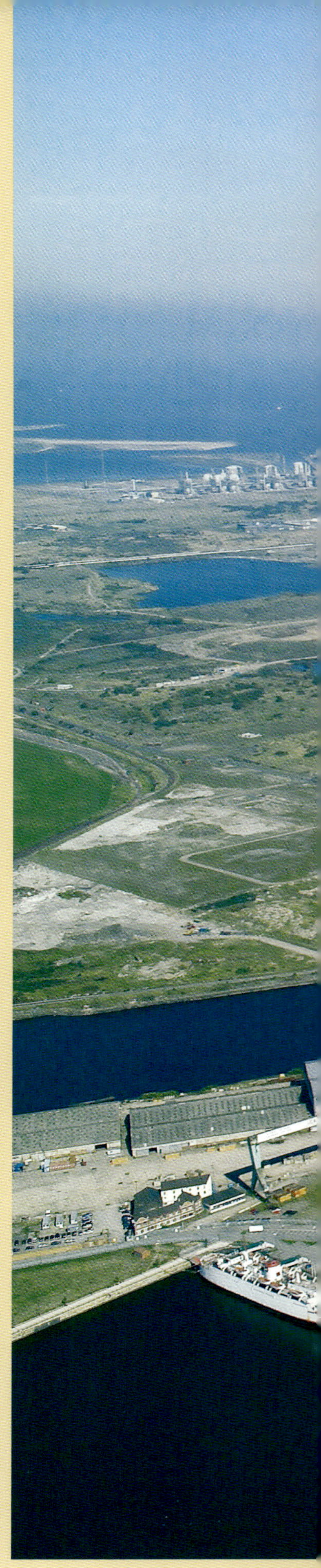

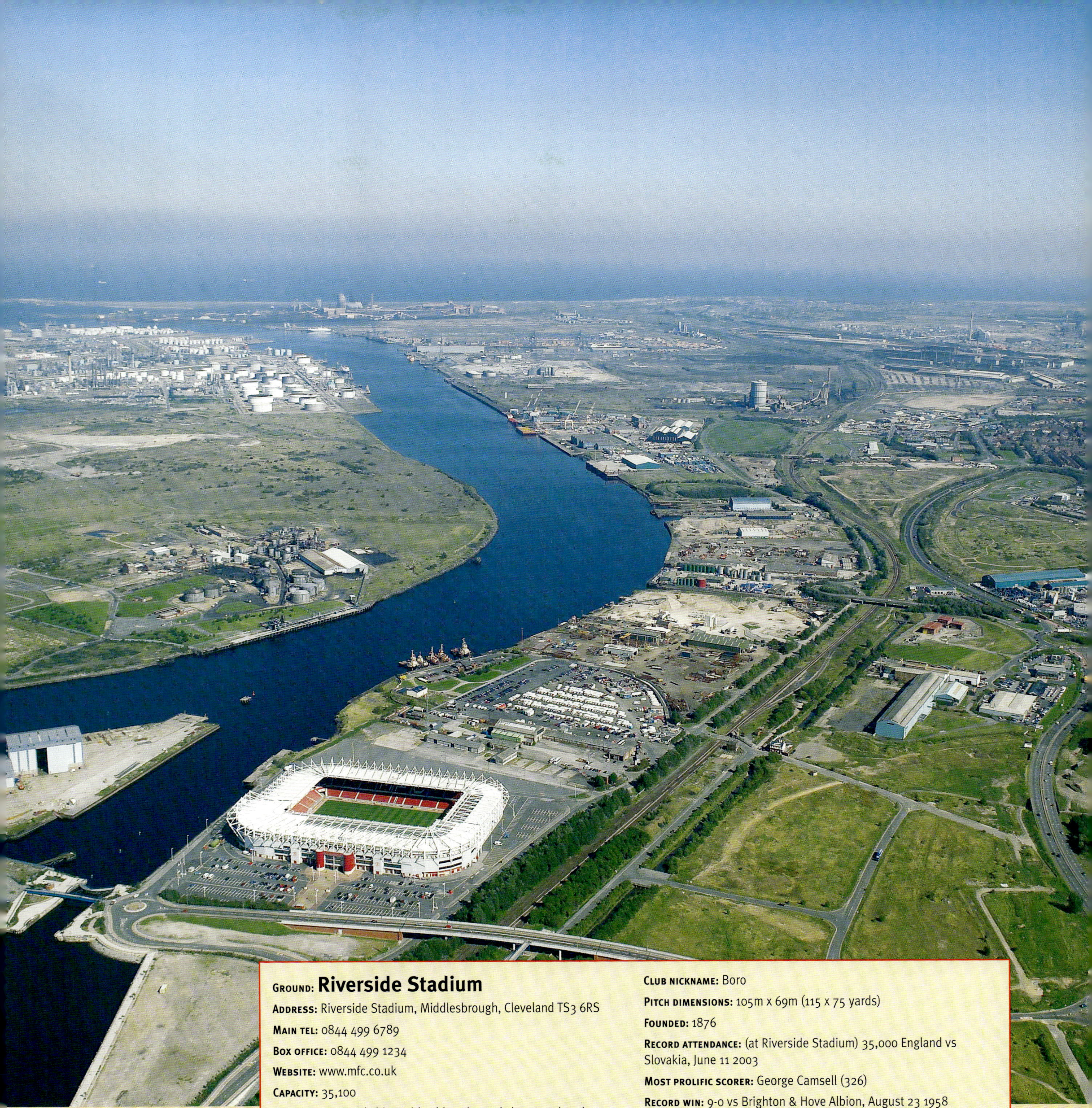

Ground: **Riverside Stadium**

Address: Riverside Stadium, Middlesbrough, Cleveland TS3 6RS

Main tel: 0844 499 6789

Box office: 0844 499 1234

Website: www.mfc.co.uk

Capacity: 35,100

Home colours: red shirts with white trim, red shorts, red socks

Club nickname: Boro

Pitch dimensions: 105m x 69m (115 x 75 yards)

Founded: 1876

Record attendance: (at Riverside Stadium) 35,000 England vs Slovakia, June 11 2003

Most prolific scorer: George Camsell (326)

Record win: 9-0 vs Brighton & Hove Albion, August 23 1958

Record defeat: 0-9 vs Blackburn Rovers, November 6 1954

Millennium Stadium

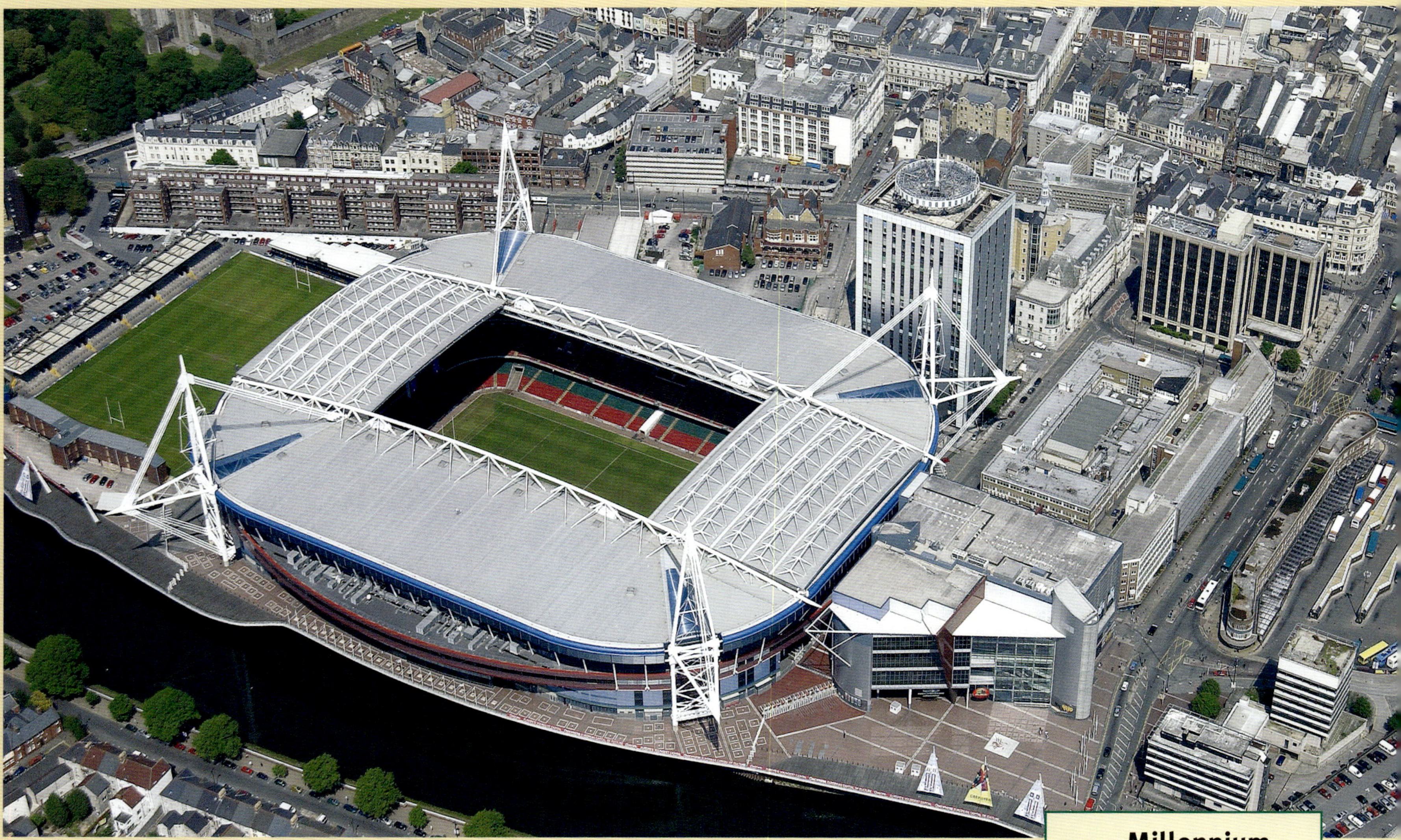

The Millennium Stadium was opened in October 1999 on the site of Cardiff Arms Park. The ground dates back to the 17th century but was not called Cardiff Arms Park until 1787. Cricket was the first sport played at the ground from 1848; rugby was played there from 1876. The Grandstand was opened in 1885, a year before football was first played there. An extension to the Grandstand was added in 1890, and a grand pavilion was built in 1904. The Grandstand was replaced by the South Stand in 1912. The Park's owner Lord Bute sold the ground in 1922 and the rugby and cricket clubs set up a joint company to take it over. The North Stand opened in 1934 and the South Stand was rebuilt in 1956 after Cardiff was selected to stage the 1958 Commonwealth Games. In 1968, the Welsh Rugby Union (WRU) took over Cardiff Arms Park and there followed a 16-year period of redevelopment. A new two-tiered stand was erected in place of the North Stand. The East Terrace opened in 1980 and the South Stand opened in 1984. Football returned to Cardiff Arms Park in 1989. Just six years later the WRU decided the ground's 53,500 capacity was insufficient and submitted plans to the Millennium Commission for an ambitious 75,000-seater stadium to be created on the site of the Park. The Commission stumped up £50m and the other £114m was funded by commercial sources. The ground was built in time for the 1999 Rugby World Cup and quickly established itself as a unique sporting venue. The ground is home to Britain's first retractable roof and the grass is grown outside the ground and brought in when needed. It is completely enclosed with curved corners and three tiers on three sides. The North Stand remains a two-tier structure as it backs onto a rugby club, leaving no room for a third tier. Capacity is now 74,500; as well as rugby, the stadium stages football play-off finals, British Speedway Grand Prix races and concerts. During the construction of the new Wembley Stadium the Millennium Stadium was also used for FA Cup finals; the last one was the 2006 match between Liverpool and West Ham United. The game took place on May 13 with Liverpool winning after a penalty shoot-out.

Ground: Millennium Stadium

Address: Millennium Stadium, Westgate Street, Cardiff CF10 1NS

Main tel: 0870 013 8600

Box office: 0870 558 2582

Website: www.millenniumstadium.com

Capacity: 74,500

Pitch dimensions: 101m x 66m (110 yards x 72 yards)

Opened: 1999

Previous name: Cardiff Arms Park

Right: the Millennium Stadium sits on the banks of the river Taff. Adjoining the stadium is the ground of Cardiff Rugby Club. Sophia Gardens, home of Glamorgan Cricket Club, lies further along the river

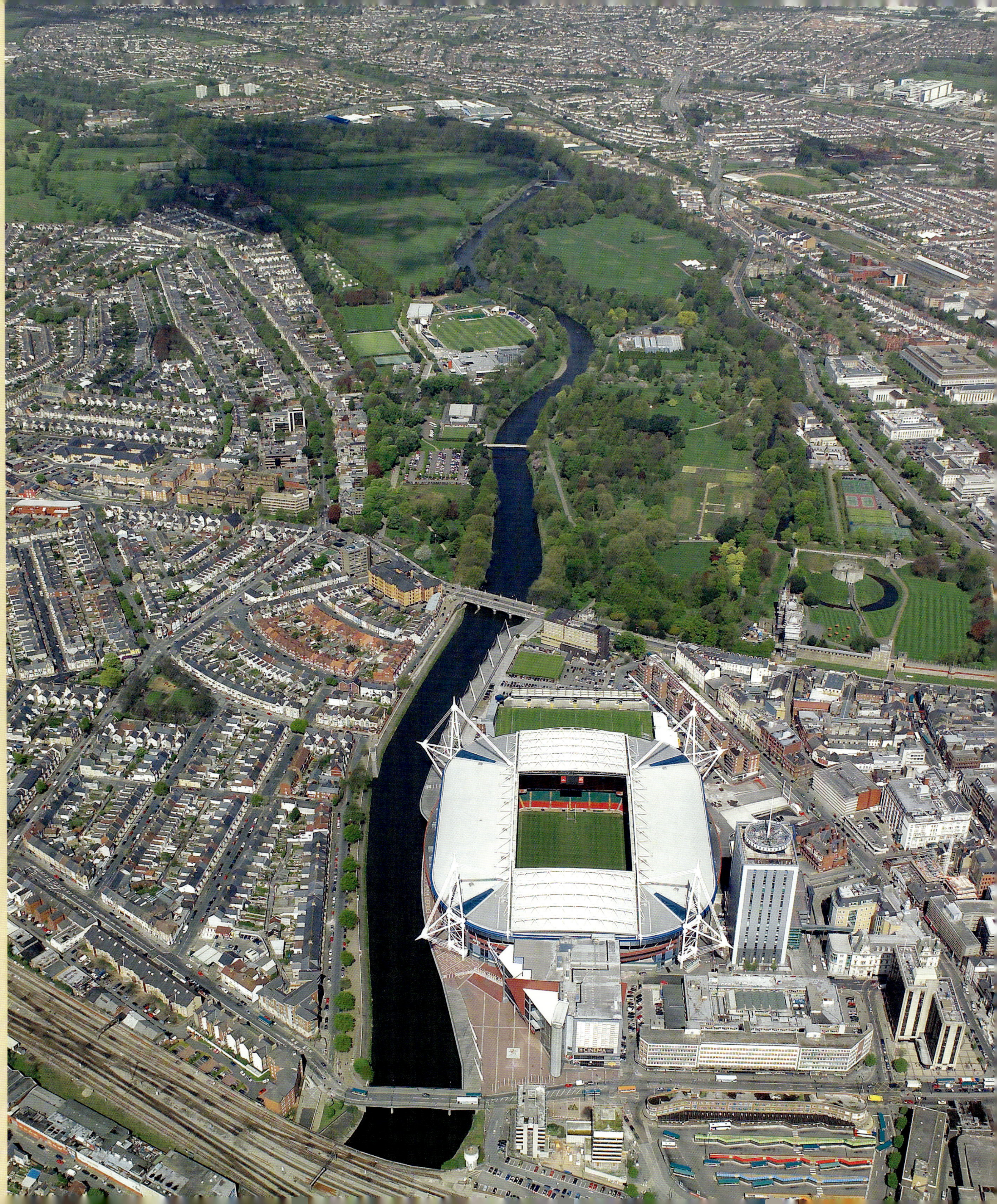

Millwall

Millwall Rovers was formed in 1885 by workers from Morton's Jam factory on the Isle of Dogs. Most of the workers at the factory were Scottish, so the kit was blue and white to reflect the Scottish flag. The club played at four different grounds on the Isle of Dogs and changed their name to Millwall Athletic, before finally relocating south of the river to The Den, Cold Blow Lane, in 1910. When The Den opened, only the Main Stand had been built, with banking on the other three sides. In 1920 Millwall joined League Division Three and dropped "Athletic" from their name. The ground developed during the following decade and saw its highest attendance of 48,672 in an FA Cup tie against Derby County on February 20, 1937. Millwall's development was interrupted by the outbreak of the Second World War. New Cross suffered badly during the Blitz and the Main Stand was severely damaged. With compensation from the War Damages Commission, the club began rebuilding the stands. They covered the Ilderton Road End in 1947 and the two remaining sides during the 1950s. Little changed inside the ground for the next 40 years, except an extension to the Ilderton Road End and seating in the paddock. Millwall played their last game at The Den in 1993, 83 years after arriving. They moved a quarter of a mile away to a new 20,000 all-seater stadium which cost £16m, also called The Den. One of the many reasons for this move, was the hope that the livelier elements of some sections of the Millwall faithful might be tamed by the constrictions of an all-seater stadium. Similar to the old ground, the new ground was designed by Scottish architects and engineers. The Den now consists of four stands which, from inside the stadium, appear almost identical. However, only the North Stand and Cold Blow Lane End are the same.

Ground: **The Den**

Address: The Den, Zampa Road, London SE16 3LN

Main tel: 020 7232 1222

Box office: 020 7231 9999

Website: www.millwallfc.co.uk

Capacity: 20,146

Home colours: blue shirt, white shorts, blue socks

Club nickname: the Lions

Pitch dimensions: 96m x 62m (105 x 68 yards)

Founded: 1885

Record attendance: 48,672 vs Derby County, February 20 1937

Most prolific scorer: Teddy Sheringham (93)

Record win: 9-1 vs Torquay United, September 29 1927

Record defeat: 1-9 vs Aston Villa, January 28 1946

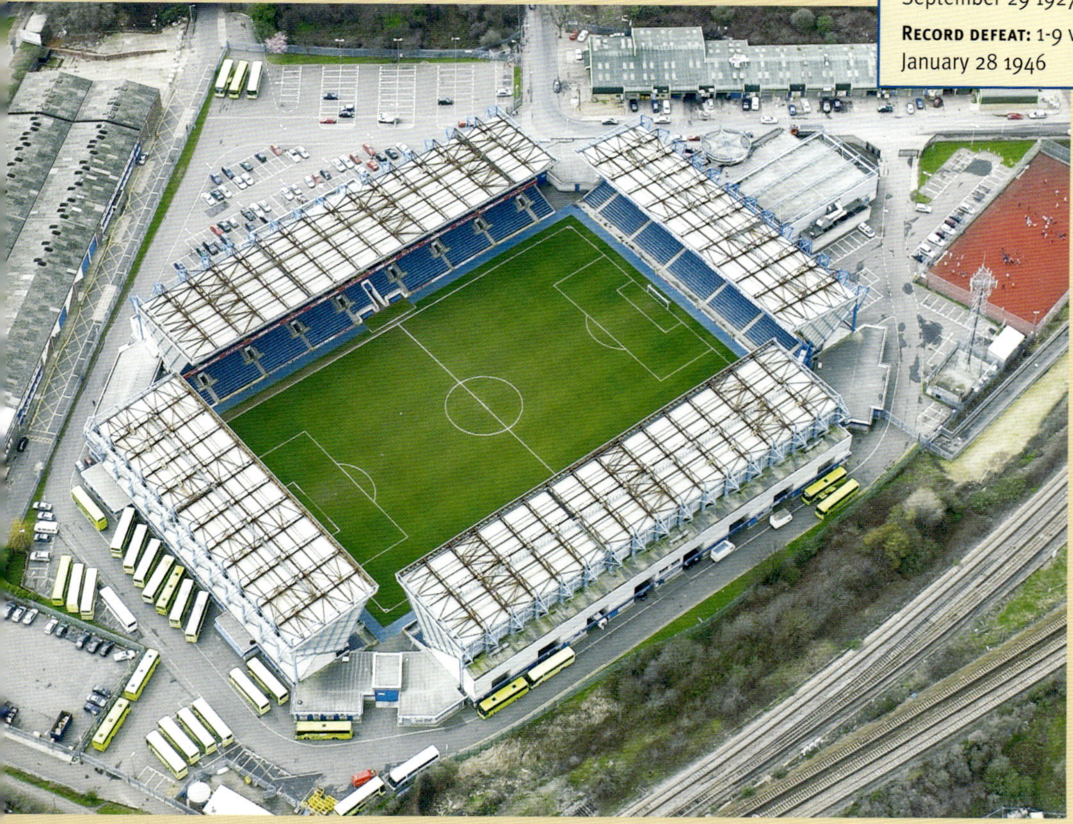

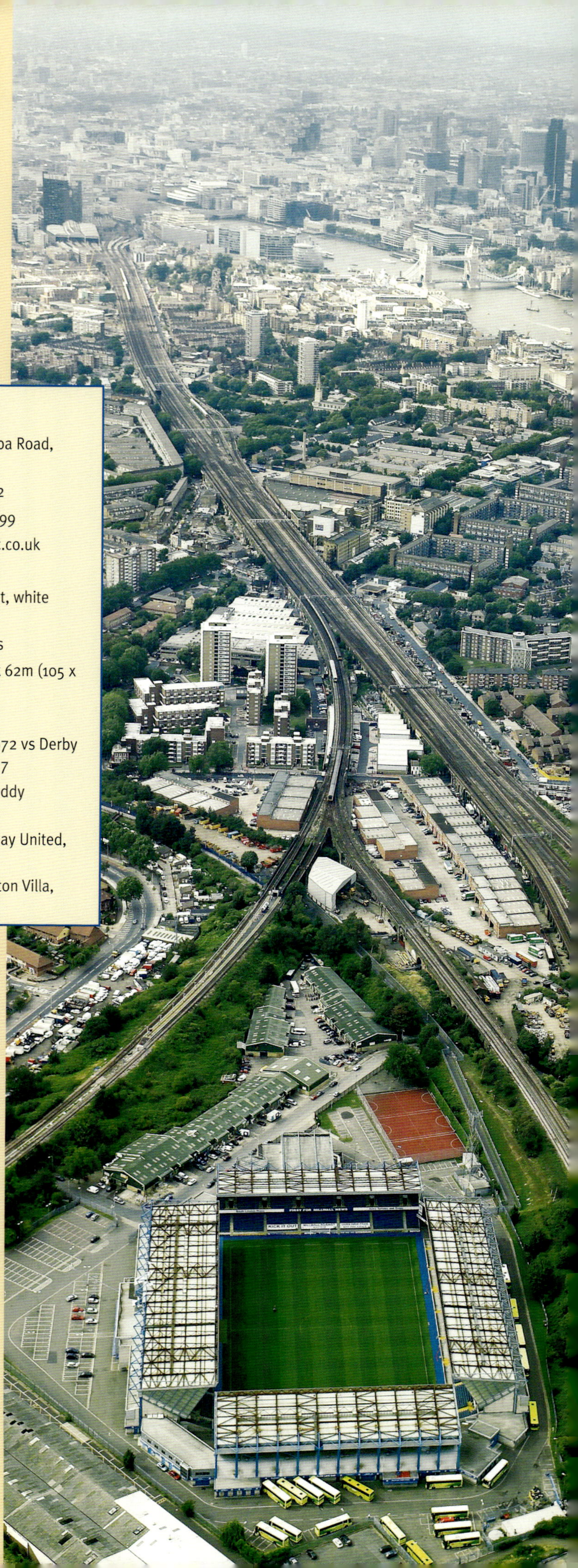

Right: The New Den, with London Bridge Station, Tower Bridge and the City in the distance

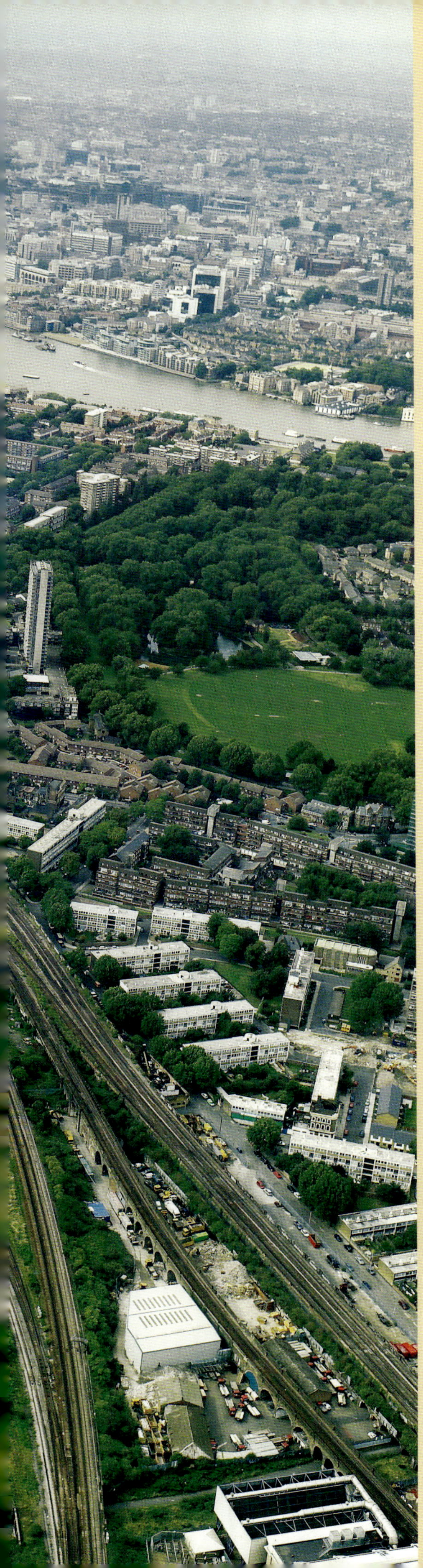

Milton Keynes Dons

Wimbledon FC formed in 1889 and played their early games on local parks. After merging with Wimbledon Borough in 1912, the club moved to Plough Lane, the site of a former refuse tip. The club bought the South Stand from Clapton Orient in 1923, erected a stand along the north side of the pitch, a terrace on the east side and banking to the west. The South Stand suffered bomb damage during the Second World War but the stand was repaired and it was used until the Dons left Plough Lane in 1991. In 1959 the Main Stand was built along the north side after the club bought the ground from the local council. In 1960 the club added a cover to the West Stand and concreted the terracing. After winning the Amateur Cup in 1963, Wimbledon FC turned professional but it was another 14 years before they managed to join the Football League. Once they did, achievements on the pitch were quick to follow: they reached the First Division in 1986, and won the FA Cup in 1988. Despite the team's meteoric success, in 1990 Plough Lane only had 2,050 seats and, following the Taylor report, could not meet the minimum standards required of a First Division football ground. In 1991 the club bade farewell to Plough Lane and entered into a ground-sharing agreement with Crystal Palace. Plough Lane was still used for reserve team games until 2002, when it was finally demolished. The Dons found a new home in Milton Keynes in 2003, at the National Hockey Stadium. Despite stiff resistance from some fans, the club changed its name to Milton Keynes Dons at the start of the 2004/05 season. At the beginning of the 2007 season, the Dons moved to the spectacular new stadium:mk in the Denbigh district of the town. The stadium will eventually seat 32,000 spectators, although it is likely that the Dons will use only the lower tier of the stadium's seating, with a capacity of 22,000.

Ground: **stadium:mk**

Address: Stadium Way West, Milton Keynes MK1 1ST

Main tel: 01908 622 922

Box office: 01908 622 900

Website: www.mkdons.co.uk

Capacity: 22,000

Home colours: white shirts, white shorts, white socks

Club nickname: the Dons

Pitch dimensions: 101m x 68m (110 x 74 yards)

Founded: 1889

Record attendance: 13,037 vs Lincoln City, October 14 2007

Most prolific scorer: Alan Cork (145)

Record win: 6-0 vs Newport County, September 3 1983

Record defeat: 0-8 vs Everton, August 29 1978

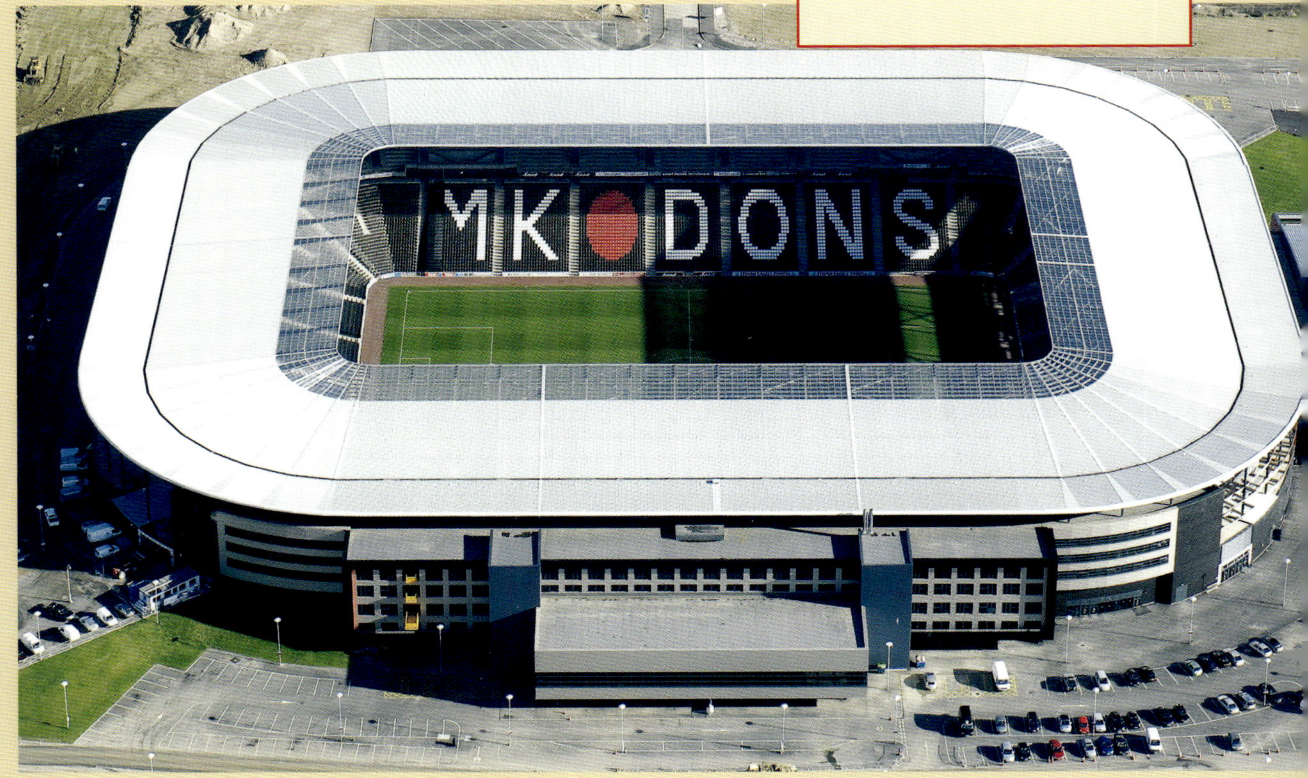

MOTHERWELL

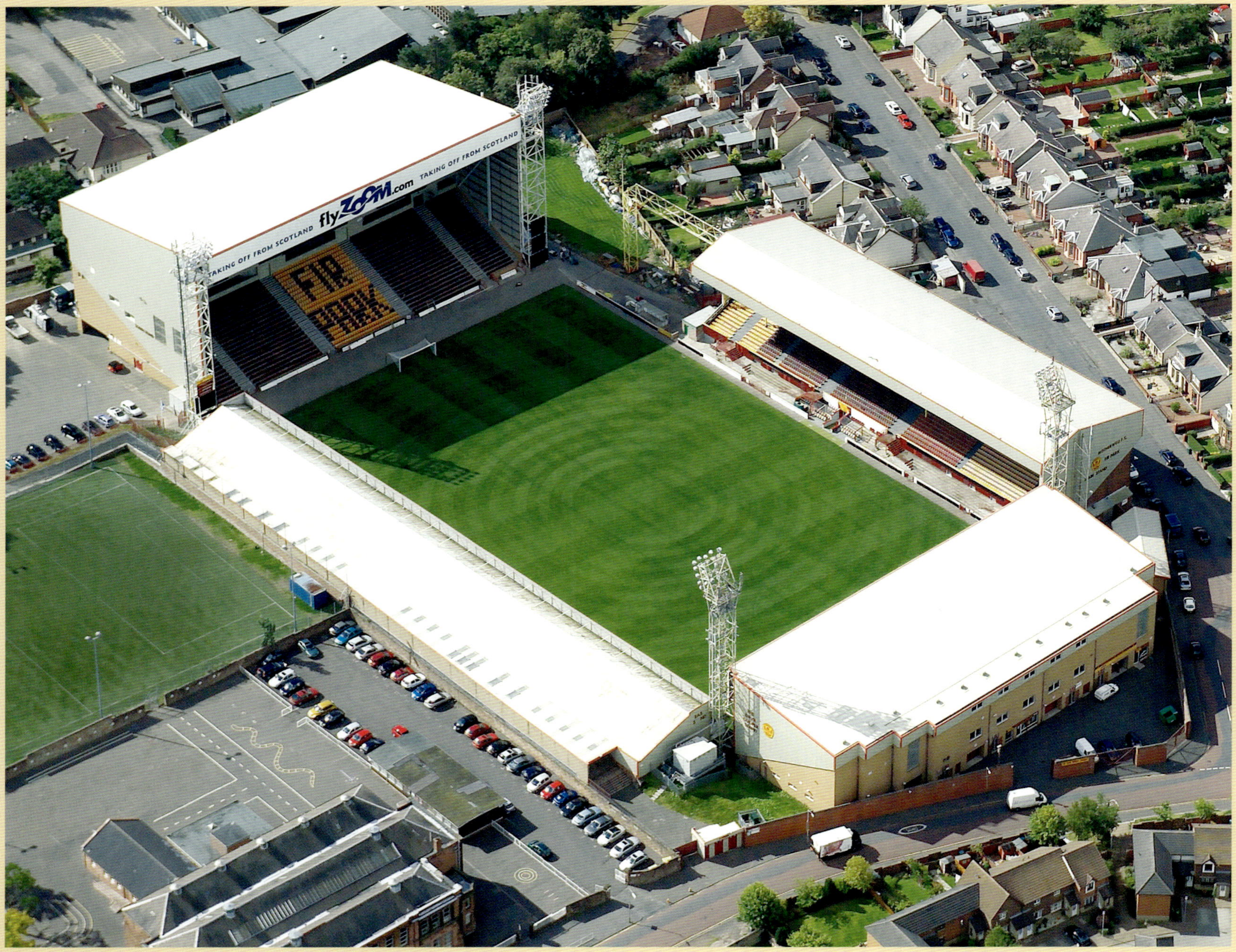

Motherwell FC formed in 1886 and from 1889 played their games at Dalziel Park. The first game played at Dalziel Park was against Rangers. The only stand at Dalziel Park was a pavilion on the west side of the ground. The club moved to Fir Park in 1895, where they have remained ever since. Due to the Well's low attendances in 1900, there were rumours that Hibernian would take over Fir Park that year, but these did not materialise. The first stand to be built at Motherwell was a pavilion along the east side of the pitch. By 1912 Motherwell was a well-established member of the Scottish Football League and a two-tiered grandstand had been erected on the west side along with banking at each end. Very little else changed to the structure at Fir Park for a number of years but the team enjoyed varying success. The club won the League in 1932 and a record 35,632 fans saw Motherwell beat Rangers in a replay of a Cup game in 1952; they went on to win the Cup that season. In 1962 two players (one of whom was Ian St John) were sold to fund the building of the new main stand. A local resident's objection to the plans for the new stand meant it was never constructed along the full length of the pitch. Following the Taylor report, Fir Park was completely redeveloped as an all-seater stadium. The South Stand is the largest of all the stands. It is a two-tiered structure, which also contains executive boxes. The Main Stand is single-tiered, capable of seating 3,385. It has windshields at each side to offer protection to the fans. Along the north end of the ground is the Davie Cooper Stand, named after a former Motherwell player. This stand is fairly small and single-tiered. The East Enclosure, also a single-tiered structure, had seats added but unusually, the stand does not run the full length of the stadium due to a planning dispute. Capacity at Fir Park stands at 13,742.

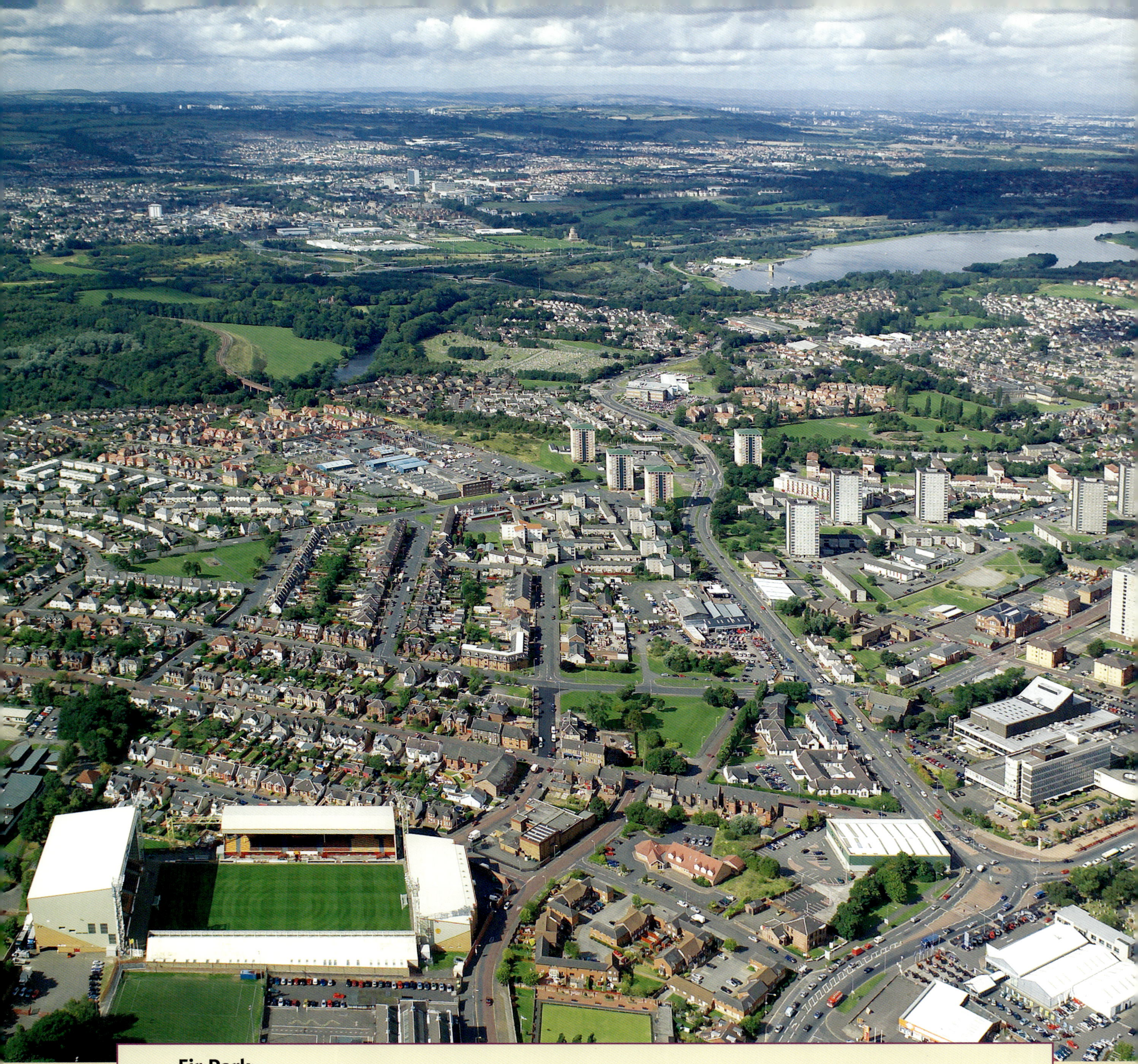

Ground: Fir Park

Address: Fir Park Stadium, Firpark Street, Motherwell ML1 2QN

Main tel: 01698 333 333

Box office: 01698 338 002

Website: www.motherwellfc.co.uk

Capacity: 13,742

Home colours: amber shirts with claret trim, amber shorts with claret trim, amber socks with claret trim

Club nickname: the Well or the Steelmen

Pitch dimensions: 101m x 69m (110 x 75 yards)

Founded: 1886

Record attendance: 35,632 vs Rangers, March 12 1952

Most prolific scorer: Hugh Ferguson (283)

Record win: 12-1 vs Dundee United, January 23 1954

Record defeat: 0-8 vs Aberdeen, March 26 1979

Newcastle United

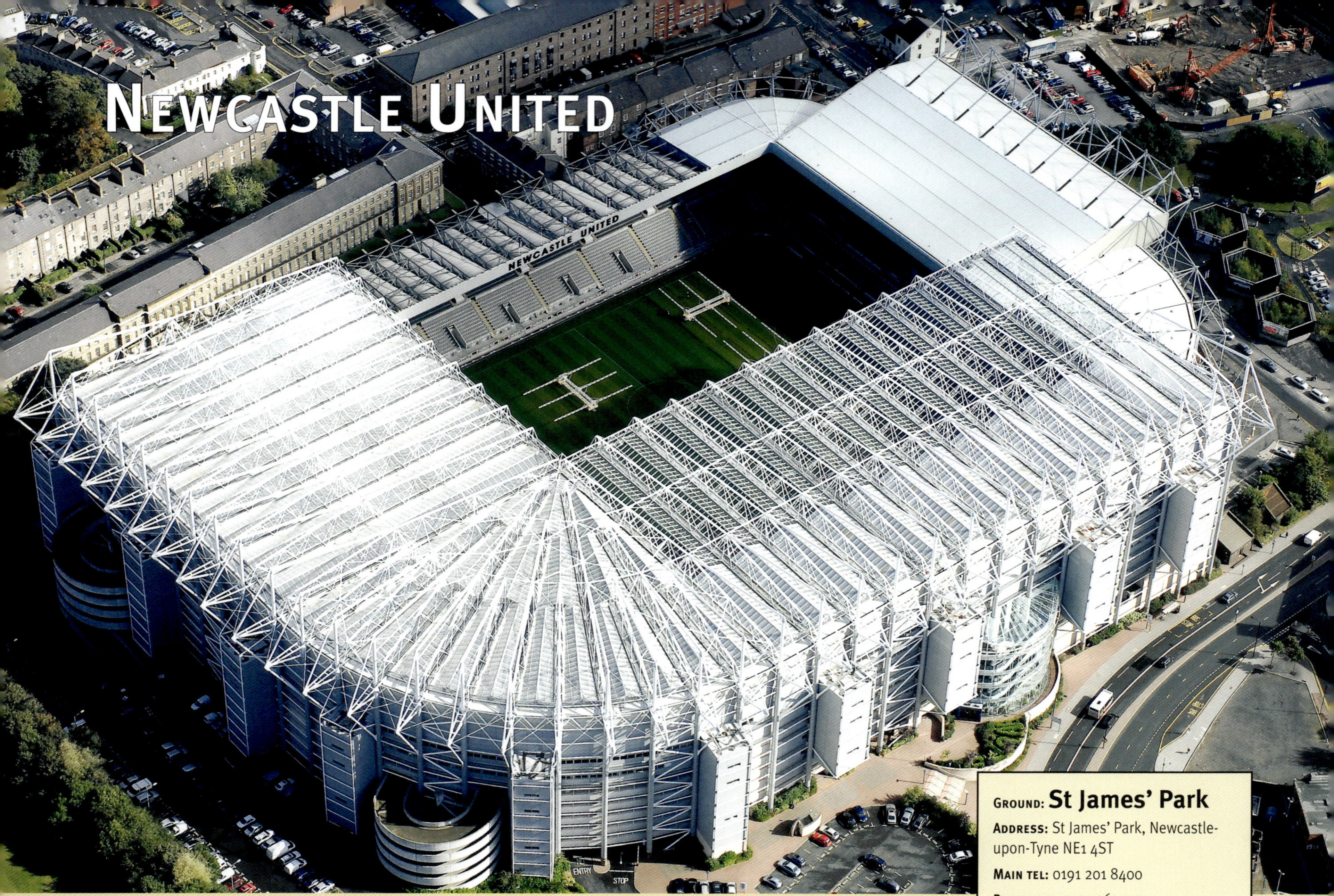

Ground: St James' Park

Address: St James' Park, Newcastle-upon-Tyne NE1 4ST

Main tel: 0191 201 8400

Box office: 0191 261 1571

Website: www.nufc.co.uk

Capacity: 52,327

Home colours: black and white striped shirts with blue trim, black shorts, black socks with white trim

Club nickname: the Magpies, the Toon

Pitch dimensions: 101m x 67m (110 x 73 yards)

Founded: 1881

Record attendance: 68,386 vs Chelsea, September 3 1930

Most prolific scorer: Alan Shearer 206

Record win: 13-0 vs Newport County, October 5 1946

Record defeat: 0-9 vs Burton Wanderers, April 15 1895

Newcastle United began life as East End FC. The club formed in 1881 and first played at Chillingham Road in Heaton; they moved to St James' Park in 1892. Early facilities were very basic and the pitch had a distinctive slant. Following the club's promotion in 1898, the ground's capacity of 15,000 was severely stretched. The next year an extra four acres were leased to the club, so they relocated the pitch and moved tons of soil to even out the surface. Terracing was cut into banks at the Leazes Park End and Leazes Terrace. In 1905 after losing the FA Cup final but winning the League, Newcastle drew the largest crowds in the League and began revamping the stadium. The wooden stands were cleared, three sides of banking were expanded and terraces and wire barriers added. The West Stand was built with seating for 4,680, beneath which was a swimming pool for the players. The ground opened in November 1905 with a new capacity of 65,000. The 1920s saw more improvements, with yet another pitch laid. A new cover was put on the Leazes Park End in 1930 and plans were drawn up to extend the other sides, although the council rejected these. The same year a record crowd of 68,386 saw Newcastle take on Chelsea; at this time the average gate was over 56,000. The Magpies had three FA Cup victories between 1951-55, which sent profits soaring; however every attempt to expand the ground was rejected and a feud developed between the club and the local council. In 1971 the club was finally granted a 99-year lease on the ground and given planning permission to build a new 3,400-seater stand backing on to Leazes Terrace. The next major development came in 1987 when the 6,607-seater Jackie Milburn Stand was built. Sir John Hall joined the board in 1992 and took full control of the club in 1994. He spent £23.5m on completely redeveloping St James' Park, with all-seater stands at each end and corner and additional tiers on the north and west sides and the north-west corner, raising capacity to 52,327.

Right: St James' Park with the Tyne bridges and the distinctive shape of the Sage Centre on the opposite bank

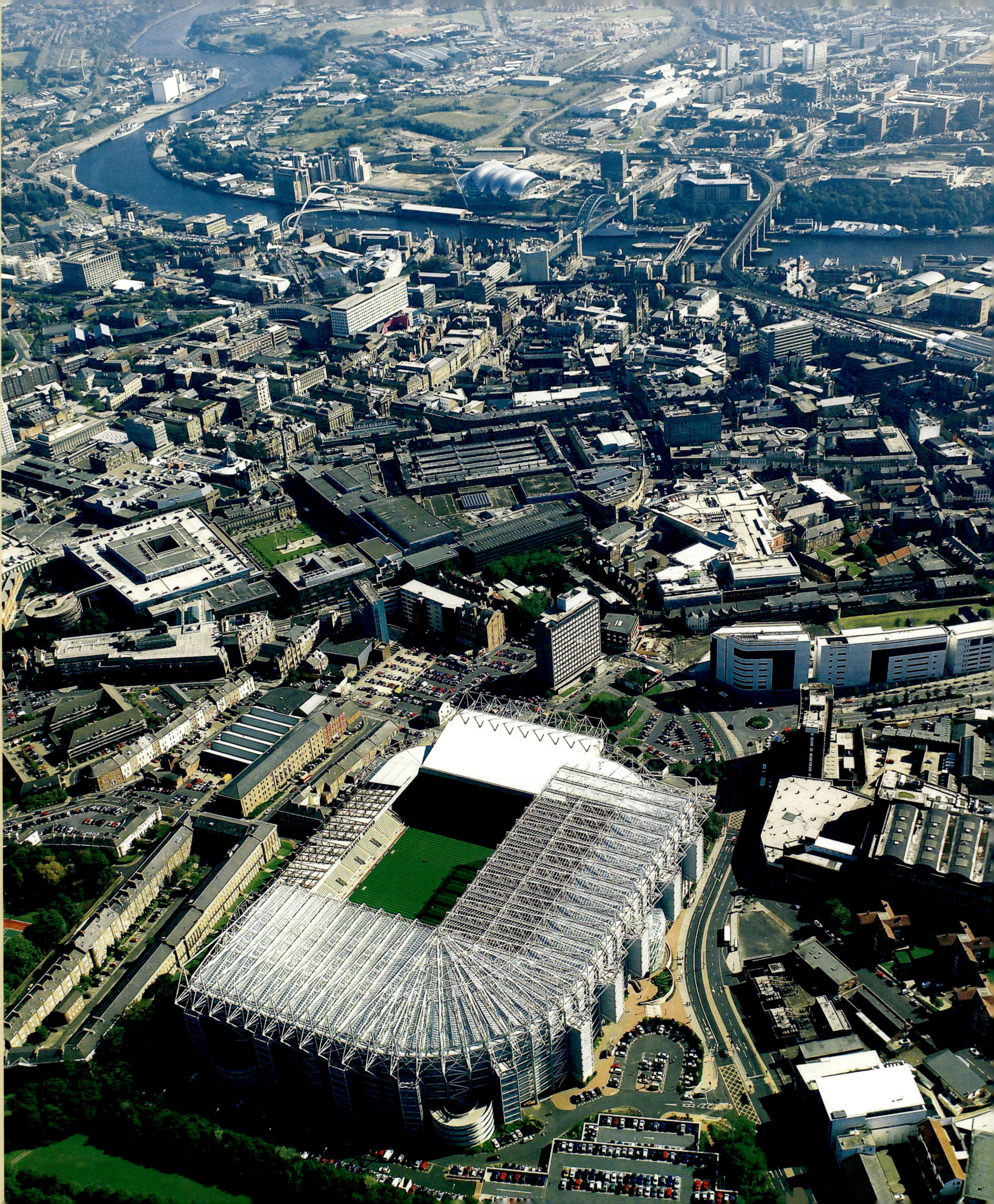

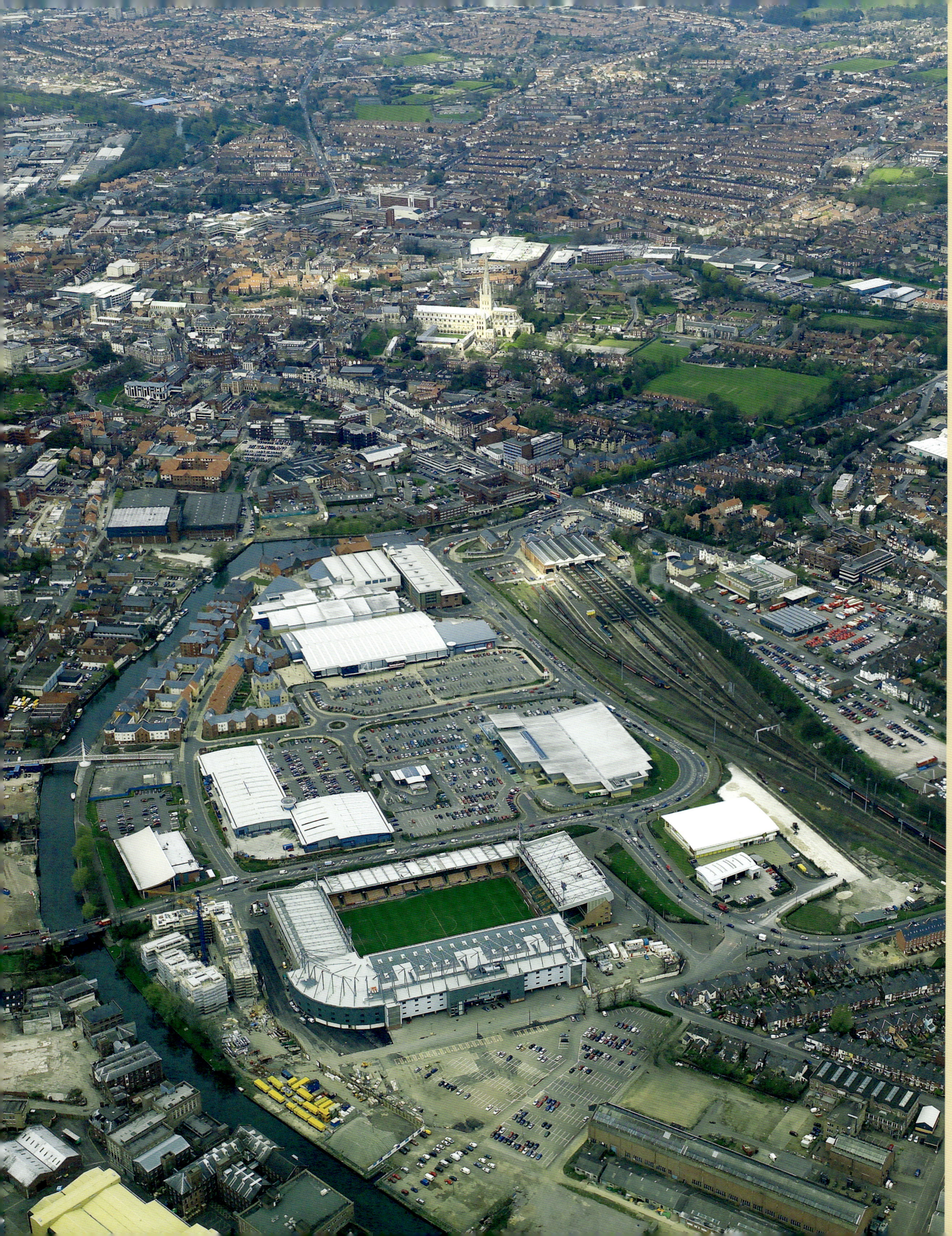

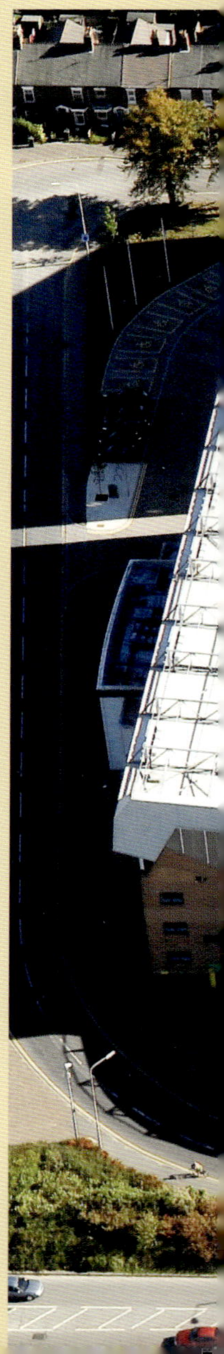

Norwich City

Football has been played in Norwich since 1868 but Norwich City did not form until 1902. Their first ground on Newmarket Road belonged to the Norfolk County FA. The Canaries turned professional in 1905, yet there were problems with the rented ground. Their chairman John Pyke thought he had solved these when he bought a disused chalkpit on Rosary Road. A wooden stand was brought with the club to the new ground, which labourers spent the summer of 1908 preparing for football. The ground was named the Nest but it was not a particularly suitable home for the Canaries as houses were very close to the pitch at the west end and there was a steep concrete verge at the east end. In 1922 barriers on top of the verge collapsed and a boy was badly injured. Despite these problems, the club continued to play on the ground until 1935. That year the club moved to Carrow Road, a sports ground owned by Colman's Mustard. In just 82 days the club built a 3,500-seater main stand and paddock on one side and embankments on the other three sides. In 1937 the first terrace cover went up at the Station End, renamed the Barclay End, but it was not until 1959, when the Canaries reached the semi-finals of the FA Cup and won promotion, that they could afford further ground improvements. The terrace opposite the Main Stand was covered and in 1963 the South Stand was built. Fire destroyed the central section of the Main Stand in October 1984, which was replaced the following season. The 1990s saw the ground almost completely rebuilt, with new stands on each side. The most recent is the Jarrold Road South Stand which opened in 2004; this can hold 8,000 fans. There are two-tiered stands at either end and the Geoffrey Watling City Stand is a smaller single-tiered stand.

Left: Carrow Road with the sunlit Norwich Cathedral in the background

Ground: Carrow Road

Address: Carrow Road, Norwich NR1 1JE

Main tel: 01603 760 760

Box office: 0870 444 1902

Website: www.canaries.co.uk

Capacity: 26,034

Home colours: yellow shirts, green shorts

Club nickname: the Canaries

Pitch dimensions: 101m x 69m (114 x 74 yards)

Founded: 1902

Record attendance: 43,984 vs Leicester City, March 30 1963

Most prolific scorer: Johnny Gavin (122)

Record win: 10-2 vs Coventry City, March 15 1930

Record defeat: 2-10 vs Swindon Town, September 5 1908

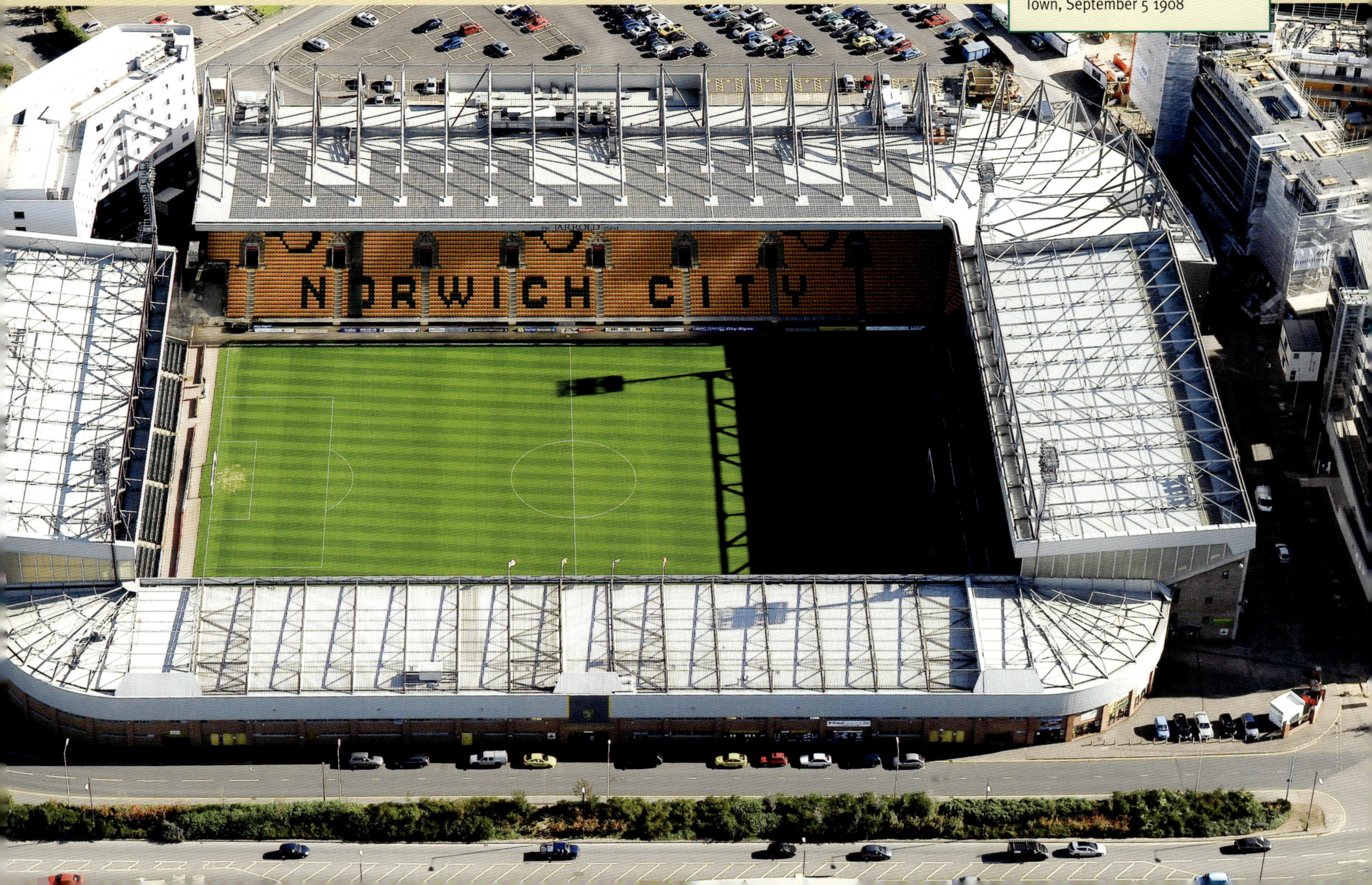

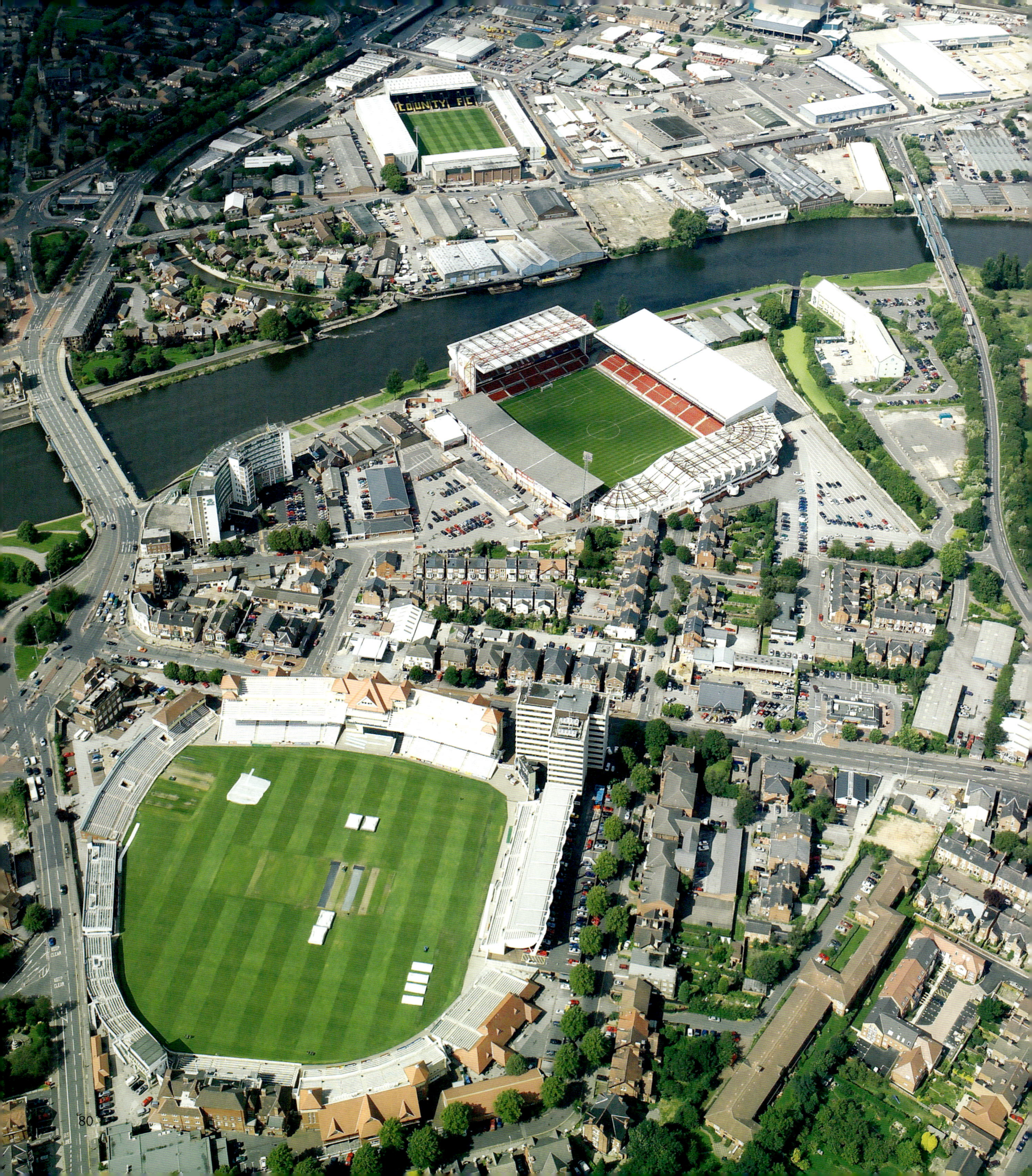
COUNTY FC

Notts County

Notts County formed in 1862 and is the oldest club that still play in the Football League. The team played early games at the Meadows Cricket Ground before moving to Trent Bridge Cricket Ground in 1882. Trent Bridge had a pavilion and the club added a stand along the west side of the pitch. Despite enjoying playing at Trent Bridge, the ground-sharing arrangement was not without its problems. The football team had to find an alternative venue for home games during the cricket season. The club eventually opted to move to Meadow Lane in 1910. Along one side of the ground was a stream, Tinkers Brook. It was on this side that the first cover was added; the Main Stand was built opposite in 1910. There was an embankment at the west end and the club brought the stand they had built at Trent Bridge and installed it at the east end. It was not until 1925 that any new structures were built. That year a new stand, the County Road Stand, was built on the Tinkers Brook side. The Main Stand was damaged during the Second World War but this was repaired in time for Meadow Lane's highest-ever recorded attendance of 47,310 when the Magpies took on York City in the FA Cup in 1955. The following years saw the team sink to the Fourth Division and then rise up to the First Division in 1981. The oldest stand, which the club had brought from Trent Bridge, was finally demolished in 1978 following new safety regulations. The 1990s saw a complete renovation of Meadow Lane, making it an all-seater stadium. In 1992 stands were built at either end and along the north side. In 1994 the new Main Stand was built bringing capacity at Meadow Lane up to 20,300.

Ground: Meadow Lane

Address: Meadow Lane, Nottingham NG2 3HJ

Main tel: 0115 952 9000

Box office: 0115 955 7204

Website: www.nottscountyfc.co.uk

Capacity: 20,300

Home colours: black and white striped shirts, black shorts and black socks

Club nickname: the Magpies

Pitch dimensions: 104m x 69m (114 x 76 yards)

Founded: 1862

Record attendance: 47,310 vs York City, March 12 1955

Most prolific scorer: Les Bradd (124)

Record win: 11-1 vs Newport County, January 15 1949

Record defeat: 1-9 vs Blackburn Rovers, November 16 1889

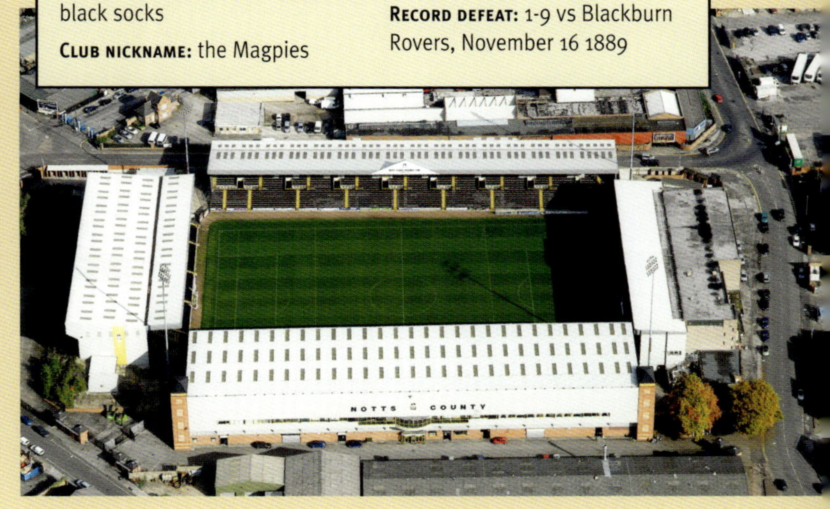

Nottingham Forest

Nottingham Forest was formed in 1865 and the club played their first games at the Forest Recreation Ground. They moved in 1879 to the Meadows and just a year later moved on to Trent Bridge, the cricket ground. The club then had a number of different homes and it was not until 1890 that they settled for a while at the Town Ground. It cost the club £1,000 to prepare the ground for football. Forest joined the League in 1892 and in 1898 won their first FA Cup final. This success brought increased numbers of supporters and that year the Reds moved to the City Ground, spending £3,000 on getting it up to scratch. The club built a wooden main stand and a wooden shelter at the Trent End. The City Ground survived the war with very little damage – repairing the ground when the Trent burst its banks in 1947 was more costly. After winning the Third Division title in 1950 they drew up plans for redevelopment. In 1954 the Trent End Terrace was extended and covered, and three years later the club built the East Stand and expanded the Bridgford End Terrace. Between 1962-65 the Main Stand was redeveloped, in time for Forest's highest gate ever when 49,946 fans saw them take on Manchester United in 1967. The following season fire engulfed the Main Stand in a game against Leeds United – fortunately, no fans were injured. The club had to make a temporary move to Meadow Lane, Notts County's ground, for six games while The City Ground was repaired. The late 1970s saw Forest win the League title, the European Cup and the League Cup twice in successive seasons. The money earned from this success funded the building of the two-tiered, all-seater Executive Stand (now called the Brian Clough Stand) in place of the East Stand, at a cost of a cool £2.5m. After a wrangle with the local council over a strip of land behind the Trent End, Forest began developing the Bridgford End in 1992, followed shortly afterwards by the Trent End which brought the capacity up to 30,602. Current plans include redevelopment of the Main Stand.

Left: Nottingham's three major sports grounds – Meadow Lane (top), the City Ground (centre) and Trent Bridge, home of Nottingham County Cricket (foreground)

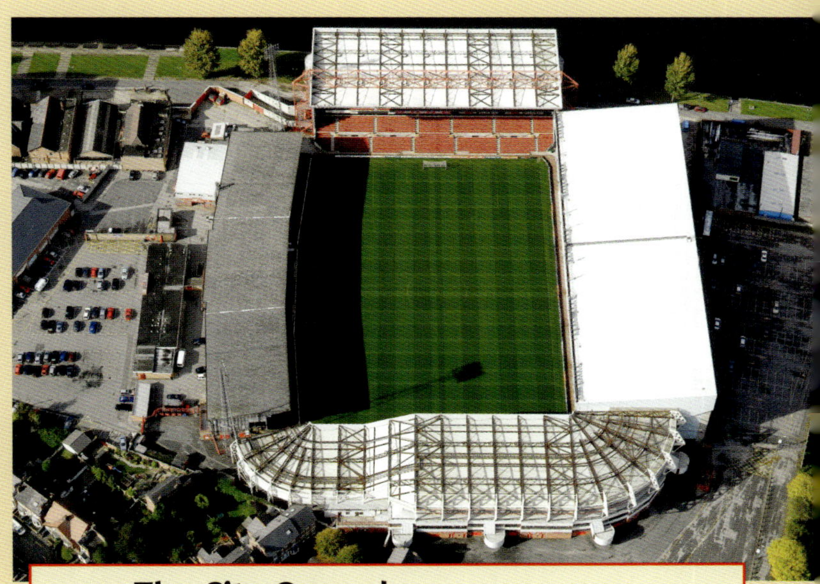

Ground: The City Ground

Address: The City Ground, Nottingham NG2 5FJ

Main tel: 0115 982 4444

Box office: 0871 226 1980

Website: www.nottinghamforest.co.uk

Capacity: 30,602

Home colours: red shirts, white shorts with red trim, red socks

Club nickname: the Reds

Pitch dimensions: 105m x 68m (115 x 78 yards)

Founded: 1865

Record attendance: 49,946 vs Manchester United, October 28 1967

Most prolific scorer: Grenville Morris (119)

Record win: 14-0 vs Clapton, January 17 1891

Record defeat: 1-9 vs Blackburn Rovers, April 10 1937

Oldham Athletic

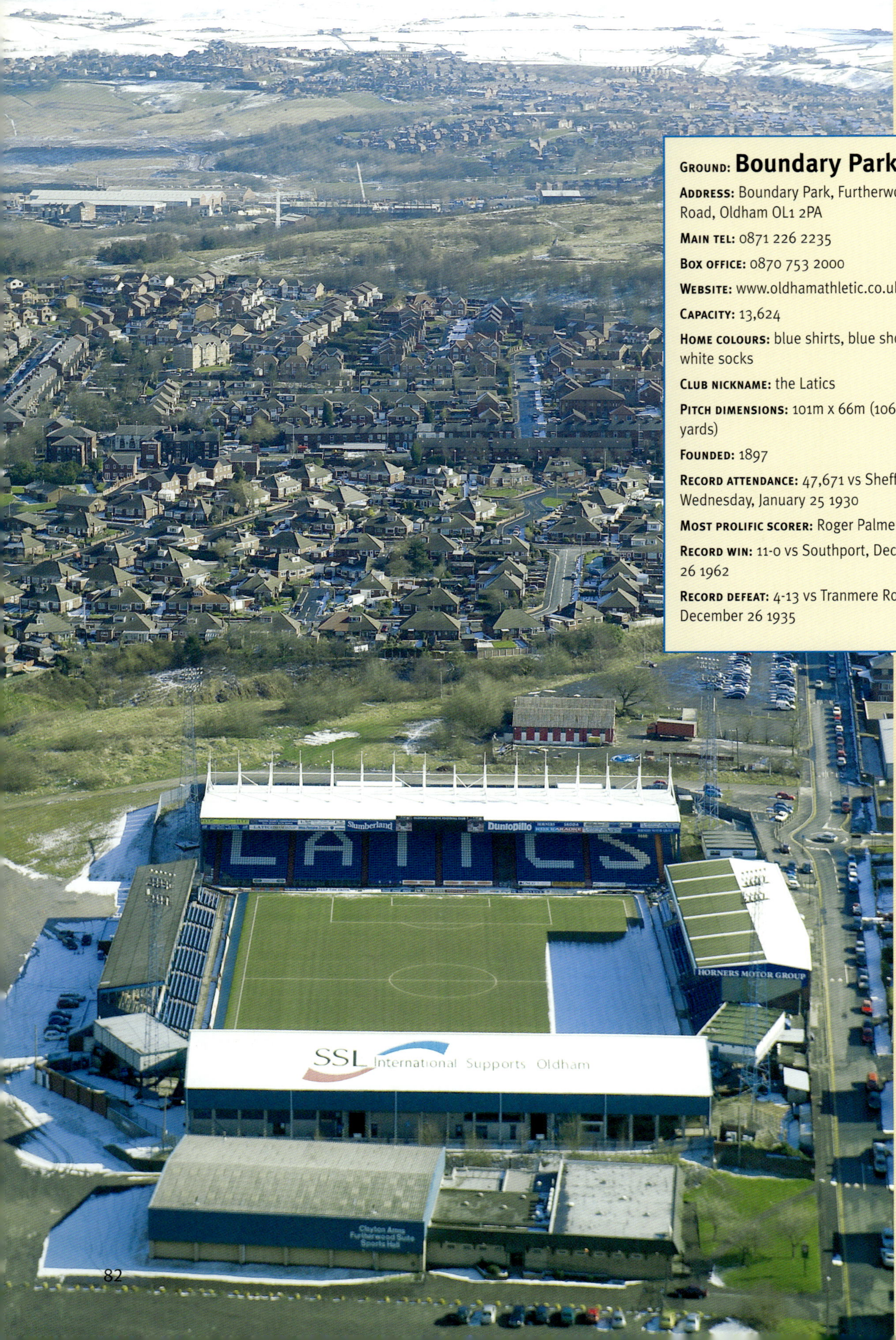

Ground: **Boundary Park**

Address: Boundary Park, Furtherwood Road, Oldham OL1 2PA

Main tel: 0871 226 2235

Box office: 0870 753 2000

Website: www.oldhamathletic.co.uk

Capacity: 13,624

Home colours: blue shirts, blue shorts, white socks

Club nickname: the Latics

Pitch dimensions: 101m x 66m (106 x 72 yards)

Founded: 1897

Record attendance: 47,671 vs Sheffield Wednesday, January 25 1930

Most prolific scorer: Roger Palmer (141)

Record win: 11-0 vs Southport, December 26 1962

Record defeat: 4-13 vs Tranmere Rovers, December 26 1935

Oldham Athletic was formed from a pub team, Pine Villa, which started playing football in 1897. The club's first game was played at Pine Mill but the team moved to Boundary Park in 1899 when Oldham County FC folded. The club changed its name to Oldham Athletic and remained at Boundary Park (then called the Athletics Ground) for just one more season. A dispute with the landlord prompted a temporary move to Hudson Fold but they returned once again to Boundary Park in 1906. By that time the ground had two stands, the Main Stand on the south side and the Broadway Stand on the north side. The original Main Stand was replaced in 1913 owing to increasing crowds and Oldham's election to the Football League. In 1927 a cover was added to the Chadderton Road End but this was blown down by a gale just before the terrace reopened and it took two years for it to be replaced. This was just in time for the Latics to record their highest ever attendance, 47,671, in a Cup game against Sheffield Wednesday. Very little changed at Boundary Park over the next 50 years; floodlights were installed in 1961 and in 1971 the Broadway Stand was replaced. The pitch's position and altitude meant it often froze in the depths of winter so the club installed undersoil heating in the 1980s. This proved to be an expensive option and in 1986 the Latics dug up the pitch and the undersoil heating and replaced it with an artificial pitch. This lasted until 1991 when a new pitch was laid. In the same season Oldham returned to the First Division and seats were added to the Chadderton Road End. In 1992 the Rochdale Road Stand was built at the east end of the ground. This brought capacity at Boundary Park up to 13,624. There are plans to build a new 20,000-seater stadium, either at Boundary Park or nearby.

Oxford United

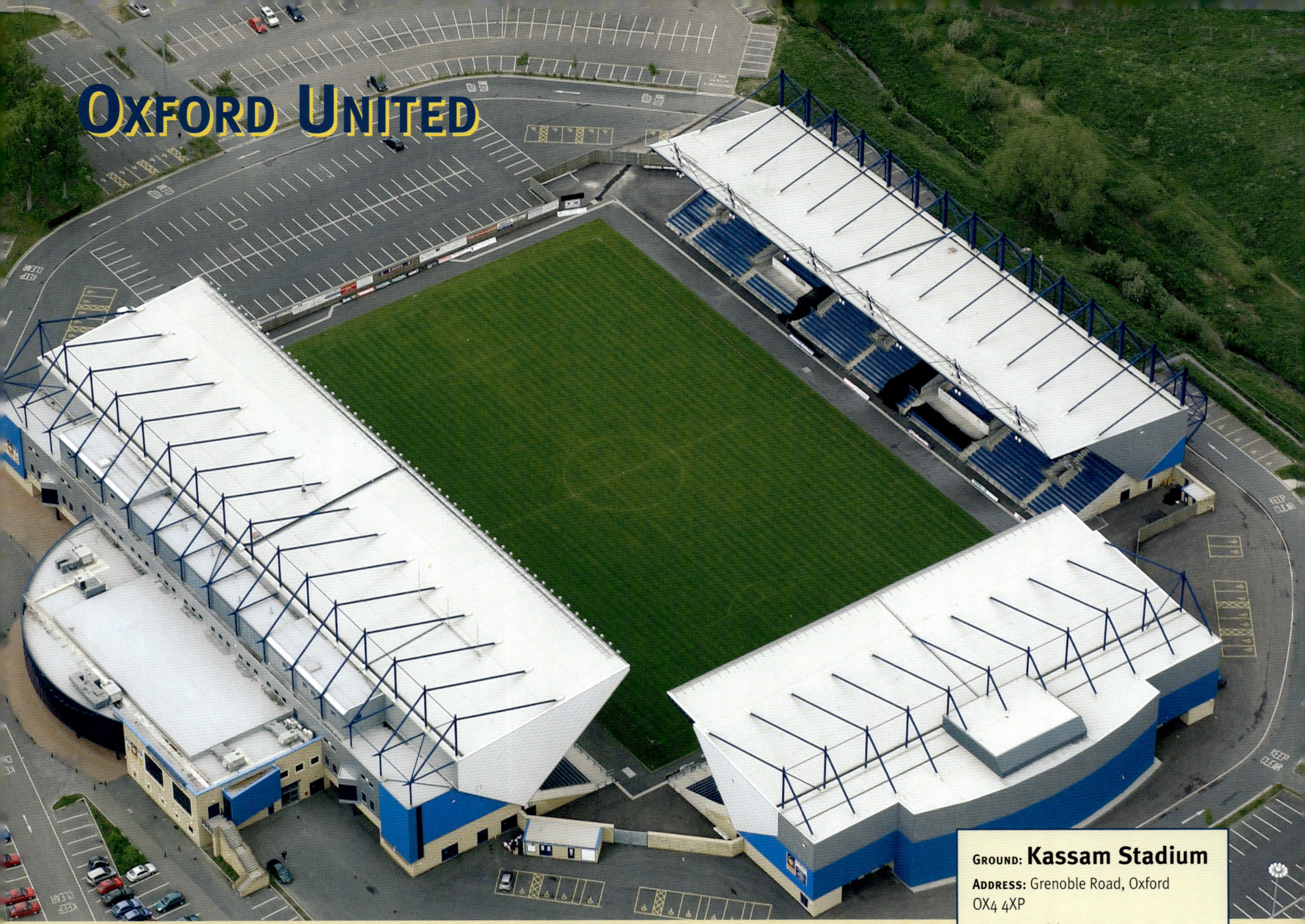

Oxford United was formed in 1893 and the club was originally called Headington FC. The team played their early games on local farm fields before arriving, in 1898, on land that would eventually become the Manor Ground. In 1902 the owners refused to renew the lease and it was not until 1925 that the club returned for good. Along with football, the ground was also home to cricket, bowls and tennis clubs. The original facilities included a pavilion along the west side and a smaller structure on the east side. In 1949 the cricket team moved out, Headington FC turned professional, joined the Southern League and installed floodlights a year later. In the 1950s a new stand, the Beech Road Stand, was built and in 1959 the club's supporters bought the ground's lease outright. In 1960 Headington FC became Oxford United and in 1962 they joined the Fourth Division of the Football League. By this time the ground had a main stand along the west side, two stands and a terrace to the north, a terrace with a cover along the east side and an uncovered terrace along the south side. Just two years later, in 1964, Oxford United recorded its highest ever attendance of 22,750 in the sixth round of the FA Cup against Preston North End. Although two small stands were added to the east side in the 1980s, the ground's capacity was still seriously restricted and its location meant it would be hard to expand, so the club decided to build a new stadium on the site of a former sewage farm. The Kassam Stadium (named after United's chairman Firoz Kassam) opened in 2001. Unusually, the ground has stands on three sides with an open end onto the car park; the two-tiered South Stand, the single-tiered North Stand and the single-tiered Oxford Mail Stand to the east. There are plans for a fourth stand to be built at the west end in the future.

Ground: Kassam Stadium

Address: Grenoble Road, Oxford OX4 4XP

Main tel: 01865 337 500

Box office: 01865 337 533

Website: www.oufc.co.uk

Capacity: 12,500

Home colours: yellow shirts with navy trim, navy shorts, navy socks

Club nickname: the Us

Pitch dimensions: 102m x 71m (112 x 78 yards)

Founded: 1893

Record attendance: (at the Kassam Stadium) 12,243 vs Leyton Orient, May 6 2006

Most prolific scorer: Graham Atkinson (77)

Record win: 7-0 vs Barrow, December 19 1964

Record defeat: 0-7 vs Sunderland, September 19 1998

Peterborough United

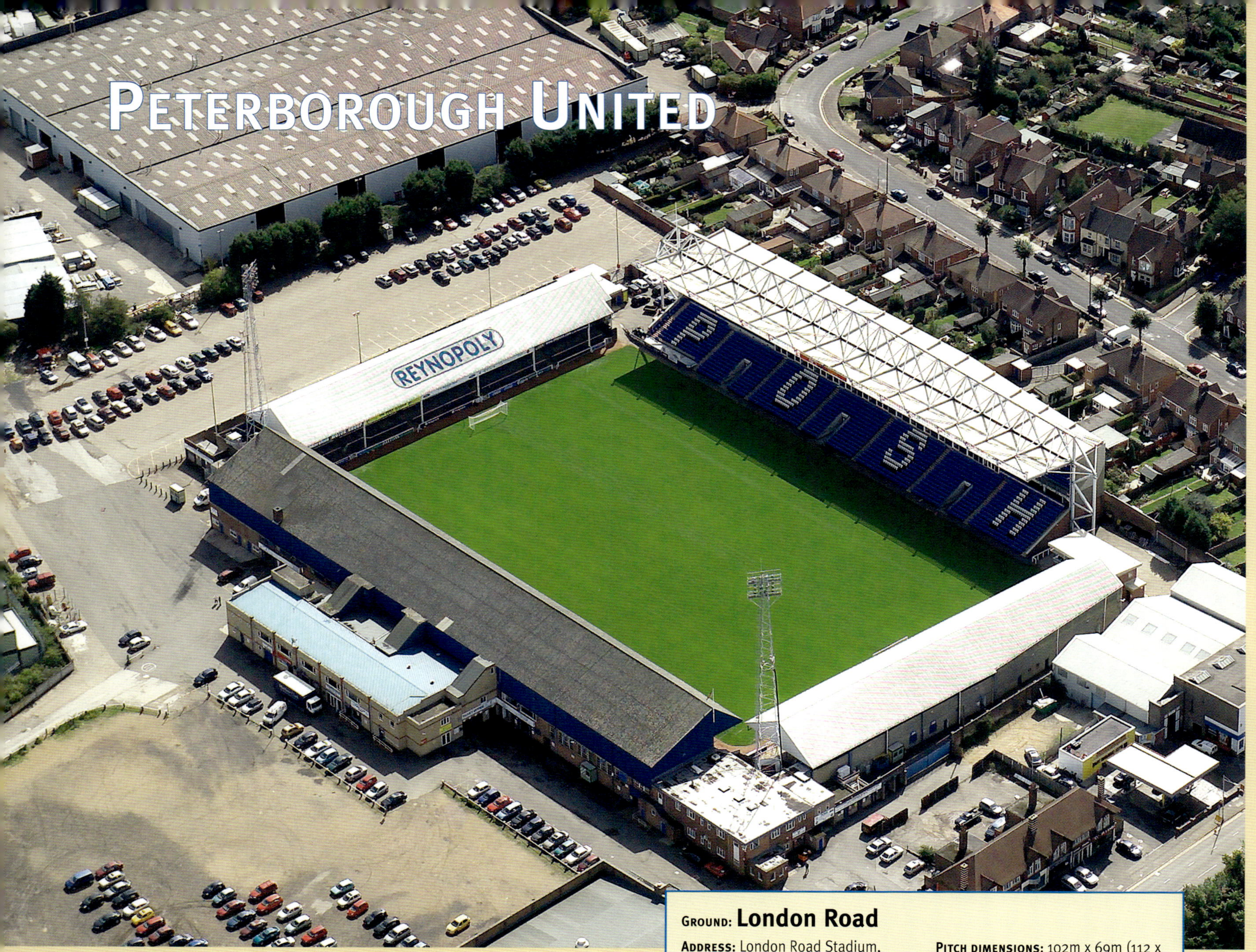

Ground: London Road

Address: London Road Stadium, London Road, Peterborough PE2 8AL

Main tel: 01733 563 947

Box office: 01733 865 674

Website: www.theposh.com

Capacity: 15,314

Home colours: royal blue shirts, white shorts, blue socks with white tops

Club nickname: the Posh

Pitch dimensions: 102m x 69m (112 x 76 yards)

Founded: 1934

Record attendance: 30,096 vs Swansea Town, February 20 1965

Most prolific scorer: Jim Hall (122)

Record win: 9-1 vs Barnet, September 5 1998

Record defeat: 1-8 vs Northampton Town, December 14 1946

Peterborough United was founded in 1934 and evolved from a club called Fletton United, formed in 1923. Fletton already had the nickname Posh, so when Peterborough formed, the nickname stuck. The club's home ground, London Road, was home to a number of football teams before the Posh moved in. In the early days the ground had only one stand, on the north side of the ground, which had 400 seats. In the 1950s major development at London Road took place: covers were added to either end of the ground and the Main Stand, which took three years to build, opened in 1958 when the original stand was demolished.

The south side also had terracing laid during the 1950s. In 1960 Peterborough's success on the pitch saw them join the Fourth Division of the Football League. The following season they were promoted to the Third Division after finishing as champions. Three years later a record attendance of 30,096 saw Peterborough take on Swansea Town and reach the quarter-finals of the FA Cup. The terraces along the sides of the pitch were extended, but then the club's momentum faltered. The team's performances began to slide and the development of London Road ceased completely. It was not until the 1990s that any further improvements to the ground took place. The paddock of the Main Stand had seats added in 1993 in time to meet the new safety regulations required by the Taylor report. In 1996 a new two-tiered stand was built along the south side of the pitch, bringing total capacity at London Road up to 15,314.

Plymouth Argyle

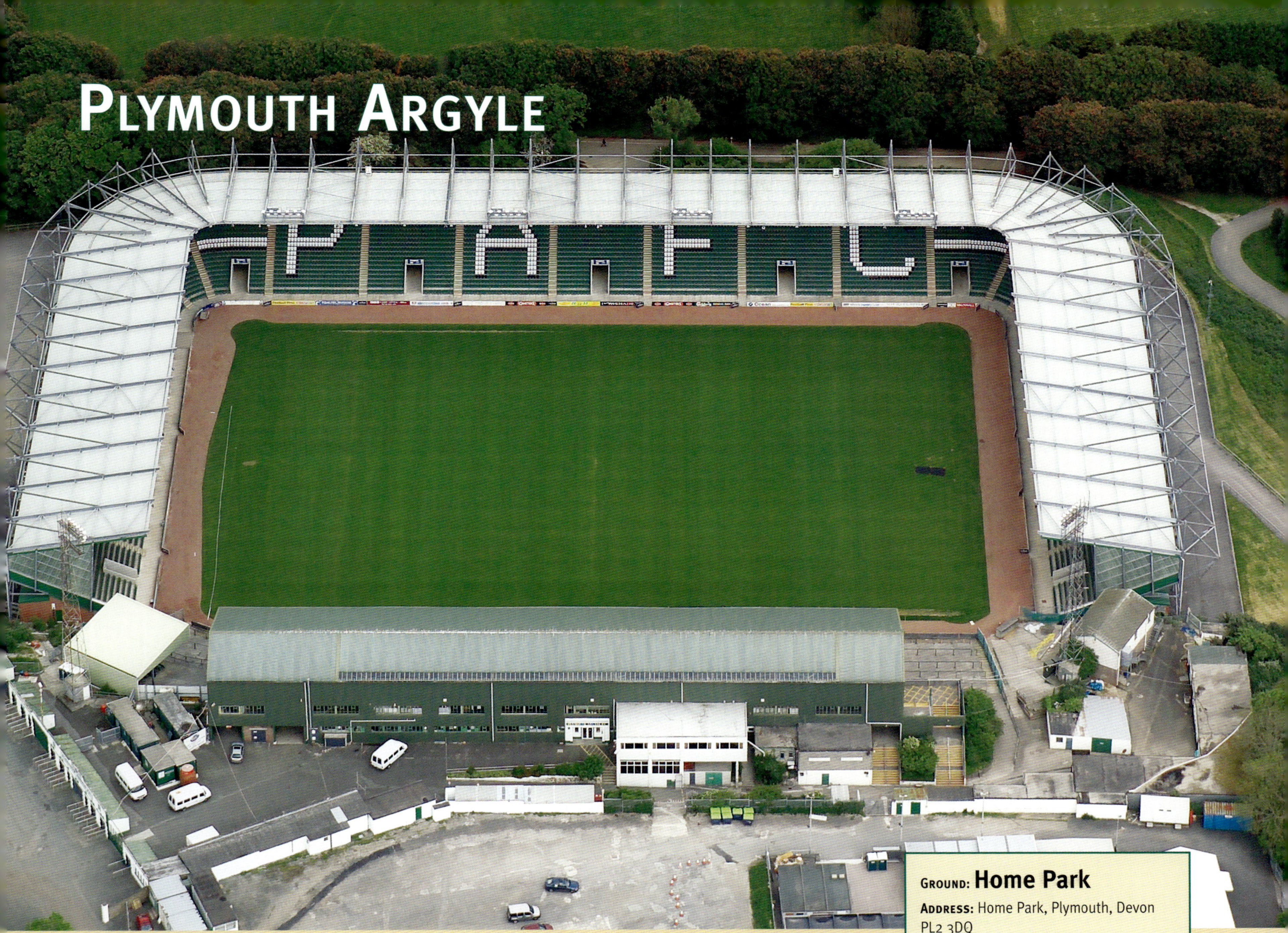

Ground: **Home Park**

Address: Home Park, Plymouth, Devon PL2 3DQ

Main tel: 01752 565 561

Box office: 0845 338 7232

Website: www.pafc.co.uk

Capacity: 19,500

Home colours: green shirts, white shorts, white socks

Club nickname: the Pilgrims

Pitch dimensions: 102m x 66m (112 x 72 yards)

Founded: 1903

Record attendance: 43,596 vs Aston Villa, October 10 1936

Most prolific scorer: Sammy Black (180)

Record win: 8-1 vs Millwall, January 16 1932

Record defeat: 0-9 vs Stoke City, December 17 1960

Plymouth Argyle FC have their roots in Argyle Athletic Club, which was established in 1886. The Athletic Club moved to Home Park in 1901, an area that had been used as a sporting venue since 1894, when rugby was played there. The Athletic Club also had a football, cricket and rugby club under its wing but it was the football club that enjoyed most success. By the time Plymouth Argyle FC turned professional in 1903, Home Park had grown from being little more than a cinder track to a much more sophisticated ground with stands at the west end and the south side. In 1920, the Pilgrims joined the League and 10 years later they built a new grandstand along the south side of the ground. The west end also saw development with a terrace being laid and a cover added. This was in time for Home Park's largest ever crowd of 43,596 for a match against Aston Villa in October 1936. Home Park was badly damaged during the Second World War; the pitch was bombed and the Grandstand burned down in 1941. Home Park reopened for football in 1946. For the first post-war game, a double-decker bus parked along the edge of the pitch served as a temporary dressing room for players. The Grandstand was rebuilt in 1952 and a cover was added to the north side in 1965. The roof above the west end was taken down in 1980 and replaced in 1984 and seats were added to the north side in 1990. In 2001 Home Park was completely redeveloped, when the east, west and north sides were rebuilt. Now a horseshoe-shaped single-tiered stand covers these three sides. The Grandstand remains, although there are plans to develop this in the future to make the ground more uniform.

Port Vale

Opinions vary as to the exact formation date of Port Vale although the club badge states that it was 1876. The Valiants played at various grounds in their early days including a ground close to Burslem station when they adopted the name Burslem Port Vale and turned professional in 1885. The following year the club moved to the Cobridge Athletic Ground. Financial insolvency threatened in 1896, and despite a hard fight, the club were declared bankrupt in 1907. A church team re-formed the club as Port Vale and in 1913 they moved to the Old Recreation Ground where they remained for almost 40 years. After joining the League in 1919, the team bought the ground's freehold. However after the Second World War the club realised they needed a bigger ground and in 1950 they moved to Vale Park. The ground had terracing on three sides but was completely uncovered. A few months after Vale Park opened, a roof was added to the north end of the ground. A new stand was built along the west side in 1954 and floodlights were installed four years later. Terracing was added to the north end of the ground in 1959 and the following season Vale Park recorded its highest ever attendance of 49,768 when the Valiants took on Aston Villa in the FA Cup. Very little changed at Vale Park until the 1990s. However, events off the pitch saw Port Vale expelled from the League for financial irregularity in 1968, although they were allowed to rejoin, albeit in the Fourth Division, a season later. In 1991 seats were installed along the west side and a roof was added to the south end. A new cover and seats were added to the north end and stands were added to two of the ground's corners. The Main Stand was finally opened in 2001 and current capacity at Vale Park is 18,392.

Ground: Vale Park

Address: Vale Park, Hamil Road, Burslem, Stoke-on-Trent ST6 1AW

Main tel: 01782 655 800

Box office: 01782 655 832

Website: www.port-vale.co.uk

Capacity: 18,392

Home colours: white shirts, black shorts, black socks

Club nickname: the Valiants

Pitch dimensions: 104m x 70m (114 x 77 yards)

Founded: 1876

Record attendance: 49,768 vs Aston Villa, February 20 1960

Most prolific scorer: Wilf Kirkham (154)

Record win: 9-1 vs Chesterfield, September 24 1932

Record defeat: 0-10 vs Sheffield United, December 10 1892

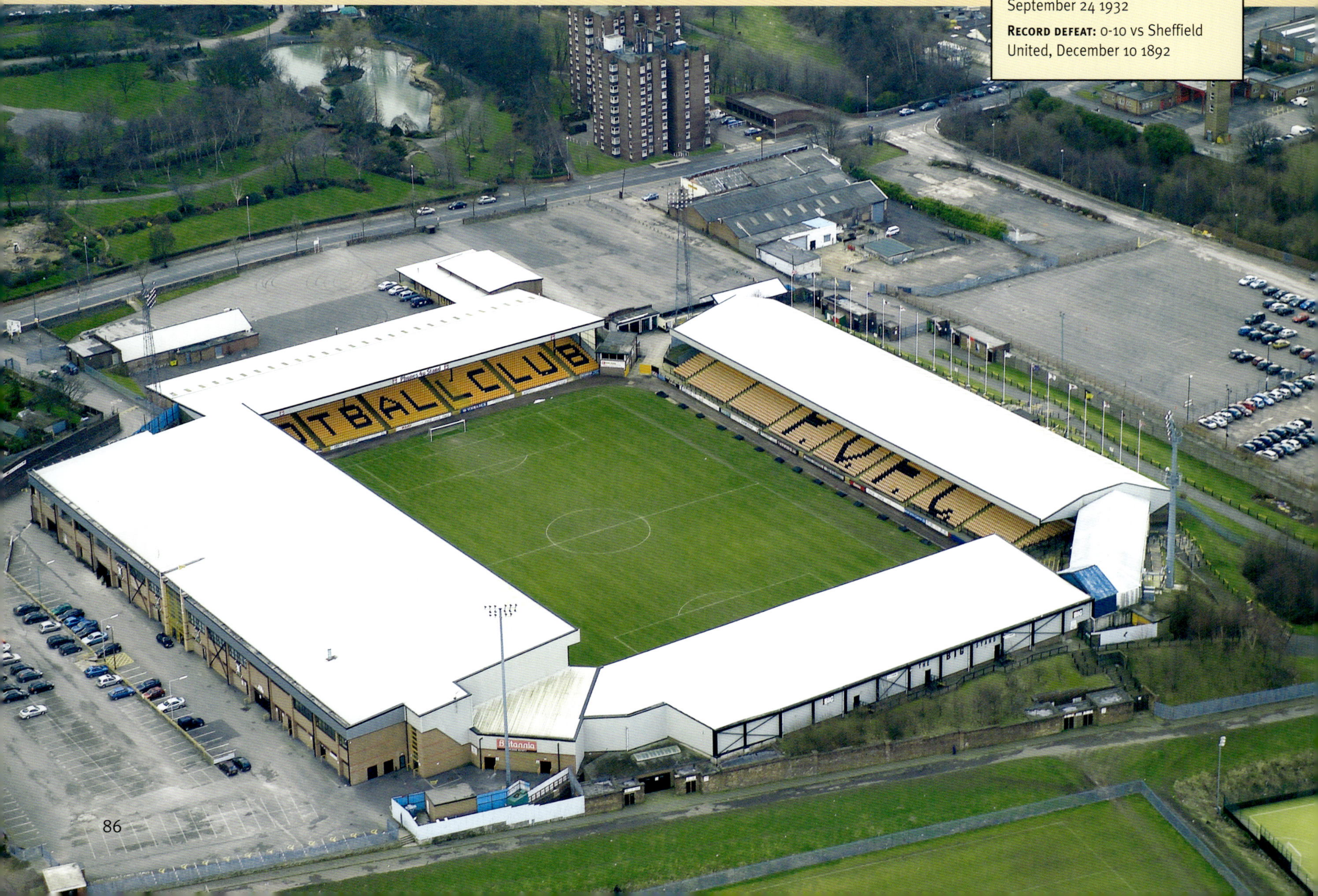

PORTSMOUTH

Portsmouth formed in 1898 after the town's other football club, the Royal Artillery, was suspended by the FA for breaching amateur regulations. The club bought land near Fratton railway station and Fratton Park was opened in September 1899. The club progressed well at the start of the 20th century, generating enough money to build a mock-Tudor pavilion at the Frogmore Road entrance complete with clock tower. In 1920 the club joined the League and were soon promoted to Division Two. In 1925 they opened the South Stand, which had 4,000 seats, a paddock and a balcony. Despite losing in the 1929 and 1934 FA Cup finals, club profits continued to rise and they were able to fund the building of the North Stand in 1935. Pompey finally got their hands on the FA Cup in 1939, when they thrashed Wolves 4-1. After the Second World War, Portsmouth won the League in 1949 and 1950 and were drawing average gates of 39,000. They notched up their largest crowd ever in February 1949 when 51,385 people saw them take on Derby County in the FA Cup. The Fratton End was covered in 1956 but it was not until 1988 when any further development took place at Fratton Park. Jim Gregory bought the club and between 1988 and 1994 funded a £4m refurbishment programme. The Fratton End was demolished in 1988 but plans for the replacement all-seater stand had to be shelved when British Rail refused to sell land behind the ground. In April 1993 the club unveiled plans for a move to Parkway Stadium in Farlington, although these were turned down by Whitehall. In 1995 the ground was partly rebuilt and made all-seater bringing the capacity up to 20,288. Following the club's successful promotion to the Premiership in 2003, there were plans to massively redevelop the ground. However, Pompey have since announced ambitious plans to sell Fratton Park and move to a purpose-built 36,000 all-seater stadium at the city's dockyard designed by leading architects Herzog and deMeuron.

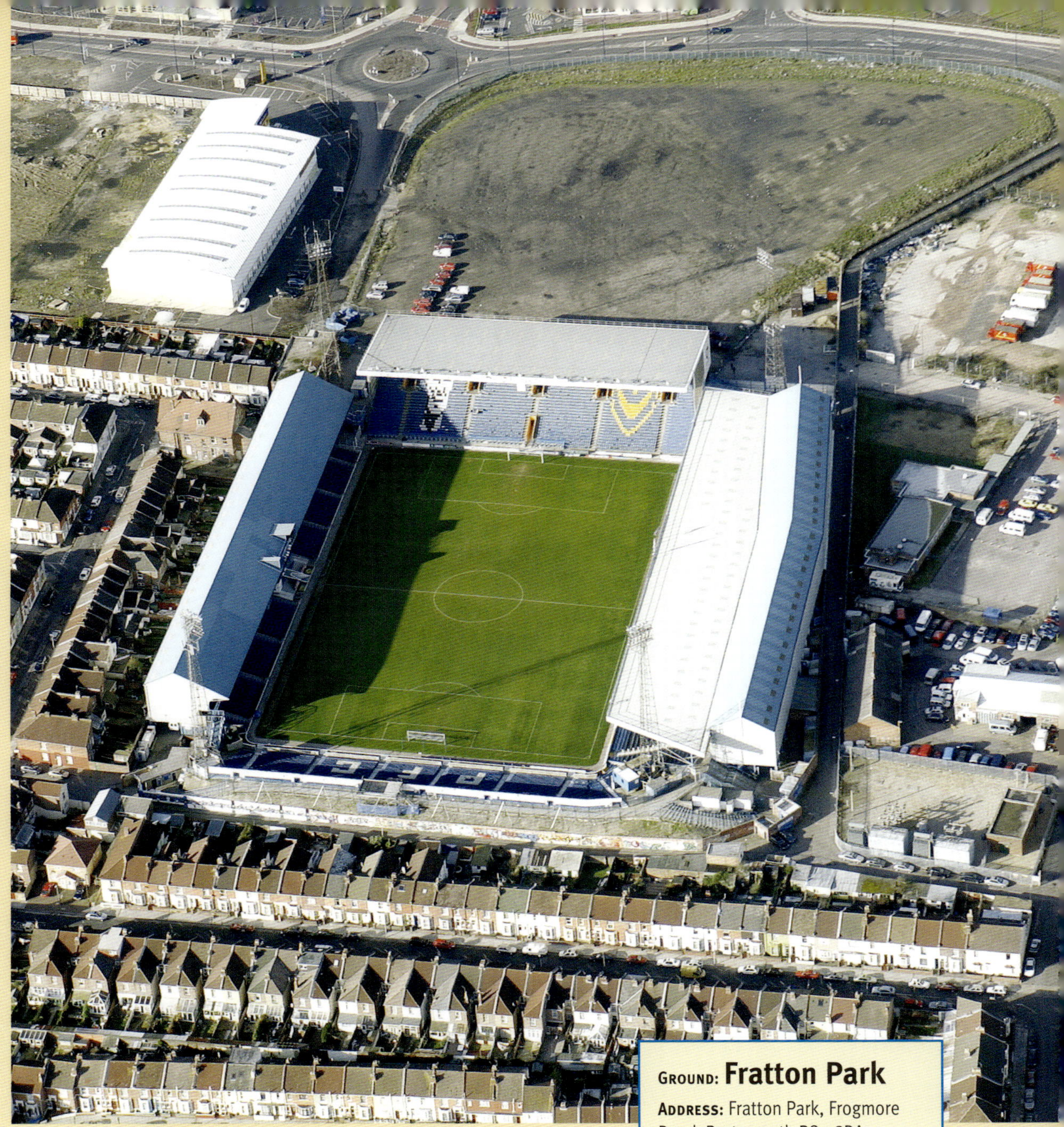

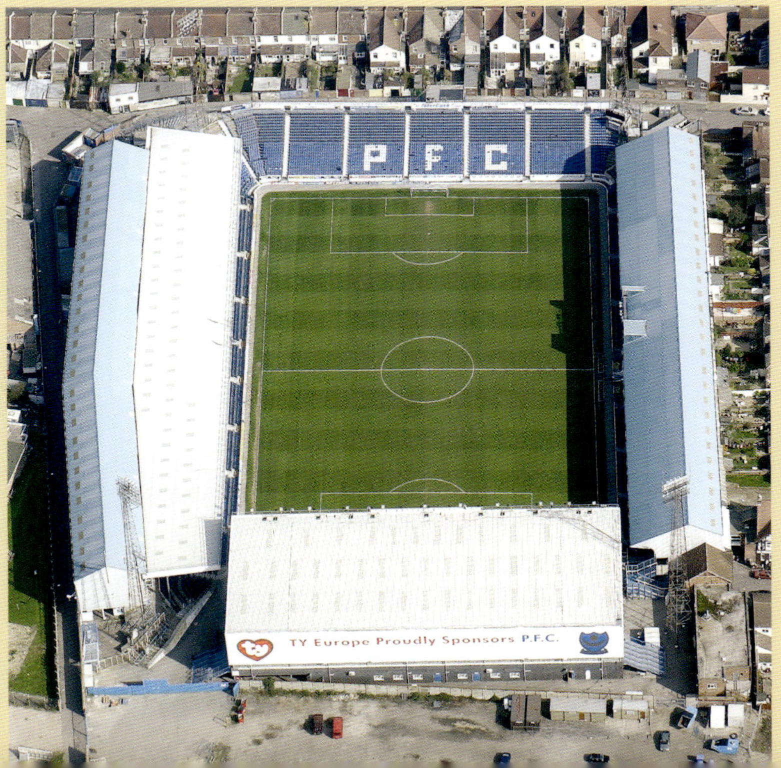

GROUND: Fratton Park

ADDRESS: Fratton Park, Frogmore Road, Portsmouth PO4 8RA

MAIN TEL: 023 9273 1204

BOX OFFICE: 0844 847 1898

WEBSITE: www.portsmouthfc.co.uk

CAPACITY: 20,288

HOME COLOURS: blue shirts, white shorts, red socks

CLUB NICKNAME: Pompey

PITCH DIMENSIONS: 105m x 67m (115 x 73 yards)

FOUNDED: 1898

RECORD ATTENDANCE: 51,385 vs Derby County, February 26 1949

MOST PROLIFIC SCORER: Peter Harris (194)

RECORD WIN: 9-1 vs Notts County, April 9 1927

RECORD DEFEAT: 0-10 vs Leicester City, October 20 1928

PRESTON NORTH END

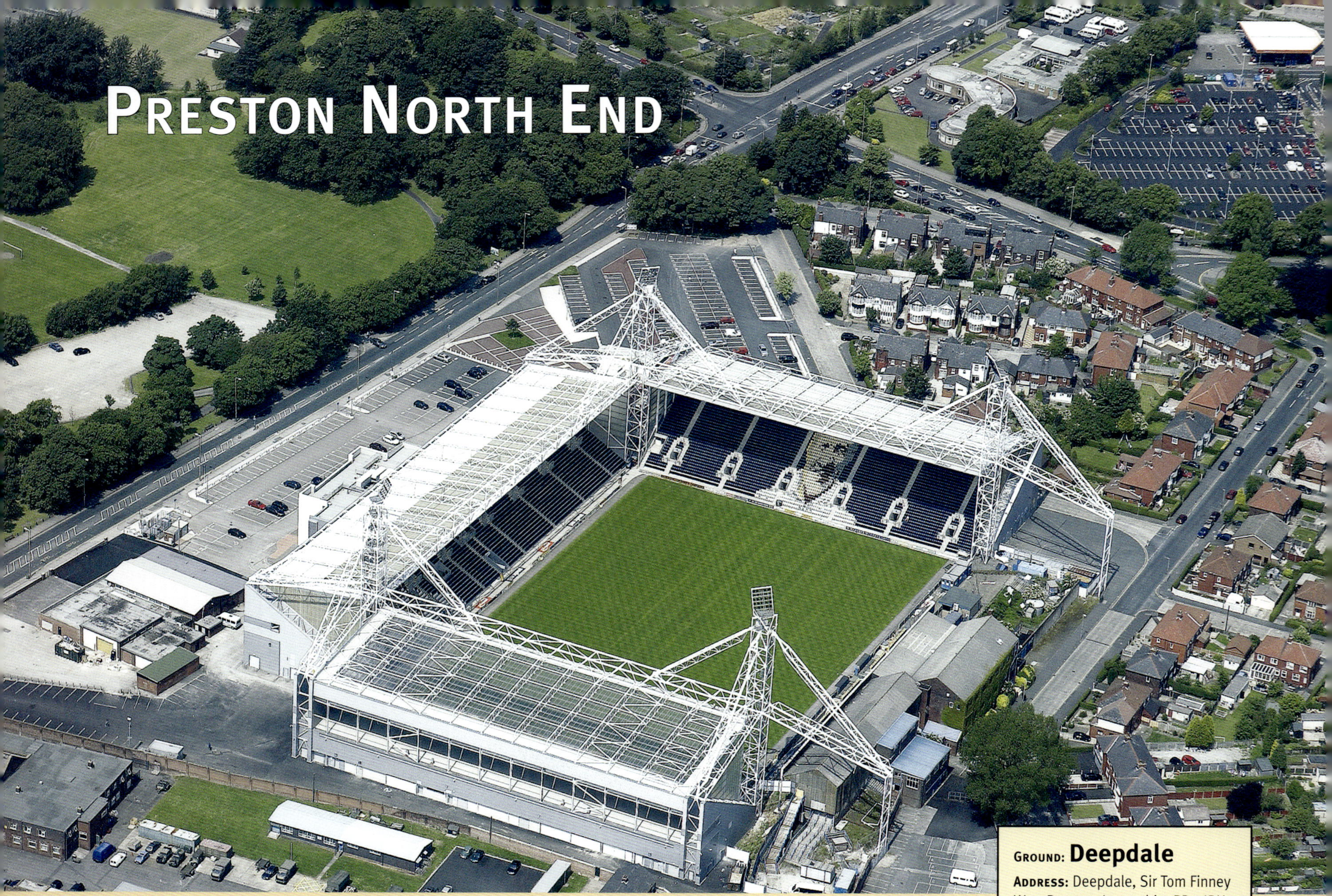

Preston North End FC was formed in 1881, although its roots go back much further. In 1863 North End was formed as a cricket club, the name originating from the club's location in the north of the town. North End moved to Deepdale, little more than a field at the time, in 1875. The club swapped from playing cricket to rugby in 1877, although this was not a particularly successful venture and just a year later North End played their first game of football. In 1881 the switch to football was made permanent. By this time, Deepdale had two stands on the west side and uncovered stands at the east and north ends. Preston were expelled from the Cup in 1884 after it was discovered they were paying their players and the Lilywhites formed Britain's first professional football team in 1885. In 1888 they were founder members of the Football League and won the FA Cup the same season. There were plans to extend the facilities at Deepdale but little happened until the Grandstand was opened in 1906. It was 1921 when Deepdale next saw some improvement when the Kop was erected at the Fulwood Road End. During the 1930s a cover was added to the Town End, a pavilion was built along the east side and a second pavilion was erected on the south side in 1936. Two years later Deepdale drew its largest ever attendance of 42,684 when they took on Arsenal in the League. That same season Preston North End won the FA Cup. The Lilywhites had to leave Deepdale during the war as the ground was taken over by the army. In the post-war years very little changed, although the club installed an artificial pitch in 1986, which was removed in 1994. In 1996 the West Stand was replaced by a new single-tiered stand and a new stand was built where the North Terrace had once stood. The final stand to be replaced was the pavilion at the south end. The old pavilion still remains along the east side of the pitch, although there are plans to replace this at some point in the future. The National Museum of Football is now located at Deepdale and is housed in two sides of the stadium.

GROUND: Deepdale

ADDRESS: Deepdale, Sir Tom Finney Way, Preston, Lancashire PR1 6RU

MAIN TEL: 0870 442 1964

BOX OFFICE: 0870 442 1966

WEBSITE: www.pne.com

CAPACITY: 19,525

HOME COLOURS: white shirts with navy trim, white shorts, white and navy socks

CLUB NICKNAME: the Lilywhites or North End

PITCH DIMENSIONS: 101m x 66m (110 x 72 yards)

FOUNDED: 1881

RECORD ATTENDANCE: 42,684 vs Arsenal, April 23 1938

MOST PROLIFIC SCORER: Tom Finney (187)

RECORD WIN: 10-0 vs Stoke City, September 14 1889

RECORD DEFEAT: 0-7 vs Blackpool, May 1 1948

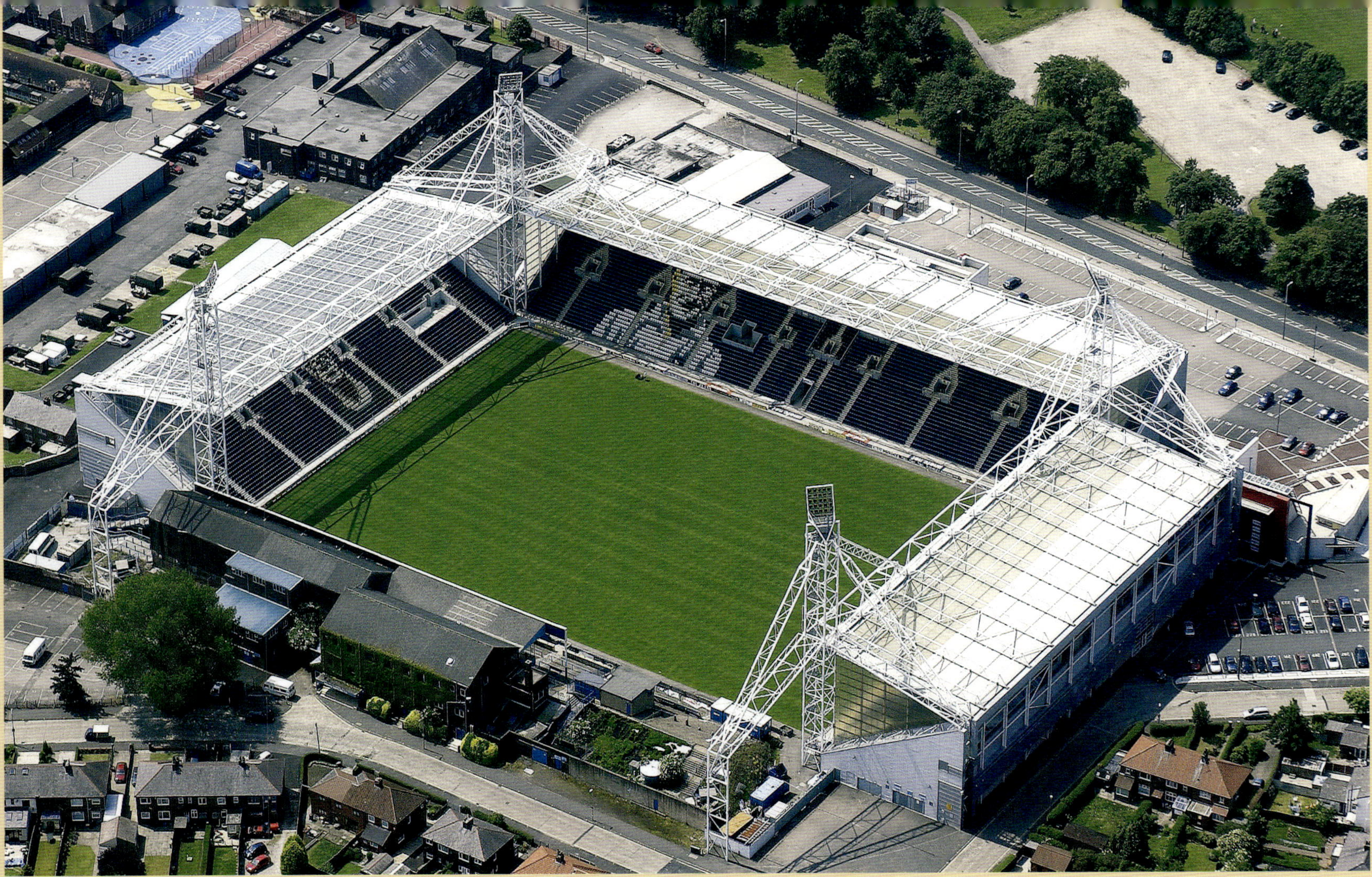

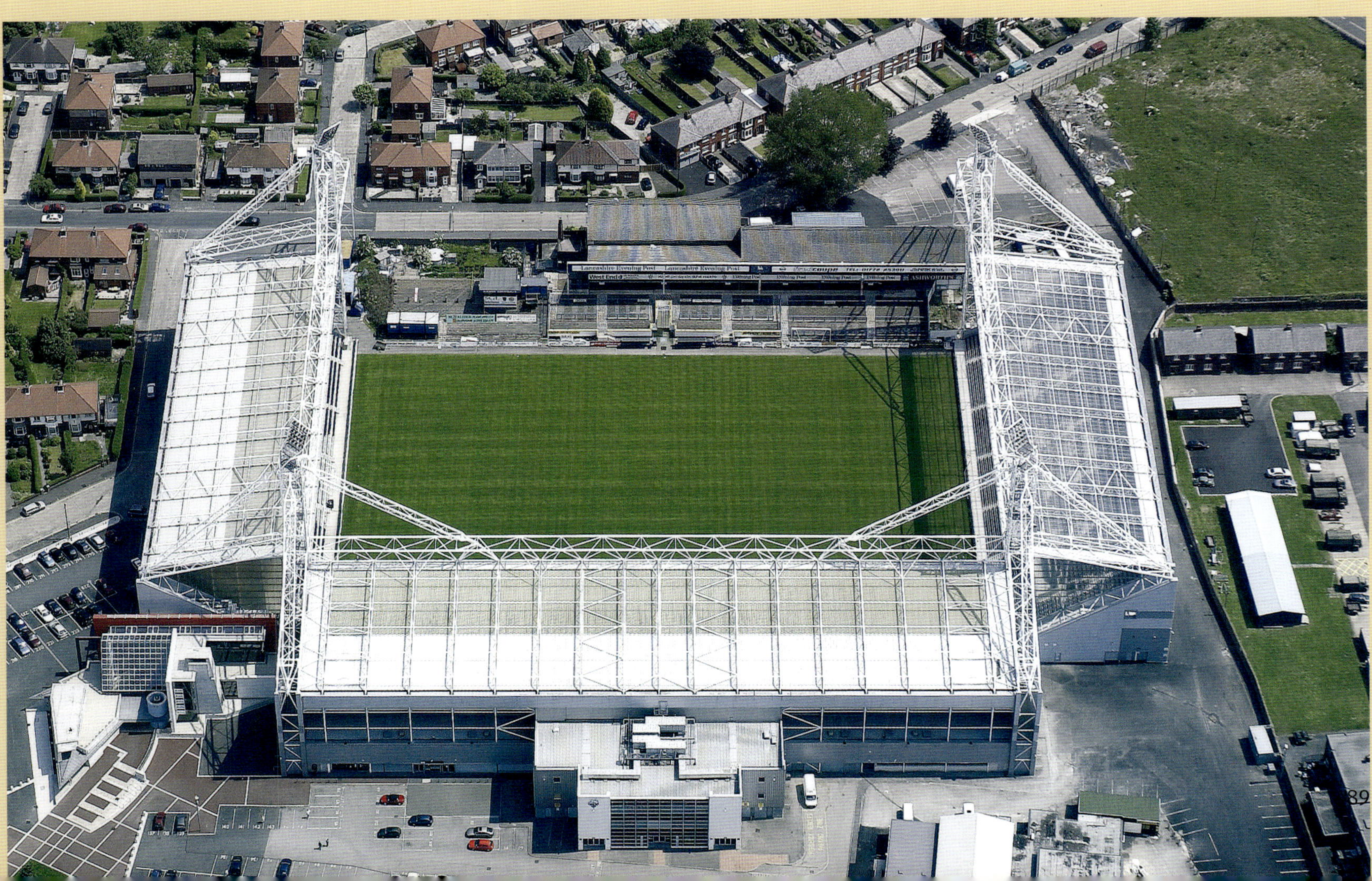

Queens Park Rangers

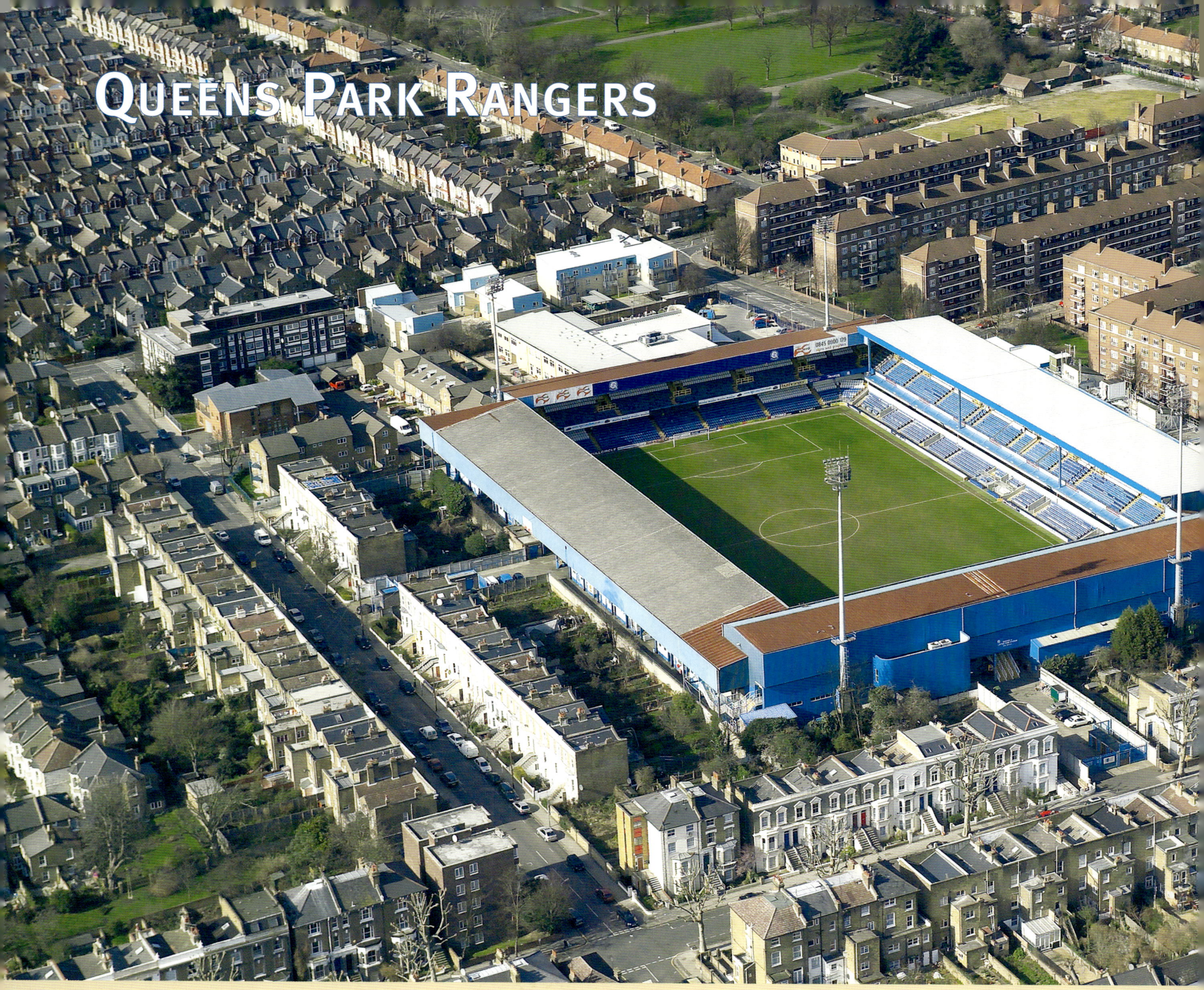

In 1882, old boys from Droop Street Board School formed Queens Park Rangers. In the early days they were known as St Judes. In 1886, when they merged with Christchurch Rangers, the club took on the name Queens Park Rangers as many of the players came from an area called Queen's Park. QPR's early days were noted for their frequent ground changes. Their first proper home was a waste ground near Kensal Rise Athletic Ground followed by a stint at Park Royal. The army took over Park Royal during the First World War and QPR had to reside at Stamford Bridge. In 1917 they moved to Loftus Road, former home of Shepherd's Bush FC, who had played there since 1904. They brought with them a stand from Park Royal and erected it on the south side of the pitch. On the other three sides were uncovered banks. Between then and the Second World War the only addition was a roof over the terrace at the east end. QPR left Loftus Road in 1930 due to crowd trouble. They played one game at Highbury and for two seasons played at White City, a purpose-built Olympic stadium with a capacity of 60,000. Crowds dropped and the stadium was so large that it lacked atmosphere, so the club returned to Loftus Road in 1933. In 1948 the club bought the freehold of Loftus Road and concreted all the terraces. Despite some improvements, the ground still felt cramped and in 1962 the club moved back to the White City. Once again, the lack of atmosphere saw them return to Loftus Road where the club opted to develop the stadium. A two-tier stand was built on

GROUND: Loftus Road

ADDRESS: Loftus Road Stadium, South Africa Road, London W12 7PA

MAIN TEL: 020 8743 0262

BOX OFFICE: 0844 477 7007

WEBSITE: www.qpr.co.uk

CAPACITY: 19,100

HOME COLOURS: blue and white hoops, white shorts, white socks

CLUB NICKNAME: the Superhoops

PITCH DIMENSIONS: 102m x 66m (112 x 72 yards)

FOUNDED: 1882

RECORD ATTENDANCE: 35,353 vs Leeds United, April 27 1974

MOST PROLIFIC SCORER: George Goddard (172)

RECORD WIN: 9-2 vs Tranmere Rovers, December 3 1960

RECORD DEFEAT: 1-8 vs Manchester United, March 19 1969

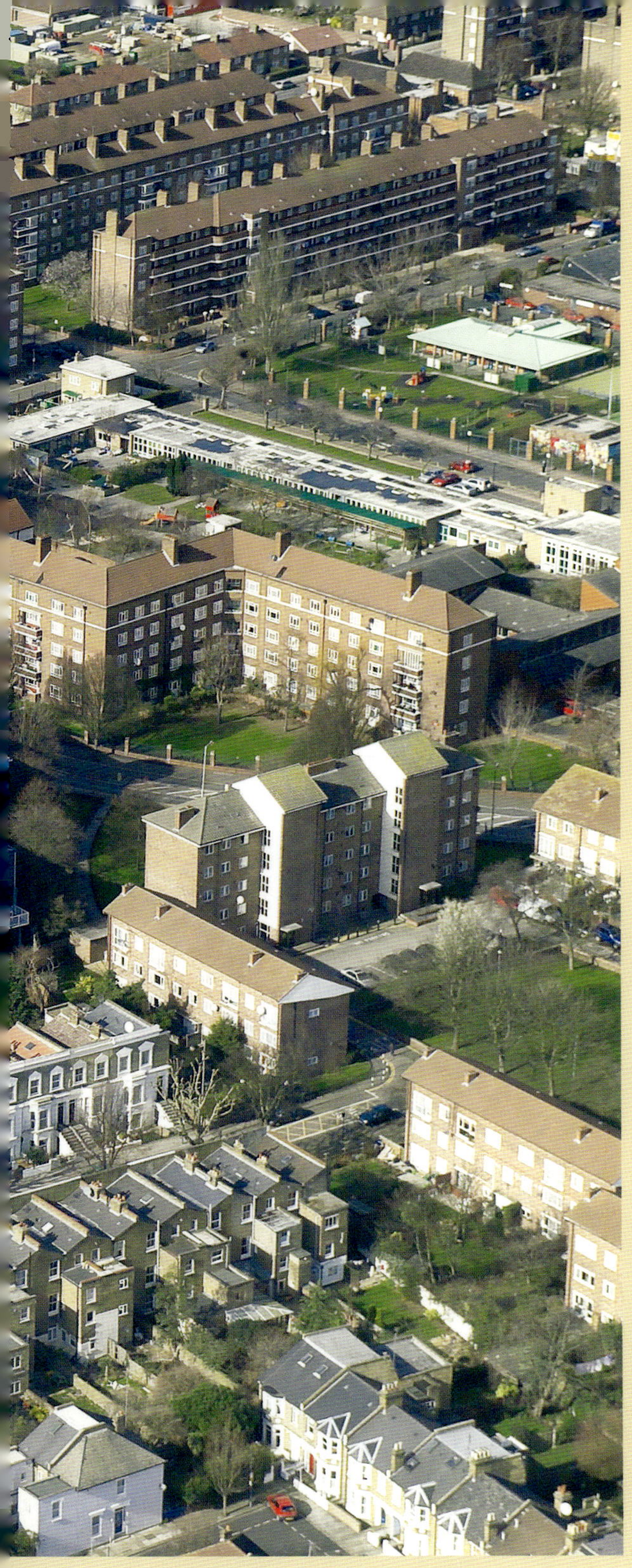

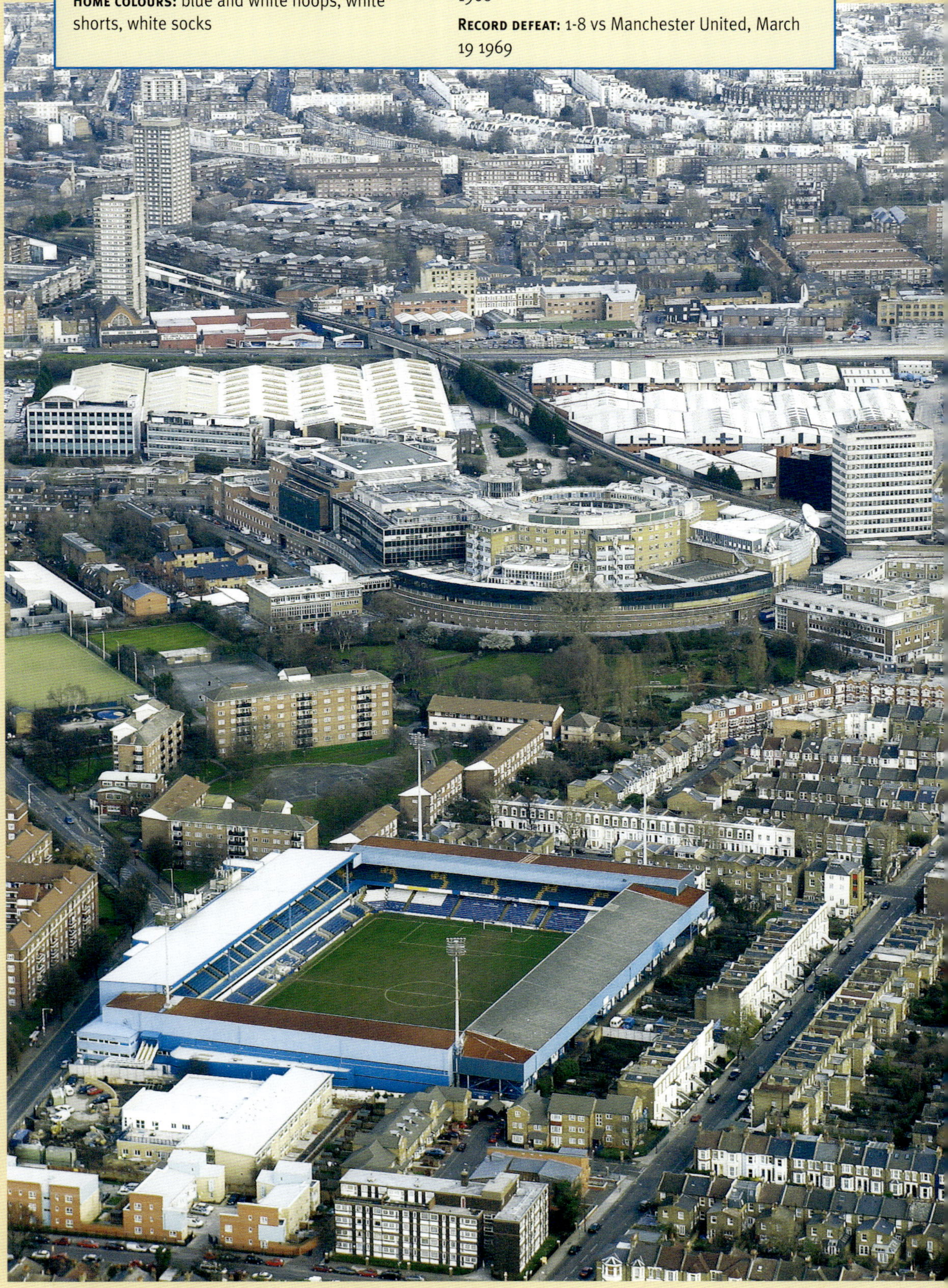

Right: Loftus Road with the BBC Televsion Centre in the background

the north side in 1966 and a new south stand opened in 1972, two years before the record 35,353 attendance at Loftus Road for a game against Leeds United on April 27 1974. By 1981 there were two-tiered stands at either end and that year QPR unveiled the world's first artificial pitch, which remained until 1987 when it was replaced by grass. Its capacity now stands at 19,100.

RANGERS

Rangers was formed in 1873 and played their first games on Glasgow Green. They moved twice again before arriving at Ibrox in 1887 to a ground which borders their current stadium. The original Ibrox ground was such a success that it hosted the 1890 Cup Final and three internationals. However, when local rivals Celtic opened the more sophisticated Celtic Park, Rangers began to make plans to build an even grander headquarters. In 1899, after winning the League without losing a game, Rangers began building on the land next to their existing pitch. When it opened the new ground boasted an oval track, a pavilion and a stand. In 1900 Scottish architect Archibald Leitch built terracing behind the west goal capable of holding 36,000 fans. However, the terracing was unstable and in a game between England and Scotland in 1902 there was a tragic collapse, killing 26 and injuring 500. By 1910 Leitch had again been commissioned to expand Ibrox and increase its capacity to 63,000. Rangers won the League and Cup double in 1928 and this funded the building of the 10,000-seater double-decker South Stand. The Gers continued to enlarge the banking and in 1939 a record 118,567 turned up for an Old Firm derby. Tragedy struck again at Ibrox in 1971, when 66 people died and 145 were injured as the notorious Stairway 13 in the ground's north-east corner collapsed at the end of a game against Celtic. Following the tragedy, the club planned to completely rebuild all sides

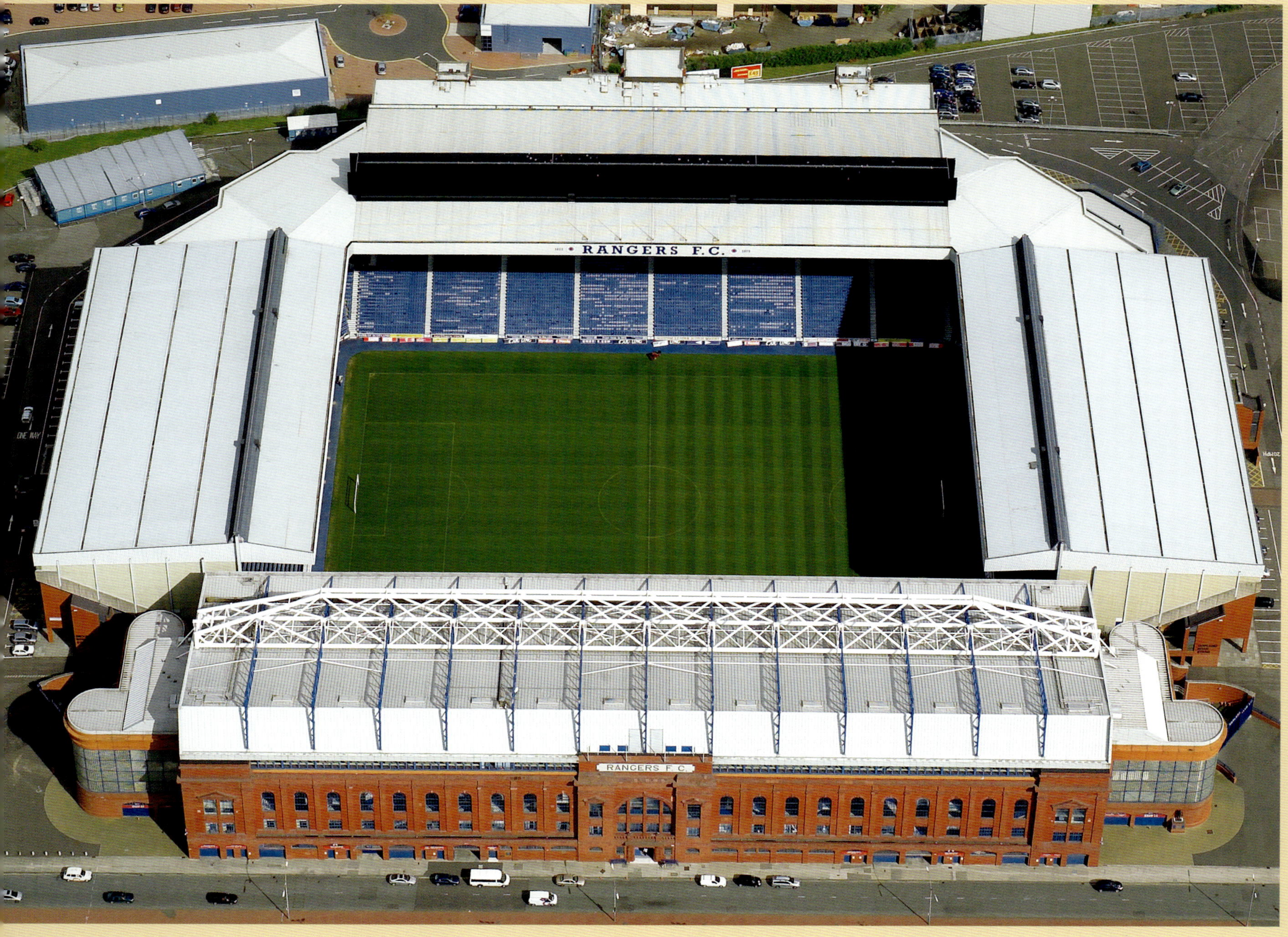

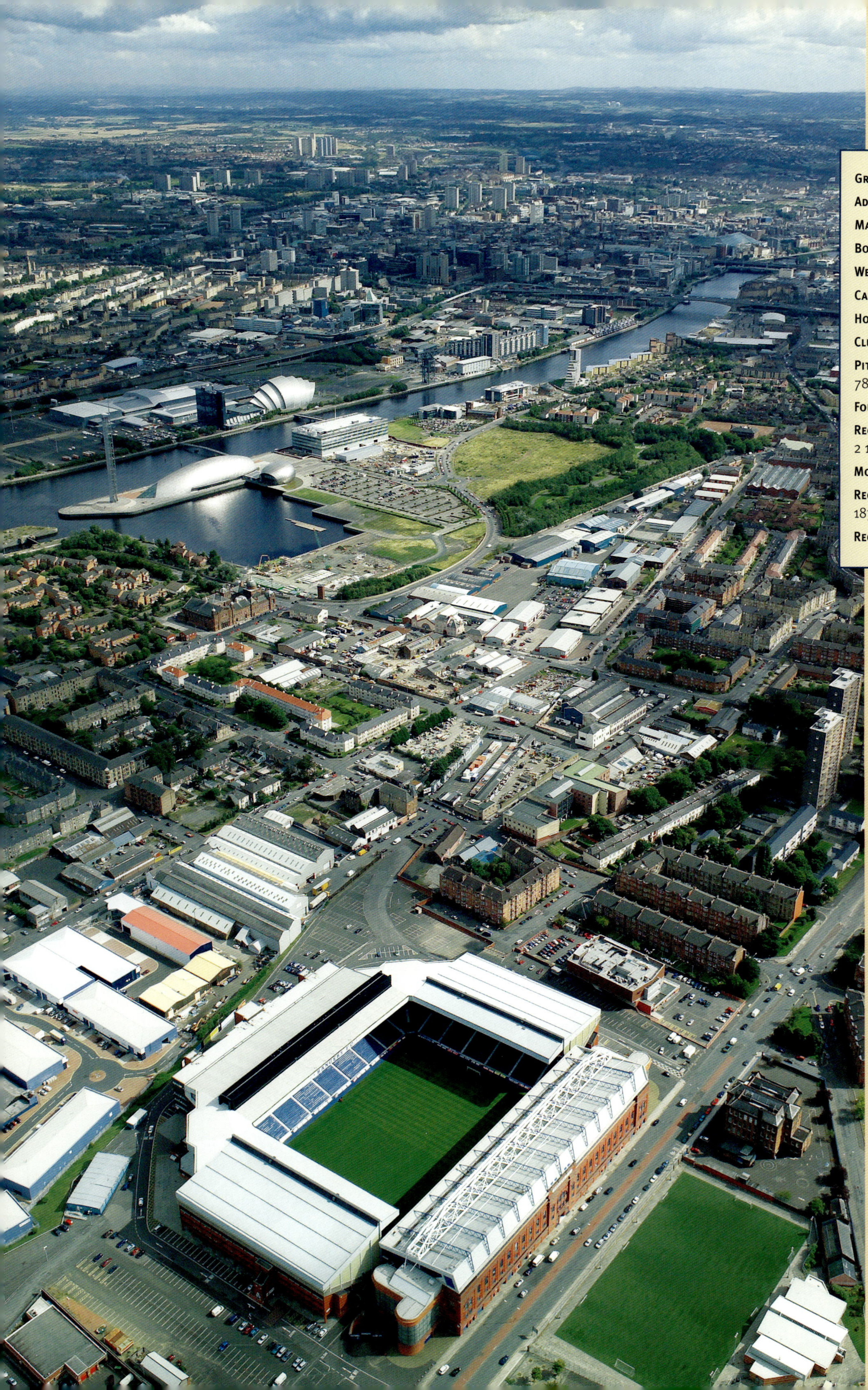

GROUND: Ibrox

ADDRESS: Ibrox Stadium, Glasgow, G51 2XD

MAIN TEL: 0871 702 1972

BOX OFFICE: 0871 702 1972

WEBSITE: www.rangers.co.uk

CAPACITY: 50,411

HOME COLOURS: blue, red and white

CLUB NICKNAME: the Gers or Teddy Bears

PITCH DIMENSIONS: 105m x 69m (115 x 78 yards)

FOUNDED: 1873

RECORD ATTENDANCE: 118,567 vs Celtic, January 2 1939

MOST PROLIFIC SCORER: Ally McCoist (355)

RECORD WIN: 13-0 vs Possilpark, October 6 1877

RECORD DEFEAT: 1-7 vs Celtic, October 19 1957

of the ground except for Leitch's South Stand and make the three new stands all-seater. Work began in 1978 and the new Ibrox opened in 1981 at a cost of £10 m. However, hard times followed and attendances dropped. Heavy investment in 1986 saw the club's fortunes reverse and in 1988 they spent £4m on the rear of the Govan Stand. Yet more investment came when new chairman David Murray took over; he spent £20m adding another tier to the South Stand, making it all-seater. An innovative move to increase capacity involved the lowering of the pitch by 12 inches, in 1991, and the corners at either side of the Govan Stand were also completed in 1996, bringing Ibrox's all-seated capacity up to 50,411.The club has proposed adding a third tier to the Govan Stand bringing overall capacity at Ibrox to around 50,411

Left: Ibrox Stadium with the Glasgow Science Centre on the near side of the river Clyde and the Scottish Exhibition and Conference Centre on the far bank

Reading

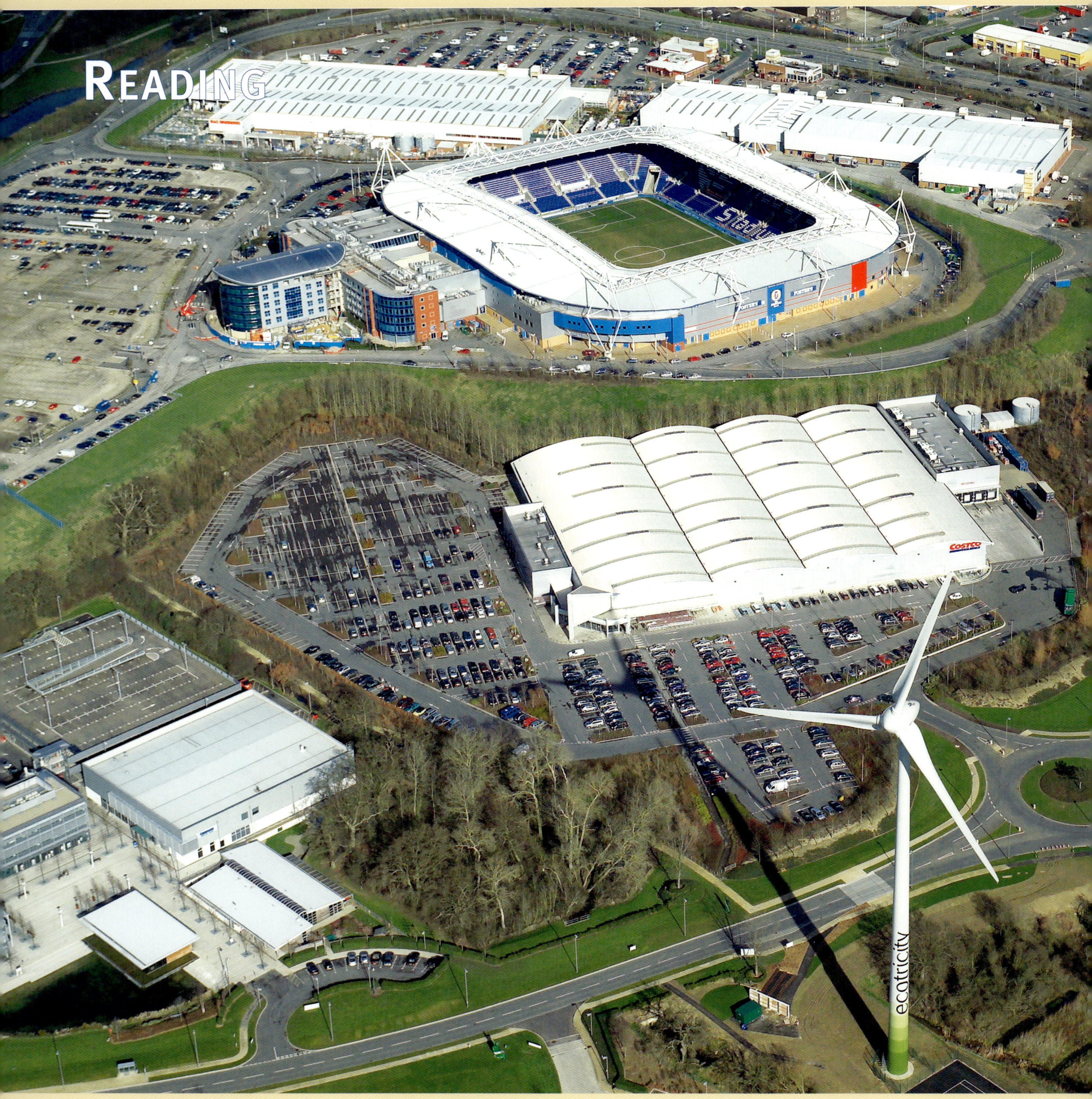

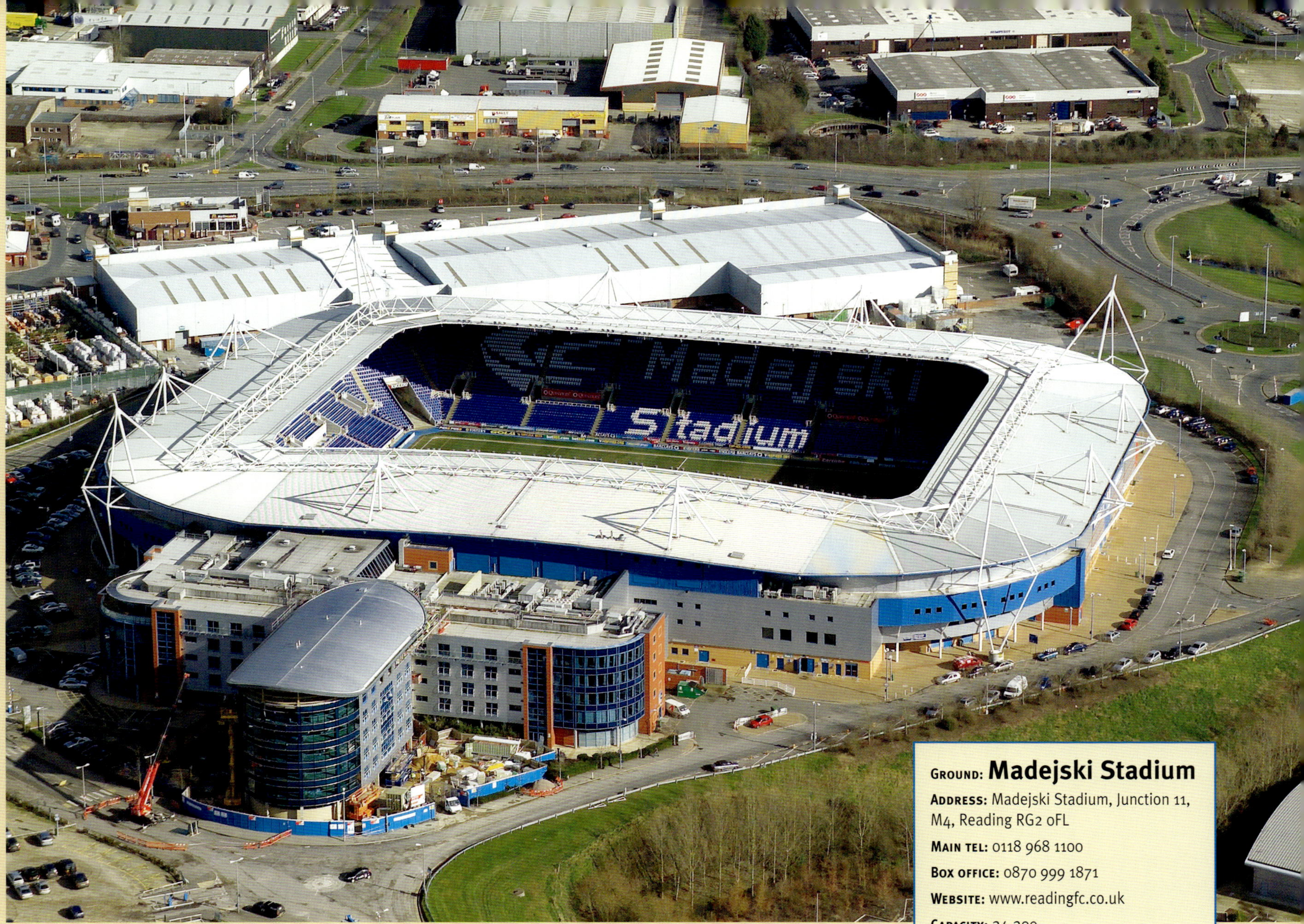

Ground: Madejski Stadium

Address: Madejski Stadium, Junction 11, M4, Reading RG2 0FL

Main tel: 0118 968 1100

Box office: 0870 999 1871

Website: www.readingfc.co.uk

Capacity: 24,200

Home colours: royal blue and white hooped shirts, blue shorts, blue socks with white hoops

Club nickname: the Royals

Pitch dimensions: 102m x 70m (112 x 77 yards)

Founded: 1871

Record attendance: (at Madejski Stadium) 24,135 vs Manchester United, January 19 2008

Most prolific scorer: Ronnie Blackman (158)

Record win: 10-2 vs Crystal Palace, September 4 1946

Record defeat: 0-18 vs Preston North End, January 27 1893

Reading FC formed in 1871 and played their first games at the Reading Recreation Ground. They moved several times and eventually in 1896 left the flood-prone Caversham Cricket Ground, their home for five years, for the drier option of Elm Park. When the Royals arrived, Elm Park had a small wooden main stand on the north side of the pitch and turfed terraces around the other three sides. In 1925 a cover, which had been added to offer protection over one of the terraces, blew down in a gale. The Main Stand was also damaged in the storm and a year later was replaced, in time for Elm Park to record its highest-ever attendance of 33,042 for a match against Brentford. In 1936 a roof was built over the terrace running along the south side of the ground. This roof was extended over both ends by the late 1950s. Little else changed at Elm Park until the 1980s when Robert Maxwell, then chairman of local rivals Oxford United, announced the two clubs were going to merge into one team to be called Thames Valley Royals. The announcement brought sweeping changes in the Reading boardroom and management. A merger was avoided and a period of success on the pitch then followed. Elm Park needed a large amount of investment to meet new safety regulations. Some ground improvements were made but the club's close proximity to local housing meant it would be impossible to expand capacity beyond a certain point. In 1990 chairman Roger Smee resigned and businessman John Madejski stepped in with the much needed cash investment. In 1998 Reading FC bade farewell to Elm Park and moved to a purpose-built 24,200 seater stadium, the Madejski Stadium, built on a greenfield site on the outskirts of Reading. The Madejski is a totally enclosed stadium, with single-tiered stands on three sides and a two-tiered stand on the west side of the pitch. It is also home to the London Irish Rugby Club. Adding extra tiers to the three single-tiered stands would bring total capacity to 38,000. This planned expansion was given the go-ahead in May 2007.

Rotherham United

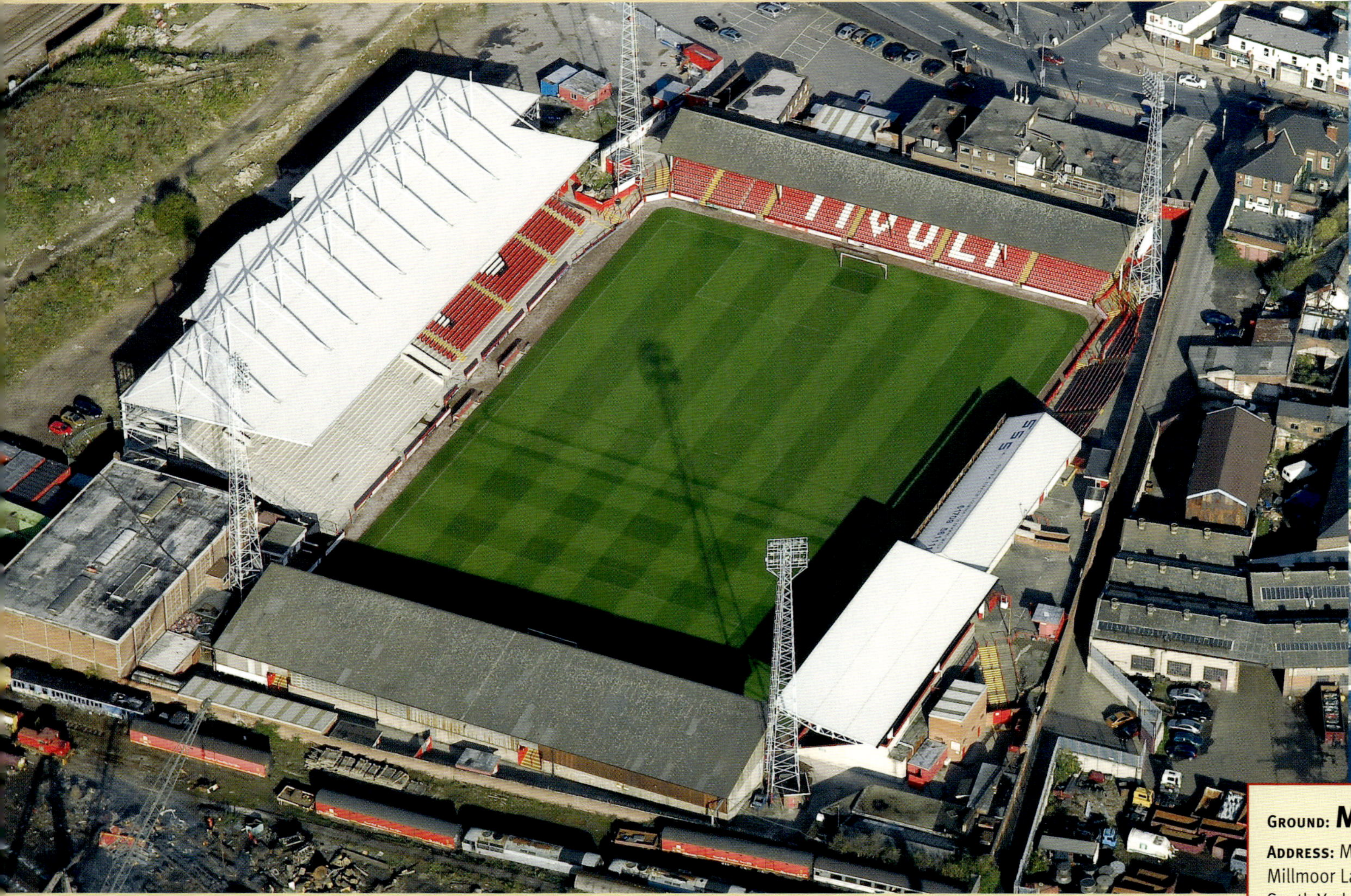

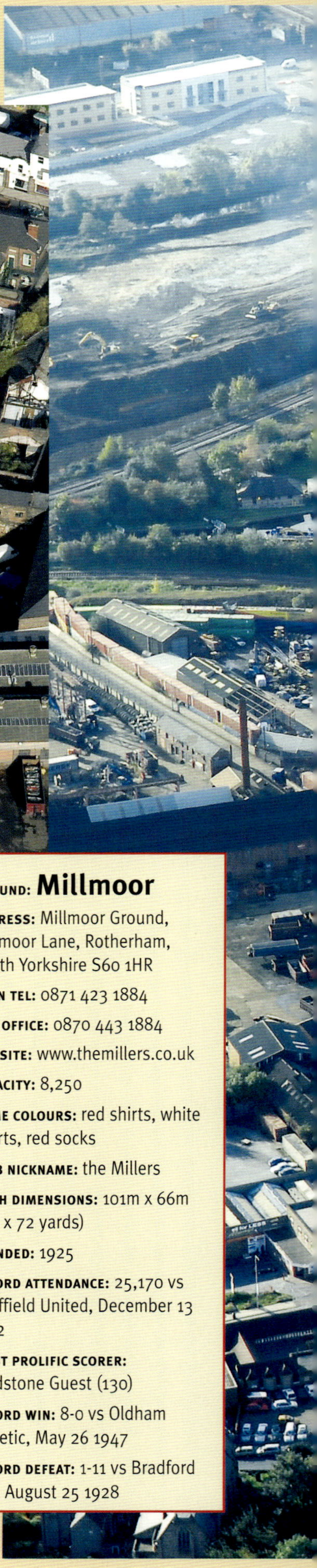

Ground: Millmoor

Address: Millmoor Ground, Millmoor Lane, Rotherham, South Yorkshire S60 1HR

Main tel: 0871 423 1884

Box office: 0870 443 1884

Website: www.themillers.co.uk

Capacity: 8,250

Home colours: red shirts, white shorts, red socks

Club nickname: the Millers

Pitch dimensions: 101m x 66m (110 x 72 yards)

Founded: 1925

Record attendance: 25,170 vs Sheffield United, December 13 1952

Most prolific scorer: Gladstone Guest (130)

Record win: 8-0 vs Oldham Athletic, May 26 1947

Record defeat: 1-11 vs Bradford City, August 25 1928

Rotherham United officially formed in 1925 but it had its roots in a number of clubs playing in the Rotherham area almost 50 years earlier. Two main clubs helped to form the Rotherham of today. The two sides were Thornhill, which was formed in 1877 and went on to become Rotherham County in 1905, and Rotherham Town. Rotherham County moved from the very confined Red House ground to Millmoor in 1907. They brought with them two small stands and these, together with an embankment along the east side, formed the basic facilities at Millmoor in its early days. A cover was added to the South End Terrace a few years later and the Main Stand was built in 1920. In 1925 Rotherham Town, who played at Clifton Lane, agreed to merge with County and play under the new name of Rotherham United. Three years after the merger a roof was added to the East Terrace and a track was laid for greyhound racing in the 1930s in a bid to raise much needed revenue. After the war, many improvements were made to Millmoor; the Millers bought the lease in 1949, concreted the terraces and the north end (the Tivoli End) was expanded. In 1952 Millmoor recorded its highest ever attendance of 25,170 in a game against local rivals Sheffield United. Development at Millmoor continued throughout the 1950s and 1960s. A roof was added to the south end (the Railway End), the roof over the Main Stand was extended and a roof was added to the Tivoli End. Seats were added to the former East Terrace in the 1970s. The 1980s saw Rotherham United beset with financial problems as their chairman quit leaving them more than a quarter of a million pounds in debt. A new chairman, local businessman Ken Booth, stepped in and saved the club. An additional cover was added to the East Stand and seats were fitted. Further seating was added to the Main Stand bringing capacity up to 8,250. There are plans to replace and further expand the Main Stand at some point in the future.

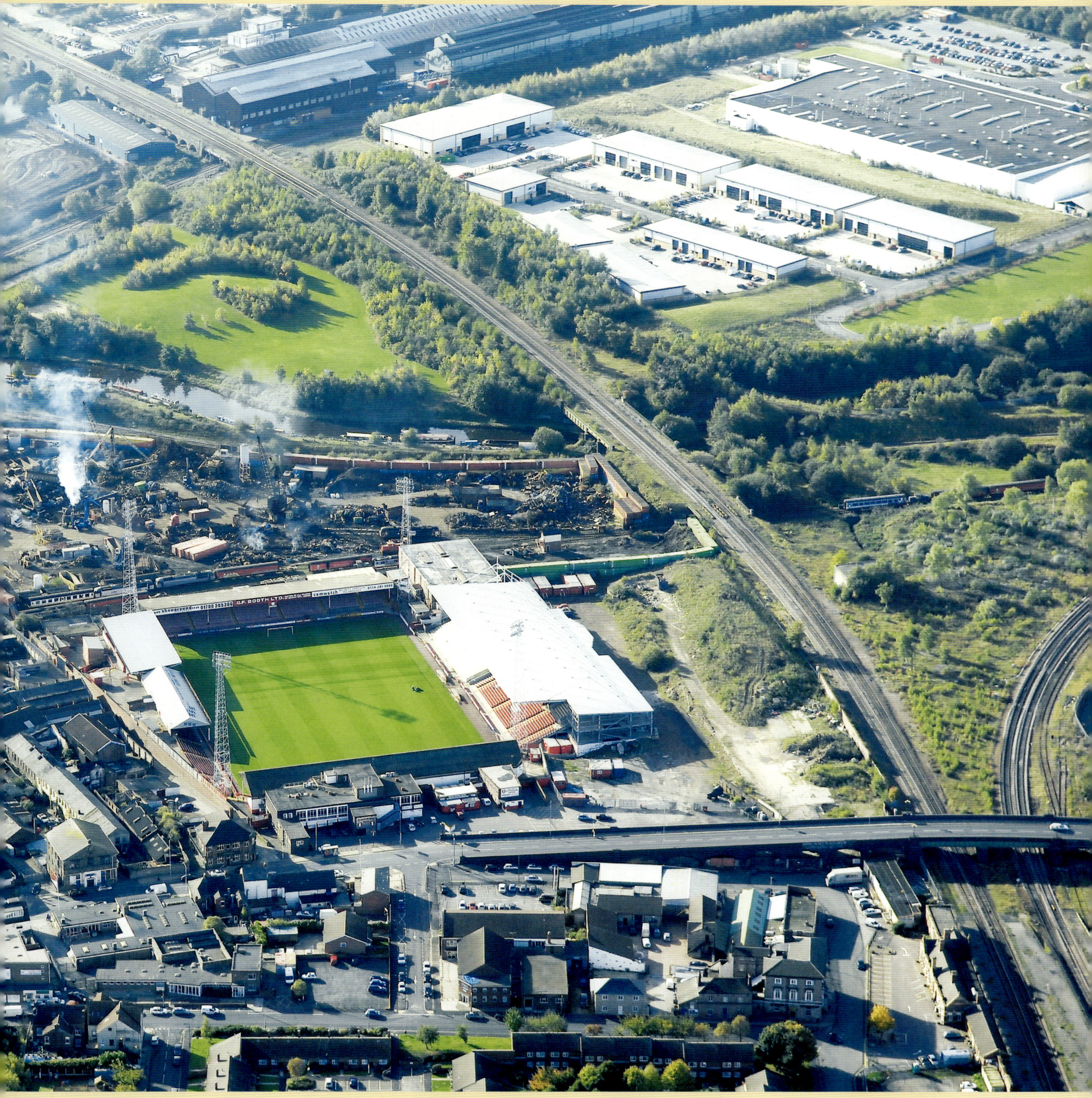
01700 305386
C.F. BOOTH LTD.
camwatch
0114 281 9999

SHEFFIELD UNITED

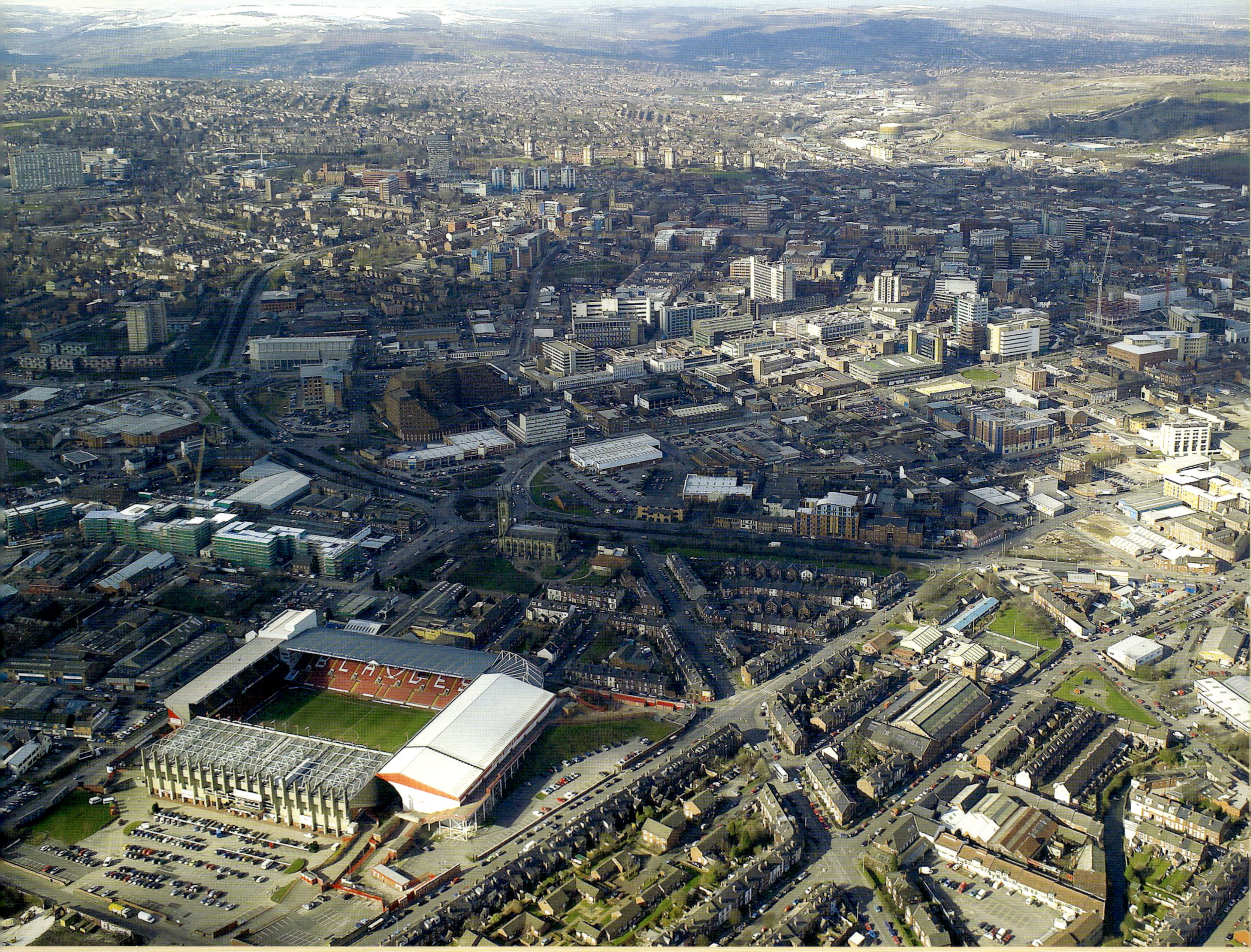

Bramall Lane was originally used as a cricket ground by Sheffield United Cricket Club from 1854. The ground also hosted various sporting activities; in 1874 an exhibition baseball match was played at Bramall Lane and bowls, lacrosse, cycling, tennis and athletics were also played there. Football was first played at the ground in 1862 when Hallam FC took on Sheffield FC, the world's oldest football club. It was not until 1889 that Sheffield United Football Club formed. Success was rapid; in 1892 they were elected to the Second Division, earning promotion just a year later and winning their only League championship in 1898. Two stands were built at this time, at the Shoreham Street End and on John Street. Glaswegian engineers were behind the 1902 design of the John Street Stand, replacing the earlier one that had been gutted by fire. The Blades won the FA Cup that season for the second time in their history. Just before the First World War terracing was extended along the Bramall Lane End, known to fans as the Kop. A roof was added in 1935 and just a year later

Above and right: Bramall Lane, the home of Sheffield United, is one of the oldest grounds in the English football league. Located close to the heart of Sheffield's bustling city centre, the ground is just a 10-minute walk from the main railway station

Bramall Lane notched up its highest attendance ever, with 68,287 fans cramming in to see the Blades take on Leeds United, many of whom sat on the new roof. Bramall Lane was bombed 10 times during WWII, damaging the John Street Stand, the Kop roof and the pitch. It took until 1954 to replace the John Street Stand. The South Stand opened in 1975, at a cost of £1m. The ground had a capacity of 49,000, yet the club's fortunes were faltering.

By 1981, the Blades were in the Fourth Division with gates of fewer than 15,000. The 1990s saw a new owner and further development of the ground. The John Street Stand was demolished in 1994 and a new stand opened in 1996. Two of the ground's corners have been completed bringing the capacity to 32,609. There are plans to build a leisure complex behind the South Stand and to fill in the corner between this stand and the Kop.

Ground: **Bramall Lane**

Address: Bramall Lane, Sheffield S2 4SU

Main tel: 0871 222 1899

Box office: 0871 222 1899

Website: www.sufc.co.uk

Capacity: 32,609

Home colours: red and white striped shirts, black shorts, red socks

Club nickname: the Blades

Pitch dimensions: 103m x 66m (112 x 72 yards)

Founded: 1889

Record attendance: 68,287 vs Leeds United, February 15 1936

Most prolific scorer: Harry Johnson (205)

Record win: 10-0 vs Port Vale, December 10, 1892

Record defeat: 0-13 vs Bolton Wanderers, February 1 1890

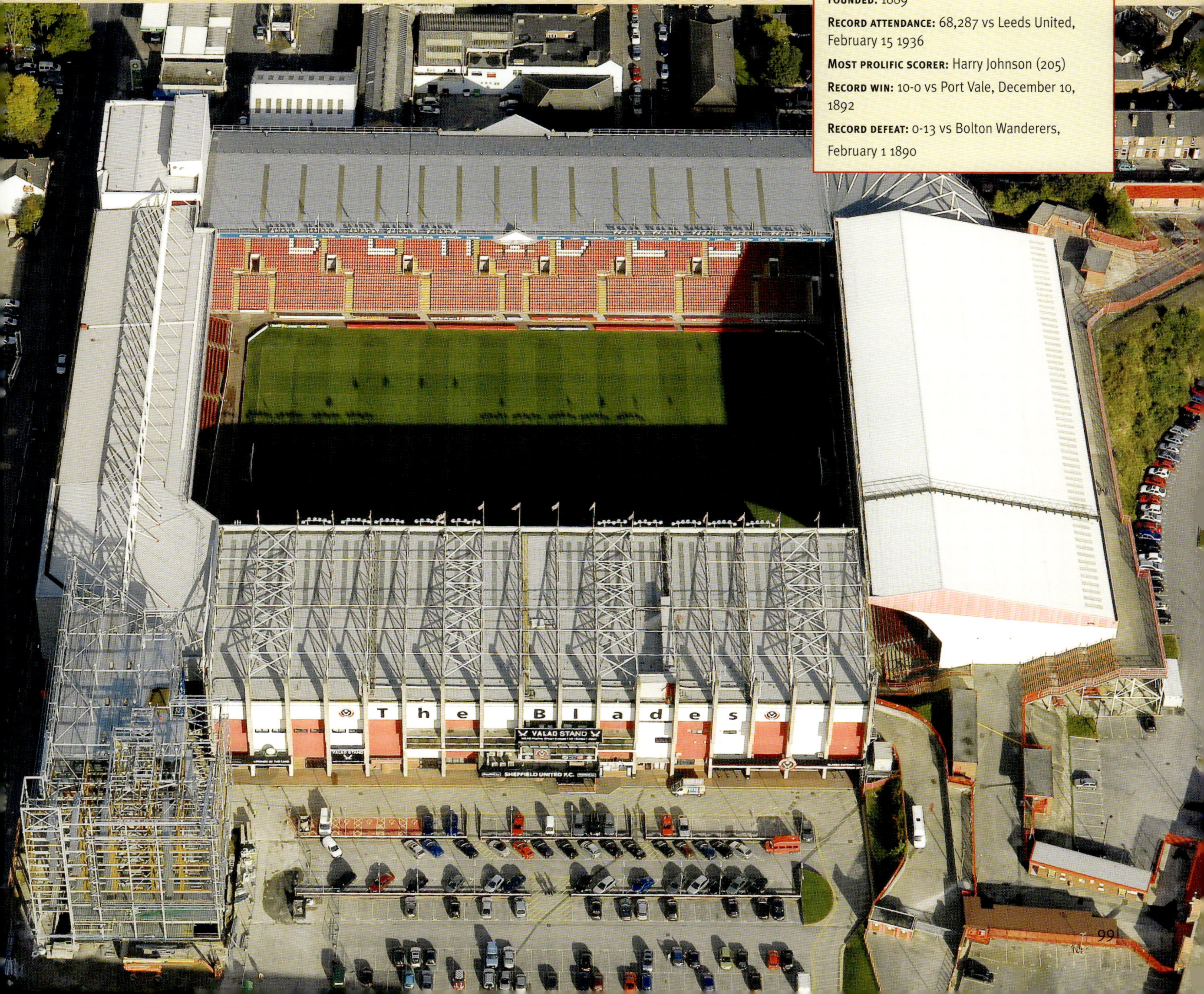

Sheffield Wednesday

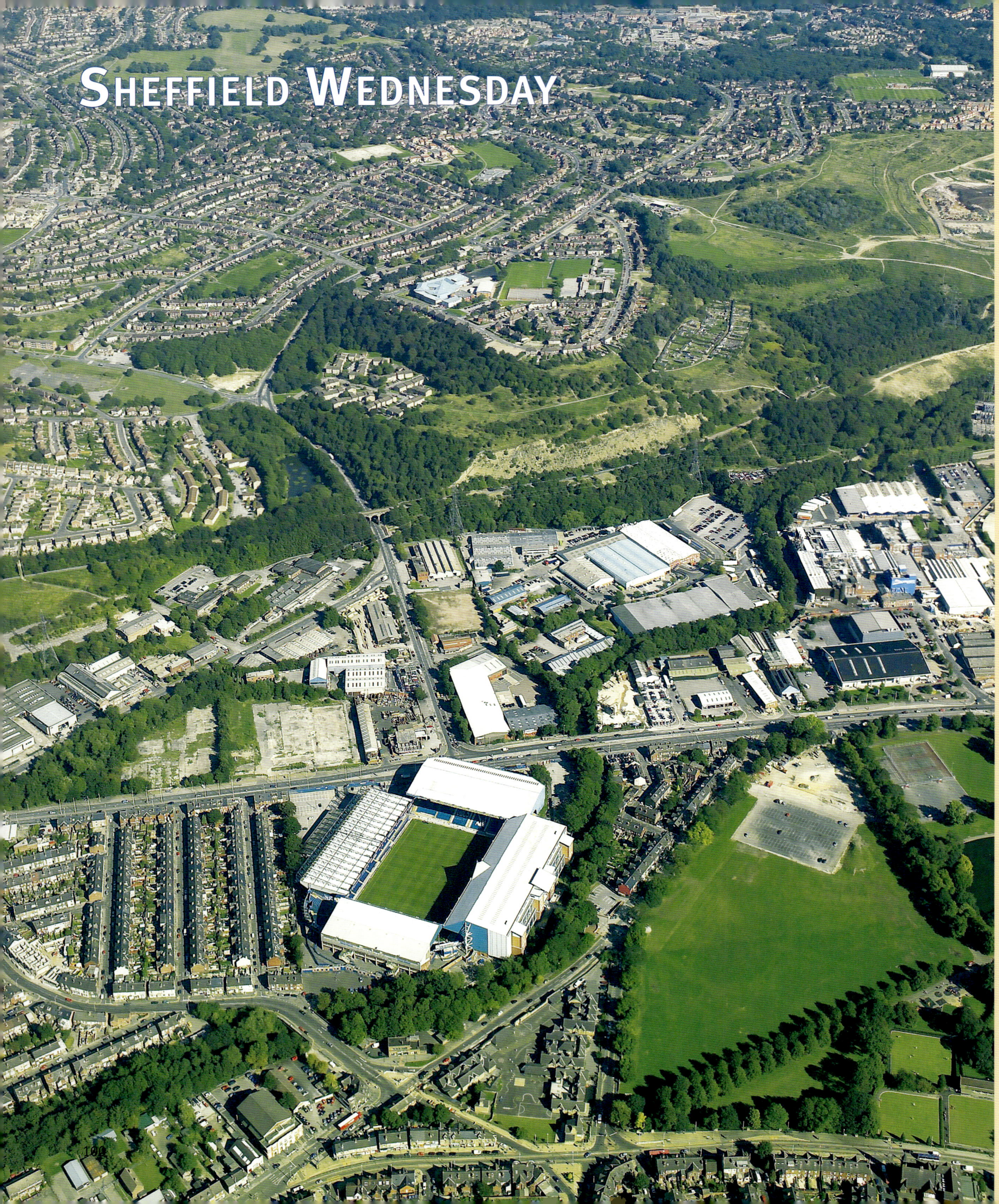

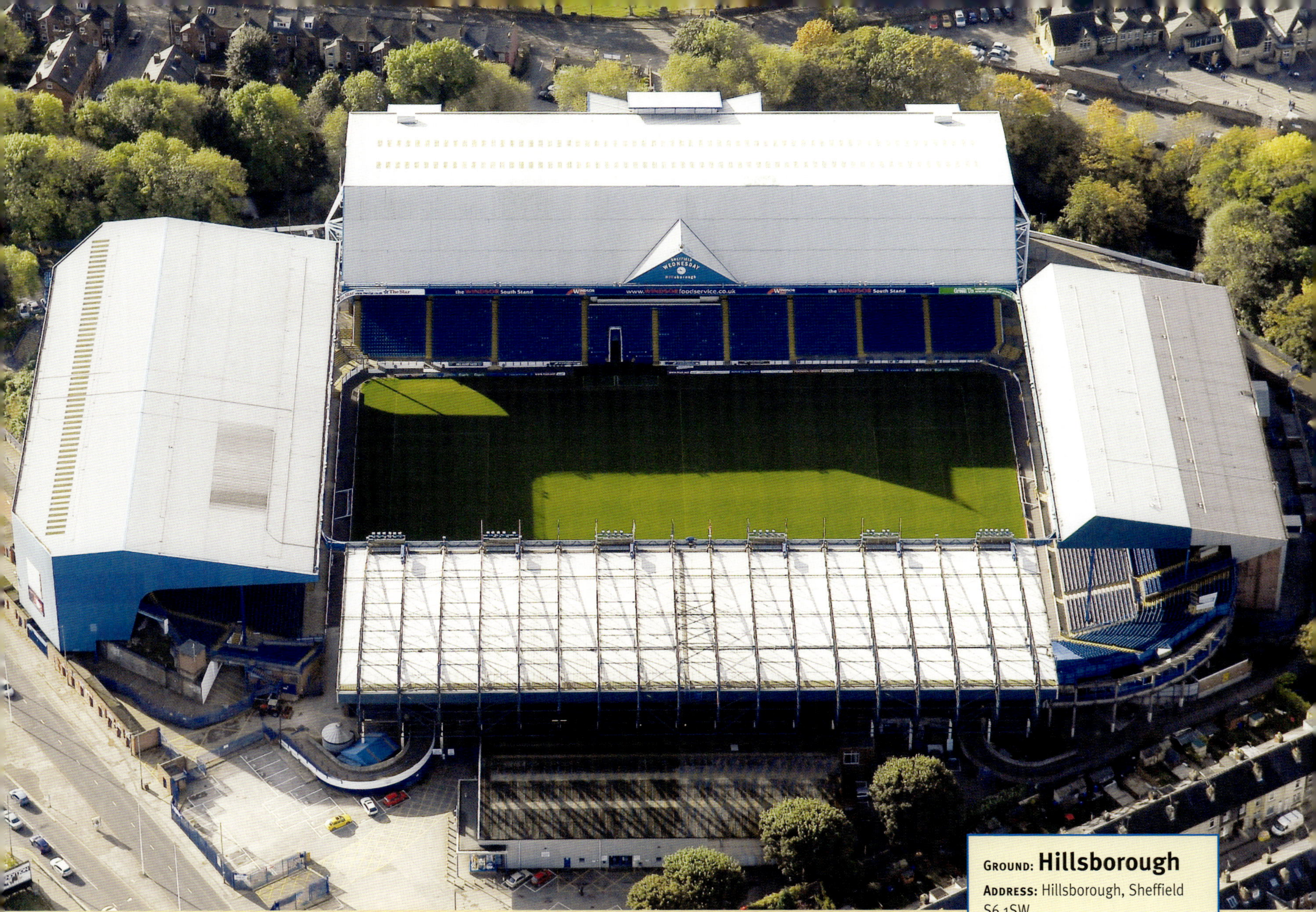

Ground: **Hillsborough**

Address: Hillsborough, Sheffield S6 1SW

Main tel: 0870 999 1867

Box office: 0871 230 1867

Website: www.swfc.co.uk

Capacity: 39,814

Home colours: blue and white striped shirts, black shorts, black socks

Club nickname: the Owls

Pitch dimensions: 105m x 69m (115 x 75 yards)

Founded: 1867

Record attendance: 72,841 vs Manchester City, February 17 1934

Most prolific scorer: Andy Wilson (199)

Record win: 12-0 vs Halliwell, January 17 1891

Record defeat: 0-10 vs Aston Villa, October 5 1912

Sheffield Wednesday was established in 1867 as the football playing section of Wednesday Cricket Club. The club played at various grounds before severing ties with the cricket club and moving to Olive Grove in 1887. In 1892 the club joined the League and in 1896 won the FA Cup. This success financed the building of the Main Stand. The lease of the ground ended in 1898 and Wednesday found themselves homeless. The supporters were invited to help choose a new ground. None of the selected grounds were suitable and in 1899 the club moved to a ground in Owlerton bringing with them the Main Stand from the Olive Grove. The new ground seemed to bring the club good fortune; in 1903 and 1904 they won the League title and in 1907 won the FA Cup for a second time. It was not until 1913 that further ground development took place, with the Spion Kop and the South Stand being built. The club changed the ground's name to Hillsborough in 1914 and when the Kop finally opened later that year the capacity was 50,000. In 1927 the Leppings Lane End was expanded and by 1934 a record 72,841 fans packed in to see the Owls take on Manchester City. A cantilevered grandstand, the North Stand, capable of seating 9,882 fans, replaced the Olive Grove Stand in 1961. Hillsborough was selected as a venue for some of the games in the 1966 World Cup, so Wednesday built the new West Stand and added seats to the South Stand paddock. On April 15 1989 the ground saw its darkest day when 96 Liverpool fans were crushed to death in the Leppings Lane End. This event changed the future of British football and the resulting Taylor report required all top clubs in England, Wales and Scotland to become all-seater by the start of the 1994 season. The Owls spent £10m on ground improvements, adding seats to the South Stand, the lower tier of the West Stand and the Kop. The ground can now seat 39,814 spectators.

SOUTHAMPTON

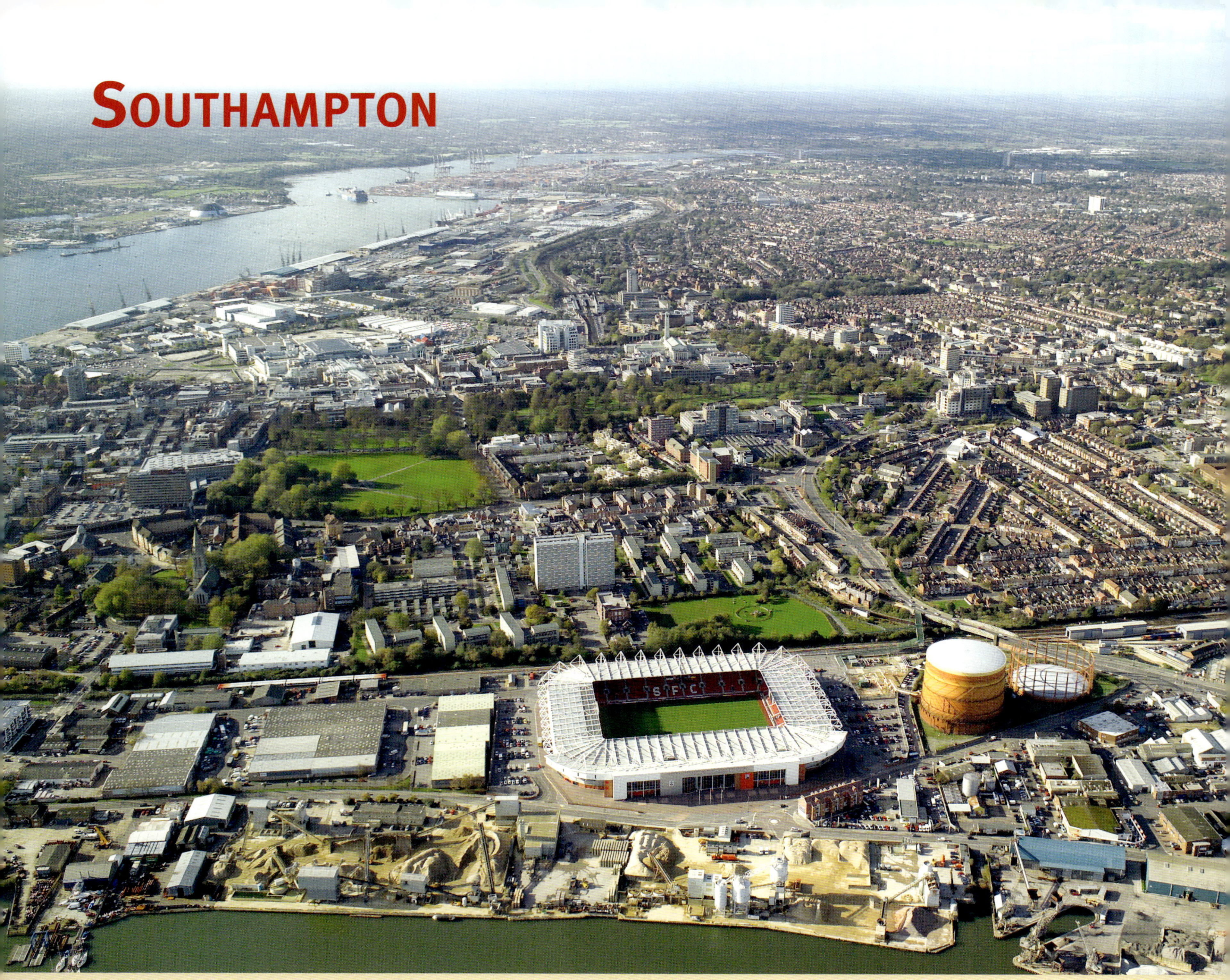

Southampton FC was founded in 1885. Due to their ties with the local St Mary's church, the club was originally called Southampton St Mary's FC. The team played their first games on the site of the County Bowling Club. A year after formation, the club moved to the Antelope Cricket Ground, previously home to Hampshire County Cricket Club. The team's success meant that the club became professional in 1894. Two years later they changed their name to Southampton FC and in 1898 moved to The Dell. Fortune shone on the Saints and a local fish merchant George Thomas funded the development of The Dell. Both ends were terraced and stands were erected on the east and west sides. The club's good fortune off the pitch was not matched by results on the pitch and by 1906 soaring debts meant that there was a threat of having to leave The Dell. The Saints held on and after two years in the Second Division they won promotion to the First in 1922. This success meant they were able to expand the ground, and they began with an £8,000 extension of the East Stand. In 1927 the West Stand was torn down and a new one was erected in 1928. The late 1940s brought high attendances to The Dell and three concrete platforms known as the chocolate boxes were fixed above the Milton Road End Terrace. Little changed at The Dell for the following 30 years. During that time the Saints won promotion to the top flight and attracted their record gate of 31,044 in a League game against Manchester United. The Taylor report brought the ground's capacity down to 15,352, so the club began to look for a site for a larger stadium elsewhere. The late 1990s saw these plans become a reality, and in August 2001 the new £32m all-seater St Mary's Stadium was opened on the site of a former gasworks. The totally enclosed stadium has one tier all the way round, and a much healthier capacity of 32,689.

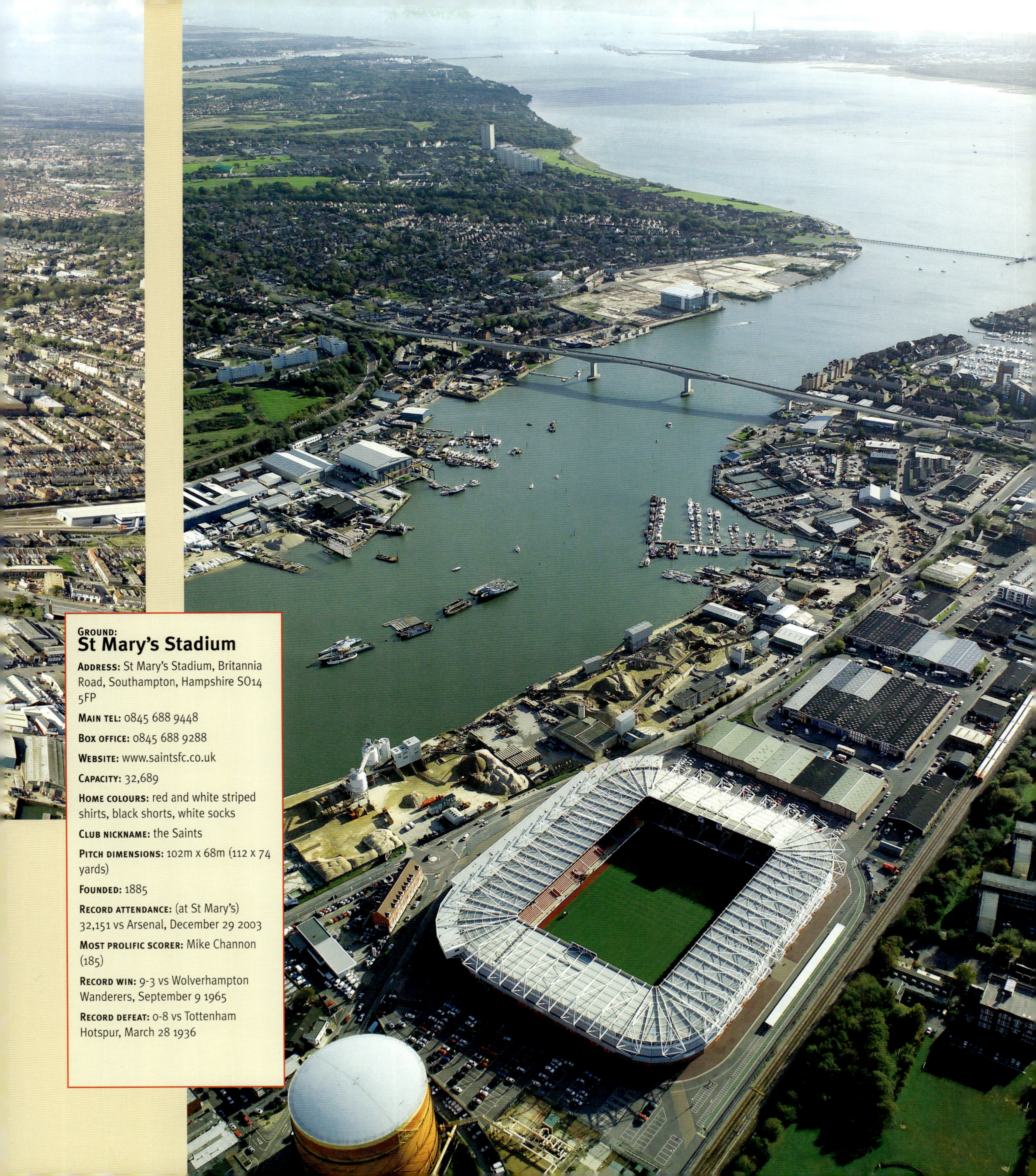

GROUND:
St Mary's Stadium

ADDRESS: St Mary's Stadium, Britannia Road, Southampton, Hampshire SO14 5FP

MAIN TEL: 0845 688 9448

BOX OFFICE: 0845 688 9288

WEBSITE: www.saintsfc.co.uk

CAPACITY: 32,689

HOME COLOURS: red and white striped shirts, black shorts, white socks

CLUB NICKNAME: the Saints

PITCH DIMENSIONS: 102m x 68m (112 x 74 yards)

FOUNDED: 1885

RECORD ATTENDANCE: (at St Mary's) 32,151 vs Arsenal, December 29 2003

MOST PROLIFIC SCORER: Mike Channon (185)

RECORD WIN: 9-3 vs Wolverhampton Wanderers, September 9 1965

RECORD DEFEAT: 0-8 vs Tottenham Hotspur, March 28 1936

Stockport County

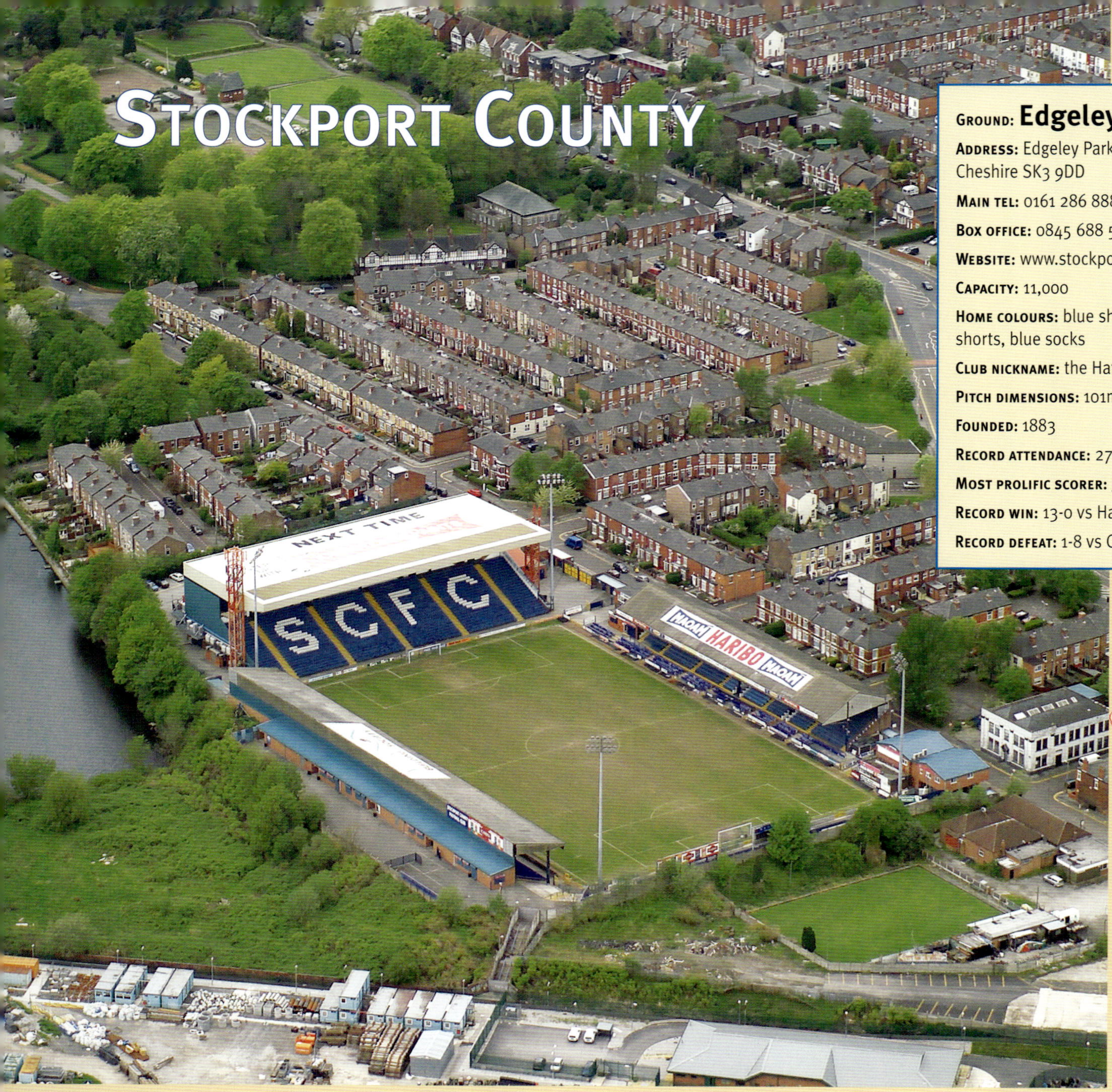

Ground: **Edgeley Park**

Address: Edgeley Park, Hardcastle Road, Edgeley, Stockport, Cheshire SK3 9DD

Main tel: 0161 286 8888

Box office: 0845 688 5799

Website: www.stockportcounty.com

Capacity: 11,000

Home colours: blue shirts with vertical white chest band, blue shorts, blue socks

Club nickname: the Hatters

Pitch dimensions: 101m x 65m (111 x 71 yards)

Founded: 1883

Record attendance: 27,833 vs Liverpool, February 11 1950

Most prolific scorer: Jack Connor (132)

Record win: 13-0 vs Halifax Town, January 6 1934

Record defeat: 1-8 vs Chesterfield, April 19 1902

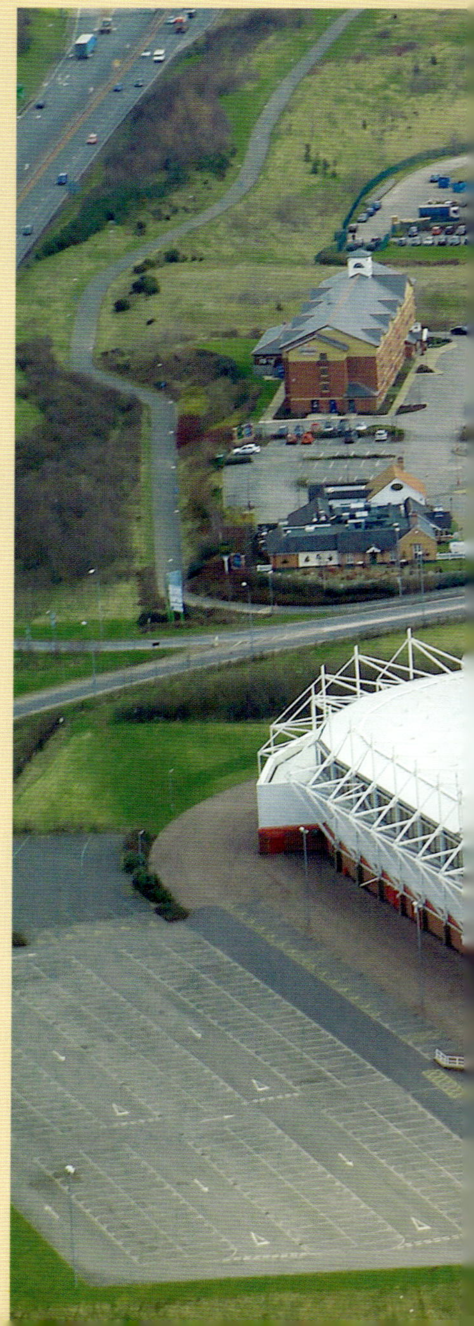

Stockport County formed in 1883 under the name of Heaton Norris Rovers. The club played at several grounds before moving to Edgeley Park in 1902; during this time they also merged with local rivals Heaton Norris and changed their name to Stockport County. Edgeley Park was originally built as a rugby ground and Stockport Rugby Club still played there when the Hatters moved in, although the rugby club closed down a year later. In 1903 a cover was added to the south side of the ground. Development was slow and it was a further 10 years before the Main Stand was built. A cover was erected at the west end and an uncovered stand with seats was built at the east end during the 1920s. In 1934 County notched up their highest home win ever, 13-0, in a game against Halifax Town. Fire destroyed the Main Stand in 1935, and this was replaced with a new stand a year later. After the Second World War the cover over the south edge was extended and Edgeley Park entertained its largest crowd ever, 27,833 for a game against Liverpool in the FA Cup. The 1970s and 1980s saw sweeping changes at Edgeley Park owing to new safety regulations. In 1978 the rear of the South Terrace was sealed off and the West Stand was demolished a few years later, the Railway (east) End had its height reduced and the standing area of the Main Stand was closed down. All of these safety measures had a major impact on the capacity at Edgeley Park. At the start of the 1990s it was down to 6,000 but things were about to change. The Hatters' new chairman Brendan Elwood invested in the ground, adding seats to the South Stand and building a new stand at the west end of the ground, bringing capacity up to 11,000.

Stoke City

Stoke City can trace their history back to 1863. The club was formed from Stoke Ramblers and after merging with the Stoke Victoria Athletic Club in 1878 they took over their home, the Athletic Ground, and changed their name to Stoke. They moved to the Victoria Ground in 1883; it had a running track around the edge, one stand on the west side and banking around the other three sides. Before the turn of the century a pavilion was built next to the stand and in 1904 a cover was added to the banking opposite. In 1922 the original stand was replaced with a new main stand. Three years later Stoke FC changed its name to Stoke City FC. By 1930 the running track was dug up so the banking at the south end of the ground could be extended to cope with rising crowds. The covered banking on the east side of the pitch was replaced by a new 5,000-seater stand in 1936 at a time when the Potters boasted one of football's all-time greats, Stanley Matthews. A year later the Victoria Ground saw its highest ever attendance of 51,380 for a game against Arsenal. The 1930s also saw the terraces concreted and the pitch shifted southwards. It was another 30 years before any further significant development took place. In 1963 the Main Stand was replaced for the second time and the roof was replaced on the Butler Street Stand (East Stand) after a gale blew it off. A new two-tiered stand was built on the site of the North Terrace in 1979. The Potters opted to sell the Victoria Ground in 1997 and moved to the Britannia Stadium, which was built on the site of a former colliery and ironworks. The new stadium has one stand curving round the north and east side and two separate stands on the south and west sides. It has a capacity of 28,384.

Ground: Britannia Stadium

Address: Britannia Stadium, Stanley Matthews Way, Stoke-on-Trent ST4 4EG

Main tel: 0871 663 2008

Box office: 0871 663 2007

Website: www.stokecityfc.com

Capacity: 28,384

Home colours: red and white striped shirts, white shorts, red and white hooped socks

Club nickname: the Potters

Pitch dimensions: 105m x 69m (115 x 75 yards)

Founded: 1863

Record attendance: (at Britannia Stadium) 28,218 vs Everton, January 5 2002

Most prolific scorer: Freddie Steel (142)

Record win: 10-3 vs West Bromwich Albion, February 4 1937

Record defeat: 0-10 vs Preston North End, September 14 1889

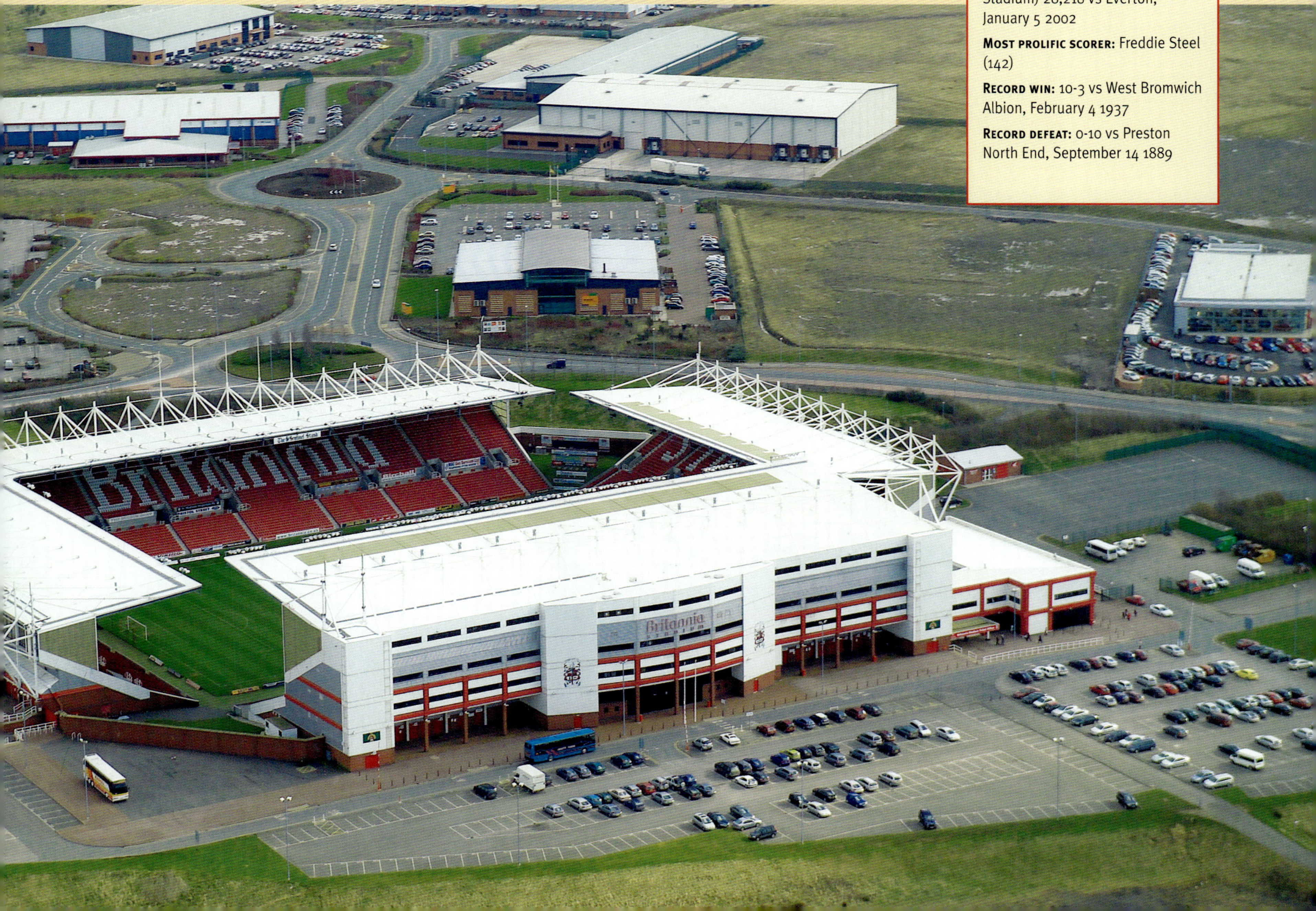

Sunderland

Sunderland AFC was formed in 1879 by Glaswegian teacher Jimmy Allen. They played their first games at Blue House field, close to Allen's school. The club moved four more times before settling, temporarily, at Newcastle Road, the district's best ground at the time. The new ground was already enclosed on three sides, so the club only had to build one further stand on the east side to complete the work. In 1888 the legendary Tom Watson took over as manager at Newcastle Road. He brought in new players and, after joining the League in 1890, they won three successive championships. The team's success meant increasing support and it was not long before the club had to look for a new ground. In 1898 the club moved to Roker Park, where it would stay for 99 years. During the summer two stands were built – the Grandstand and the Clock Stand; the other two ends were left open. In 1908 the capacity of Roker Park was 50,000. The 1920s saw further development; in 1925 the Fulwell End was expanded bringing capacity up to 60,000 and the Main Stand was erected in 1929. March 8 1933 saw a record 75,118 fans cram into Roker Park to see Sunderland take on Derby County in the FA Cup. The Clock Stand was replaced in 1936, and no further development took place until after the war. Roker Park was selected as a venue to stage games during the 1966 World Cup. This led to the pitch being expanded by three yards while seats were added in the Clock Stand and the Fulwell End was covered. The next major changes came in the 1990s when, following the Taylor report, the club had to decide whether to redevelop or relocate. After a lengthy battle with the nearby Nissan car plant, a new site was found in 1996, on the site of the former Monkwearmouth Colliery. The Stadium of Light opened in 1997, with three two-tier stands on the north, south and east sides linking to the Main Stand on the west. The capacity was expanded to 49,000 in 2001 when the Carling (North) Stand and north-west corner were expanded to three tiers.

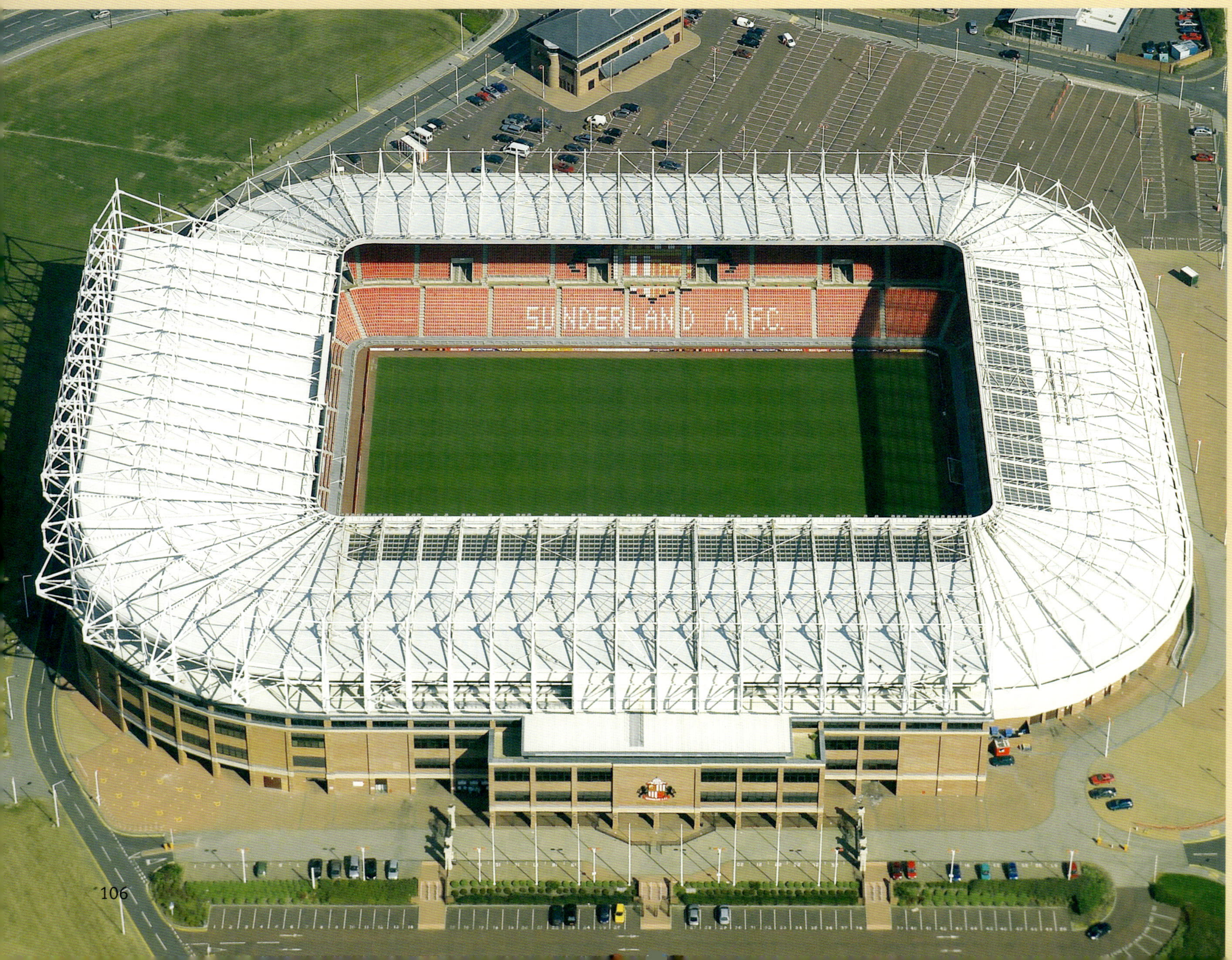

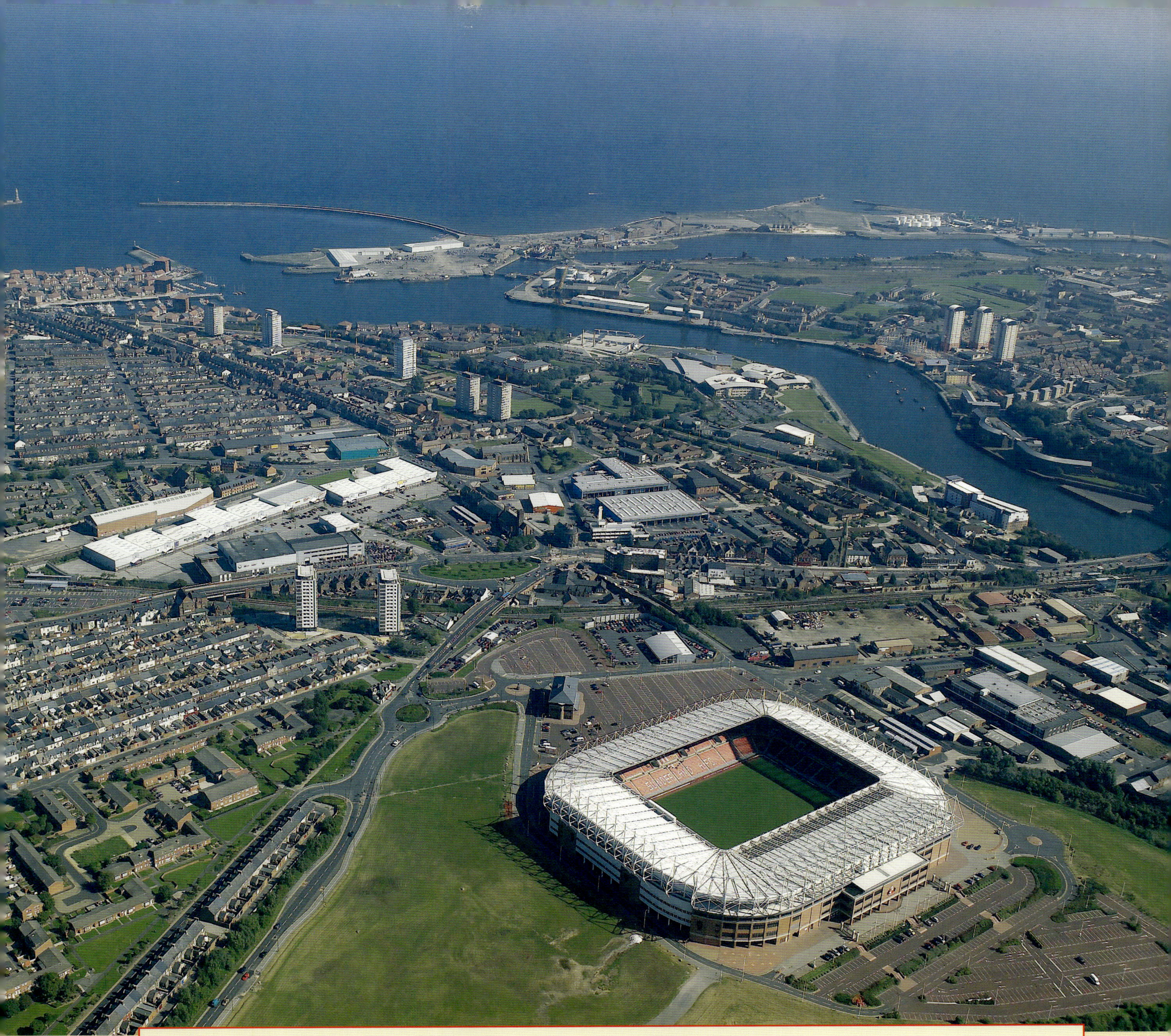

Ground: **Sunderland Stadium of Light**
Address: The Sunderland Stadium of Light, Sunderland SR5 1SU
Main tel: 0191 551 5000
Box office: 0845 671 1973
Website: www.safc.com
Capacity: 49,000
Home colours: red and white striped shirts, black shorts, black socks with a red trim

Club nickname: the Black Cats
Pitch dimensions: 105m x 68m (115 x 74 yards)
Founded: 1879
Record attendance: (at the Stadium of Light) 48,353 vs Liverpool, April 13 2002
Most prolific scorer: Charlie Buchan (209)
Record win: 11-0 vs Fairfield, February 2 1895
Record defeat: 0-8 vs West Ham United, October 19 1968

Swansea City

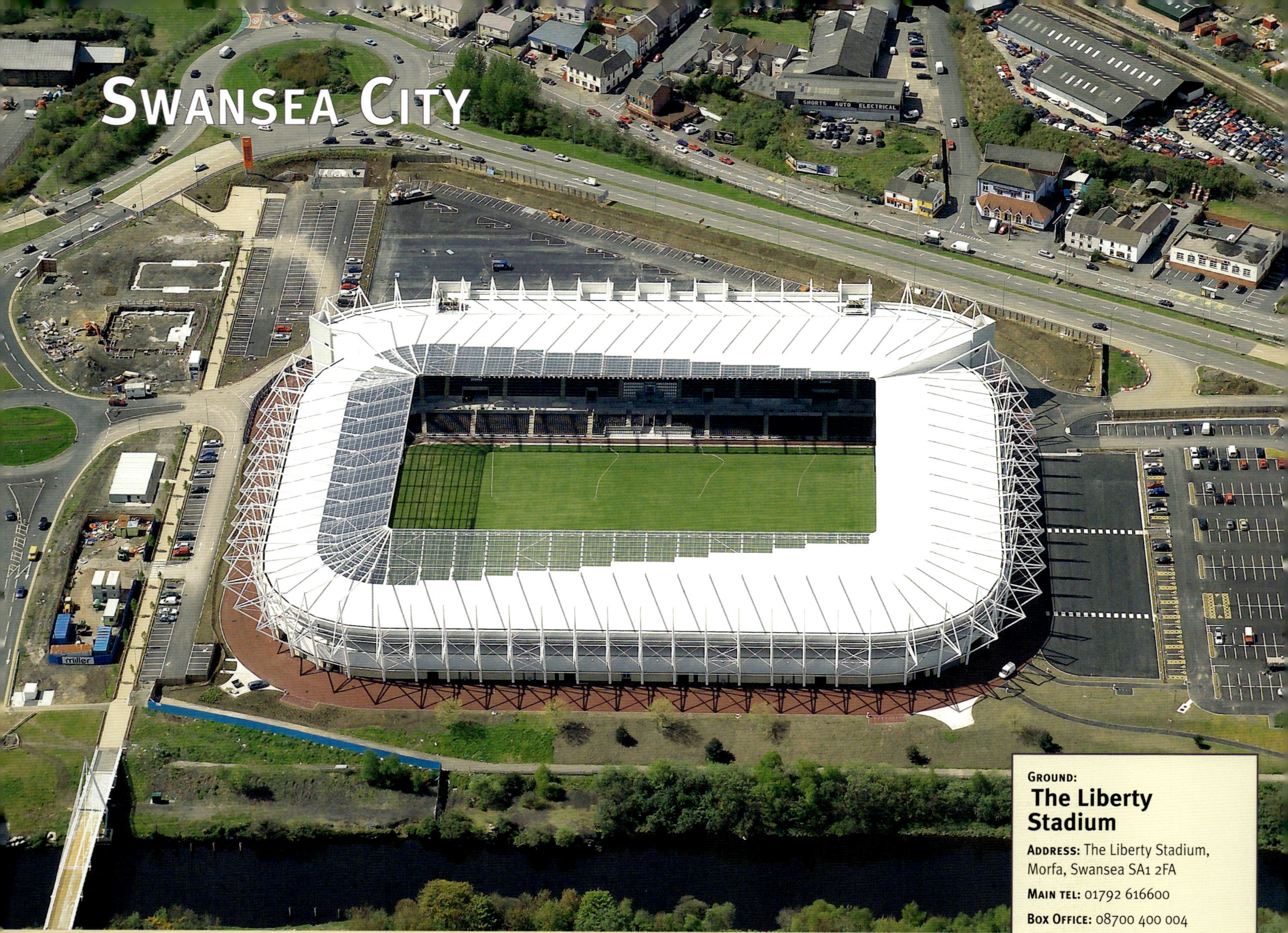

Swansea Town FC formed in 1912. Their first ground, The Vetch Field, had open banking on all four sides. A year later they opened the ground's first stand along the south edge of the pitch. After joining the Football League in 1920, Swansea Town built a small stand at the south-west corner of the pitch. Five years later they extended the banking along the north side of the ground and in 1927 they erected a two-tiered stand at the west end of the pitch. The Vetch Field escaped damage during the Second World War and it was not developed further until the 1950s. In 1959 a roof was erected over the terrace along the north side of the pitch, paid for by the Swans' supporters club. Support reached a record high in the 1960s when, in 1968, Swansea took on Arsenal in the FA Cup and attracted a crowd of 32,796. In 1970 the club changed its name from Swansea Town to Swansea City. The early 1970s saw the team's performances on the pitch falter and the club slump out of the League for a short time. Once they rejoined, their fortunes took a turn for the better. Under manager John Toshack (who was appointed in 1978), the Swans leapt up the divisions and found themselves in the First Division in just three seasons. The club's new status highlighted the need for development at The Vetch Field and so the club built a two-tiered stand at the east end of the ground. The top tier of the West Stand was closed for safety reasons in 1990 and was later removed.

At the start of the 2005/2006 season, Swansea City moved to the Liberty Stadium, a brand new, state-of the-art sports facility which they share with the regional rugby team, the Ospreys.

Above: The Liberty Stadium opened for the start of the 2005-06 season, signalling the end of the old Vetch Field site, right.

Ground:
The Liberty Stadium

Address: The Liberty Stadium, Morfa, Swansea SA1 2FA

Main tel: 01792 616600

Box Office: 08700 400 004

Website: www.swanseacity.net

Capacity: 20,500

Home colours: white shirts, white shorts, white socks

Club nickname: the Swans or Jacks

Pitch dimensions: 101m x 68m (110 x 74 yards)

Founded: 1912

Record attendance: (at The Liberty Stadium) 19,288 vs Yeovil Town, November 18 2005

Most prolific scorer: Ivor Allchurch (166)

Record win: 8-0 vs Hartlepool United, April 1 1978

Record defeat: 0-8 vs Liverpool, January 9 1990

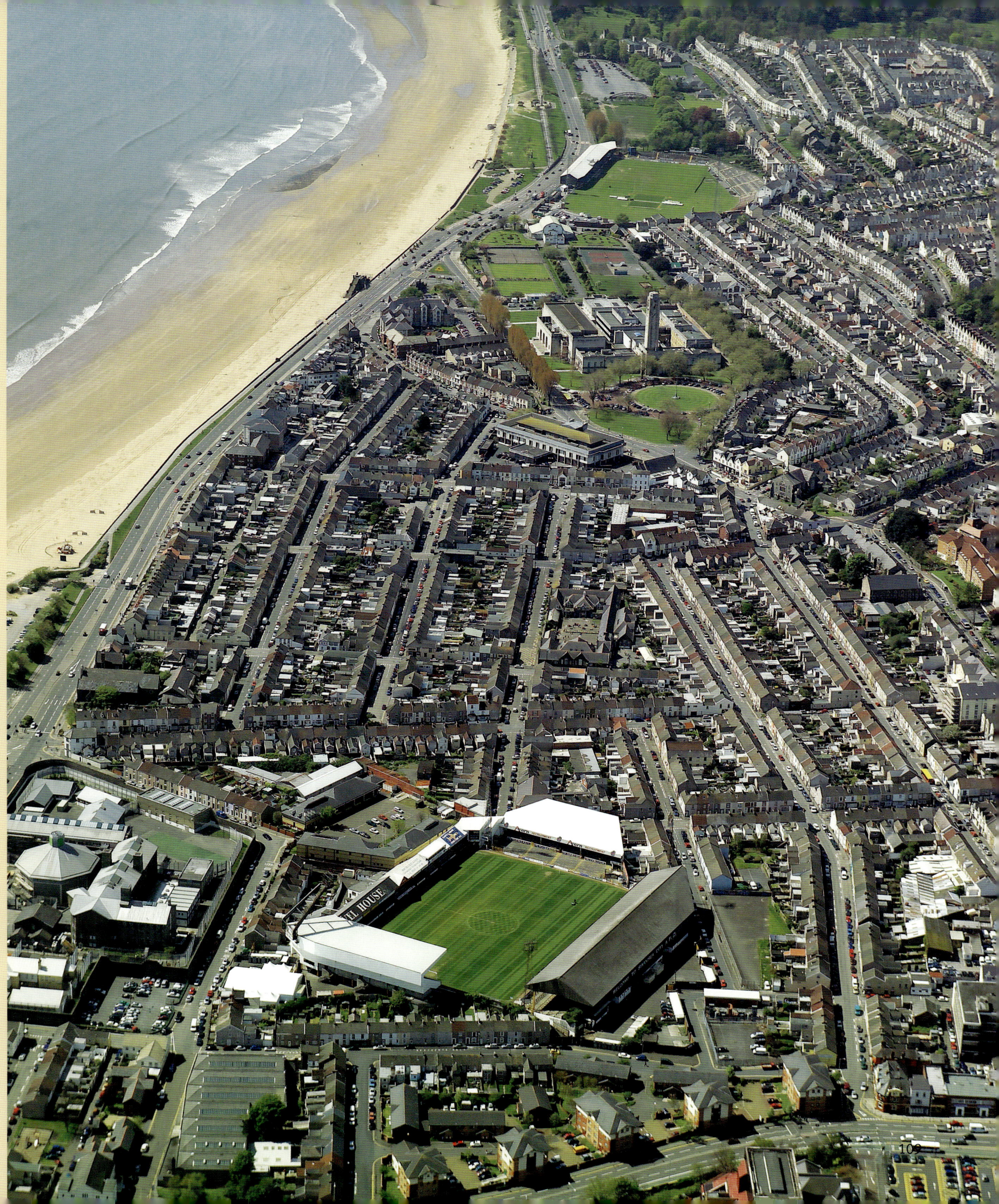
EL HOUSE

Swindon Town

Swindon Town formed in 1881 as part of the Spartans Cricket Club. Their early games were played at various venues, including the Croft, where they stayed for 10 years. They moved to the County Ground in 1894 after joining the Southern League. At the time, the County Ground had a stand along the north side of the pitch, which was extended to run the length of the pitch in 1911. Terracing was laid in 1908 and covers were added to the south and western edges in the 1930s. The County Ground was used to house prisoners of war during the Second World War. In 1958 the Shrivenham Road covered terrace (on the south side) was replaced by a new stand, which the club bought from the Aldershot Military Tattoo. Known as the Tattoo Stand, it was a two-tiered structure with seats on the upper tier and terracing below. It was the 1970s before the County Ground underwent any further development. The new North Stand was installed in 1971 with 5,300 seats one year before the County Ground recorded its highest ever attendance of 32,000 when the Robins took on Arsenal in the FA Cup. During the 1980s the new safety regulations saw capacity at the County Ground drop significantly. The upper tier of the Tattoo Stand was closed, as it was a predominantly wooden structure. The terraces also had to be resurfaced to guarantee safety. In 1990 the club's chairman was sent to prison for financial irregularities and despite winning promotion to the First Division this saw the club demoted back to the Second Division. After the dust had settled, plans were made to leave the County Ground. However, these did not come to fruition and instead the club turned its attention to redeveloping the ground. Seats were added to the front of the Main Stand and to both ends and a new stand was built along the south side of the pitch.

Ground: **County Ground**
Address: County Ground, Swindon, Wiltshire SN1 2ED
Main tel: 0871 423 6433
Box office: 0871 223 2300
Website: www.swindontownfc.co.uk
Capacity: 15,728
Home colours: red shirts, red shorts, red socks
Club nickname: the Robins
Pitch dimensions: 101m x 69m (110 x 75 yards)
Founded: 1881
Record attendance: 32,000 vs Arsenal, January 15 1972
Most prolific scorer: Harry Morris (216)
Record win: 9-1 vs Luton Town, August 28 1920
Record defeat: 1-10 vs Manchester City, January 25 1930

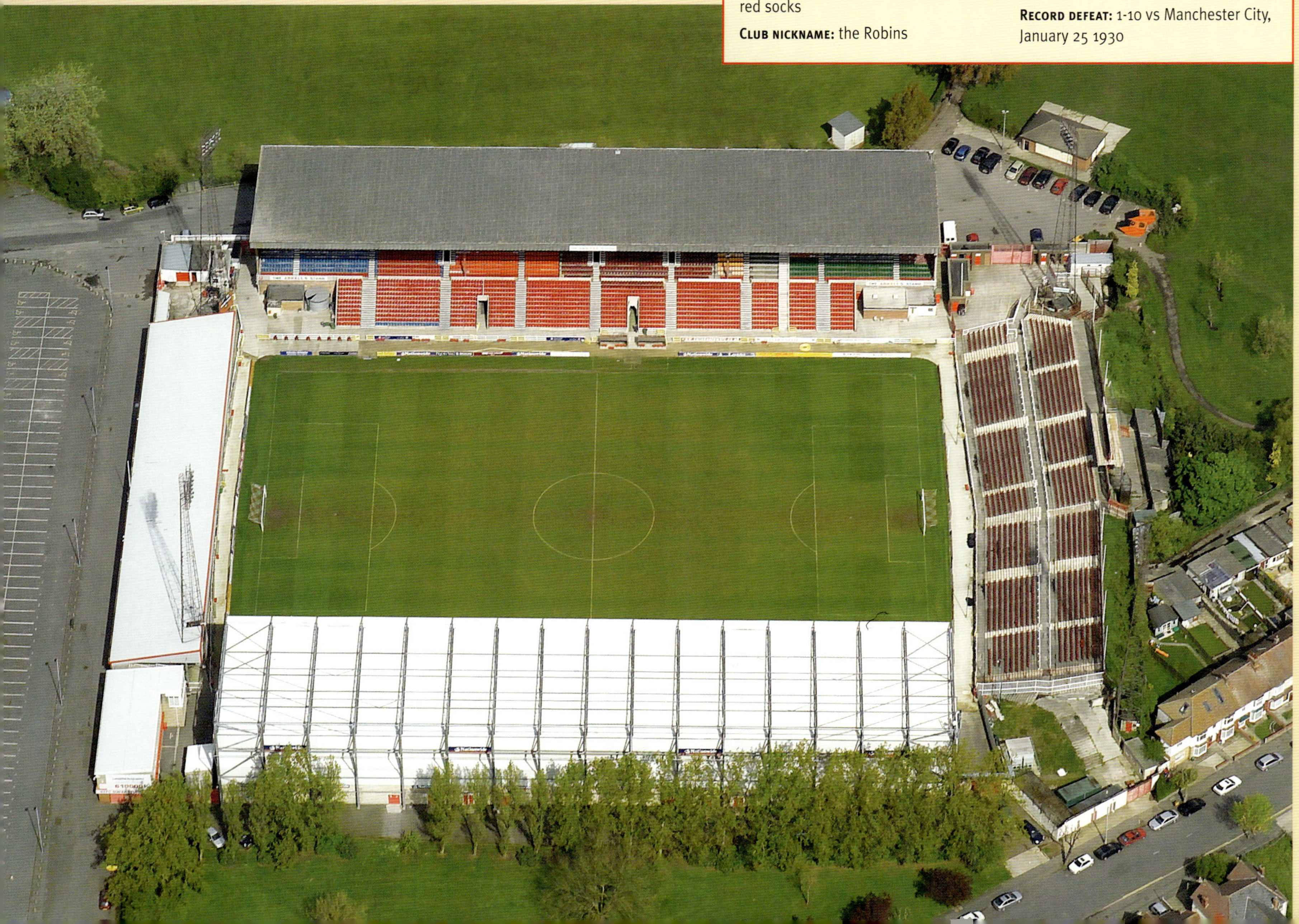

TORQUAY UNITED

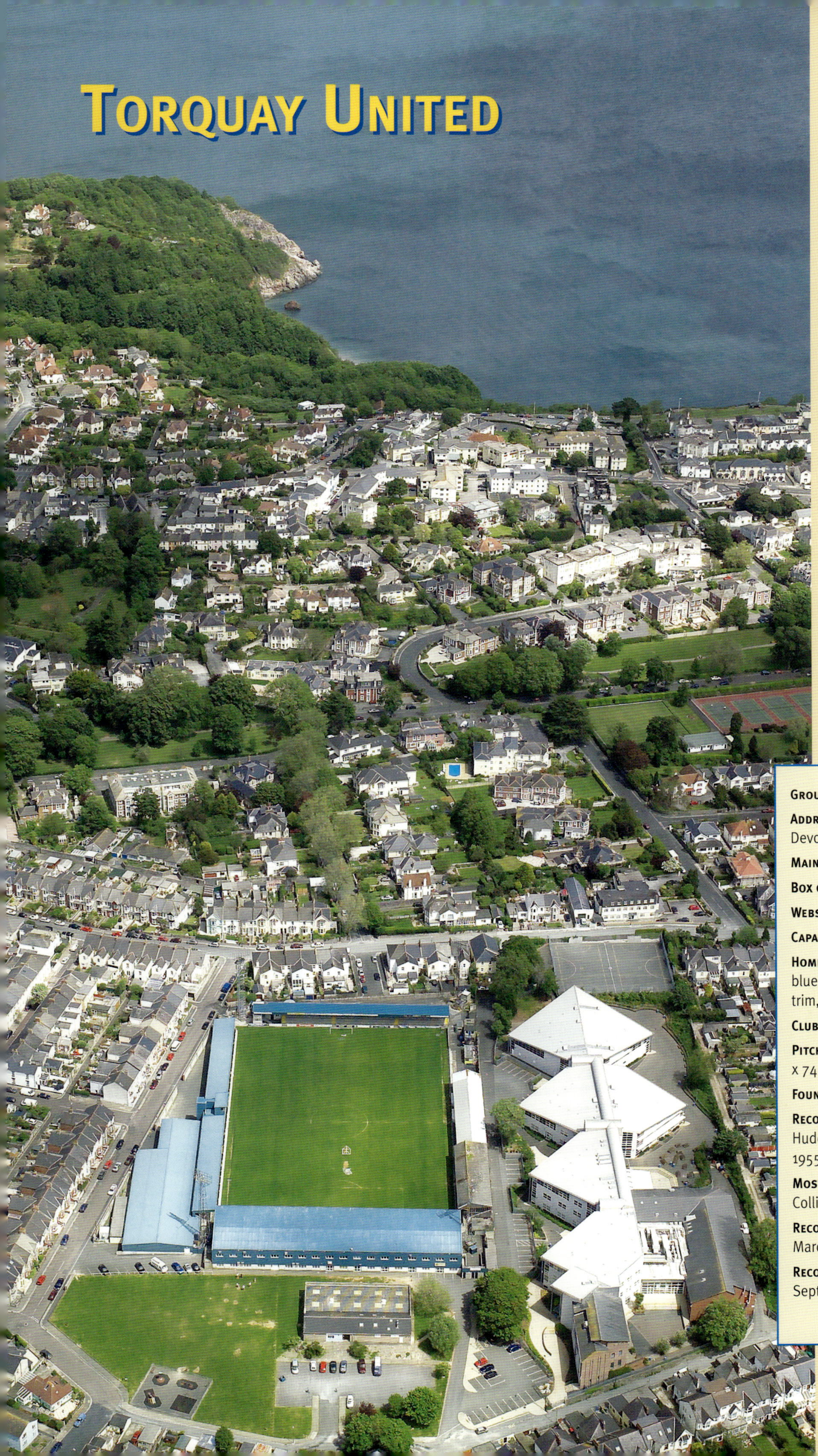

Torquay United formed in 1898 and played their early games at the Recreation Ground. At the time, Plainmoor was used by Torquay Athletic Rugby Union FC. In 1905 Plainmoor was taken over by another local football club, Ellacombe. Eventually, Ellacombe and Torquay merged to form Torquay Town FC in 1910. Further changes came when Babbacombe FC, who also used Plainmoor as a home ground, merged with the team in 1921 and the name was changed back to Torquay United FC. In 1927 the Gulls joined the Football League. By then the club had installed a stand purchased from Buckfastleigh Racecourse along the east side of the ground. A cover was added to the terrace running along the south end of the pitch in 1933 but there were few improvements to Plainmoor until after the Second World War. In the early 1950s a cover was added to the terrace on the west side of the pitch (the Popular Side) in time for Plainmoor's highest ever attendance of 21,908 for an FA Cup match against Huddersfield Town in January 1955. This match helped to fund the extension of the Main Stand on the east side of the pitch. In the 1960s a new stand was built at the south end of the ground bringing capacity up to 22,000. A fire destroyed the Main Stand in 1985; this was rebuilt in 1986, but with a much reduced capacity. The club introduced an ID card scheme and for almost two seasons banned away fans completely. The 1990s saw a new stand built at the south end of the ground and a cover added to the west side. Capacity at Plainmoor is now up to 6,000 and the club hope to increase this by replacing the Main Stand.

GROUND: Plainmoor

ADDRESS: Plainmoor, Torquay, Devon TQ1 3PS

MAIN TEL: 01803 328 666

BOX OFFICE: 01803 328 666

WEBSITE: www.torquayunited.com

CAPACITY: 6,000

HOME COLOURS: yellow shirts with blue trim, blue shorts with yellow trim, yellow socks

CLUB NICKNAME: the Gulls

PITCH DIMENSIONS: 102m x 68m (112 x 74 yards)

FOUNDED: 1898

RECORD ATTENDANCE: 21,908 vs Huddersfield Town, January 29 1955

MOST PROLIFIC SCORER: Sammy Collins (204)

RECORD WIN: 9-0 vs Swindon Town, March 8 1952

RECORD DEFEAT: 2-10 vs Fulham, September 7 1931

Tottenham Hotspur

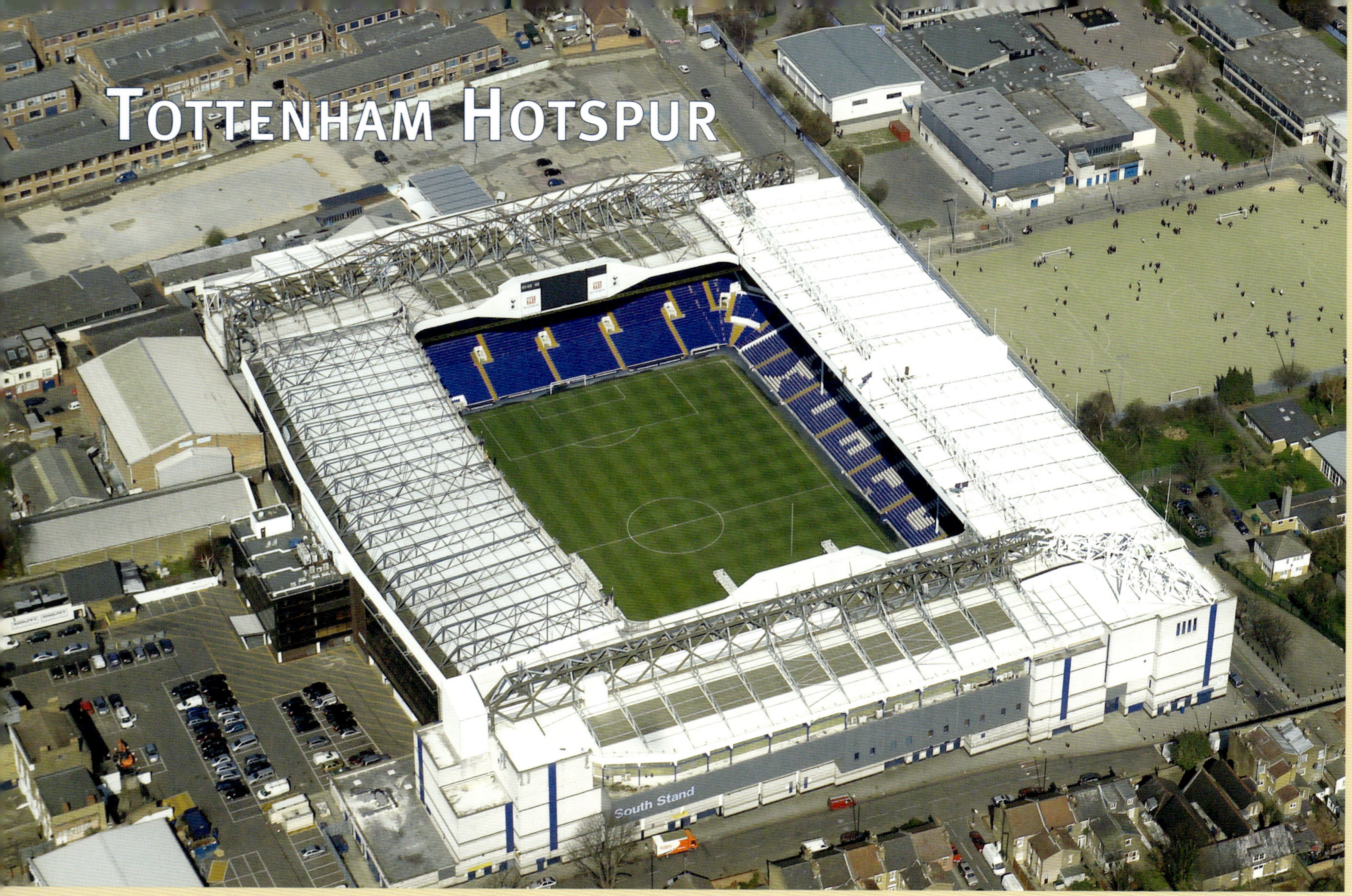

Tottenham Hotspur was formed by a group of cricketers in 1882. The team, then called Hotspur FC, first played games on Tottenham Marshes. By 1885 the club had added the prefix "Tottenham" and three years later moved to their first ground, Northumberland Park. In 1899 the club moved again to a ground owned by a local brewery then called the High Road Ground. In 1901, Spurs became the first non-League team since 1888 to win the FA Cup. The club's first major stand, the West Stand, was opened in 1909. The stand came complete with a mock-Tudor gable and a year later a copper cockerel perched on a ball was placed on the roof. In 1919 the ground adopted the name of the local station – White Hart Lane. Spurs won the FA Cup for the second time in 1921 and this funded the covering of the Paxton Road End and the Park Lane End. It was not until 1934 that the final terrace – the East Terrace – was built. The East Stand was a two-tier stand erected on top of the terracing, so that it resembled three tiers. This stand had a capacity of 24,000 and when Spurs took Sunderland on in the FA Cup in 1938 a record 75,038 fans looked on. The cockerel moved to the East Stand in 1958 in time to see the club go through their most successful era, winning the double in 1961, the FA Cup in 1962 and 1967, the League Cup in 1971 and 1973, the European Cup Winners' Cup in 1963 and the UEFA Cup in

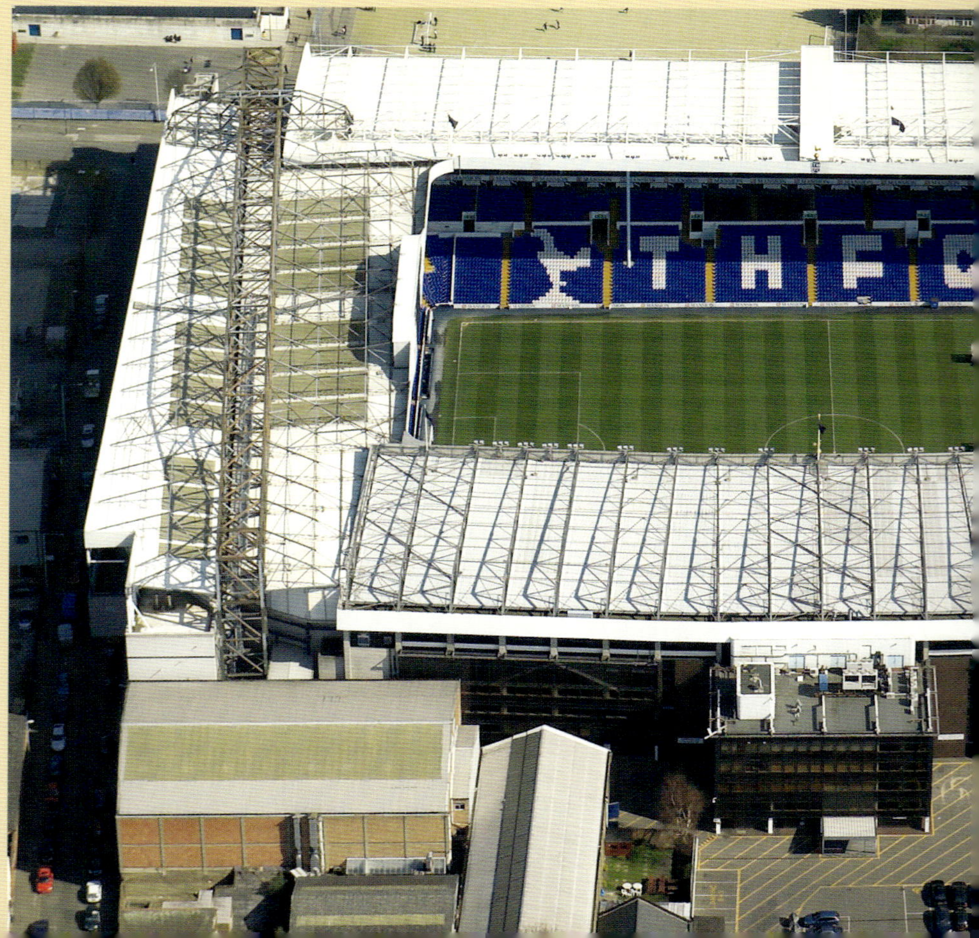

Ground: **White Hart Lane**

Address: Bill Nicholson Way, 748 High Road, Tottenham, London N17 0AP

Main tel: 0844 499 5000

Box office: 0844 499 5000

Website: www.tottenhamhotspur.com

Capacity: 36,214

Home colours: white shirts, navy blue shorts, navy blue socks

Club nickname: Spurs

Pitch dimensions: 100m x 67m (109 x 73 yards)

Founded: 1882

Record attendance: 75,038 vs Sunderland, March 5 1938

Most prolific scorer: Jimmy Greaves (220)

Record win: 13-2 vs Crewe Alexandra, February 3 1960

Record defeat: 0-7 vs Liverpool, September 2 1978

1972. In the 1980s, the club became nearly bankrupt since the building of the West Stand cost almost double the original estimated fee. The redevelopment of the East Stand in 1987 again caused crippling debt as costs spiralled. However, the club managed its debts and after adding seats to the East Terrace, the Park Lane Terrace and the Shelf, the new South Stand was built in 1995, and a new upper tier was added to the Paxton Road End, bringing the capacity up to 36,214.

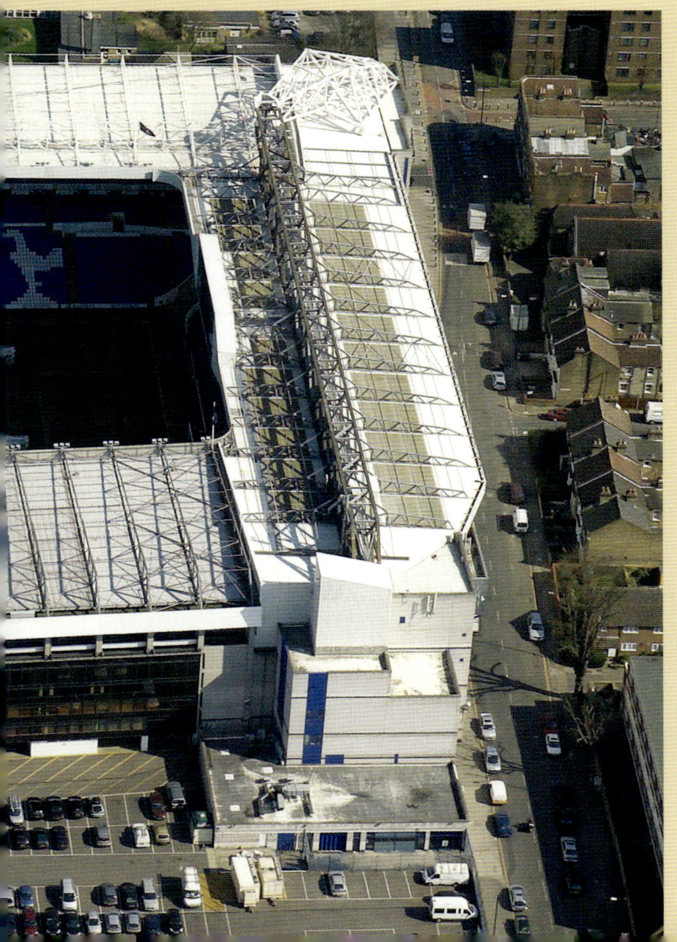

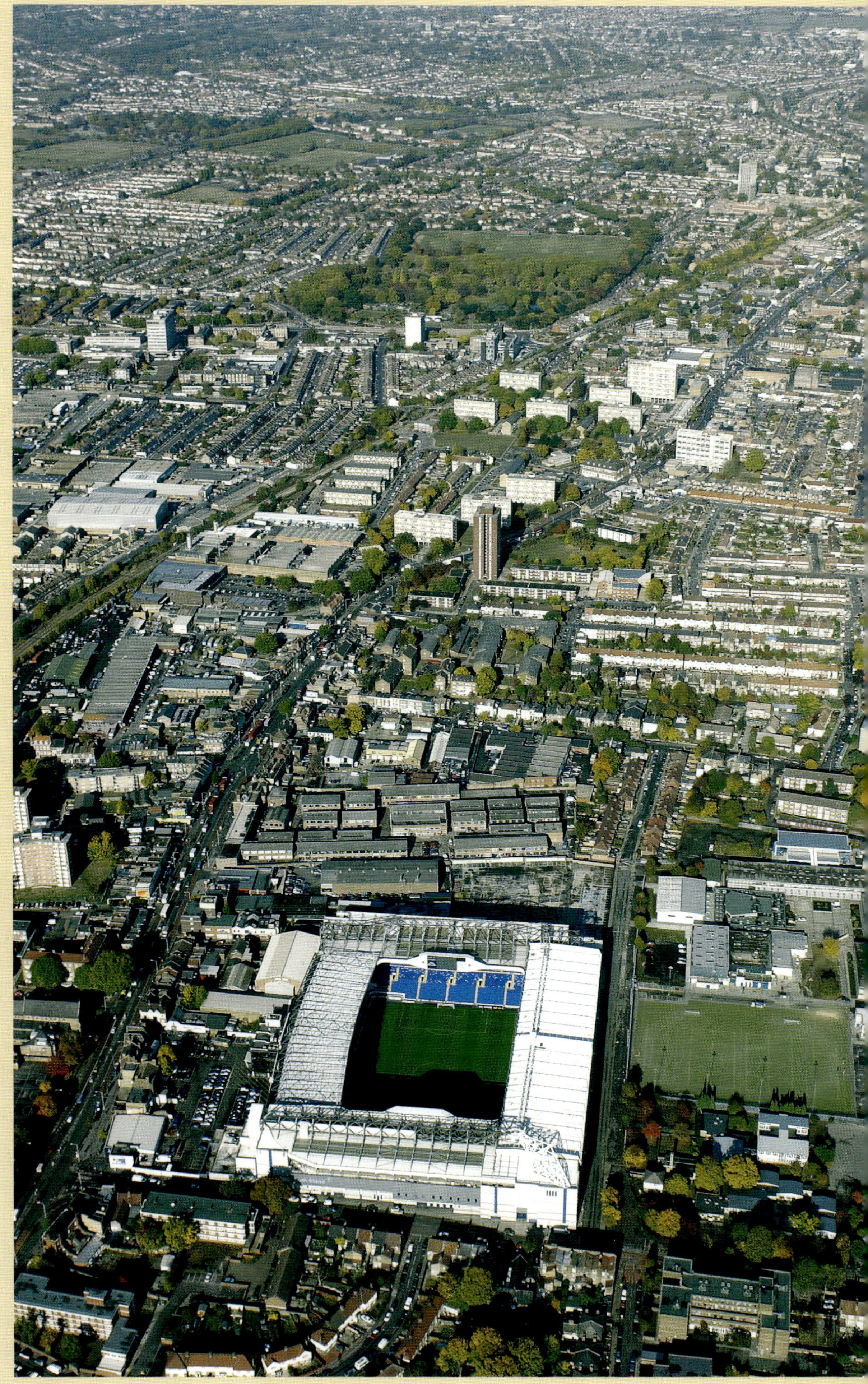

Tranmere Rovers

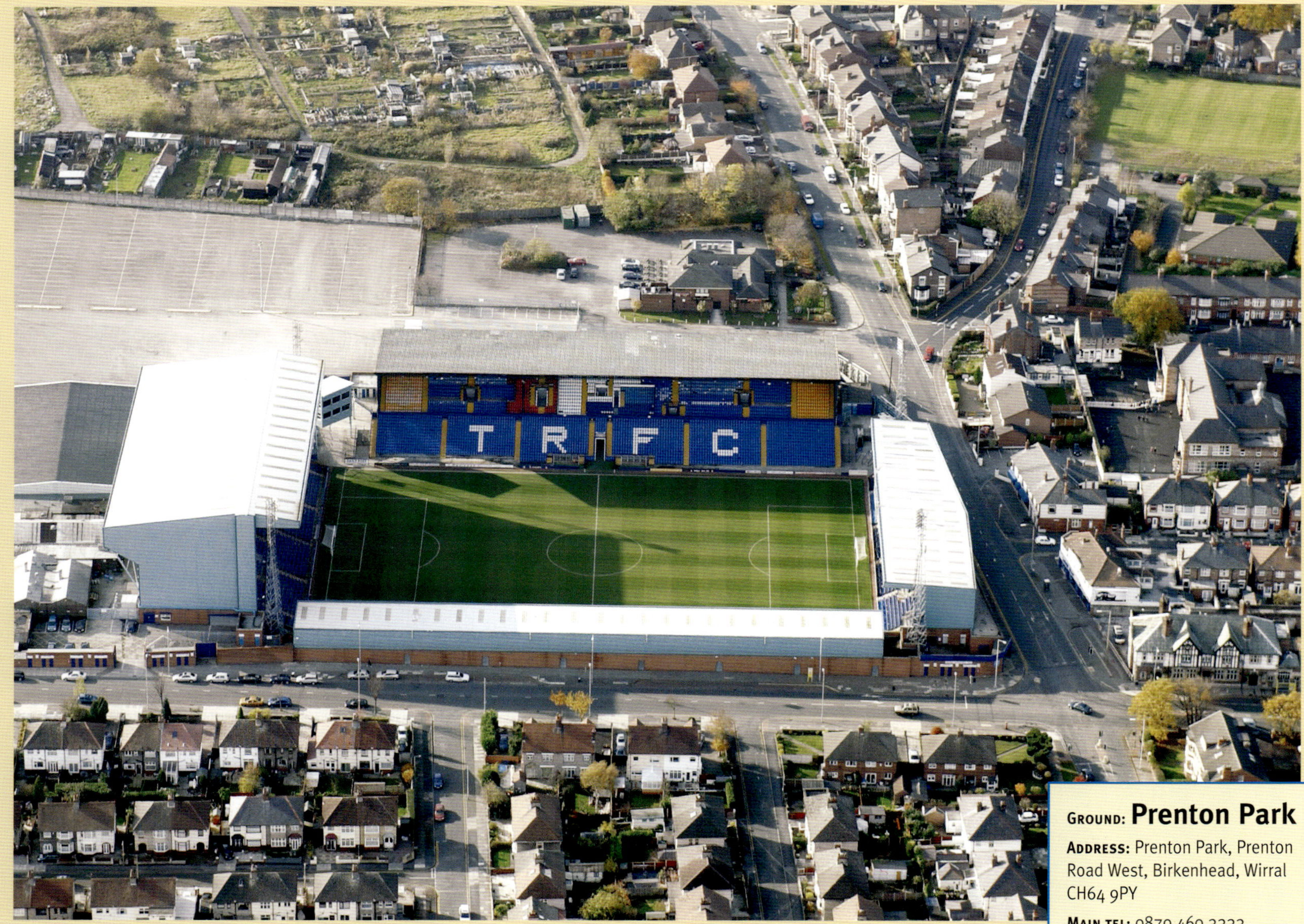

Tranmere Rovers formed in 1884 and was initially known as Belmont FC. The club changed its name to Tranmere Rovers a year later. The team played at Borough Park from 1887 until 1912, when they moved to Prenton Park. The club brought with them a small stand from Borough Park and then built a new main stand on the west side of the ground. In 1913 they built a Kop at one end of the ground and bought a further stand from a local sports ground a year later. In the 1920s a roof was added to the east side of the ground. In the same decade, Rovers joined the Football League and bought the lease to Prenton Park. A roof was added to the terracing at the north end and the Kop at the south end was further extended. During the Second World War the roof over the east side was destroyed by a bomb. After the war the club struck up a deal with the local council, which saw them exchange a few feet of land on the east side of the ground for tank traps. These were lifted to the south end, where they were used as the foundations for extra banking. Further developments took place in the 1960s when the Main Stand and the stand bought from the sports club were taken down and replaced by a new stand with a capacity of 4,000. For the next 20 years few further improvements took place and the ground fell into a bad state of repair. The new safety regulations of the 1980s meant Rovers had to reduce capacity to 8,000 since the club could not afford to make the necessary safety repairs. In 1994 a new owner brought funds into the club and a major redevelopment took place. Prenton Park was turned into an all-seater stadium, with the new Kop dominating the ground and the smaller John King Stand opposite. The stadium now has a healthy capacity of 16,587.

Ground: Prenton Park

Address: Prenton Park, Prenton Road West, Birkenhead, Wirral CH64 9PY

Main tel: 0870 460 3333

Box office: 0870 460 3332

Website: www.tranmererovers.co.uk

Capacity: 16,587

Home colours: white shirts, white shorts, white socks

Club nickname: Rovers

Pitch dimensions: 102m x 66m (112 x 72 yards)

Founded: 1884

Record attendance: 24,424 vs Stoke City, February 5 1972

Most prolific scorer: Ian Muir (141)

Record win: 13-4 vs Oldham Athletic, December 26 1935

Record defeat: 1-9 vs Tottenham Hotspur, January 14 1953

WALSALL

Walsall's roots can be traced back to 1888 when two clubs, Walsall Swifts and Walsall Town, merged to form Walsall Town Swifts – which was shortened to Walsall in 1895. The club played their early games at The Chuckery and West Bromwich Road before moving to Hillary Street in 1896. Hillary Street had a laundry in one corner of the ground; by the First World War a stand had been built along its south side and embankments around the other sides. Hillary Street was renamed Fellows Park in 1930. Soon after the new main stand was built to replace the stand on the south side and a roof was added to the north side. After recording its highest ever attendance of 25,453 in a game against Newcastle United in 1961, the ground was further developed, with a roof being added to the West End Terrace. The laundry was bought and replaced by a terrace and an extension was added to the Main Stand. The club first considered moving to a new ground in the 1940s but it was not until 1990 that they actually moved to the Bescot Stadium, situated on a former sewage farm. The new ground was built with two all-seater stands along either side, terracing at each end and a continuous roof around all four sides. A year after it opened, Bescot entertained England's B team as they took on Switzerland in an international. The William Sharp Stand at the south end of the pitch had seats added in 1992. In 2003 the Gilbert Alsop Stand at the north end of the ground was replaced by the Purple Stand, a massive two-tiered structure with a slightly larger upper tier than lower. The Bescot Stadium was re-named the Banks's Stadium in May 2007.

GROUND: Banks's Stadium

ADDRESS: Banks's Stadium, Bescot Crescent, Walsall, West Midlands Ws1 4SA

MAIN TEL: 01922 613 202

BOX OFFICE: 0871 663 0111/0222

WEBSITE: www.saddlers.co.uk

CAPACITY: 11,300

HOME COLOURS: red shirts, white shorts, red socks

CLUB NICKNAME: the Saddlers

PITCH DIMENSIONS: 101m x 67m (110 x 73 yards)

FOUNDED: 1888

RECORD ATTENDANCE: 11,049 vs Rotherham United, May 9 2004

MOST PROLIFIC SCORER: Colin Taylor (181)

RECORD WIN: 10-0 vs Darwen, March 4 1899

RECORD DEFEAT: 0-12 vs Birmingham City, December 17 1892

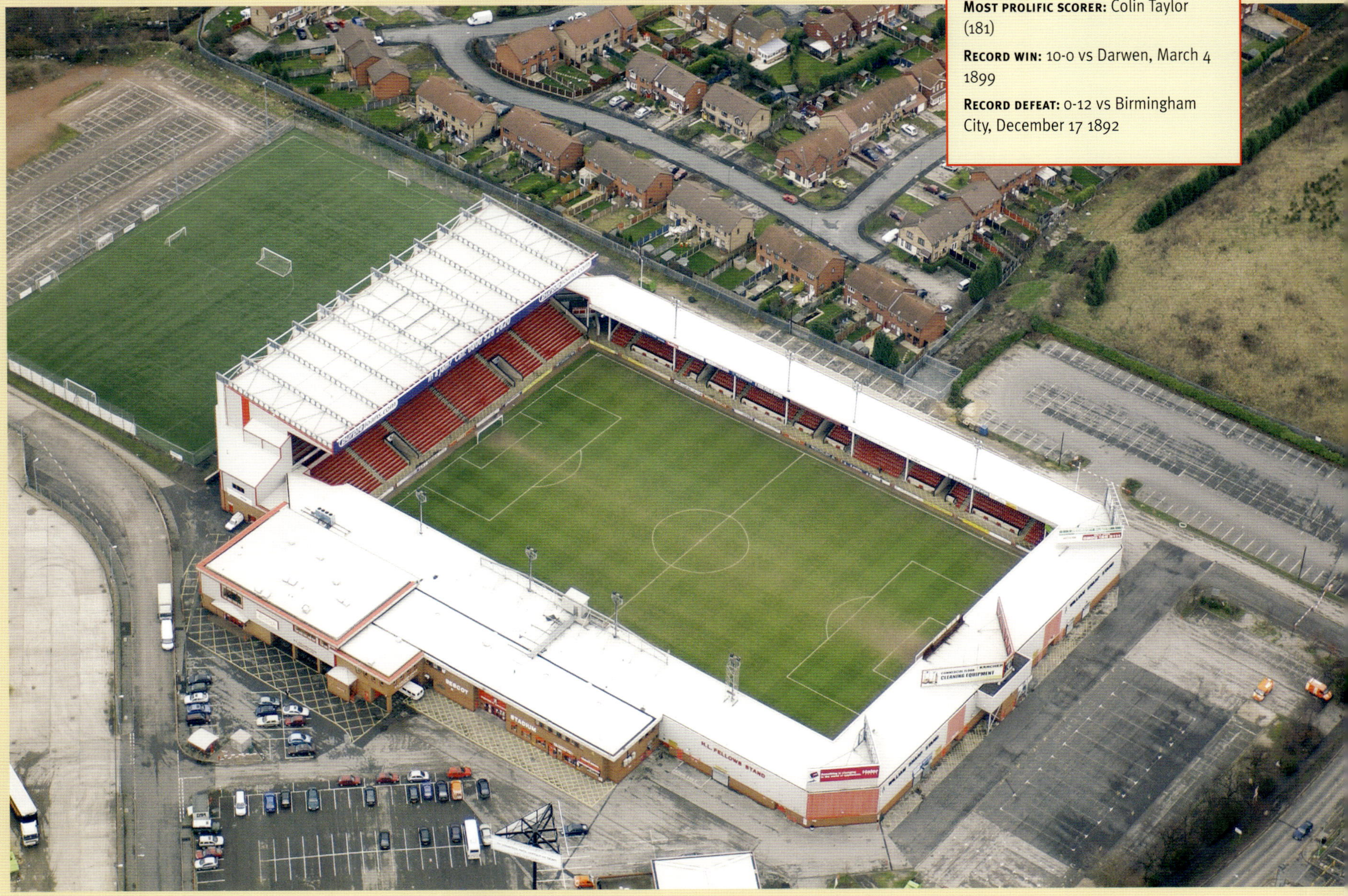

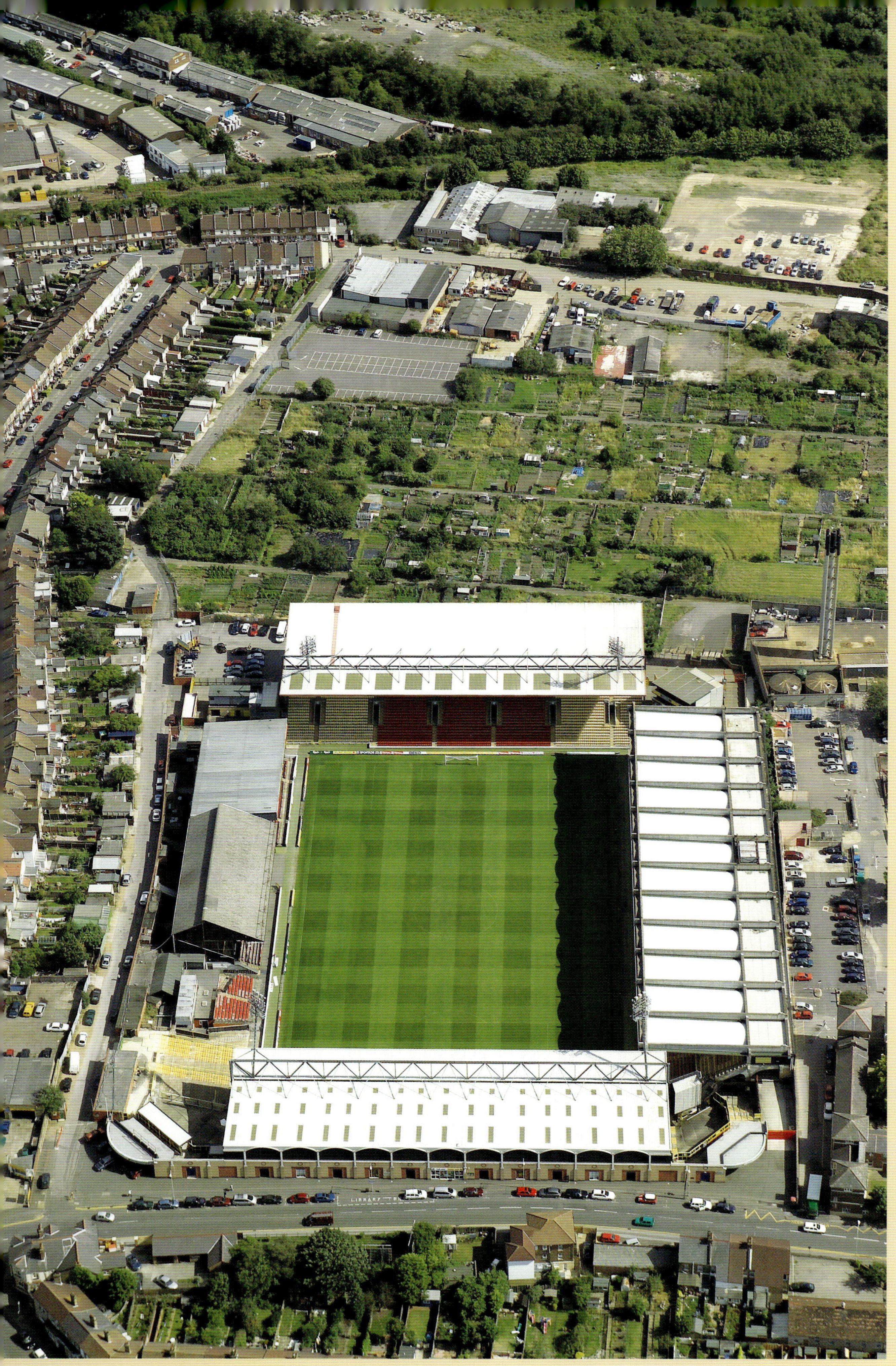

WATFORD

Watford can trace its roots back to 1881 and a team called Watford Rovers. Rovers played at Cassiobury Park before moving to Rose and Crown Park, followed by a stint at Colney Butts Meadow. The club changed their name to West Herts in 1891 and moved to the West Herts Sports Ground. Along one side of the pitch stood a pavilion, which had low covered stands on either side. Attendances grew in the post-war period and in 1922 Watford moved to Vicarage Road, a former gravel pit. The Hornets built a new 3,500-seater main stand on the east side of the ground and brought with them stands from the sports ground which were installed on the west and south edges. At the north end they built a large embankment. In 1928 the club introduced greyhound racing to Vicarage Road and the 1930s saw concrete terracing replace the ashen slopes, which had proved hazardous for some fans. After the Second World War, Watford added a roof to the South End. On February 3 1969, Vicarage Road notched up its highest attendance ever of 34,099 for a game against Manchester United. Growing attendances prompted the club to end greyhound racing at the ground and extend the Main Stand. Greyhound racing returned between 1975-79 but has not been welcomed back since. In 1976 long-time fan and pop star Sir Elton John became chairman and Graham Taylor took over as manager of the club. This marked the Hornets' most successful era, when they leapt up the divisions and reached the FA Cup final for the first time in their history. In 1986 the Hornets' chairman opened a brand new two-tiered stand, the Rous Stand on the west side of the ground. During the 1990s the Hornets built new, single-tiered stands at either end and further developed the front of the Rous Stand. The oldest stand, the East Stand, still remains but the club have plans for its redevelopment.

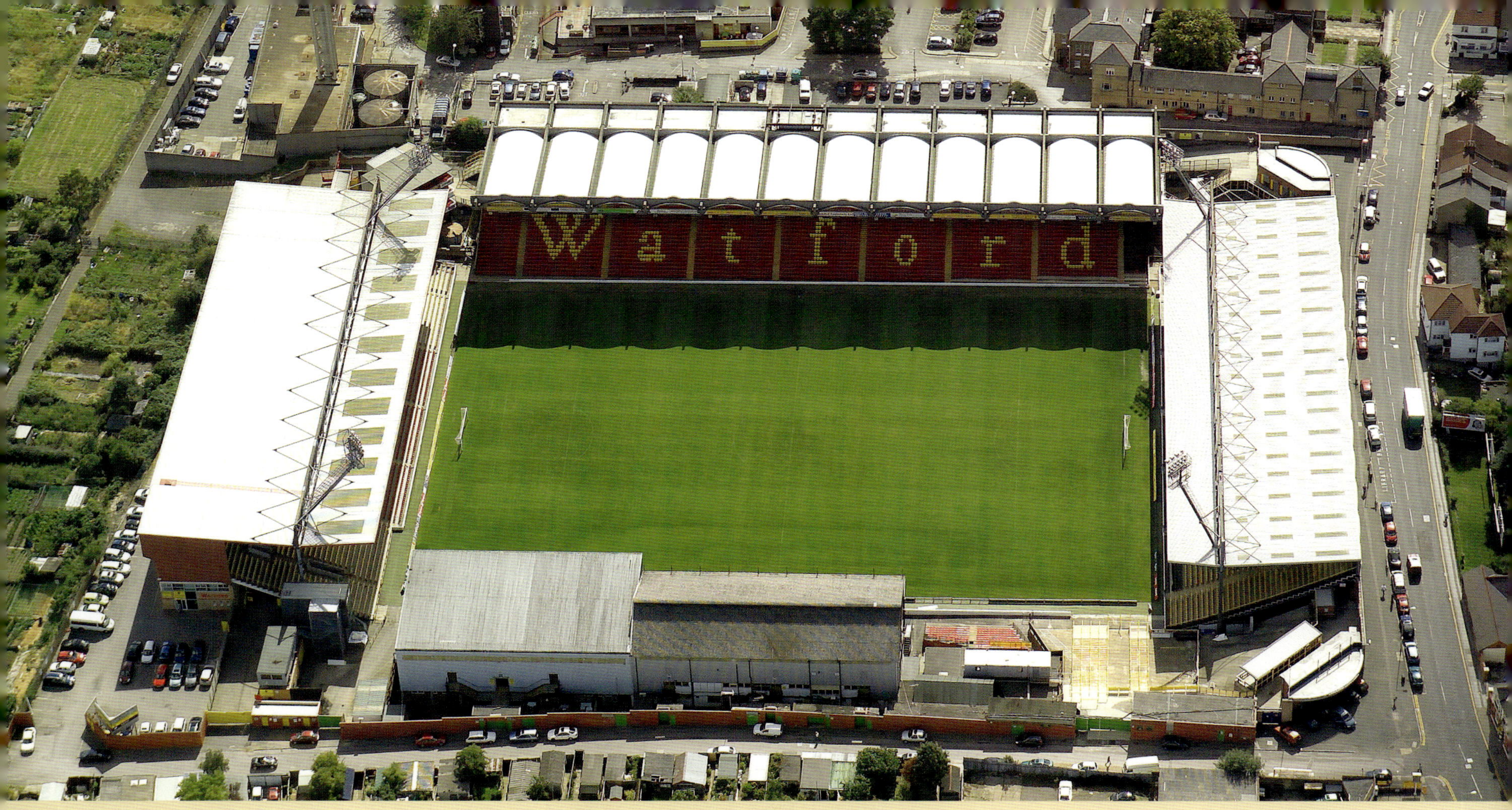

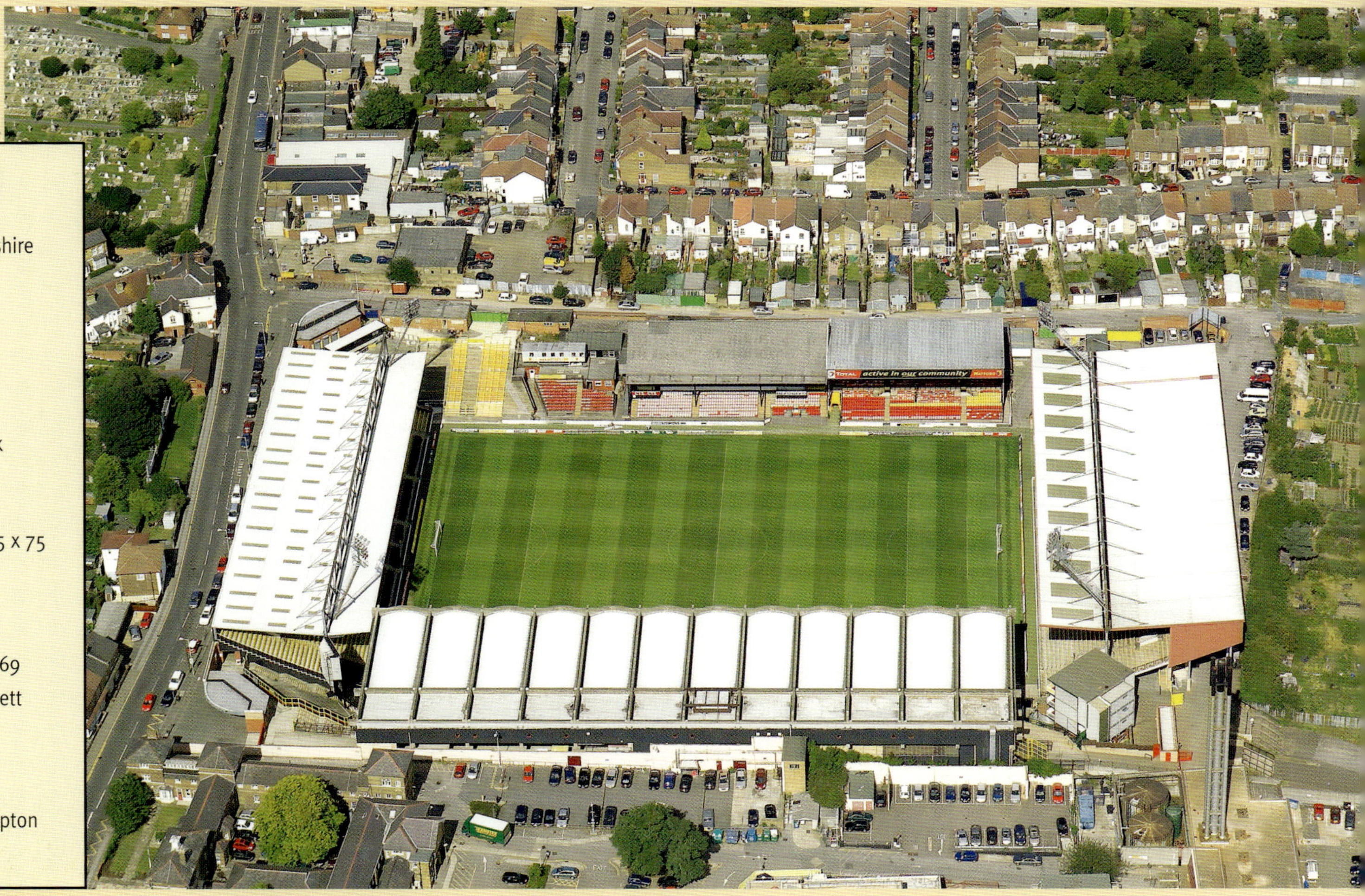

Ground: Vicarage Road

Address: Vicarage Road Stadium, Vicarage Road, Watford, Hertfordshire WD18 0ER

Main tel: 0845 442 1881

Box office: 0845 442 1881

Website: www.watfordfc.com

Capacity: 19,900

Home colours: yellow shirts, black shorts, yellow socks

Club nickname: the Hornets

Pitch dimensions: 105m x 69m (115 x 75 yards)

Founded: 1881

Record attendance: 34,099 vs Manchester United, February 3 1969

Most prolific scorer: Luther Blissett (158)

Record win: 8-0 vs Sunderland, September 25 1982

Record defeat: 0-10 vs Wolverhampton Wanderers, January 24 1912

Wembley Stadium

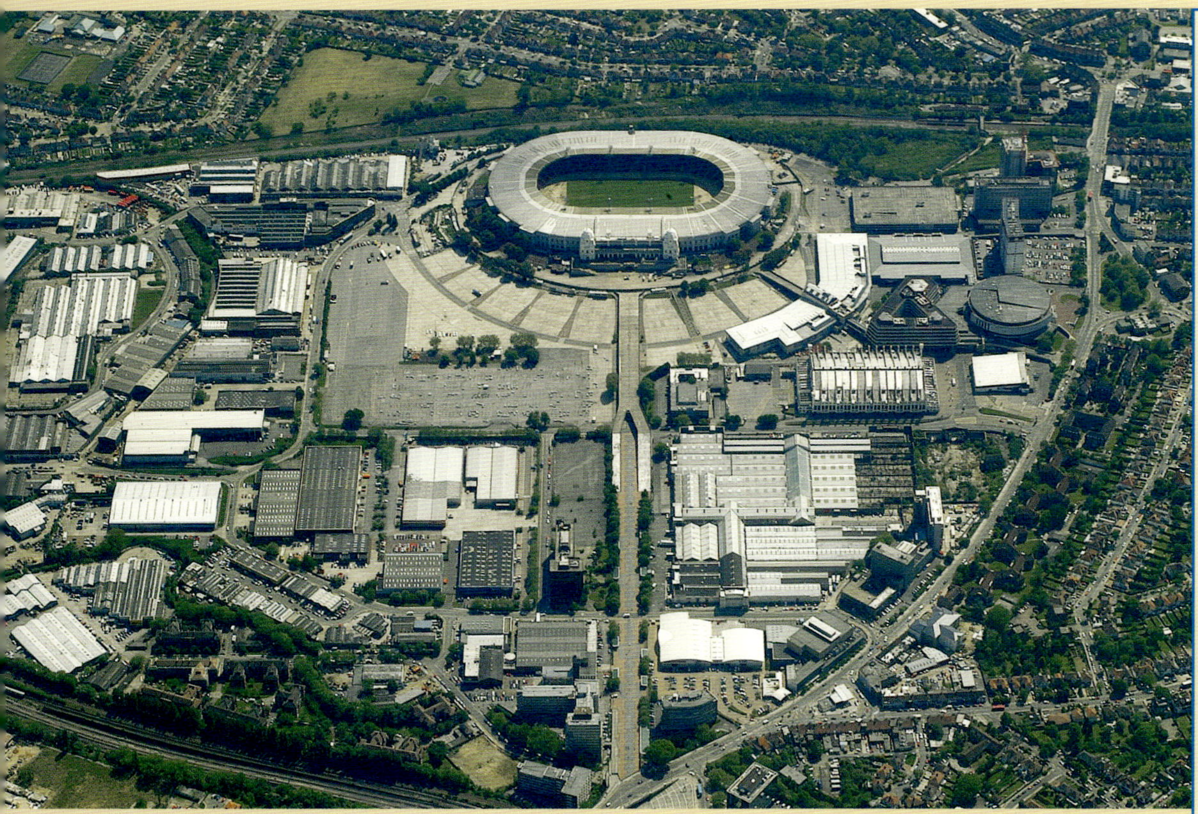

Ground: Old Wembley Stadium

Opened: 1923

Closed: 2000

Capacity: 80,000

Pitch dimensions: 105m x 68m (115 x 74 yards)

Officially recorded record attendance: 126,047

Ground: New Wembley Stadium

Address: Wembley National Stadium, Wembley, London HA9 OWS

Main tel: 0844 980 8001

Box office: contact the FA or Ticketmaster

Website: www.wembleystadium.com

Capacity: 90,000

Pitch dimensions: 105m x 68m (115 x 74 yards)

Record attendance: 89,826 Chelsea vs Manchester United, FA Cup final, May 19 2007

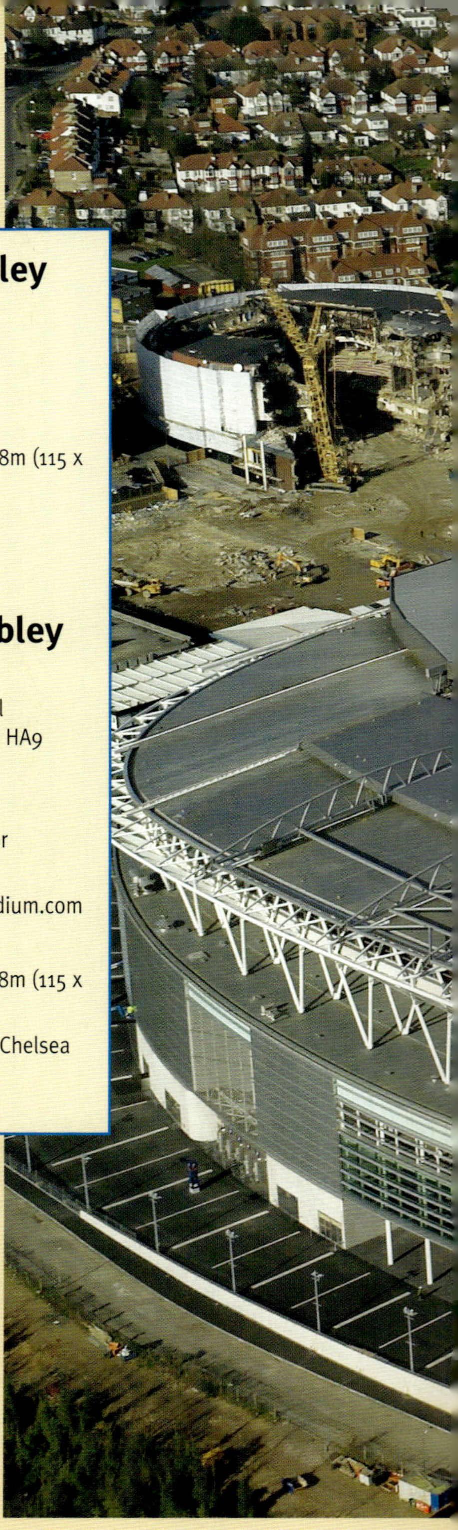

Sport was played on the site occupied by Wembley Stadium as early as the 1880s when Wembley Park Leisure Grounds had football and cricket pitches and a running track. In 1889 the site's owners decided to build a main attraction at the site and started work on a huge four-legged tower to rival the newly constructed Eiffel Tower in Paris. Work began but the tower was never completed and in 1907 the base of the construction was dynamited. The first Wembley Stadium was a project devised by the government in 1918 in the aftermath of the First World War. Plans were drawn up for a British Empire Exhibition with a national sporting stadium as its centrepiece. The stadium was originally named the Empire Stadium, designed by architects Sir John Simpson and Maxwell Ayerton; it took just 300 days to complete. George V officially opened the Empire Exhibition in 1924, although the first event held at the stadium was the 1923 Cup Final between West Ham United and Bolton Wanderers. During that game, although the officially recorded attendance was 126,047 an estimated 200,000 crammed in to see the game. Spectators spilled onto the pitch and the game became known as the "white horse final" because newsreel film captured the memorable sight of a policeman on a white horse vainly trying to clear the pitch. At this time, the ground was oval-shaped and the pitch was surrounded by a running track. The north and south ends of the stadium had seated stands, while the remaining sides had open terracing. Floodlights were added to the stadium in 1955 and the encircling roof and electronic scoreboards were added in 1963. In 1990, following the Taylor report, the ground became all-seater and had a capacity of 80,000. Apart from these developments, very little changed in Wembley's structure from its original 1920s design. The stadium has been used for a wide variety of events from the venue for England's 1966 World Cup triumph against West Germany to the place where Pope John Paul II celebrated Mass in 1982. However, its poor facilities, coupled with its difficult access, led to calls for Wembley to be closed and a new national stadium built in a more central location. Despite various suggestions for alternative venues, in the end the Football Association came to the conclusion that Wembley was the best place for corporate clients and the decision was taken to build a new Wembley Stadium on the site of the old ground in 2002. The first Wembley Stadium was finally closed in 2000 and demolition of the buildings began. The iconic twin towers came down in December 2002.

After many delays, the new Wembley was completed on March 9 2007 when the keys of the stadium were handed over to the Football Association. The first FA Cup final at the new Wembley was between Manchester

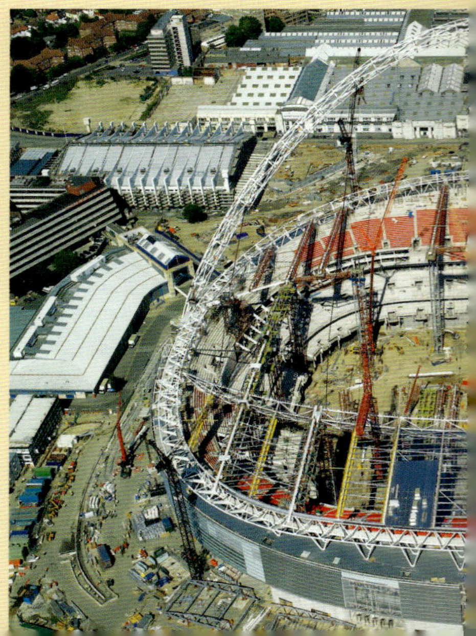

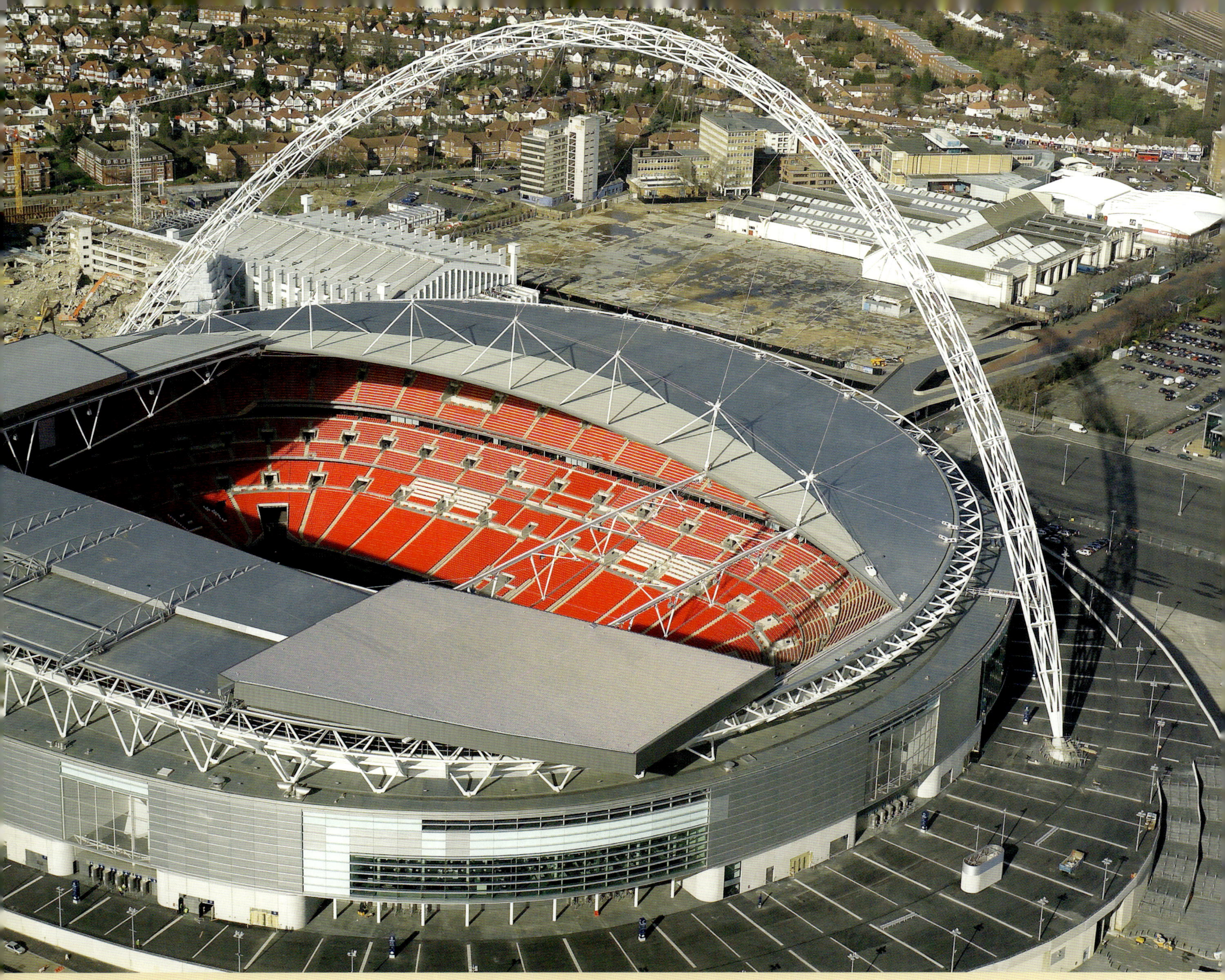

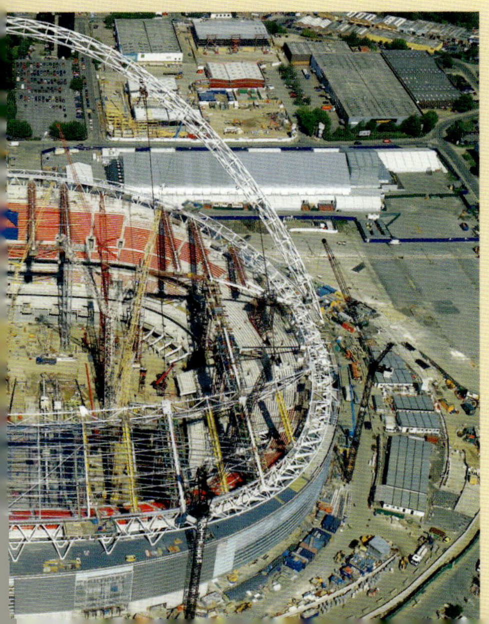

Above: the new Wembley stadium nears completion in spring 2007

United and Chelsea on May 19 2007.

The 90,000-seater venue will primarily stage football, rugby and music events but it will also host major athletics events. To turn the stadium into an athletics venue there is a removable steel and concrete platform, 6m above the football pitch with a 400m running track. The most unusual feature of the new stadium, however, is its arch – a 133m (436ft) tall structure located above the North Stand. Made of steel, it is 315m (1034ft) long and is the longest single roof structure in the world. The arch supports the weight of the north roof as well as some of the south and sits at an angle of 68° from the horizontal which enables the roof to slide back to let light on to the pitch. It towers above the level of the external concourse and it is estimated that the London Eye could sit comfortably between the pitch and the top of the arch. The new stadium boasts many state of the art facilities, including two giant screens, escalators, over 2,000 toilets and, most importantly, more leg room in every seat than there was in the royal box of the old Wembley. In 2012 the new Wembley Stadium will host the football competition as part of the London Olympics.

West Bromwich Albion

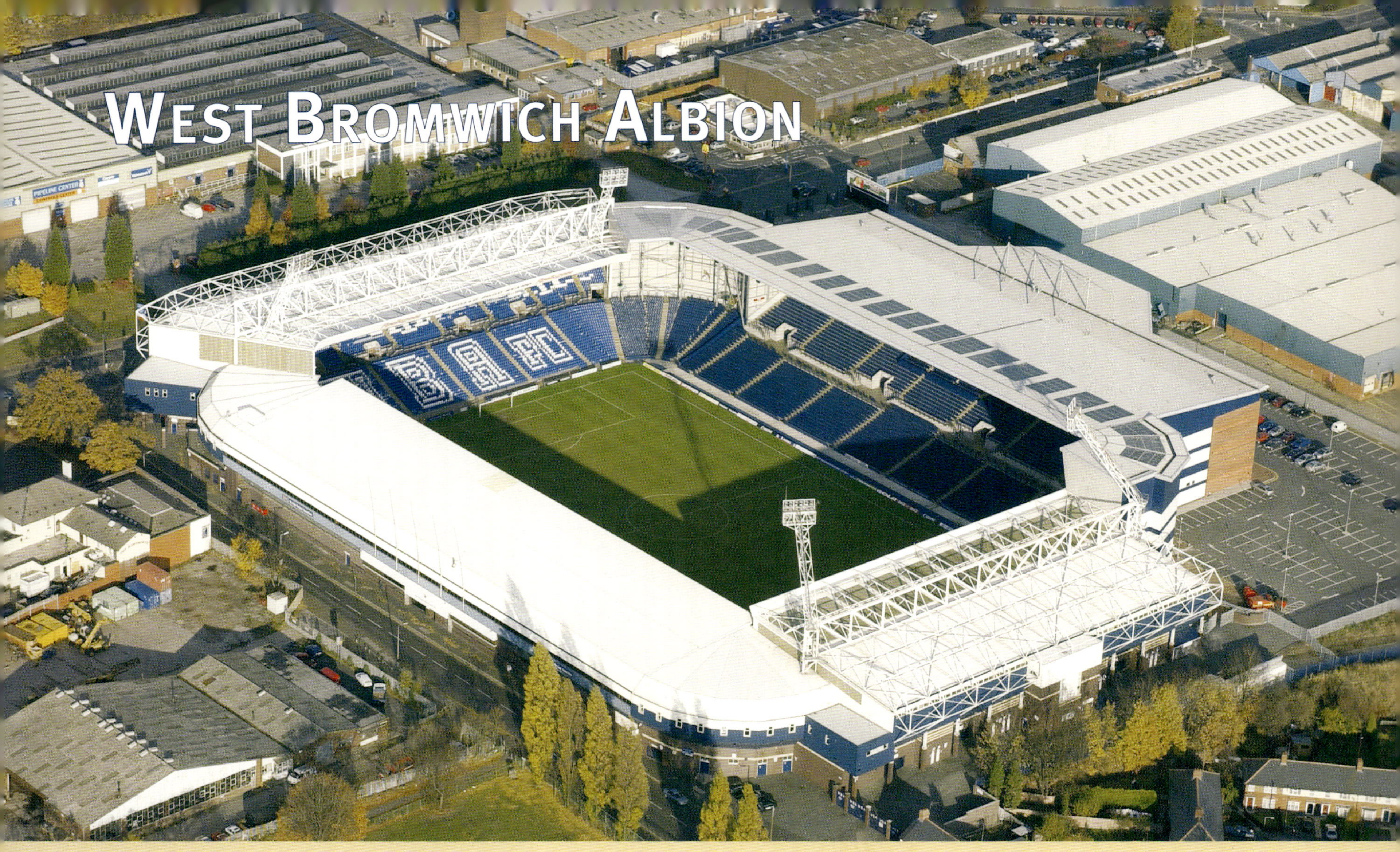

West Bromwich Albion FC was created by a group of workers from Salter's Spring Works in 1878. More than 100 years after they formed, they are one of only a few English football clubs to have won all three major honours – the League title, the FA Cup and the League Cup. They originally called themselves the West Bromwich Strollers after walking to nearby Wednesbury to buy themselves a ball. The name stuck until 1880, when they changed their name to the more familiar Albion. The club played at five different grounds before settling at The Hawthorns in 1900, a name that developed because the ground was once surrounded by hawthorn bushes. Situated between Birmingham and Sandwell, the initial capacity was 35,500 but when the club bought the ground's freehold in 1913 it began developing the stands. Concrete terracing was installed in 1920 and by 1924 the capacity reached 65,000. Terracing was completed on all four sides of the ground in 1931, the year the club won the FA Cup for the third time and gained promotion to the First Division. In 1937 the ground saw a record attendance as 64,815 fans watched the Baggies take on Arsenal in the sixth round of the FA Cup. The more familiar stands of today were constructed between the 1940s and the 1960s. The East Stand, known as the Rainbow Stand because of its multi-coloured seats, was built on the site of the former Handsworth Stand. Improvements continued to the Birmingham Road End, which was covered in 1964, and the Halfords Lane side. The 1960s also saw the emergence of the Baggies' two most prolific scorers, Jeff Astle and Tony Brown. Following the Taylor report, a £4.15m all-seater stadium was opened in 1995. The Rainbow Stand was finally demolished in 2001 to make way for the new East Stand. When it opened in 2002 to a 1-0 defeat by Grimsby, The Hawthorns finally became fully enclosed.

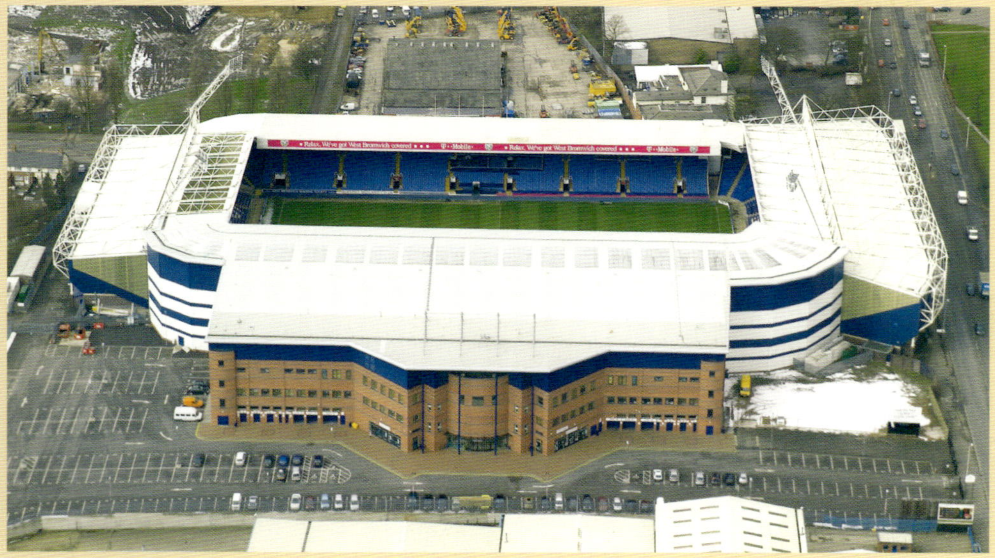

Ground: **The Hawthorns**

Address: The Hawthorns, West Bromwich, West Midlands B71 4LF

Main tel: 0871 271 1100

Box office: 0871 271 9780

Website: www.wba.co.uk

Capacity: 28,003

Home colours: navy blue and white striped shirts, white shorts, blue and white socks

Club nickname: the Baggies

Pitch dimensions: 105m x 68m (115 x 74 yards)

Founded: 1878

Record attendance: 64,815 vs Arsenal, March 6 1937

Most prolific scorer: Tony Brown (218)

Record win: 12-0 vs Darwen, April 4 1892

Record defeat: 3-10 vs Stoke City, February 4 1937

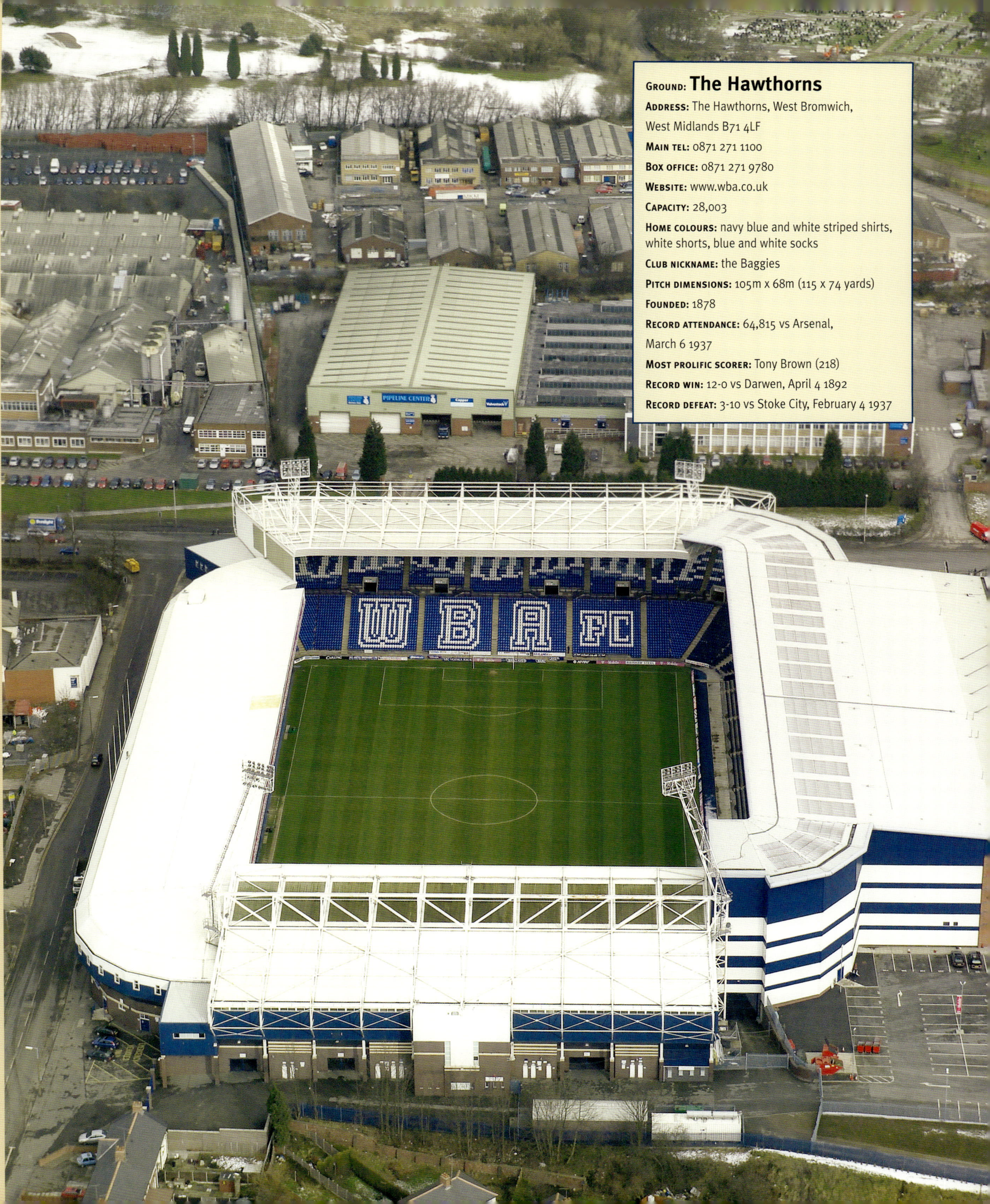

West Ham United

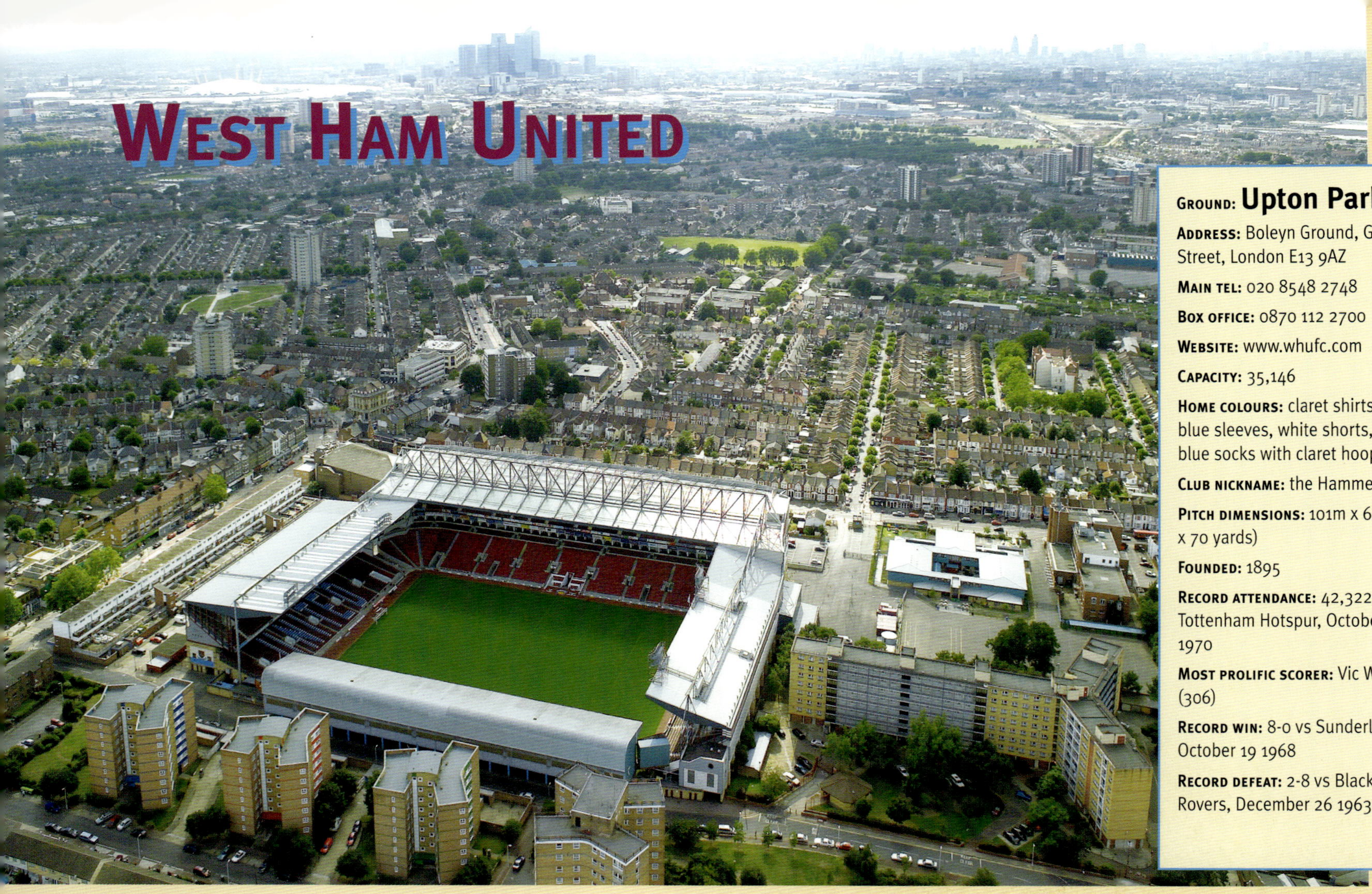

Ground: Upton Park

Address: Boleyn Ground, Green Street, London E13 9AZ

Main tel: 020 8548 2748

Box office: 0870 112 2700

Website: www.whufc.com

Capacity: 35,146

Home colours: claret shirts with blue sleeves, white shorts, light blue socks with claret hoops

Club nickname: the Hammers

Pitch dimensions: 101m x 64m (110 x 70 yards)

Founded: 1895

Record attendance: 42,322 vs Tottenham Hotspur, October 17 1970

Most prolific scorer: Vic Watson (306)

Record win: 8-0 vs Sunderland, October 19 1968

Record defeat: 2-8 vs Blackburn Rovers, December 26 1963

West Ham United began as Thames Ironworks, a team set up by Arnold Hills in 1895. Hills was a shipyard owner and the club's nickname, the Hammers, refers to the tools used by shipyard workers. The team originally played at Hermit Road in Canning Town before eventually moving to Upton Park in 1904, four years after renaming themselves West Ham United. The club's ground is called the Boleyn Ground, named after a 16th century house that stood next door to the ground. Attendances climbed and in 1913 the new West Stand was built, which was extended in 1925 to a two-tier structure. During this time the South Stand was covered, as was the East Stand. The Second World War saw severe damage to the South Stand when a V1 bomb landed on the ground. The 1960s brought sweeping changes to Upton Park, beginning with the covering of the North Bank. Another bay was added to the West Stand and the East Stand was completely rebuilt, significantly raising Upton Park's capacity, so much so that a record 42,322 fans saw the Hammers take on Spurs in a First Division derby in 1970. As with many other clubs, the ground had to reduce its capacity following the Taylor report. In 1991, the club bought land behind the West Stand, which they rebuilt and expanded. However, the club encountered financial difficulties and in November 1991 launched a disastrous bond scheme. Boycotts and pitch protests followed and gates dropped below 16,000.

To try and lure fans back, the club slashed the price of season tickets and eventually began redeveloping the South Stand (now the Centenary Stand) in 1993. The Bobby Moore Stand opened in 1994; the millennium brought further redevelopment to the Dr Marten's Stand and the East Stand, raising the capacity to 35,146. Plans for further development have been put on temporary hold.

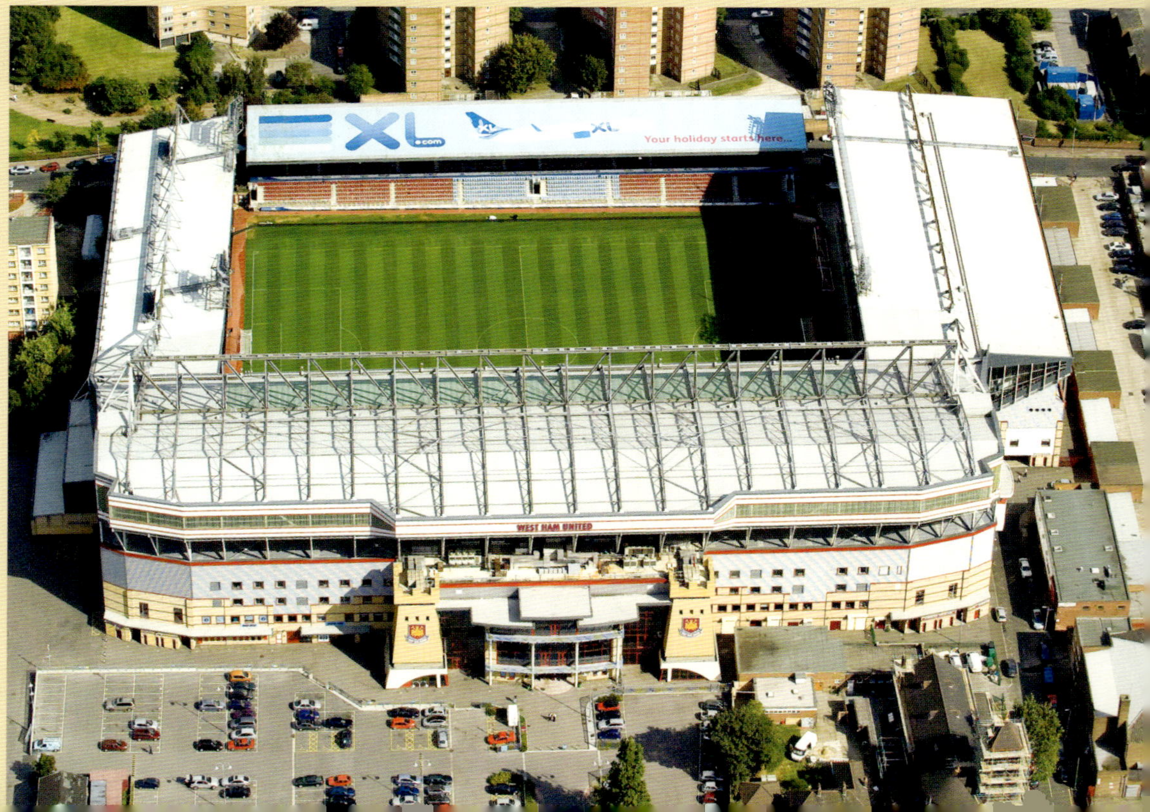

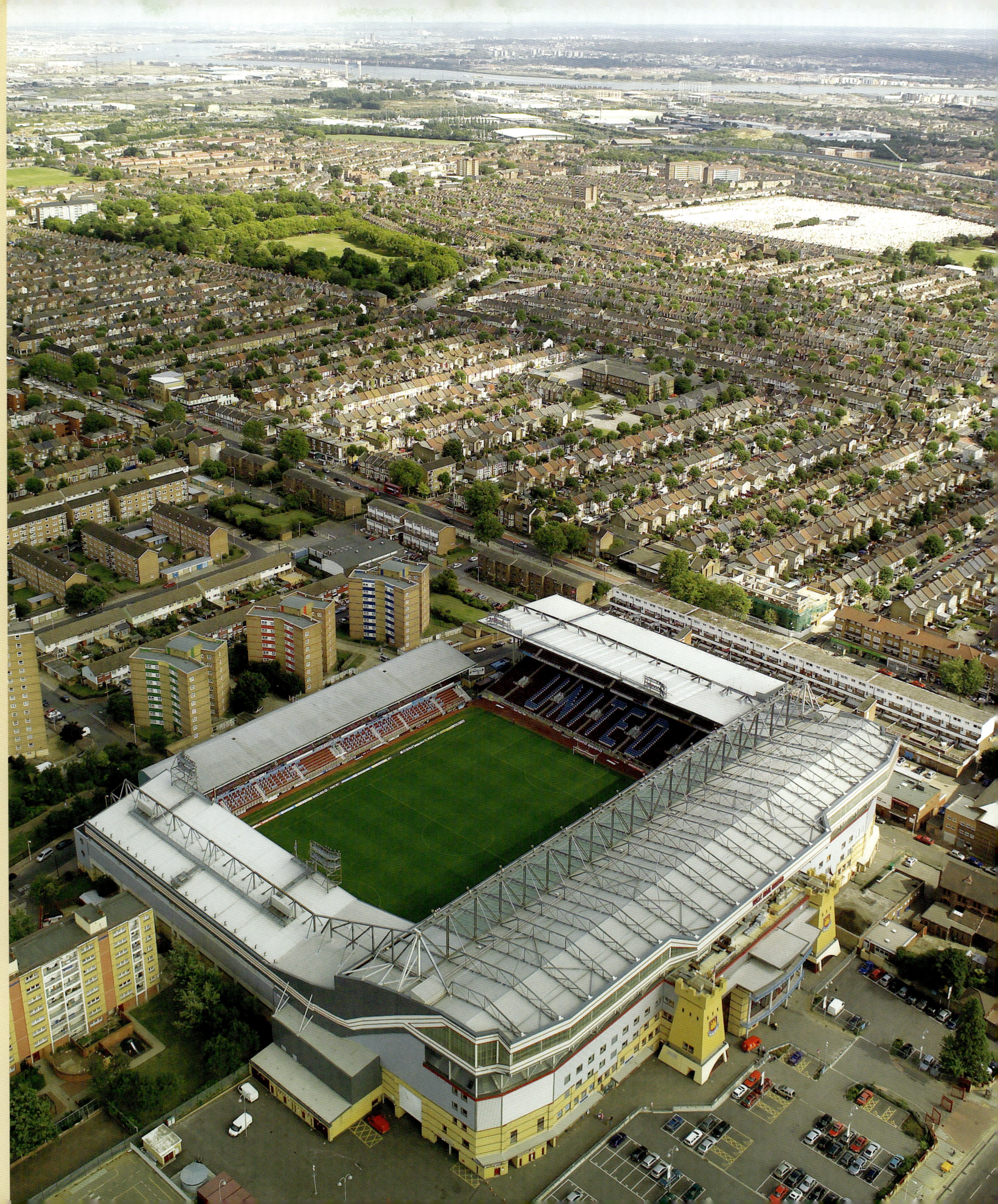
UNITED

Wigan Athletic

Springfield Park, Wigan's original home ground, was first used for football in 1897 by Wigan County. Before then the ground was a sports ground with a horse trotting track, a concrete cycle track and a running track. Following Wigan County's demise, a succession of Wigan clubs formed and disbanded, Wigan Borough being the most successful, lasting from 1919 to 1932. During Borough's ownership of the ground the original stands were replaced and the new main stand created. The Shevington End Stand and the Popular Side Stand were also constructed during this period. When Wigan Athletic formed in 1932, they bought Springfield Park and this remained the Latics home for the next 67 years. The Latics' first game at Springfield Park was against Port Vale Reserves, which ended in a 2-0 defeat for the home side. The club fought for League status until 1978. During this time the club drew the largest crowd in its history. More than 27,500 fans turned up to see the Latics beat Hereford United 4-1 in the third round of the FA Cup; in the next round the club faced Newcastle United. The Latics finally made it into the Football League after 34 attempts in 1978. They marked the occasion by losing 3-0 to Grimsby Town. The Latics had mixed success after joining the League. An impressive start saw them promoted to the Third Division at the end of the 1981/82 season. They stared bankruptcy and relegation to the Conference in the face after a bad run of results in the 1992/3 season, but their fortunes were reversed when local businessman Dave Whelan bought the club in 1995. He subsidised the building of a new stadium, the JJB Stadium, which they moved to in 1999. The new stadium is shared with local rugby league team Wigan Warriors who moved from Central Park in 1999.

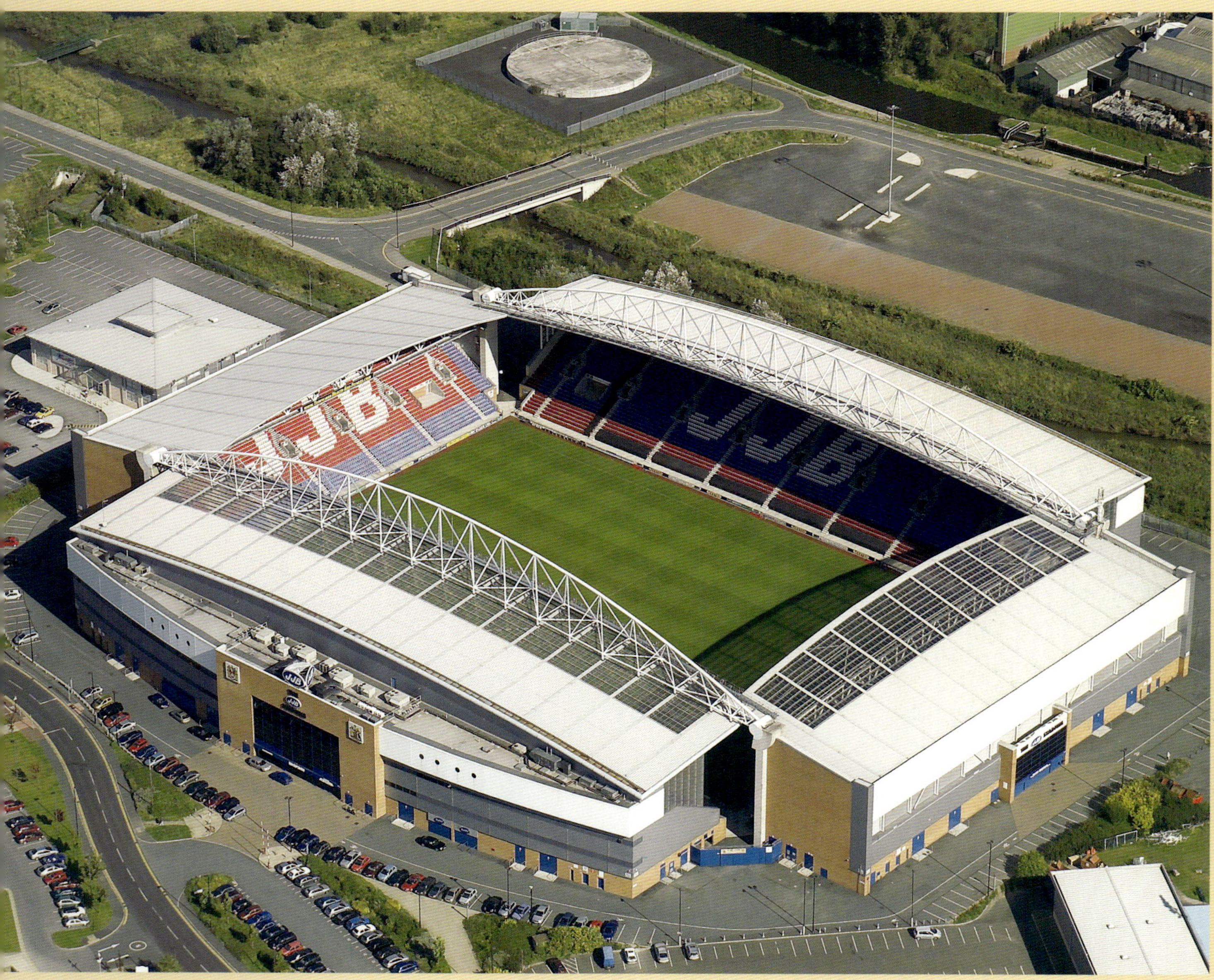

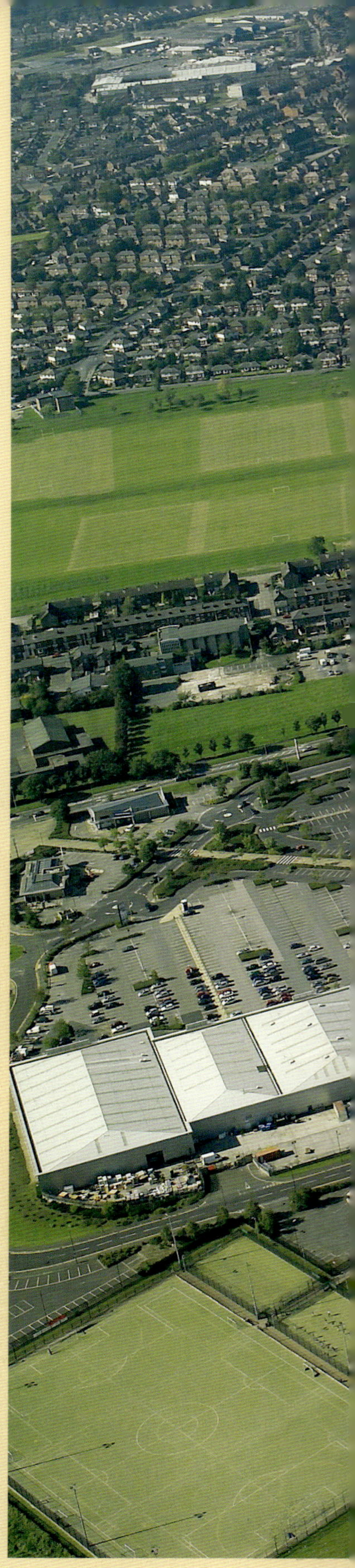

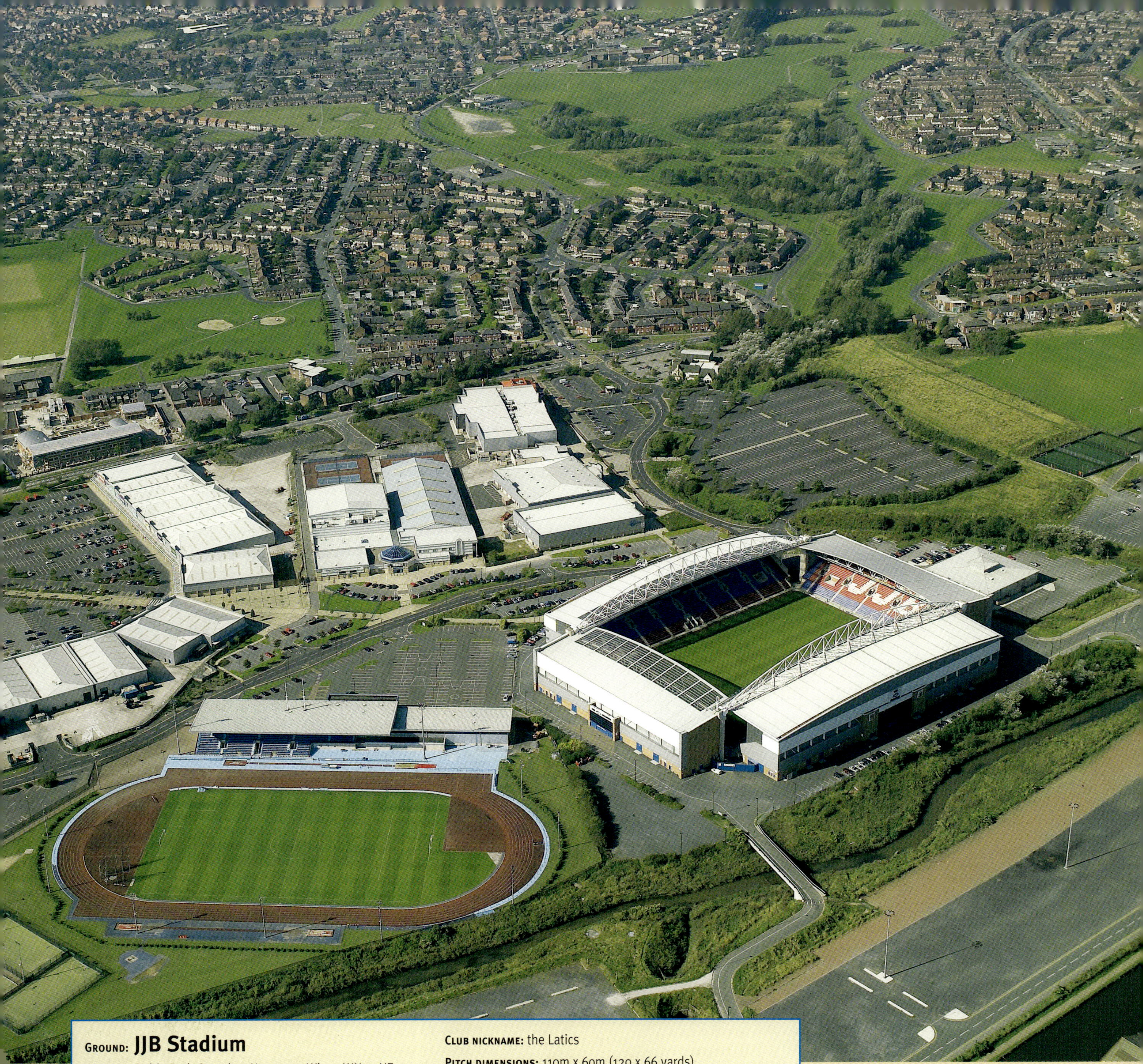

GROUND: **JJB Stadium**

ADDRESS: Robin Park Complex, Newtown, Wigan WN5 0UZ

MAIN TEL: 01942 774 000

BOX OFFICE: 0871 663 3552

WEBSITE: www.wiganlatics.com

CAPACITY: 25,023

HOME COLOURS: blue with white and green

CLUB NICKNAME: the Latics

PITCH DIMENSIONS: 110m x 60m (120 x 66 yards)

FOUNDED: 1932

RECORD ATTENDANCE: (at the JJB Stadium) 25,023 vs Liverpool, February 11 2006

MOST PROLIFIC SCORER: Peter Houghton (62)

RECORD WIN: 7-1 vs Scarborough, March 1997

RECORD DEFEAT: 1-6 vs Bristol Rovers, March 1990

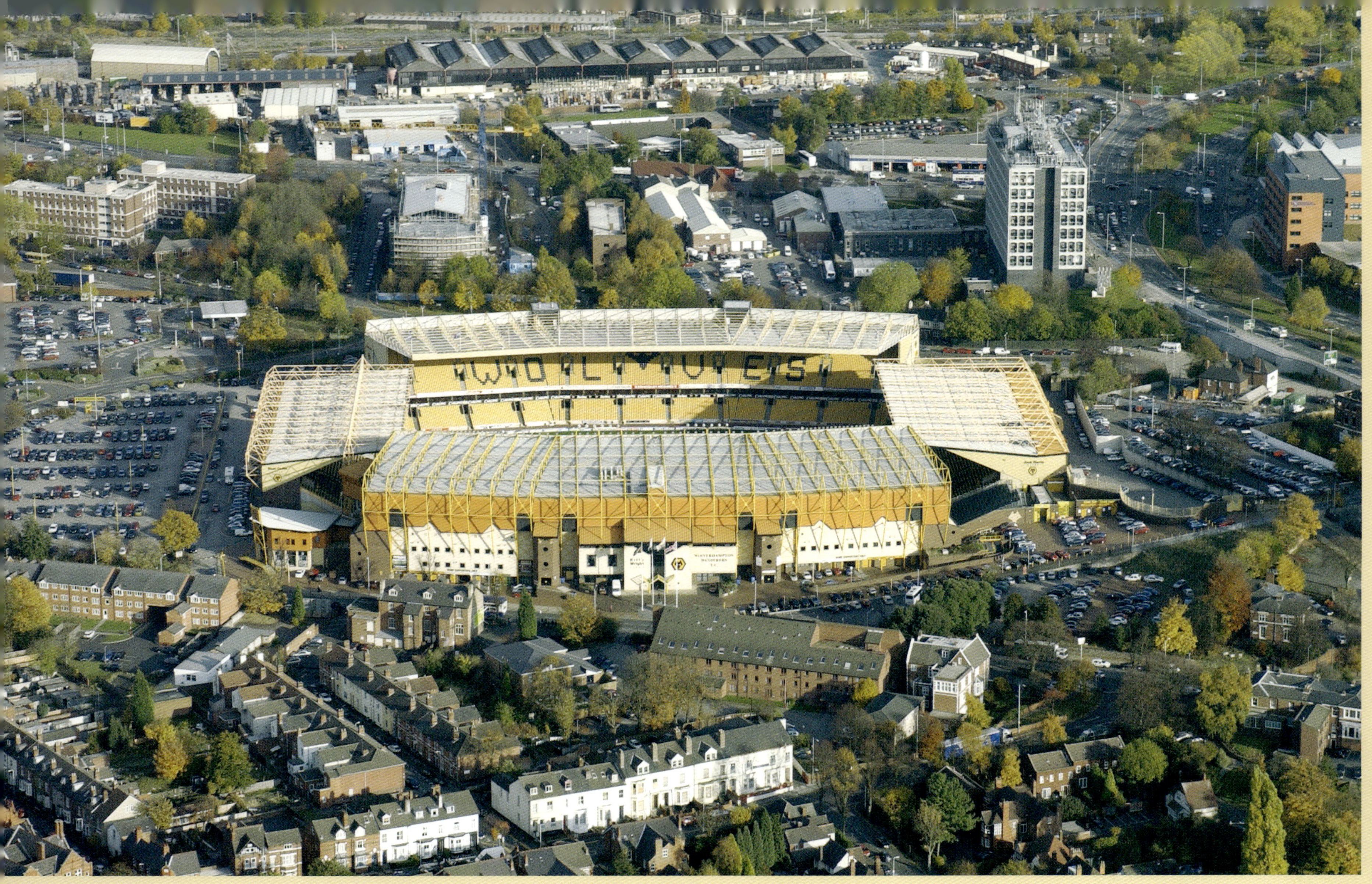

Wolverhampton Wanderers

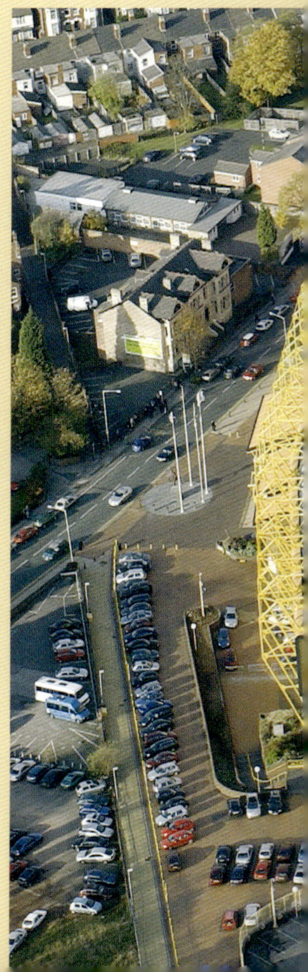

Wolves formed from a schoolboys team, St Lukes, in 1877, which then merged with a local cricket and football team, The Wanderers, in 1879 to form Wolverhampton Wanderers. After playing home games at Goldthorn Hill and Dudley Road, in 1889 the club moved to Molineux, a ground with a long history of hosting sporting events. A grandstand was built which could seat 300 spectators with shelter for a further 4,000 fans. Wolves played their first League game in 1889 against Notts County, which they won 2-0. Despite boasting a capacity of 20,000, it was not until 1925 that the major stands were built. The first was erected on the Waterloo Road side of the ground. The Molineux Street Stand was rebuilt in 1932 after a gale blew the old cover down. This distinctive structure had a multi-span roof, with a clock mounted in the centre. The 1930s saw the north and south end terracing covered to shelter the large crowds that flocked to home games. During this period, 61,315 fans turned up to see Wolves take on Liverpool, the largest crowd ever recorded at the ground. During the 1950s, Molineux was best known for its newly installed floodlights. Top European clubs flocked to the Midlands ground to enjoy the opportunities of midweek evening games made possible by this novel invention. In 1978, new legislation led to the demolition of the Molineux Street Stand and in its place a £2m grandstand was erected. This stand almost led to the club folding as they struggled to cope with the debt but in 1986 they were saved by the local council, who bought the ground for £1.12m. In May 1990 Sir Jack Hayward purchased Molineux and paid an estimated £20m, redeveloping the ground into one of the then most modern in the country. The stadium is now made up of four separate stands. The oldest, the Steve Bull Stand, was opened in 1979. The original timepiece that sat on top of the old Molineux Street Stand since the 1930s was incorporated into the Stan Cullis Stand. Three other stands were subsequently added, the last of which was the Jack Harris Stand, completed in December 1993. Outside the ground are two famous statues – one of Billy Wright, the other of player and manager Stan Cullis.

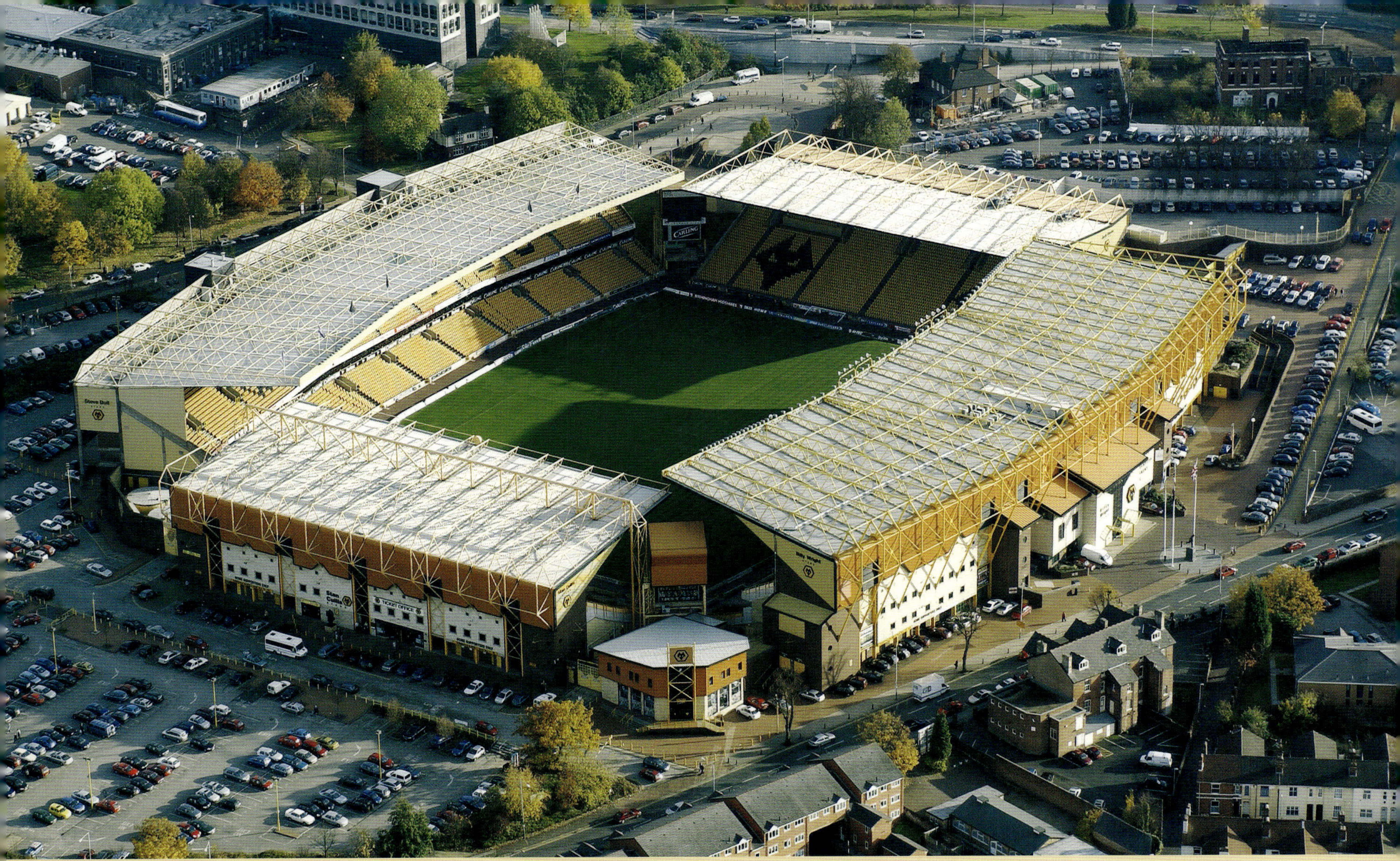

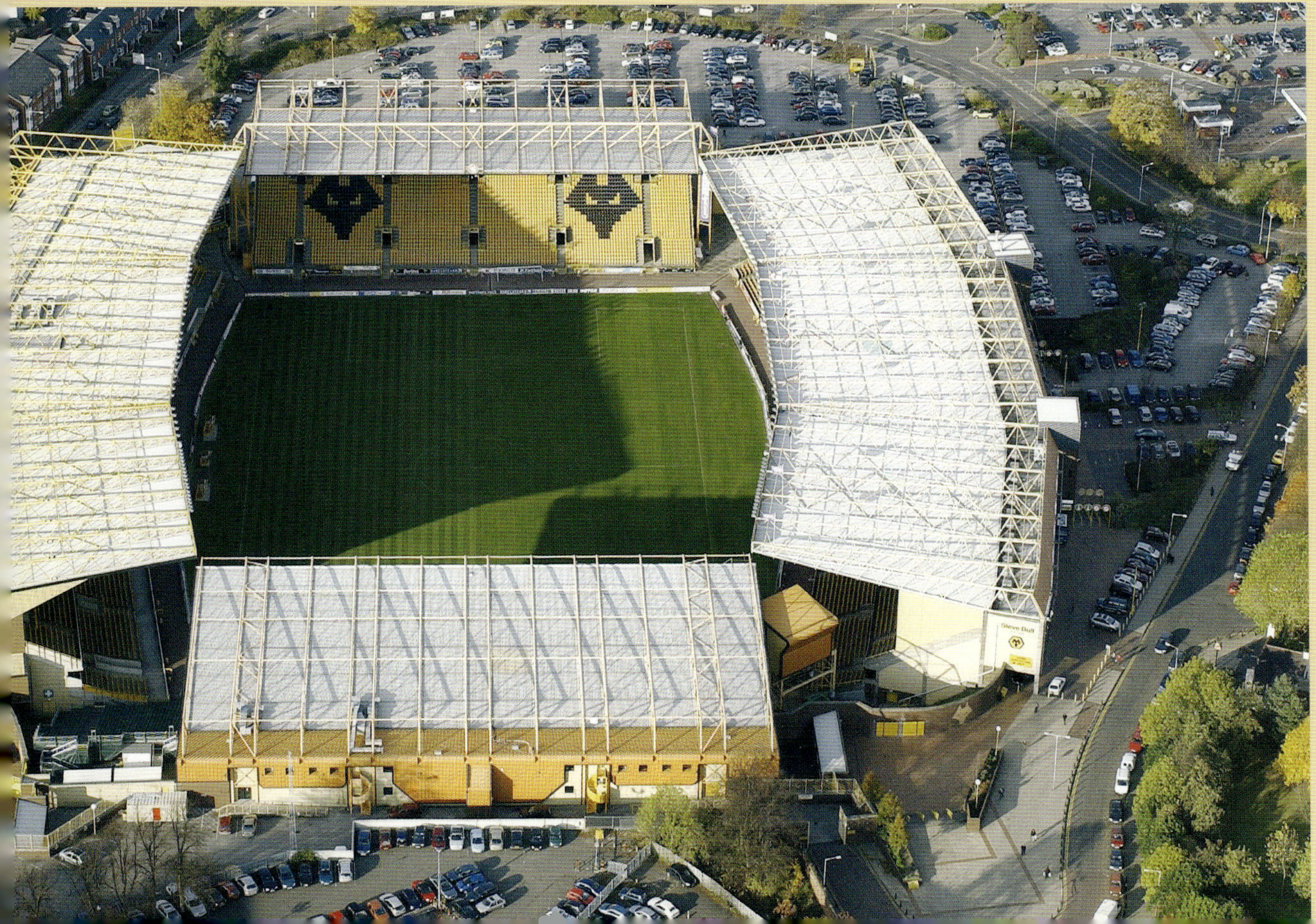

Ground: **Molineux**

Address: Molineux Stadium, Waterloo Road, Wolverhampton WV1 4QR

Main tel: 0871 880 8442

Box office: 0871 880 8443

Website: www.wolves.co.uk

Capacity: 28,500

Home colours: gold shirts, black shorts

Club nickname: Wolves

Pitch dimensions: 106m x 68m (116 x 74 yards)

Founded: 1877

Record attendance: 61,315 vs Liverpool, February 11 1939

Most prolific scorer: Steve Bull (247)

Record win: 10-1 vs Leicester City, 15 April 1938

Record defeat: 1-10 vs Manchester United, October 15 1892

Wrexham

Wrexham formed in 1872, opting to play on the cricket pitch in the middle of an unused local racecourse, where they have remained ever since. In 1902, the ground lost its oval shape and began to be shaped into a football ground. Originally a cycle track ran round the edge of the pitch, a stand stood on its south side and there was banking on the other three sides. When the Red Dragons joined the Football League in 1921, the club began to develop the ground fully. A small cover was added to part of the terrace at the west end of the pitch in 1926 and this was extended three years later to cover the remainder of the West Terrace. In the 1930s a roof was added to the terrace running along the north side of the ground and before war was declared the stand on the south of the pitch was extended to the south-west corner. After the war, the East Terrace was concreted. The Red Dragons' next piece of ground development was the installation of a stand at the east end of the ground in 1962; it was a steel structure bought from a local cinema and came with a balcony. This odd structure, which was capable of seating 700, only lasted 16 years; a cover was added to the terrace after the stand was taken down. During the 1970s Wrexham experienced their best ever spell on the pitch and were able to continue developing the ground. The two-tier Main Stand was built at the north side of the ground in 1972 and a similar stand went up at the west end in 1978. Seats were added to the North and West Terraces and finally an all-seater stand was built along the south edge in 2000.

Ground: Racecourse Ground

Address: Racecourse Ground, Mold Road, Wrexham LL11 2AN

Main tel: 01978 262 129

Box office: 01978 262 129

Website: www.wrexhamafc.co.uk

Capacity: 15,500

Home colours: red shirts, white shorts, red socks

Club nickname: the Red Dragons

Pitch dimensions: 101m x 68m (111 x 74 yards)

Founded: 1872

Record attendance: 34,445 vs Manchester United, January 26 1957

Most prolific scorer: Tom Bamford (175)

Record win: 10-1 vs Hartlepool United, March 3 1962

Record defeat: 0-9 vs Brentford, October 15 1963

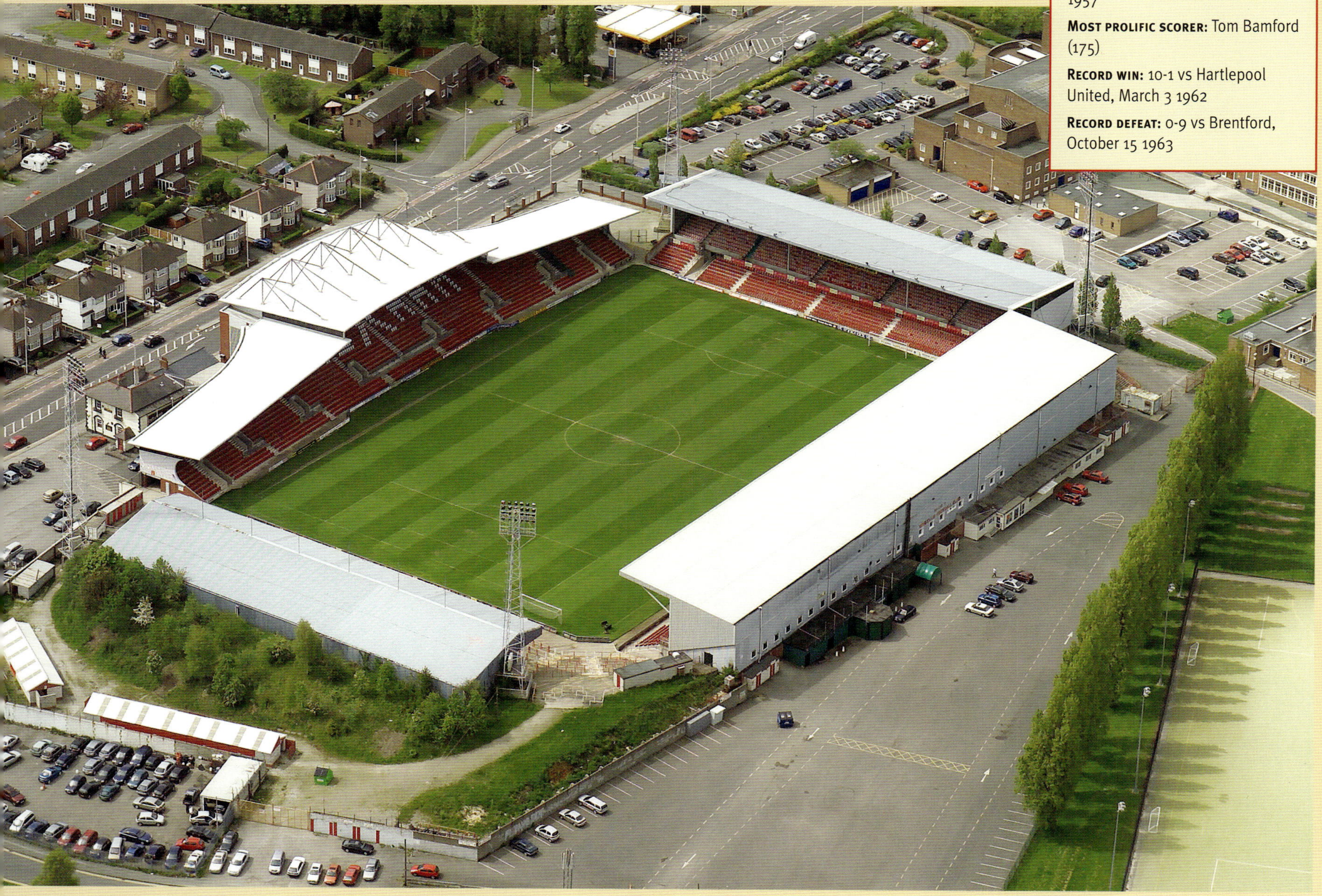